ARCTIC OCEAN
Svalbard (Norway)
RUSSIA
FINLAND
NORWAY
SWEDEN
St. Petersburg
ESTONIA
LATVIA
LITHUANIA
Moscow
DENMARK
BELARUS
GERMANY
POLAND
CZECH.
LUX.
AUSTRIA
SLOV.
HUNG.
SWITZ.
UKRAINE
MOLD.
ROMANIA
KAZAKHSTAN
MONGOLIA
ITALY
BULGARIA
ALBANIA
Istanbul
GEORGIA
ARM.
AZER.
UZBEKISTAN
KYRGYZSTAN
TURKMENISTAN
TAJIKISTAN
GREECE
TURKEY
MALTA
CYPRUS
SYRIA
LEB.
ISRAEL
Tehran
IRAN
IRAQ
Baghdad
JORDAN
KUWAIT
AFGHANISTAN
TUNISIA
Cairo
Lahore
PAKISTAN
Delhi
NEPAL
BHUTAN
CHINA
Asia
Beijing (Peking)
Shenyang
Tianjin
NORTH KOREA
Seoul
SOUTH KOREA
JAPAN
Tokyo
Osaka
Wuhan
Chongqing
Shanghai
PACIFIC OCEAN
Tropic of Cancer
LIBYA
EGYPT
BAHRAIN
QATAR
U.A.E.
SAUDI ARABIA
OMAN
Karachi
Ahmadabad
BANGLADESH
Dacca
Kolkata (Calcutta)
BURMA (Myanmar)
Hong Kong
TAIWAN
Africa
NIGER
CHAD
SUDAN
ERITREA
YEMEN
DJIBOUTI
Mumbai (Bombay)
INDIA
Hyderabad
Chennai (Madras)
Bangalore
LAOS
THAILAND
Bangkok
CAMBODIA
VIETNAM
Ho Chi Minh City
Manila
PHILIPPINES
NORTHERN MARIANAS
Guam (U.S.A.)
MARSHALL IS.
NIGERIA
Lagos
CAMEROON
CENTRAL AFRICAN REP.
ETHIOPIA
SOMALI REP.
SRI LANKA
MALDIVES
BRUNEI
MALAYSIA
SINGAPORE
Sumatra
Borneo
PALAU
FEDERATED STATES OF MICRONESIA
EQUATORIAL GUINEA
GABON
CONGO
UGANDA
KENYA
Equator
KIRIBATI
Kinshasa
CABINDA (Angola)
CONGO (Dem. Rep. of the)
RWANDA
BURUNDI
TANZANIA
SEYCHELLES
INDIAN OCEAN
INDONESIA
Jakarta
New Guinea
PAPUA NEW GUINEA
TUVALU
EAST TIMOR
Cocos Islands (Australia)
Christmas Island (Australia)
ANGOLA
ZAMBIA
MALAWI
MOZAMBIQUE
COMOROS
ZIMBABWE
MADAGASCAR
MAURITIUS
NAMIBIA
BOTSWANA
Réunion (Fr.)
Oceania
FIJI
New Caledonia (Fr.)
Tropic of Capricorn
AUSTRALIA
SWAZILAND
SOUTH AFRICA
LESOTHO
Sydney
NEW ZEALAND
Prince Edward Islands (South Africa)
Crozet Is. (Fr.)
Kerguelen Is. (Fr.)
SOUTHERN OCEAN
Antarctic Circle
Antarctica
East from Greenwich

CONTENTS

NOTE:
For reasons of safety or politics, there may be times when it is not advisable, or desirable, to visit one or more of the countries described in the Gazetteer of Nations section. If in doubt, please check with the US Department of State (www.state.gov/travel).

Philip's, a division of Octopus Publishing Group Limited, 2–4 Heron Quays, London E14 4JP

Cartography by Philip's

CITY PLANS
Page 29, Dublin: The town plan of Dublin is based on Ordnance Survey Ireland by permission of the Government Permit Number 7978. © Ordnance Survey Ireland and Government of Ireland.

Page 31, London: This product includes mapping data licensed from Ordnance Survey® with the permission of the Controller of Her Majesty's Stationery Office. © Crown copyright 2005. All rights reserved. Licence number 100011710.

Vector data: Courtesy of Gräfe and Unser Verlag GmbH, München, Germany (city-center maps of Bangkok, Cape Town, Mexico City, Singapore, Sydney, and Tokyo).

Published in North America by Oxford University Press, Inc., 198 Madison Avenue, New York, NY 10016

www.oup.com/us/atlas

OXFORD UNIVERSITY PRESS Oxford is a registered trademark of Oxford University Press

Library of Congress Cataloging-in-Publication Data available

ISBN-13 978-0-19-530026-0
ISBN-10 0-19-530026-2

Printing (last digit): 9 8 7 6 5 4 3 2 1

Printed in Hong Kong

Country/Territory	Area (1,000 sq km)	Area (1,000 sq mi)	Population (1,000s)	Capital City	Annual Income US$
Afghanistan	652	252	28,514	Kabul	700
Albania	28.7	11.1	3,545	Tirana	4,400
Algeria	2,382	920	32,129	Algiers	5,400
American Samoa (US)	0.20	0.08	58	Pago Pago	8,000
Andorra	0.47	0.18	70	Andorra La Vella	19,000
Angola	1,247	481	10,979	Luanda	1,700
Anguilla (UK)	0.10	0.04	13	The Valley	8,600
Antigua & Barbuda	0.44	0.17	68	St John's	11,000
Argentina	2,780	1,074	39,145	Buenos Aires	10,500
Armenia	29.8	11.5	2,991	Yerevan	3,600
Aruba (Netherlands)	0.19	0.07	71	Oranjestad	28,000
Australia	7,741	2,989	19,913	Canberra	26,900
Austria	83.9	32.4	8,175	Vienna	27,900
Azerbaijan	86.6	33.4	7,868	Baku	3,700
Azores (Portugal)	2.2	0.86	236	Ponta Delgada	15,000
Bahamas	13.9	5.4	300	Nassau	15,300
Bahrain	0.69	0.27	678	Manama	15,100
Bangladesh	144	55.6	141,340	Dhaka	1,800
Barbados	0.43	0.17	278	Bridgetown	15,000
Belarus	208	80.2	10,311	Minsk	8,700
Belgium	30.5	11.8	10,348	Brussels	29,200
Belize	23.0	8.9	273	Belmopan	4,900
Benin	113	43.5	7,250	Porto-Novo	1,100
Bermuda (UK)	0.05	0.02	65	Hamilton	35,200
Bhutan	47.0	18.1	2,186	Thimphu	1,300
Bolivia	1,099	424	8,724	La Paz/Sucre	2,500
Bosnia-Herzegovina	51.2	19.8	4,008	Sarajevo	1,900
Botswana	582	225	1,562	Gaborone	8,500
Brazil	8,514	3,287	184,101	Brasília	7,600
Brunei	5.8	2.2	365	Bandar Seri Begawan	18,600
Bulgaria	111	42.8	7,518	Sofia	6,500
Burkina Faso	274	106	13,575	Ouagadougou	1,100
Burma (= Myanmar)	677	261	42,720	Rangoon	1,700
Burundi	27.8	10.7	6,231	Bujumbura	500
Cambodia	181	69.9	13,363	Phnom Penh	1,600
Cameroon	475	184	16,064	Yaoundé	1,700
Canada	9,971	3,850	32,508	Ottawa	29,300
Canary Is. (Spain)	7.2	2.8	1,682	Las Palmas/Santa Cruz	19,900
Cape Verde Is.	4.0	1.6	415	Praia	1,400
Cayman Is. (UK)	0.26	0.10	43	George Town	35,000
Central African Republic	623	241	3,742	Bangui	1,200
Chad	1,284	496	9,539	Ndjaména	1,000
Chile	757	292	15,824	Santiago	10,100
China	9,597	3,705	1,298,848	Beijing	4,700
Colombia	1,139	440	42,311	Bogotá	6,100
Comoros	2.2	0.86	652	Moroni	700
Congo	342	132	2,998	Brazzaville	900
Congo (Dem. Rep. of the)	2,345	905	58,318	Kinshasa	600
Cook Is. (NZ)	0.24	0.09	21	Avarua	5,000
Costa Rica	51.1	19.7	3,957	San José	8,300
Croatia	56.5	21.8	4,497	Zagreb	9,800
Cuba	111	42.8	11,309	Havana	2,700
Cyprus	9.3	3.6	776	Nicosia	13,200
Czech Republic	78.9	30.5	10,246	Prague	15,300
Denmark	43.1	16.6	5,413	Copenhagen	28,900

Listed above are the principal countries and territories of the world. If a territory is not completely independent, then the country it is associated with is named. The area figures give the total area of land, inland water, and ice. The population figures are 2004 estimates. The annual income is the Gross Domestic Product per capita in US dollars. [Gross Domestic Product per capita has been measured

Country/Territory	Area (1,000 sq km)	Area (1,000 sq mi)	Population (1,000s)	Capital City	Annual Income US$
Djibouti	23.2	9.0	467	Djibouti	1,300
Dominica	0.75	0.29	69	Roseau	5,400
Dominican Republic	48.5	18.7	8,834	Santo Domingo	6,300
East Timor	14.9	5.7	1,019	Dili	500
Ecuador	284	109	13,213	Quito	3,200
Egypt	1,001	387	76,117	Cairo	4,000
El Salvador	21.0	8.1	6,588	San Salvador	4,600
Equatorial Guinea	28.1	10.8	523	Malabo	2,700
Eritrea	118	45.4	4,447	Asmara	700
Estonia	45.1	17.4	1,342	Tallinn	11,000
Ethiopia	1,104	426	67,851	Addis Ababa	700
Faroe Is. (Denmark)	1.4	0.54	47	Tórshavn	22,000
Fiji	18.3	7.1	881	Suva	5,600
Finland	338	131	5,215	Helsinki	25,800
France	552	213	60,424	Paris	26,000
French Guiana (France)	90.0	34.7	191	Cayenne	14,400
French Polynesia (France)	4.0	1.5	266	Papeete	5,000
Gabon	268	103	1,355	Libreville	6,500
Gambia, The	11.3	4.4	1,547	Banjul	1,800
Gaza Strip (OPT)*	0.36	0.14	1,325	–	600
Georgia	69.7	26.9	4,694	Tbilisi	3,200
Germany	357	138	82,425	Berlin	26,200
Ghana	239	92.1	20,757	Accra	2,000
Gibraltar (UK)	0.006	0.002	28	Gibraltar Town	17,500
Greece	132	50.9	10,648	Athens	19,100
Greenland (Denmark)	2,176	840	56	Nuuk (Godthåb)	20,000
Grenada	0.34	0.13	89	St George's	5,000
Guadeloupe (France)	1.7	0.66	445	Basse-Terre	9,000
Guam (US)	0.55	0.21	166	Agana	21,000
Guatemala	109	42.0	14,281	Guatemala City	3,900
Guinea	246	94.9	9,246	Conakry	2,100
Guinea-Bissau	36.1	13.9	1,388	Bissau	700
Guyana	215	83.0	706	Georgetown	3,800
Haiti	27.8	10.7	7,656	Port-au-Prince	1,400
Honduras	112	43.3	6,824	Tegucigalpa	2,500
Hong Kong (China)	1.1	0.42	6,855	–	27,200
Hungary	93.0	35.9	10,032	Budapest	13,300
Iceland	103	39.8	294	Reykjavik	30,200
India	3,287	1,269	1,065,071	New Delhi	2,600
Indonesia	1,905	735	238,453	Jakarta	3,100
Iran	1,648	636	69,019	Tehran	6,800
Iraq	438	169	25,375	Baghdad	2,400
Ireland	70.3	27.1	3,970	Dublin	29,300
Israel	20.6	8.0	6,199	Jerusalem	19,500
Italy	301	116	58,057	Rome	25,100
Ivory Coast (= Côte d'Ivoire)	322	125	17,328	Yamoussoukro	1,400
Jamaica	11.0	4.2	2,713	Kingston	3,800
Japan	378	146	127,333	Tokyo	28,700
Jordan	89.3	34.5	5,611	Amman	4,300
Kazakhstan	2,725	1,052	15,144	Astana	7,200
Kenya	580	224	32,022	Nairobi	1,100
Kiribati	0.73	0.28	101	Tarawa	800
Korea, North	121	46.5	22,698	Pyŏngyang	1,000
Korea, South	99.3	38.3	48,598	Seoul	19,600
Kuwait	17.8	6.9	2,258	Kuwait City	17,500

using the purchasing power parity method. This enables comparisons to be made between countries through their purchasing power (in US dollars), showing real price levels of goods and services rather than using currency exchange rates.] The figures are the latest available, usually 2002 estimates. *OPT = Occupied Palestinian Territory; N/A = Not available.

Country/Territory	Area (1,000 sq km)	Area (1,000 sq mi)	Population (1,000s)	Capital City	Annual Income US$
Kyrgyzstan	200	77.2	5,081	Bishkek	2,900
Laos	237	91.4	6,068	Vientiane	1,800
Latvia	64.6	24.9	2,306	Riga	8,900
Lebanon	10.4	4.0	3,777	Beirut	4,800
Lesotho	30.4	11.7	1,865	Maseru	2,700
Liberia	111	43.0	3,391	Monrovia	1,000
Libya	1,760	679	5,632	Tripoli	6,200
Liechtenstein	0.16	0.06	33	Vaduz	25,000
Lithuania	65.2	25.2	3,608	Vilnius	8,400
Luxembourg	2.6	1.0	463	Luxembourg	48,900
Macau (China)	0.02	0.007	445	–	18,500
Macedonia (FYROM)	25.7	9.9	2,071	Skopje	5,100
Madagascar	587	227	17,502	Antananarivo	800
Madeira (Portugal)	0.78	0.30	241	Funchal	22,700
Malawi	118	45.7	11,907	Lilongwe	600
Malaysia	330	127	23,522	Kuala Lumpur/Putrajaya	8,800
Maldives	0.30	0.12	339	Malé	3,900
Mali	1,240	479	11,957	Bamako	900
Malta	0.32	0.12	397	Valletta	17,200
Marshall Is.	0.18	0.07	58	Majuro	1,600
Martinique (France)	1.1	0.43	430	Fort-de-France	10,700
Mauritania	1,026	396	2,999	Nouakchott	1,700
Mauritius	2.0	0.79	1,220	Port Louis	10,100
Mayotte (France)	0.37	0.14	186	Mamoundzou	600
Mexico	1,958	756	104,960	Mexico City	8,900
Micronesia, Fed. States of	0.70	0.27	108	Palikir	2,000
Moldova	33.9	13.1	4,446	Chişinău	2,600
Monaco	0.001	0.0004	32	Monaco	27,000
Mongolia	1,567	605	2,751	Ulan Bator	1,900
Montserrat (UK)	0.10	0.04	9	Plymouth	3,400
Morocco	447	172	32,209	Rabat	3,900
Mozambique	802	309	18,812	Maputo	1,100
Namibia	824	318	1,954	Windhoek	6,900
Nauru	0.02	0.008	13	Yaren District	5,000
Nepal	147	56.8	27,071	Katmandu	1,400
Netherlands	41.5	16.0	16,318	Amsterdam/The Hague	27,200
Netherlands Antilles (Neths)	0.80	0.31	218	Willemstad	11,400
New Caledonia (France)	18.6	7.2	214	Nouméa	14,000
New Zealand	271	104	3,994	Wellington	20,100
Nicaragua	130	50.2	5,360	Managua	2,200
Niger	1,267	489	11,361	Niamey	800
Nigeria	924	357	137,253	Abuja	900
Northern Mariana Is. (US)	0.46	0.18	78	Saipan	12,500
Norway	324	125	4,575	Oslo	33,000
Oman	310	119	2,903	Muscat	8,300
Pakistan	796	307	159,196	Islamabad	2,000
Palau	0.46	0.18	20	Koror	9,000
Panama	75.5	29.2	3,000	Panamá	6,200
Papua New Guinea	463	179	5,420	Port Moresby	2,100
Paraguay	407	157	6,191	Asunción	4,300
Peru	1,285	496	27,544	Lima	5,000
Philippines	300	116	86,242	Manila	4,600
Poland	323	125	38,626	Warsaw	9,700
Portugal	88.8	34.3	10,524	Lisbon	19,400
Puerto Rico (US)	8.9	3.4	3,898	San Juan	11,100
Qatar	11.0	4.2	840	Doha	20,100
Réunion (France)	2.5	0.97	766	St-Denis	5,600
Romania	238	92.0	22,356	Bucharest	7,600

Country/Territory	Area (1,000 sq km)	Area (1,000 sq mi)	Population (1,000s)	Capital City	Annual Income US$
Russia	17,075	6,593	143,782	Moscow	9,700
Rwanda	26.3	10.2	7,954	Kigali	1,200
St Kitts & Nevis	0.26	0.10	39	Basseterre	8,800
St Lucia	0.54	0.21	164	Castries	5,400
St Vincent & Grenadines	0.39	0.15	117	Kingstown	2,900
Samoa	2.8	1.1	178	Apia	5,600
San Marino	0.06	0.02	29	San Marino	34,600
São Tomé & Príncipe	0.96	0.37	182	São Tomé	1,200
Saudi Arabia	2,150	830	25,796	Riyadh	11,400
Senegal	197	76.0	10,852	Dakar	1,500
Serbia & Montenegro	102	39.4	10,826	Belgrade	2,200
Seychelles	0.46	0.18	81	Victoria	7,800
Sierra Leone	71.7	27.7	5,884	Freetown	500
Singapore	0.68	0.26	4,354	Singapore City	25,200
Slovak Republic	49.0	18.9	5,424	Bratislava	12,400
Slovenia	20.3	7.8	2,011	Ljubljana	19,200
Solomon Is.	28.9	11.2	524	Honiara	1,700
Somalia	638	246	8,305	Mogadishu	600
South Africa	1,221	471	42,719	Cape Town/Pretoria/Bloemfontein	10,000
Spain	498	192	40,281	Madrid	21,200
Sri Lanka	65.6	25.3	19,905	Colombo	3,700
Sudan	2,506	967	39,148	Khartoum	1,400
Suriname	163	63.0	437	Paramaribo	3,400
Swaziland	17.4	6.7	1,169	Mbabane	4,800
Sweden	450	174	8,986	Stockholm	26,000
Switzerland	41.3	15.9	7,451	Bern	32,000
Syria	185	71.5	18,017	Damascus	3,700
Taiwan	36.0	13.9	22,750	Taipei	18,000
Tajikistan	143	55.3	7,012	Dushanbe	1,300
Tanzania	945	365	36,588	Dodoma	600
Thailand	513	198	64,866	Bangkok	7,000
Togo	56.8	21.9	5,557	Lomé	1,400
Tonga	0.65	0.25	110	Nuku'alofa	2,200
Trinidad & Tobago	5.1	2.0	1,097	Port of Spain	10,000
Tunisia	164	63.2	9,975	Tunis	6,800
Turkey	775	299	68,894	Ankara	7,300
Turkmenistan	488	188	4,863	Ashkhabad	6,700
Turks & Caicos Is. (UK)	0.43	0.17	20	Cockburn Town	9,600
Tuvalu	0.03	0.01	11	Fongafale	1,100
Uganda	241	93.1	26,405	Kampala	1,200
Ukraine	604	233	47,732	Kiev	4,500
United Arab Emirates	83.6	32.3	2,524	Abu Dhabi	22,100
United Kingdom	242	93.4	60,271	London	25,500
United States of America	9,629	3,718	293,028	Washington, DC	36,300
Uruguay	175	67.6	3,399	Montevideo	7,900
Uzbekistan	447	173	26,410	Tashkent	2,600
Vanuatu	12.2	4.7	203	Port-Vila	2,900
Vatican City	0.0004	0.0002	1	Vatican City	N/A
Venezuela	912	352	25,017	Caracas	5,400
Vietnam	332	128	82,690	Hanoi	2,300
Virgin Is. (UK)	0.15	0.06	22	Road Town	16,000
Virgin Is. (US)	0.35	0.13	109	Charlotte Amalie	19,000
Wallis & Futuna Is. (France)	0.20	0.08	16	Mata-Utu	2,000
West Bank (OPT)*	5.9	2.3	2,311	–	800
Western Sahara	266	103	267	El Aaiún	N/A
Yemen	528	204	20,025	Sana'	800
Zambia	753	291	10,462	Lusaka	800
Zimbabwe	391	151	12,672	Harare	2,100

	Population (1,000s)
Afghanistan	
Kabul	2,602
Algeria	
Algiers	1,722
Angola	
Luanda	2,697
Argentina	
Buenos Aires	12,024
Córdoba	1,368
Rosario	1,279
Mendoza	934
Armenia	
Yerevan	1,407
Australia	
Sydney	4,086
Melbourne	3,466
Brisbane	1,627
Perth	1,381
Adelaide	1,096
Austria	
Vienna	1,807
Azerbaijan	
Baku	1,792
Bangladesh	
Dhaka	12,519
Chittagong	3,651
Khulna	1,442
Rajshahi	1,035
Belarus	
Minsk	1,717
Belgium	
Brussels	964
Bolivia	
La Paz	1,487
Santa Cruz	1,035
Brazil	
São Paulo	17,962
Rio de Janeiro	10,652
Belo Horizonte	4,224
Pôrto Alegre	3,757
Recife	3,346
Salvador	3,238
Fortaleza	3,066
Curitiba	2,562
Brasília	2,051
Belém	1,658
Manaus	1,467
Campinas	1,434
Santos	1,270
Goiânia	1,117
São José dos Campos	972
São Luís	968
Maceió	886
Teresina	848
Campo Grande	821
Natal	806
Bulgaria	
Sofia	1,187
Burkina Faso	
Ouagadougou	831
Burma (= Myanmar)	
Rangoon	4,393
Cambodia	
Phnom Penh	1,070
Cameroon	
Douala	1,642
Yaoundé	1,420
Canada	
Toronto	4,881
Montréal	3,511
Vancouver	2,079
Ottawa	1,107
Calgary	972
Edmonton	957
Chile	
Santiago	5,467
China	
Shanghai	12,887
Beijing	10,839
Tianjin	9,156
Hong Kong	6,860
Wuhan	5,169
Chongqing	4,900
Shenyang	4,828
Guangzhou	3,893
Chengdu	3,294
Xi'an	3,123
Changchun	3,093
Harbin	2,928
Nanjing	2,740
Zibo	2,675
Dalian	2,628
Jinan	2,568
Guiyang	2,533
Linyi	2,498
Taiyuan	2,415
Qingdao	2,316
Zhengzhou	2,070
Zaozhuang	2,048
Liupanshui	2,023
Handan	1,996
Jinxi	1,821
Lu'an	1,818
Hangzhou	1,780
Tianmen	1,779
Changsha	1,775
Wanxian	1,759
Lanzhou	1,730
Nanchang	1,722
Kunming	1,701
Yantai	1,681
Tangshan	1,671
Xuzhou	1,636
Xiantao	1,614
Shijiazhuang	1,603
Heze	1,600
Yancheng	1,562
Yulin	1,558
Xinghua	1,556
Tai'an	1,503
Pingxiang	1,502
Anshan	1,453
Luoyang	1,451
Jilin	1,435
Qiqihar	1,435
Suining, Sichuan	1,428
Ürümqi	1,415
Fushun	1,413
Fuzhou	1,397
Neijiang	1,393
Changde	1,374
Zhanjiang	1,368
Huainan	1,354
Yiyang	1,343
Xintai	1,325
Baotou	1,319
Dongguan	1,319
Nanning	1,311
Weifang	1,287
Wenzhou	1,269
Hefei	1,242
Huaian	1,232
Yueyang	1,213
Suqian	1,189
Tianshui	1,187
Suzhou	1,183
Shantou	1,176
Ningbo	1,173
Yuzhou	1,173
Datong	1,165
Jingmen	1,153
Leshan	1,137
Shenzhen	1,131
Wuxi	1,127
Xiaoshan	1,124
Zaoyang	1,121
Yixing	1,108
Yongzhou	1,097
Chifeng	1,087
Huzhou	1,077
Daqing	1,076
Zigong	1,072
Mianyang	1,065
Nanchong	1,055
Fuyu	1,025
Jining, Shandong	1,019
Hohhot	978
Xinyi, Guangdong	973
Benxi	957
Jixi	949
Liuzhou	928
Xiangxiang	908
Yichun, Heilongjiang	904
Xianyang	896
Linqing	891
Changzhou	886
Zhangjiagang	886
Zhangjiakou	880
Jiamusi	874
Yichun, Jiangxi	871
Zhaotong	851
Yuyao	848
Jinzhou	834
Xuanzhou	823
Huaibei	814
Xinyu	808
Mudanjiang	801
Colombia	
Bogotá	6,771
Medellín	2,866
Cali	2,233
Barranquilla	1,683
Bucaramanga	937
Cartagena	845
Congo	
Brazzaville	1,306
Congo (Democratic Republic of the)	
Kinshasa	5,054
Lubumbashi	965
Mbuji-Mayi	806
Costa Rica	
San José	961
Croatia	
Zagreb	1,067
Cuba	
Havana	2,256
Czech Republic	
Prague	1,203
Denmark	
Copenhagen	1,332
Dominican Republic	
Santo Domingo	2,563
Santiago de los Caballeros	804
Ecuador	
Guayaquil	2,118
Quito	1,616
Egypt	
Cairo	9,462
Alexandria	3,506
Shubrâ el Kheima	937
El Salvador	
San Salvador	1,341
Ethiopia	
Addis Ababa	2,645
Finland	
Helsinki	937
France	
Paris	9,630
Lyons	1,353
Marseilles	1,290
Lille	991
Nice	889
Georgia	
Tbilisi	1,406
Germany	
Berlin	3,387
Hamburg	1,705
Munich	1,195
Cologne	963
Ghana	
Accra	1,868
Greece	
Athens	3,116
Guatemala	
Guatemala City	3,242
Guinea	
Conakry	1,232
Haiti	
Port-au-Prince	1,769
Honduras	
Tegucigalpa	949
Hungary	
Budapest	1,819
India	
Mumbai	16,086
Kolkata	13,058
Delhi	12,441
Chennai	6,353
Bangalore	5,567
Hyderabad	5,445
Ahmedabad	4,427
Pune	3,655
Surat	2,699
Kanpur	2,641
Jaipur	2,259
Lucknow	2,221
Nagpur	2,089
Patna	1,658
Indore	1,597
Vadodara	1,465
Bhopal	1,425
Coimbatore	1,420
Ludhiana	1,368
Cochin	1,340
Visakhapatnam	1,309
Agra	1,293
Varanasi	1,199
Madurai	1,187
Meerut	1,143
Nashik	1,117
Jabalpur	1,100
Jamshedpur	1,081
Asansol	1,065
Bhilainagar-Durg	1,049
Dhanbad	1,046
Allahabad	1,035
Faridabad	1,018
Vijayawada	999
Rajkot	974
Amritsar	955
Srinagar	954
Ghaziabad	928
Trivandrum	885
Calicut	875
Aurangabad	868
Gwalior	855
Solapur	853
Ranchi	844
Tiruchchirapalli	837
Jodhpur	833
Indonesia	
Jakarta	11,018
Bandung	3,409
Surabaya	2,461
Medan	1,879
Palembang	1,422
Ujung Pandang	1,051
Bandar Lampung	915
Iran	
Tehran	6,979

	Population (1,000s)
Mashhad	1,990
Esfahan	1,381
Tabriz	1,274
Karaj	1,200
Shiraz	1,124
Qom	888
Ahvaz	871
Iraq	
Baghdad	4,865
Basra	1,338
Mosul	1,131
Irbil	840
Ireland	
Dublin	985
Israel	
Tel Aviv-Yafo	2,001
Italy	
Rome	2,649
Milan	1,183
Naples	993
Turin	857
Ivory Coast (= Côte d'Ivoire)	
Abidjan	3,790
Japan	
Tokyo	12,064
Yokohama	6,427
Osaka	2,599
Nagoya	2,172
Sapporo	1,922
Kobe	1,493
Kyoto	1,468
Fukuoka	1,341
Kawasaki	1,250
Hiroshima	1,126
Kitakyushu	1,011
Sendai	1,008
Chiba	887
Jordan	
Amman	1,148
Kazakhstan	
Almaty	1,130
Kenya	
Nairobi	2,233
Korea, North	
Pyŏngyang	3,124
Hamhung	821
Korea, South	
Seoul	9,888
Pusan	3,830
Inch'on	2,884
Taegu	2,675
Taejŏn	1,522
Kwangju	1,379
Sŏngnam	1,353
Ulsan	1,340
Ansan	984
Puch'on	900
Suwŏn	876
Kuwait	
Kuwait City	879
Latvia	
Riga	811
Lebanon	
Beirut	2,070
Libya	
Tripoli	1,733
Benghazi	829
Madagascar	
Antananarivo	1,603
Malaysia	
Kuala Lumpur	1,379
Mali	
Bamako	1,114
Mexico	
Mexico City	18,066
Guadalajara	3,697
Monterrey	3,267
Puebla	1,888
Toluca	1,455
Tijuana	1,297
León	1,293
Ciudad Juárez	1,239
Torreón	1,012
San Luis Potosí	857
Mérida	849
Morocco	
Casablanca	3,357
Rabat	1,616
Fès	907
Marrakesh	822
Mozambique	
Maputo	1,094
Nepal	
Katmandu	1,176
Netherlands	
Amsterdam	1,105
Rotterdam	1,078
New Zealand	
Auckland	1,102
Nicaragua	
Managua	1,009
Nigeria	
Lagos	8,665
Ibadan	1,549
Ogbomosho	809
Pakistan	
Karachi	10,032
Lahore	5,452
Faisalabad	2,142
Rawalpindi	1,521
Gujranwala	1,325
Multan	1,263
Hyderabad	1,221
Peshawar	1,066
Panama	
Panamá	1,173
Paraguay	
Asunción	1,262
Peru	
Lima	7,443
Philippines	
Manila	9,950
Davao	1,146
Poland	
Warsaw	1,626
Lódz	815
Portugal	
Lisbon	3,861
Porto	1,940
Puerto Rico	
San Juan	2,217
Romania	
Bucharest	2,001
Russia	
Moscow	8,367
Saint Petersburg	4,635
Nizhniy Novgorod	1,332
Novosibirsk	1,321
Yekaterinburg	1,218
Omsk	1,174
Samara	1,132
Ufa	1,102
Kazan	1,063
Chelyabinsk	1,045
Perm	1,014
Rostov	1,012
Volgograd	1,000
Voronezh	918
Saratov	881
Simbirsk	864
Krasnoyarsk	840
Saudi Arabia	
Riyadh	3,180
Jedda	1,490
Senegal	
Dakar	2,078
Serbia & Montenegro	
Belgrade	1,673
Sierra Leone	
Freetown	822
Singapore	
Singapore City	4,131
Somalia	
Mogadishu	1,162
South Africa	
Johannesburg	2,950
Cape Town	2,930
Durban / eThekwini	2,391
Pretoria / Tshwane	1,590
Port Elizabeth	1,006
Spain	
Madrid	3,017
Barcelona	1,527
Sudan	
Khartoum	2,742
Sweden	
Stockholm	1,612
Switzerland	
Zürich	939
Syria	
Aleppo	2,229
Damascus	2,144
Homs	811
Taiwan	
Taipei	2,550
Kaohsiung	1,463
T'aichung	950
Tanzania	
Dar es Salaam	2,115
Thailand	
Bangkok	7,372
Tunisia	
Tunis	1,892
Turkey	
Istanbul	8,953
Ankara	3,203
Izmir	2,250
Bursa	1,184
Adana	1,133
Gaziantep	862
Uganda	
Kampala	1,213
Ukraine	
Kiev	2,621
Kharkov	1,521
Dnepropetrovsk	1,122
Donetsk	1,065
Odessa	1,027
Zaporozhye	863
United Arab Emirates	
Abu Dhabi	928
Dubai	886
United Kingdom	
London	8,089
Birmingham	2,373
Manchester	2,353
Liverpool	852
Glasgow	832
United States of America	
New York	17,800
Los Angeles	11,789
Chicago	8,308
Philadelphia	5,149
Miami	4,919
Dallas–Fort Worth	4,146
Boston	4,032
Washington	3,934
Detroit	3,903
Houston	3,823
Atlanta	3,500
San Francisco	3,229
Phoenix	2,907
Seattle	2,712
San Diego	2,674
Minneapolis–St Paul	2,389
St Louis	2,078
Baltimore	2,076
Tampa–St Petersburg	2,062
Denver	1,985
Cleveland	1,787
Pittsburgh	1,753
Portland	1,583
San Jose	1,538
San Bernardino	1,507
Cincinnati	1,503
Norfolk–Virginia Beach	1,394
Sacramento	1,393
Kansas City	1,362
San Antonio	1,328
Las Vegas	1,314
Milwaukee	1,309
Indianapolis	1,219
Providence	1,175
Orlando	1,157
Columbus	1,133
New Orleans	1,009
Buffalo	977
Memphis	972
Austin	902
Stamford	889
Salt Lake City	888
Jacksonville	882
Louisville	864
Hartford	852
Richmond	819
Uruguay	
Montevideo	1,324
Uzbekistan	
Tashkent	2,148
Venezuela	
Caracas	3,153
Maracaibo	1,901
Valencia	1,893
Maracay	1,100
Ciudad Guayana	966
Barquisimeto	923
Vietnam	
Ho Chi Minh City	4,619
Hanoi	3,751
Haiphong	1,676
Yemen	
Sana'	1,327
Zambia	
Lusaka	1,653
Zimbabwe	
Harare	1,791
Bulawayo	824

Listed above are the principal cities with more than 800,000 inhabitants. The figures are taken from the most recent census or estimate available (usually 2000), and as far as possible are for the metropolitan area or urban agglomeration.

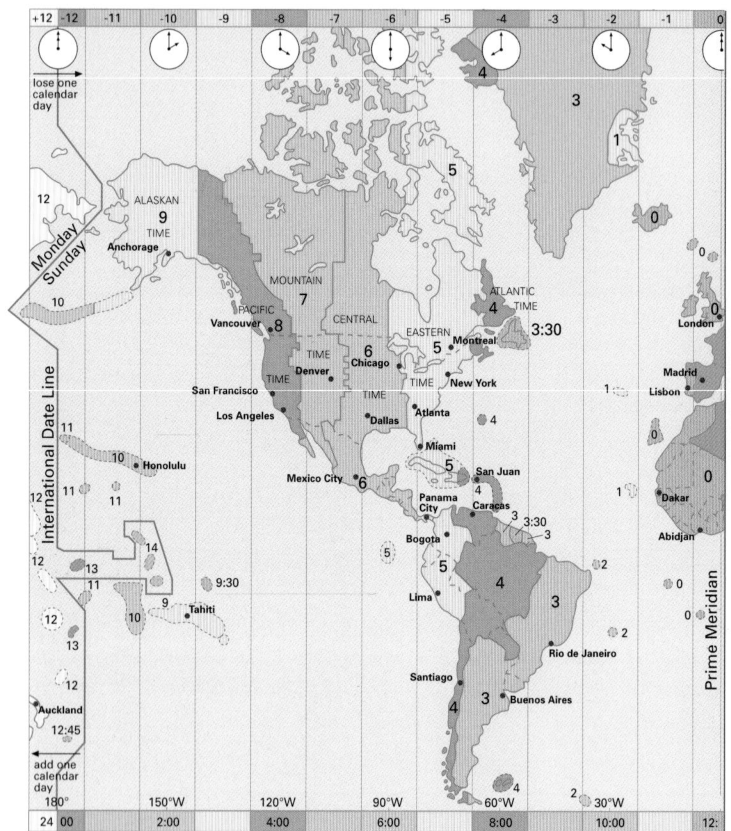

The world is divided into 24 time zones, each centered on meridians at 15° intervals, which is the longitudinal distance the Sun travels every hour. The Prime Meridian running through Greenwich in London, England, passes through the middle of the first time zone. Zones to the east of Greenwich are ahead of Greenwich Mean Time (GMT) by one hour for every 15° of longitude, while zones to the west are behind GMT by one hour.

When it is 12 noon at the Greenwich meridian, 180° east it is midnight of the same day, while at 180° west the day is only just beginning. To overcome this, the International Date Line was established in 1883 – an imaginary line which approximately follows the 180th meridian. Therefore, if one traveled eastward from Japan (140° East) toward Samoa (170° West), one would pass from Sunday night straight into Sunday morning.

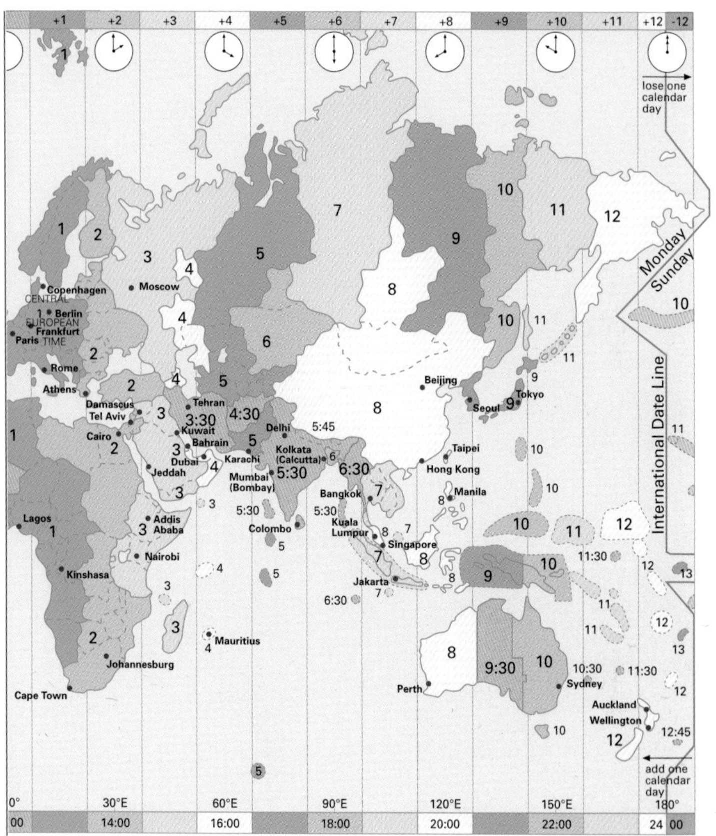

TIME DIFFERENCES FROM EASTERN STANDARD TIME

BEIJING	+13	LONDON	+5
CAIRO	+7	LOS ANGELES	–3
CHICAGO	–1	MOSCOW	+8
DALLAS	–1	MEXICO CITY	–1
DELHI	+10.5	SANTIAGO	+1
DENVER	–2	SYDNEY	+15
HONOLULU	–5	TOKYO	+14
KUWAIT	+8	VANCOUVER	–3

KEY TO TIME ZONES MAP

10 — Hours slow or fast of UT or Coordinated Universal Time

Zones ahead of UT (GMT)

Zones using UT (GMT)

Half-hour zones

Zones behind UT (GMT)

Time zone boundaries

International boundaries

International Date Line

Actual solar time, when time at Greenwich is 12:00 (noon)

Note: Certain time zones are affected by Daylight Saving Time (normally one hour ahead of Standard Time).

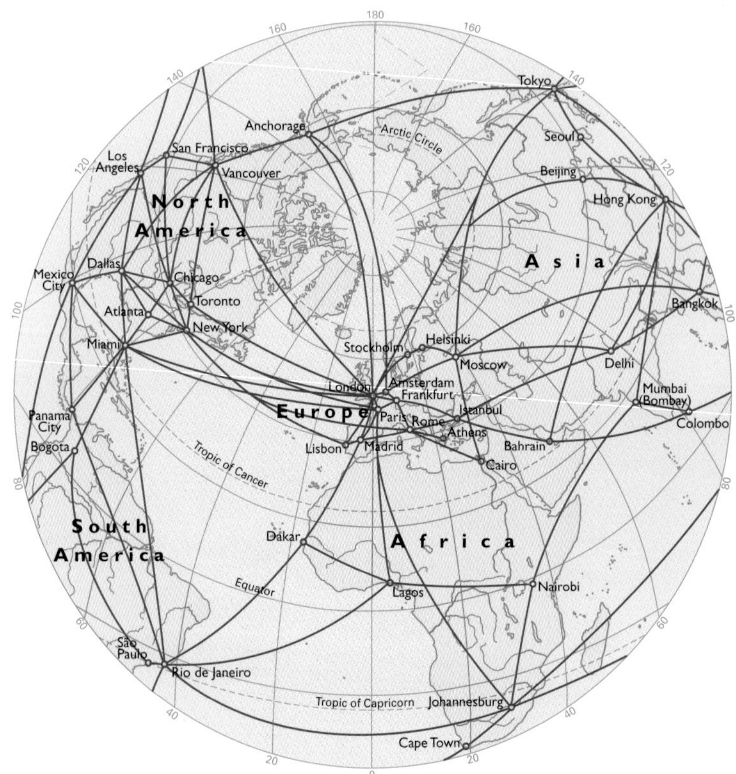

WORLD'S BUSIEST AIRPORTS

TOTAL NUMBER OF PASSENGERS IN MILLIONS (2004)

ATLANTA HARTSFIELD INTL. (ATL)	83.6
CHICAGO O'HARE INTL. (ORD)	75.4
LONDON HEATHROW (LHR)	67.3
TOKYO HANEDA (HND)	62.3
LOS ANGELES INTL. (LAX)	60.7
DALLAS/FORT WORTH INTL. (DFW)	59.4
FRANKFURT INTL. (FRA)	51.1
PARIS CHARLES DE GAULLE (CDG)	50.9
AMSTERDAM SCHIPHOL (AMS)	42.5

The flight paths shown on the maps above usually follow the shortest, most direct route from A to B, known as the ***great-circle route***. A great circle is any circle that divides the globe into equal halves. Aircraft do not always fly along great-circle routes, however. Lack of search and rescue and emergency landing provisions, together with limits on fuel consumption and minimum flying altitudes, mean that commercial aircraft do not usually fly across Antarctica.

FLIGHT TIMES FROM NEW YORK	
FRANKFURT	*8hrs 35mins*
JOHANNESBURG	*17hrs 45mins*
MEXICO CITY	*5hrs 45mins*
PARIS	*8hrs 15mins*
ROME	*9hrs 35mins*
SANTIAGO	*12hrs 55mins*
SINGAPORE	*23hrs 10mins*
TOKYO	*14hrs 35mins*
VANCOUVER	*7hrs 25mins*

FLIGHT TIMES FROM LONDON	
ATHENS	*4hrs 05mins*
AUCKLAND	*24hrs 20mins*
BANGKOK	*14hrs 30mins*
BUENOS AIRES	*14hrs 20mins*
HONG KONG	*14hrs 10mins*
LOS ANGELES	*12hrs 00mins*
MOSCOW	*3hrs 50mins*
MUMBAI (BOMBAY)	*11hrs 15mins*
NEW YORK	*6hrs 50mins*

Kms	Beijing	Bombay (Mumbai)	Buenos Aires	Cairo	Calcutta (Kolkata)	Caracas	Chicago	Hong Kong	Honolulu	Johannesburg	Lagos	London
		2956	11972	4688	2031	8947	6588	1220	5070	7276	7119	5057
			9275	2706	1034	9024	8048	2683	8024	4334	4730	4467
Kms				7341	10268	3167	5599	11481	7558	5025	4919	6917
Beijing					3541	6340	6127	5064	8838	3894	2432	2180
Bombay (Mumbai)	4757					9609	7978	1653	7048	5256	5727	4946
Buenos Aires	19268	14925					2502	10166	6009	6847	4810	4664
Cairo	7544	4355	11814					7783	4247	8689	5973	3949
Calcutta (Kolkata)	3269	1664	16524	5699					5543	6669	7360	5980
Caracas	14399	14522	5096	10203	15464					11934	10133	7228
Chicago	10603	12953	9011	3206	12839	4027					2799	5637
Hong Kong	1963	4317	18478	8150	2659	16360	12526					3118
Honolulu	8160	12914	12164	14223	11343	9670	6836	8921				
Johannesburg	11710	6974	8088	6267	8459	11019	13984	10732	19206			
Lagos	11457	7612	7916	3915	9216	7741	9612	11845	16308	4505		
London	8138	7190	11131	3508	7961	7507	6356	9623	11632	9071	5017	
Los Angeles	10060	14000	9852	12200	13120	5812	2804	11639	4117	16676	12414	8758
Mexico City	12460	15656	7389	12372	15280	3586	2726	14122	6085	14585	11071	8936
Moscow	5794	5031	13477	2902	5534	9938	8000	7144	11323	9161	6254	2498
Nairobi	9216	4532	10402	3536	6179	11544	12883	8776	17282	2927	3807	6819
New York	10988	12541	8526	9020	12747	3430	1145	12950	7980	12841	8477	5572
Paris	8217	7010	11051	3210	7858	7625	6650	9630	11968	8732	4714	342
Rio de Janeiro	17338	13409	1953	9896	15073	4546	8547	17704	13342	7113	6035	9299
Rome	8126	6175	11151	2133	7219	8363	7739	9284	12916	7743	4039	1431
Singapore	4478	3914	15879	8267	2897	18359	15078	2599	10816	8660	11145	10852
Sydney	8949	10160	11800	14418	9138	15343	14875	7374	8168	11040	15519	16992
Tokyo	2099	6742	18362	9571	5141	14164	10137	2874	6202	13547	13480	9562
Wellington	10782	12370	9981	16524	11354	13122	13451	9427	7513	11761	16050	18814

The table above shows air distances in miles and kilometers between 30 major cities.

6251	7742	3600	5727	6828	5106	10773	5049	2783	5561	1304	6700	**Beijing**
8700	9728	3126	2816	7793	4356	8332	3837	2432	6313	4189	7686	**Bombay (Mumbai)**
6122	4591	8374	6463	5298	6867	1214	6929	9867	7332	11410	6202	**Buenos Aires**
7580	7687	1803	2197	5605	1994	6149	1325	5137	8959	5947	10268	**Cairo**
8152	9494	3438	3839	7921	4883	9366	4486	1800	5678	3195	7055	**Calcutta (Kolkata)**
3612	2228	6175	7173	2131	4738	2825	5196	11407	9534	8801	8154	**Caracas**
1742	1694	4971	8005	711	4132	5311	4809	9369	9243	6299	8358	**Chicago**
7232	8775	4439	5453	8047	5984	11001	5769	1615	4582	1786	5857	**Hong Kong**
2558	3781	7036	10739	4958	7437	8290	8026	6721	5075	3854	4669	**Honolulu**
10362	9063	5692	1818	7979	5426	4420	4811	5381	6860	8418	7308	**Johannesburg**
7713	6879	3886	2366	5268	2929	3750	2510	6925	9643	8376	9973	**Lagos**
5442	5552	1552	4237	3463	212	5778	889	6743	10558	5942	11691	**London**
	1549	6070	9659	2446	5645	6310	6331	8776	7502	5475	6719	**Los Angeles**
Los Angeles		6664	9207	2090	5717	4780	6365	10321	8058	7024	6897	**Mexico City**
	Mexico City		3942	4666	1545	7184	1477	5237	9008	4651	10283	**Moscow**
		Moscow		7358	4029	5548	3350	4635	7552	6996	8490	**Nairobi**
2493			**Nairobi**		3626	4832	4280	9531	9935	6741	8951	**New York**
9769	10724			**New York**		5708	687	6671	10539	6038	11798	**Paris**
15544	14818	6344			**Paris**		5725	9763	8389	11551	7367	**Rio de Janeiro**
3936	3264	7510	11842			**Rio de Janeiro**		6229	10143	6127	11523	**Rome**
9085	9200	2486	6485	5836			**Rome**		3915	3306	5298	**Singapore**
10155	7693	11562	8928	7777	9187			**Singapore**		4861	1383	**Sydney**
10188	10243	2376	5391	6888	1105	9214			**Sydney**		5762	**Tokyo**
14123	16610	8428	7460	15339	10737	15712	10025			**Tokyo**		**Wellington**
12073	12969	14497	12153	15989	16962	13501	16324	6300			**Wellington**	Miles
8811	11304	7485	11260	10849	9718	18589	9861	5321	7823			
10814	11100	16549	13664	14405	18987	11855	18545	8526	2226	9273		

Known as "great-circle" distances, these measure the shortest routes between the cities.

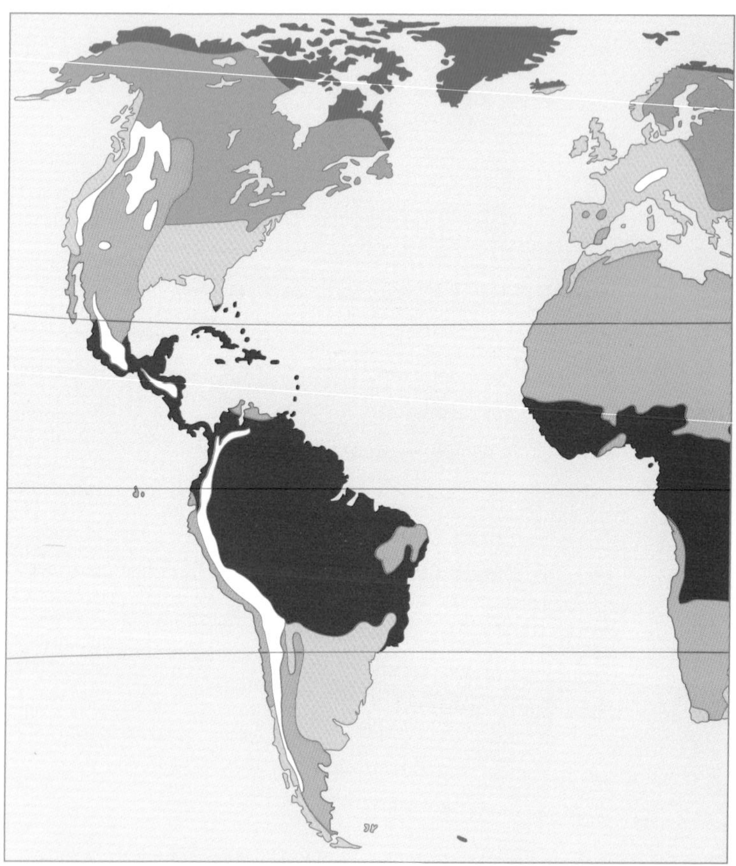

Climate is weather in the long term: the seasonal pattern of temperature and precipitation averaged over a period of time. Temperature roughly follows latitude, and is warmest near the equator and coldest near the poles. The interplay of various factors, however, namely the differential heating of land and sea, the influence of land masses and mountain ranges on winds and ocean currents, and the effect of vegetation, all combine to add complexity. Thus New York and Naples share almost the same latitude, but their resulting climates are quite different. Most scientists are now in agreement that the world's climate is changing, due partly to atmospheric pollution. By the year 2050, average world temperatures are predicted to rise by approximately 3°F to make the climate hotter than it has been at any time during the last 120,000 years. Climate statistics for 18 cities are given on pages 18 and 19.

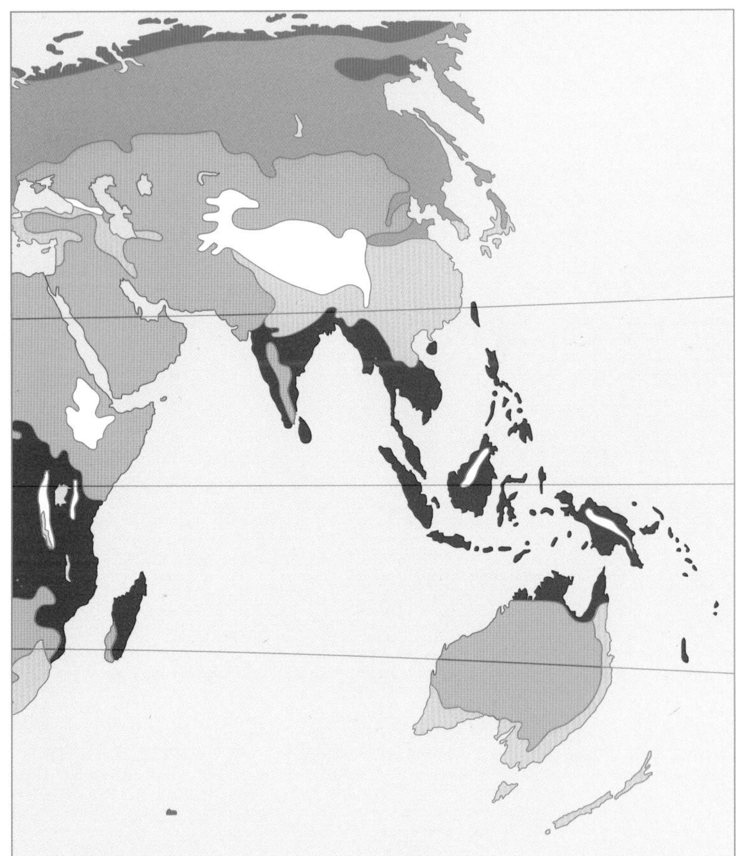

SEASONAL WEATHER EXTREMES

- **Caribbean**
  Hurricanes – August to October
- **Northern Latitudes**
  Blizzards – November to March
- **Southern Asia**
  Cyclones and typhoons – June to November
- **Southern Asia**
  Monsoon rains – July to October

CLIMATIC REGIONS

- Tropical climate (hot and wet)
- Continental climate (cold and wet)
- Dry climate (desert and steppe)
- Polar climate (very cold and dry)
- Mild climate (warm and wet)
- Mountainous areas (where altitude affects climate types)

Note: Climate comprises a description of the condition of the atmosphere over a considerable area for a long time (at least 30 years).

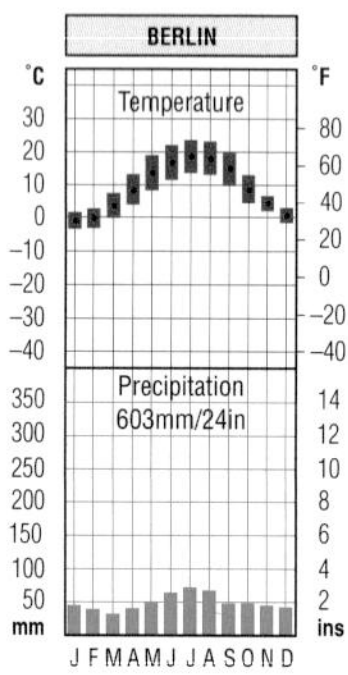
BERLIN
Temperature
Precipitation
603mm/24in

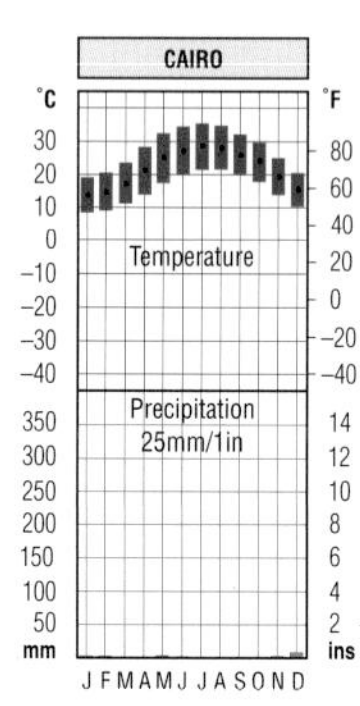
CAIRO
Temperature
Precipitation
25mm/1in

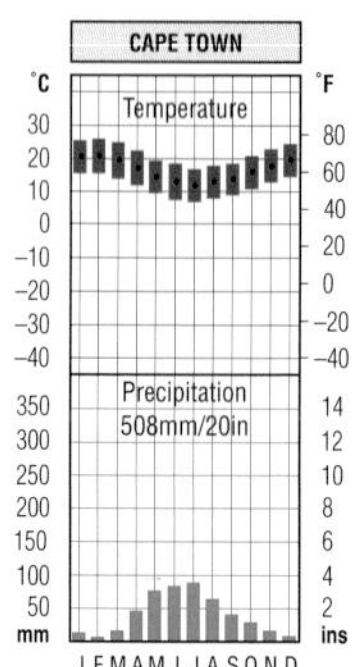
CAPE TOWN
Temperature
Precipitation
508mm/20in

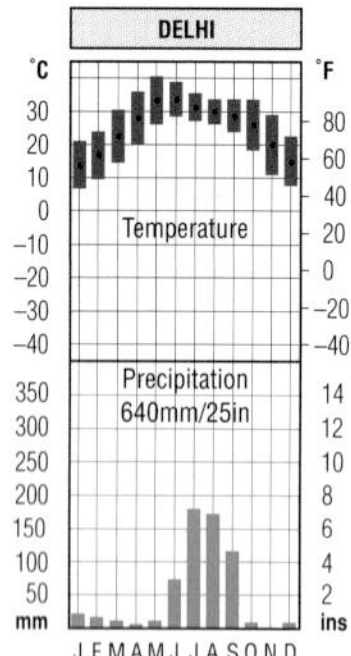
DELHI
Temperature
Precipitation
640mm/25in

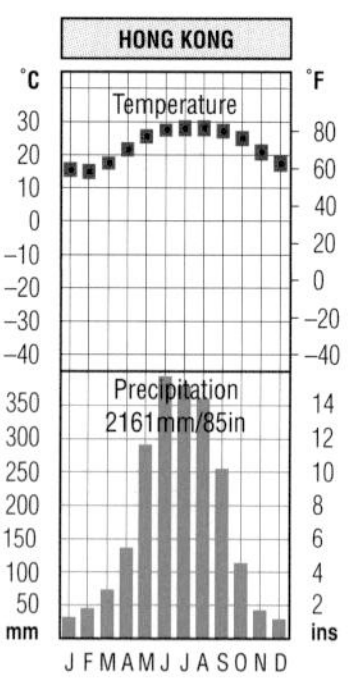
HONG KONG
Temperature
Precipitation
2161mm/85in

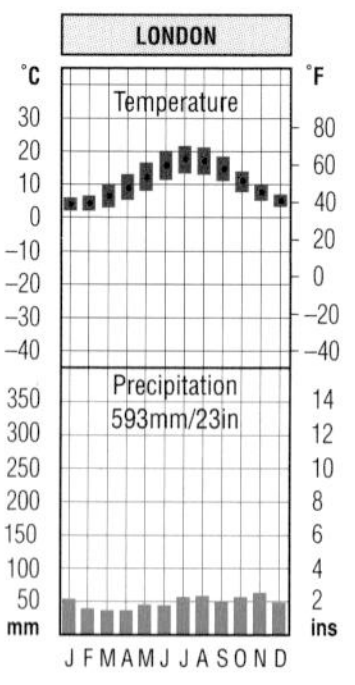
LONDON
Temperature
Precipitation
593mm/23in

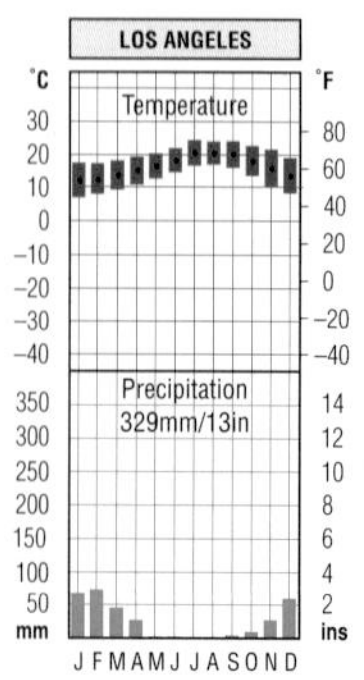
LOS ANGELES
Temperature
Precipitation
329mm/13in

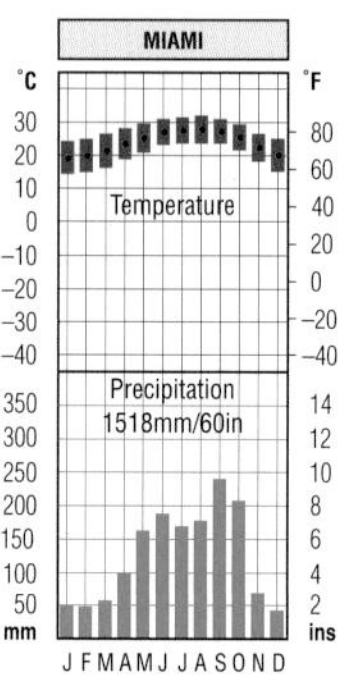
MIAMI
Temperature
Precipitation
1518mm/60in

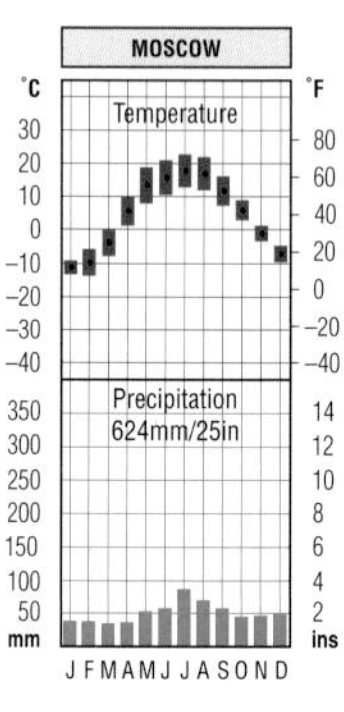
MOSCOW
Temperature
Precipitation
624mm/25in

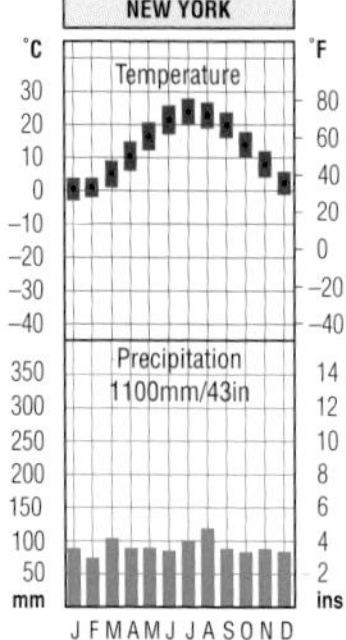
NEW YORK
Temperature
Precipitation
1100mm/43in

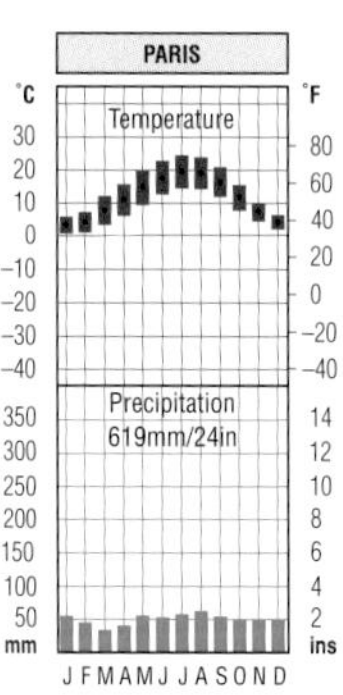
PARIS
Temperature
Precipitation
619mm/24in

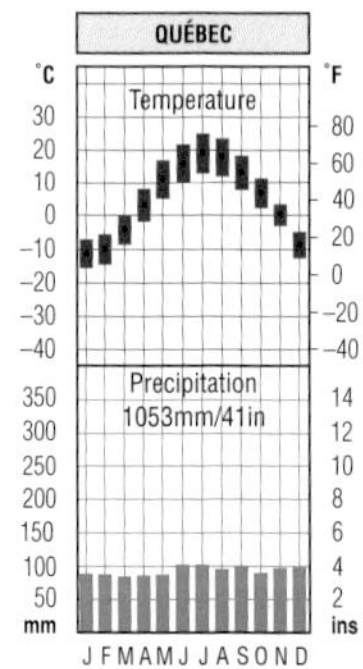
QUÉBEC
Temperature
Precipitation
1053mm/41in

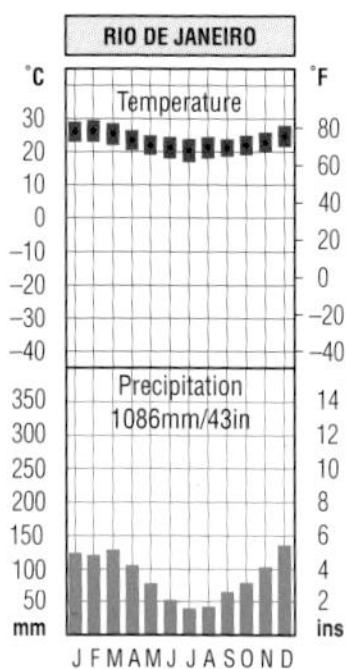
RIO DE JANEIRO
Temperature
Precipitation
1086mm/43in

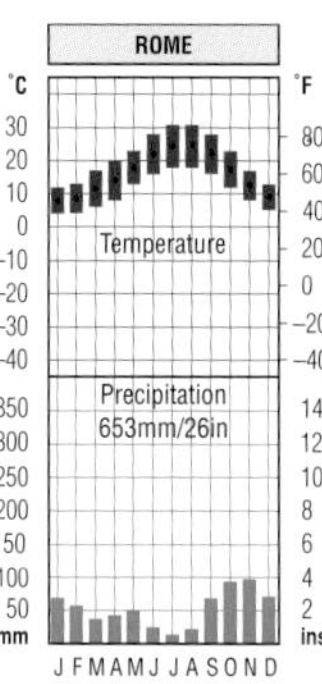
ROME
Temperature
Precipitation
653mm/26in

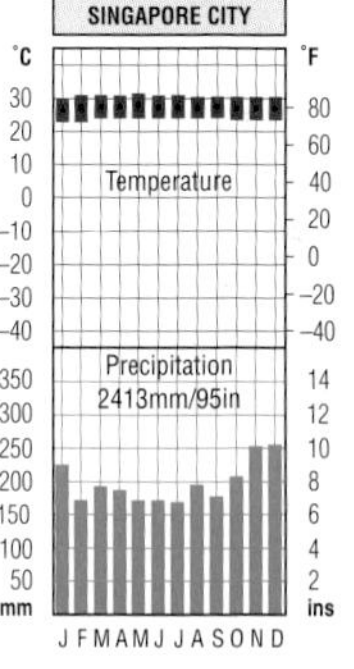
SINGAPORE CITY
Temperature
Precipitation
2413mm/95in

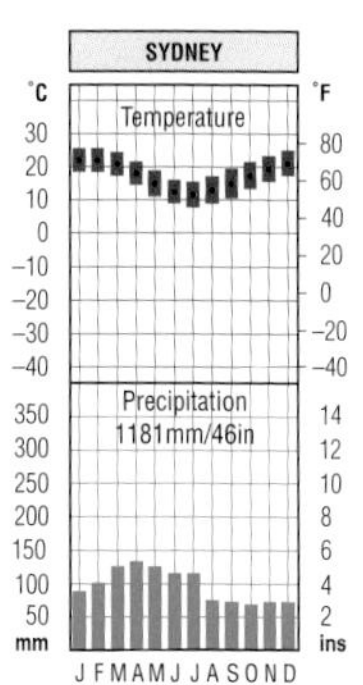
SYDNEY
Temperature
Precipitation
1181mm/46in

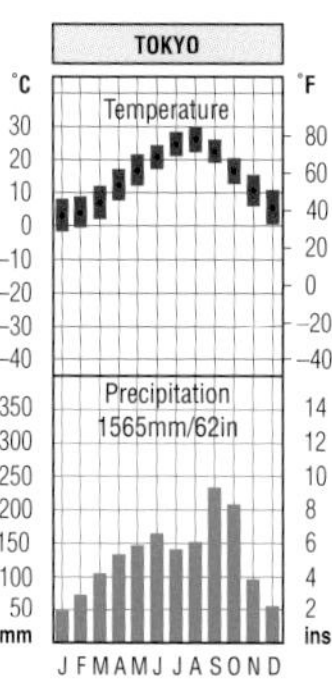
TOKYO
Temperature
Precipitation
1565mm/62in

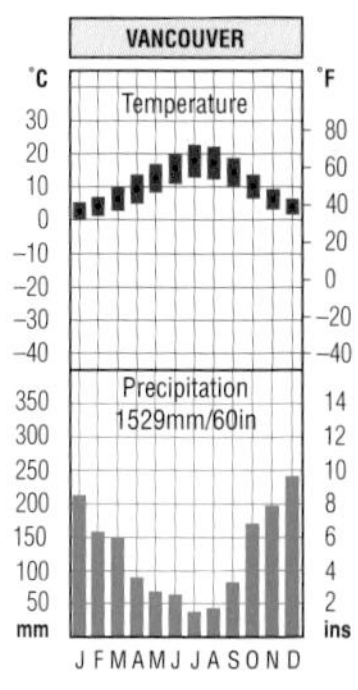
VANCOUVER
Temperature
Precipitation
1529mm/60in

TO CONVERT	INTO	MULTIPLY BY
Length		
Centimeters	Inches	0.394
Feet	Meters	0.305
Inches	Centimeters	2.540
Inches	Millimeters	25.400
Kilometers	Miles	0.621
Meters	Feet	3.281
Meters	Yards	1.094
Miles	Kilometers	1.609
Millimeters	Inches	0.039
Yards	Meters	0.914
Area		
Acres	Hectares	0.405
Hectares	Acres	2.471
Square centimeters	Square inches	0.155
Square feet	Square meters	0.093
Square inches	Square centimeters	6.452
Square kilometers	Square miles	0.388
Square meters	Square feet	10.764
Square miles	Square yards	1.195
Square yards	Square meters	0.836
Volume		
Cubic centimeters	Cubic inches	0.61
Cubic feet	Cubic meters	0.028
Cubic meters	Cubic feet	35.315
Cubic inches	Cubic centimeters	16.387
Cubic meters	Cubic yards	1.308
Cubic yards	Cubic meters	0.785
Gallons (Imperial)	Liters	4.506
Gallons (US)	Liters	3.785
Liters	Gallons (Imperial)	0.220
Liters	Gallons (US)	0.264
Liters	Ounces (fluid)	33.814
Liters	Pints	2.113
Liters	Quarts	1.057
Milliliters (cc)	Ounces (fluid)	0.034
Ounces (fluid)	Milliliters (cc)	29.573
Pints	Liters	0.473
Quarts	Liters	0.946
Weight		
Grams	Ounces	0.35
Kilograms	Pounds	2.205
Ounces	Grams	28.350
Pounds	Kilograms	0.454
Tons (2,000 lbs)	Tons metric	0.907
Tons metric	Tons (2,000 lbs)	1.102

CITY PLANS

LEGEND TO CITY PLANS

- Motorway
- Through route
- Secondary road
- Other road
- Limited access / pedestrian road
- Railroad
- Tramway/monorail
- Rail/bus station
- Underground/Metro station
- MANLY Ferry route/destination
- Abbey/cathedral
- Church of interest
- Hospital
- Mosque
- Shrine
- Synagogue
- Temple
- Tourist information center
- Public building
- Museum Place of interest

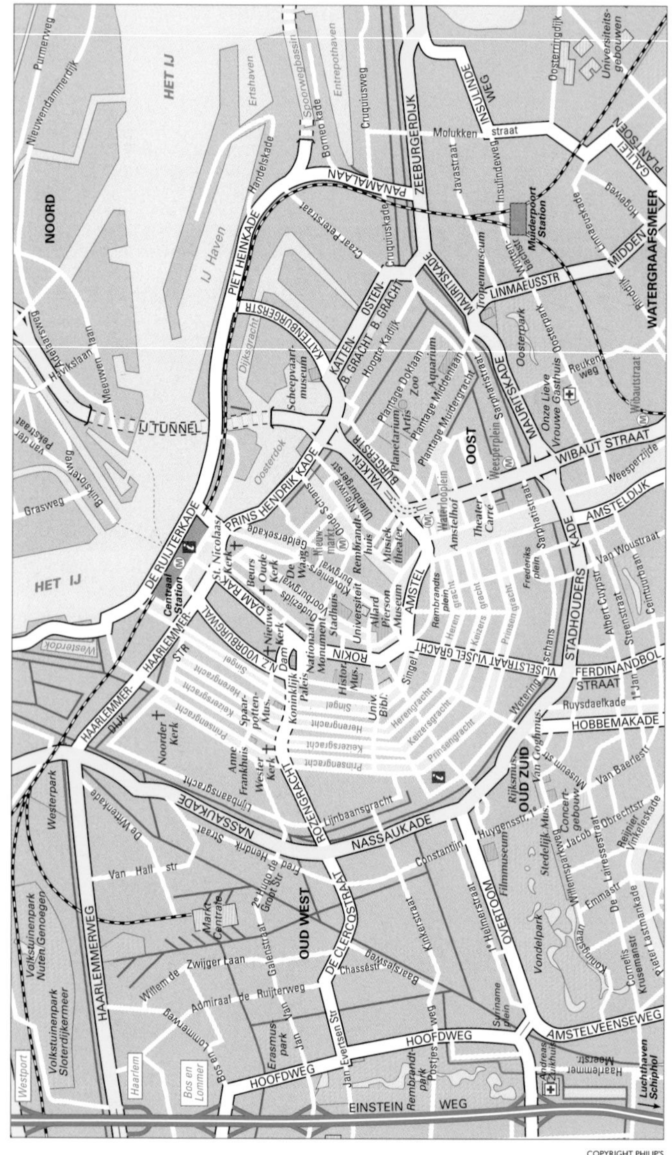
0 km 2
HET IJ
NOORD
IJ Haven
Ertshaven
Spoorwegbassin
Entrepothaven
Borneo kade
Cruquiusweg
ZEEBURGERDIJK
INSULINDE WEG
Molukken straat
Javastraat
Insulindeweg
Oosterringdijk
Universiteits-gebouwen
GALILEI PLANTSOEN
PANAMALAAN
Handelskade
PIET HEINKADE
Czaar Petersstraat
Cruquiuskade
Muiderpoort Station
Hogeweg
Linnaeuskade
MIDDEN
WATERGRAAFSMEER
MAURITSKADE
Tropenmuseum
LINMAEUSSTR
Oosterpark
Ringdijk
KATTENBURGERSTR
Dijksgracht
Scheepvaart-museum
KATTEN-BURGERGRACHT
OSTEN-B. GRACHT
Hoogte Kadijk
Plantage Doklaan
Aquarium
Zoo
Artis
Planetarium
Plantage Middenlaan
Plantage Muidergracht
Sarphatistraat
Onze Lieve Vrouwe Gasthuis
Reuken weg
Wibautstraat
Purmerweg
Nieuwendammerdijk
Adelaarsweg
Havikslaan
Meeuwen laan
IJ TUNNEL
Oosterdok
VALKEN-BURGERSTR.
OOST
Weesperplein
WIBAUT STRAAT
Weesperzijde
Van der Pekstraat
Buiksloterweg
Grasweg
HET IJ
DE RUIJTERKADE
Centraal Station
PRINS HENDRIK KADE
Nieuwe Uilenburgerstr.
Oude Schans
Waterlooplein
Amstelhof
Theater Carré
AMSTELDIJK
St. Nicolaas Kerk
Geldersekade
Nieuw-markt
Rembrandt-huis
Muziek theater
Beurs
Oude Kerk
De Waag
Kloveniersburgwal
Oudezijds Voorburgwal
Universiteit
Allard Pierson Museum
AMSTEL
Rembrandts plein
Frederiks plein
KADE
Van Woustraat
DAM RAK
Nieuwe Kerk
Stadhuis
Nationaal Monument
Dam
Koninklijk Paleis
Histor. Mus.
ROKIN
Singel
Herengracht
Keizersgracht
Prinsengracht
VIJZELSTRAAT
VIJZELGRACHT
Weteringschans
STADHOUDERS
Albert Cuypstr
Ceintuurbaan
Westerdok
HAARLEMMER-STR
N.Z. VOORBURGWAL
HAARLEMMER-DIJK
Noorder Kerk
Spaar-potten-Mus.
Univ. Bibl.
FERDINANDBOL STRAAT
1e Jan
Ruysdaelkade
HOBBEMAKADE
Anne Frankhuis
Wester Kerk
OUD ZUID
Rijksmus.
Van Goghmus.
Museum str
Van Baerlestr
Lijnbaansgracht
ROZENGRACHT
NASSAUKADE
De Wittenkade
Westerpark
Hendrik Straat
Concert-gebouw
Huygensstr.
Stedelijk Mus.
Jacob Obrechtstr
Reijnier Vinkeleskade
Van Hall str
Fred. Hugo de Groot Str
Constantijn
Markt Centrale
OUD WEST
DE CLERCQSTRAAT
Kinkerstraat
1e Helmerstraat
OVERTOOM
Filmmuseum
Vondelpark
Willemsparkweg
De Lairessestraat
Emmastr
Koningslaan
Cornelis Krusemanstr
Pieter Lastmankade
Volkstuinenpark Nuten Genoegen
Volkstuinenpark Slotedijkermeer
HAARLEMMERWEG
Willem de Zwijger Laan
Galenstraat
Admiraal de Ruijterweg
Chassestr
Baarsjesweg
Lumeriusweg
Erasmus-park
Jan van
Jan Evertsen Str
Postjes weg
Suriname plein
HOOFDWEG
AMSTELVEENSEWEG
Andreas Ziekhuis
Haarlemmer Meerstr.
Luchthaven Schiphol
Westport
Haarlem
Bos en Lommer
Rembrandt-park
EINSTEIN WEG

0 km 1

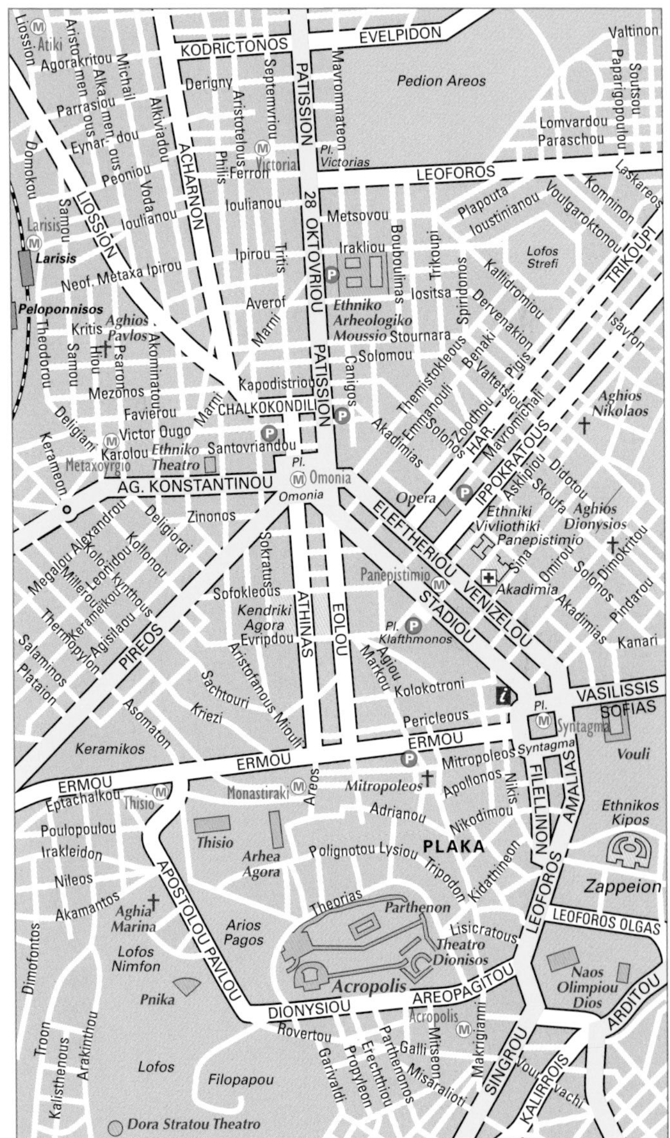

KODRICTONOS
EVELPIDON
Pedion Areos
Valtinon
Liossion
Atiki
Aristo men ous
Agorakritou
Alkamen ous
Michail
Derigny
Septemvriou
PATISSION
Mavrommateon
Parrasiou
Alkiviadou
Aristotelous
Eynar- dou
ACHARNON
Philis
Victoria
Ferron
Pl. Victorias
LEOFOROS
Papparigopoulou
Soutsou
Lomvardou
Paraschou
Laskareos
Komninon
Domokou
Peoniou
Voda
LIOSSION
Ioulianou
Samou
Larisis
28 OKTOVRIOU
Metsovou
Plapouta
Ioustinianou
Voulgaroktonou
Larisis
Irakliou
Bouboulinas
Trikoupi
Lofos Strefi
TRIKOUPI
Ipirou
Tritis
Neof. Metaxa Ipirou
Iositsa
Spiridonos
Kallidromiou
Peloponnisos
Averof
Ethniko Arheologiko Moussio
Stournara
Dervenakion
Isavrou
Kritis
Aghios Pavlos
Marni
Theodorou
Hiou
Psaron
Akominatou
Solomou
Benaki
PATISSION
Canigos
Themistokleous
Valtetsiou
Pigis
Samou
Kapodistriou
Mezonos
Emmanouli
Zoodhou
Aghios Nikolaos
Favierou
CHALKOKONDILI
Solonos
Mavromichali
Deligiani
Marni
Akadimias
HAR.
IPPOKRATOUS
Kerameon
Victor Ougo
Karolou
Ethniko Theatro
Santovriandou
Metaxoyrgio
Pl. Omonia
Omonia
Askliipiou
Didotou
AG. KONSTANTINOU
Opera
Skoufa
Ethniki Vivliothiki
Aghios Dionysios
Zinonos
Deligiorgi
ELEFTHERIOU
Panepistimio
Dimokritou
Alexandrou
Megalou
Kolonou
Kolonou
Leonidou
Millerou
Kynthous
Sokratous
Sina
Omirou
Panepistimio
VENIZELOU
Solonos
Akadimia
Pindarou
Kerameikou
Sofokleous
STADIOU
Thermopylon
Agisilaou
Kendriki Agora
Evripdou
ATHINAS
EOLOU
Pl. Klafthmonos
Akadimias
Kanari
Salaminos
PIREOS
Aristofanous
Agiou Markou
Plataion
Sachtouri
Kolokotroni
VASILISSIS SOFIAS
Kriezi
Miouli
Asomaton
Pericleous
Pl. Syntagma
Syntagma
Keramikos
ERMOU
ERMOU
Mitropoleos
Vouli
ERMOU
Eptachalkou
Thisio
Monastiraki
Areos
Mitropoleos
Apollonos
Nikis
FILELLINON
AMALIAS
Adrianou
Nikodimou
Ethnikos Kipos
Poulopoulou
Thisio
Irakleidon
Arhea Agora
Polignotou
Lysiou
PLAKA
Tripodon
Kidathineon
LEOFOROS
Zappeion
Nileos
APOSTOLOU PAVLOU
Theorias
Parthenon
Akamantos
Aghia Marina
Arios Pagos
LEOFOROS OLGAS
Lisicratous
Theatro Dionisos
Dimofontos
Lofos Nimfon
Naos Olimpiou Dios
Pnika
Acropolis
AREOPAGITOU
DIONYSIOU
ARDITOU
Acropolis
Rovertou
Makrigianni
Troon
Arakinthou
Galli
Mitseon
Garivaldi
Propyleon
Erechthiou
Parthenonos
Misaralioti
SINGROU
KALIRROIS
Vouli
Vachi
Kalisthenous
Lofos
Filopapou
Dora Stratou Theatro

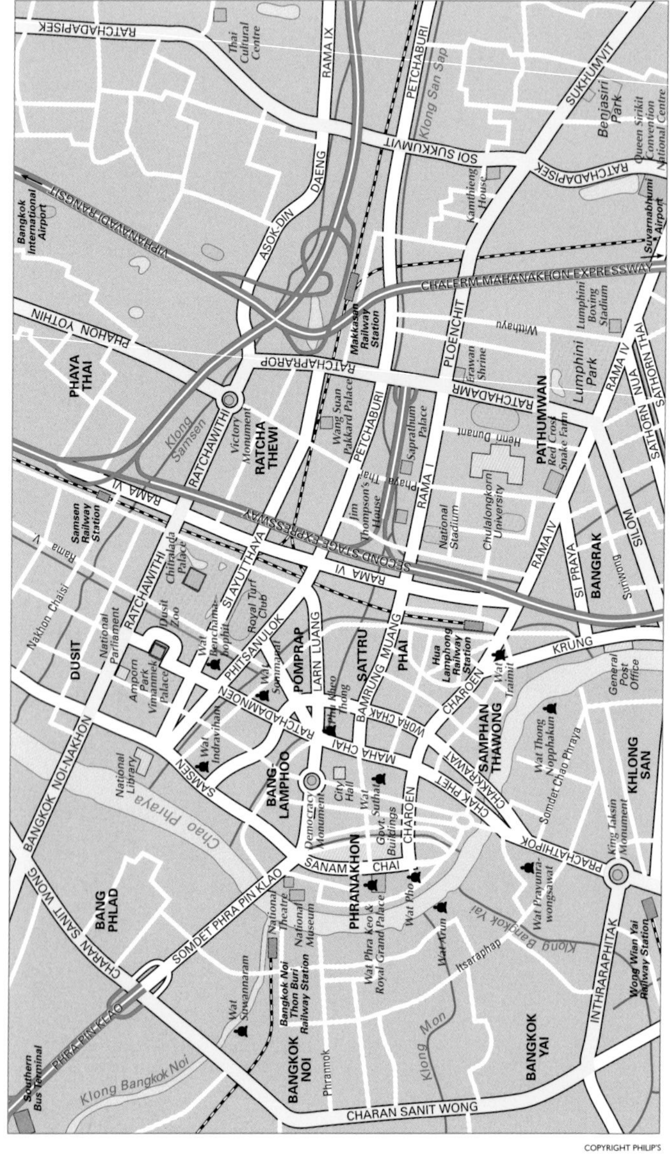
0 km 2
RATCHADAPISEK
Thai Cultural Centre
RAMA IX
PETCHABURI
Klong San Sap
SUKHUMVIT
Benjasiri Park
Queen Sirikit National Convention Centre
SOI SUKKUMVIT
RATCHADAPISEK
Kamthieng House
ASOK-DIN DAENG
VIPHANAVADI-RANGSIT
Bangkok International Airport
Suvarnabhumi Airport
CHALERM MAHANAKHON EXPRESSWAY
Makkasan Railway Station
PHAHON YOTHIN
PLOENCHIT
Witthayu
Lumphini Boxing Stadium
Erawan Shrine
Lumphini Park
RAMA IV
NUA
SATHORN THAI
SATHORN
PHAYA THAI
RATCHAPRAROP
RATCHADAMRI
PATHUMWAN
Wang Suan Pakkard Palace
Victory Monument
RATCHAWITHI
Klong Samsen
RATCHA THEWI
PETCHABURI
Sapratum Palace
Henri Dunant
Red Cross Snake Farm
RAMA VI
Phaya Thai
Jim Thompson's House
RAMA I
National Stadium
Chulalongkorn University
RAMA IV
SILOM
Samsen Railway Station
Rama V
Chitralada Palace
SI AYUTTHAYA
SECOND STAGE EXPRESSWAY
RAMA VI
SI PRAYA
BANGRAK
Suriwong
Nakhon Chaisi
RATCHAWITHI
National Parliament
Dusit Zoo
Royal Turf Club
Wat Benchamabophit
PHITSANULOK
POMPRAP
LARN LUANG
SATTRU
BAMRUNG MUANG
PHAI
Hua Lamphong Railway Station
KRUNG
Wat Traimit
General Post Office
DUSIT
Amporn Park
Vimanmek Palace
Wat Sommanat
RATCHADAMNOEN
Phu Khao Thong
WORA CHAK
CHAROEN
SAMPHAN THAWONG
Wat Thong Nopphakun
BANGKOK NOI-NAKHON
National Library
Wat Indraviharn
SAMSEN
BANG LAMPHOO
Democracy Monument
City Hall
MAHA CHAI
Wat Suthat
Govt. Buildings
CHAROEN
CHAK PHET
CHAKKRAWAT
Somdet Chao Phraya
KHLONG SAN
Chao Phraya
PRACHATHIPOK
King Taksin Monument
SANAM CHAI
PHRANAKHON
CHARAN SANIT WONG
BANG PHLAD
SOMDET PHRA PIN KLAO
National Theatre
National Museum
Wat Phra Keo & Royal Grand Palace
Wat Pho
Wat Arun
Klong Bangkok Yai
Wat Prayunrawongsawat
INTHRARAPHITAK
Wong Wian Yai Railway Station
Itsaraphap
Bangkok Noi Thon Buri Railway Station
Wat Suwannaram
PHRA PIN KLAO
Southern Bus Terminal
Klong Bangkok Noi
BANGKOK NOI
Phrannok
Klong Mon
BANGKOK YAI
CHARAN SANIT WONG

0 km 1

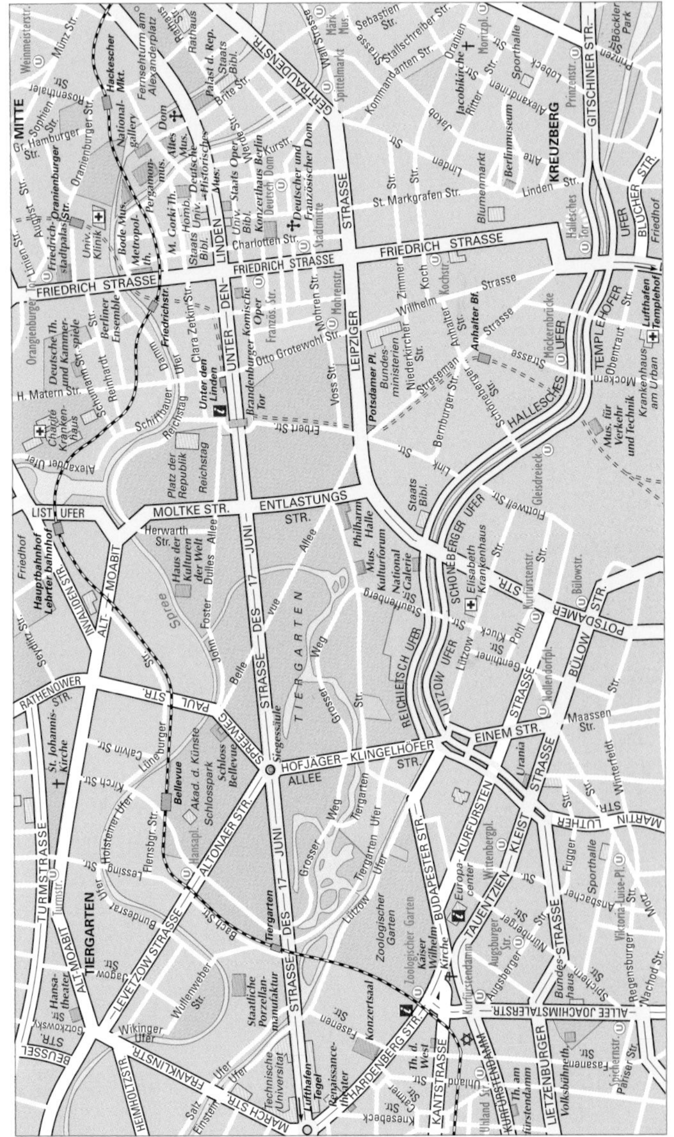
MITTE
TIERGARTEN
KREUZBERG
FRIEDRICH STRASSE
LEIPZIGER STRASSE
UNTER DEN LINDEN
MOLTKE STR.
ENTLASTUNGS STR.
STRASSE DES 17. JUNI
TIERGARTEN
HOFJÄGER ALLEE
KLINGELHÖFER STR.
POTSDAMER STR.
BÜLOW STR.
EINEM STR.
TAUENTZIEN
KURFÜRSTENDAMM
KANTSTRASSE
HARDENBERG STR.
BUDAPESTER STR.
ALTONAER STR.
LEVETZOW STRASSE
TURMSTRASSE
ALT-MOABIT
INVALIDEN STR.
PAUL STR.
SPREEWEG
RATHENOWER STR.
HALLESCHES UFER
TEMPELHOFER UFER
GITSCHINER STR.
BLÜCHER STR.
GERTRAUDENSTR.
ALLEE JOACHIMSTALERSTR.
MARTIN LUTHER STR.
Siegessäule
Brandenburger Tor
Reichstag
Platz der Republik
Potsdamer Pl.
Anhalter Bf.
Hauptbahnhof Lehrter bahnhof
Zoologischer Garten
Kulturforum
Philharm. Halle
National Galerie
Schloss Bellevue
Bellevue
Tiergarten
Haus der Kulturen der Welt
Charité Krankenhaus
Fernsehturm am Alexanderplatz
Dom
Altes Mus.
Pergamon mus.
Bode Mus.
Hackescher Mkt.
Friedrichstr.
Deutscher und Französischer Dom
Konzerthaus Berlin
Komische Oper
Staats Oper
Berlinmuseum
Jacobikirche
Mus. für Verkehr und Technik
Europa-center
Kaiser Wilhelm-Kirche
Staatliche Porzellan-manufaktur
Technische Universität
Lufthafen Tegel
Lufthafen Tempelhof
Urania
Spree
Landwehr Kanal

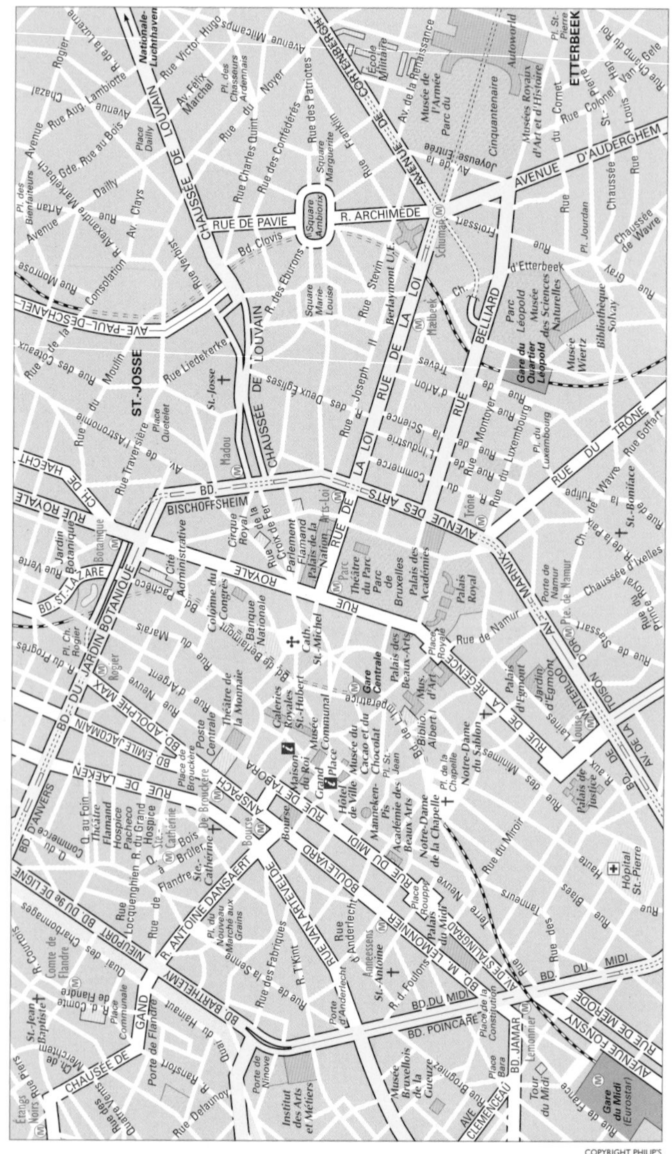

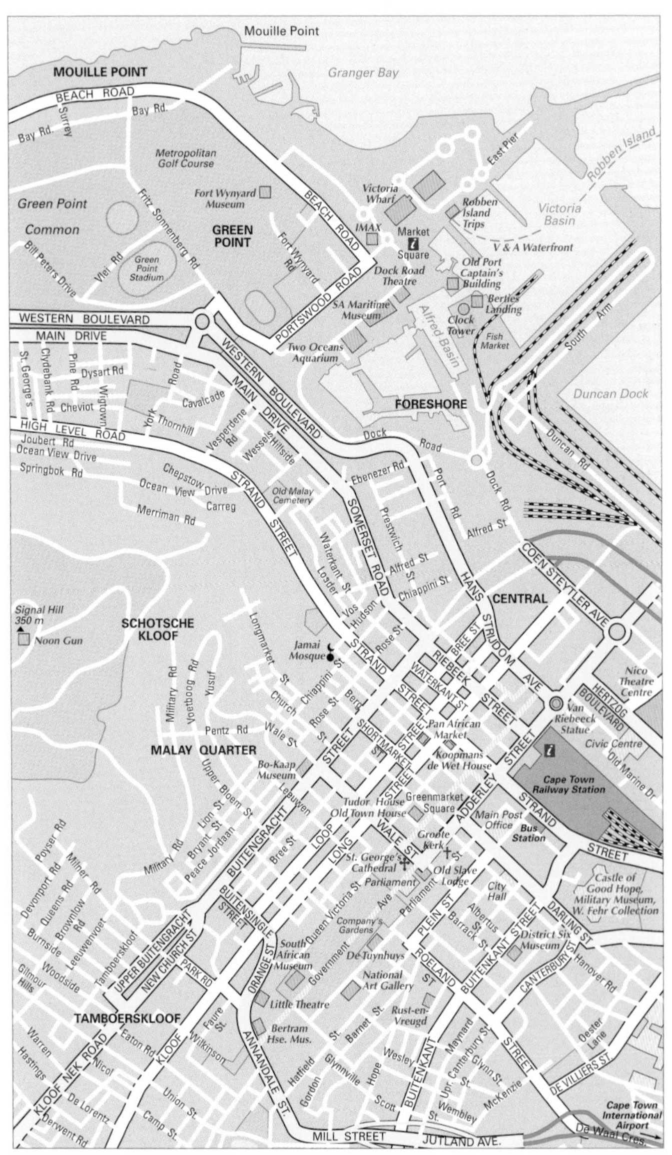
0 km 1
Mouille Point
MOUILLE POINT
Granger Bay
BEACH ROAD
Bay Rd.
Surrey
Metropolitan Golf Course
Fort Wynyard Museum
Green Point Common
GREEN POINT
Fritz Sonnenberg Rd
Bill Peters Drive
Vlei Rd
Green Point Stadium
Fort Wynyard Rd
PORTSWOOD ROAD
Victoria Wharf
IMAX
Market Square
Robben Island Trips
East Pier
Robben Island
Victoria Basin
V & A Waterfront
Dock Road Theatre
Old Port Captain's Building
Berties Landing
SA Maritime Museum
Alfred Basin
Clock Tower
Fish Market
South Arm
Two Oceans Aquarium
Duncan Dock
WESTERN BOULEVARD
MAIN DRIVE
St. George's
Clydebank Rd
Pine Rd
Dysart Rd
Cheviot
Wigtown
York Road
Cavalcade
Thornhill
HIGH LEVEL ROAD
Joubert Rd
Ocean View Drive
Springbok Rd
Vesperdene Rd
Wessels
Hillside
FORESHORE
Dock Road
Duncan Rd
Dock Rd
Ebenezer Rd
Chepstow Drive
Ocean View Drive
Carreg
Merriman Rd
STRAND STREET
Old Malay Cemetery
SOMERSET ROAD
Prestwich St
Port Rd
Alfred St
Waterkant St
Loader
Chiappini St
HANS STRIJDOM AVE
COEN STEYTLER AVE
CENTRAL
Signal Hill 350 m
Noon Gun
SCHOTSCHE KLOOF
Longmarket St
Vos
Hudson
Rose St
Jamai Mosque
BREE ST
RIEBEEK STREET
WATERKANT ST
Nico Theatre Centre
HERTZOG BOULEVARD
Military Rd
Voetboog Rd
Yusuf
Church
Chiappini St
Rose St
Berg
Van Riebeeck Statue
Pentz Rd
Wale St
SHORTMARKET ST
Pan African Market
Civic Centre
Old Marine Dr
MALAY QUARTER
Bo-Kaap Museum
Koopmans de Wet House
Cape Town Railway Station
Upper Bloem St
Leeuwen
Tudor House
Greenmarket Square
ADDERLEY STREET
STRAND STREET
Old Town House
Main Post Office
Bus Station
Lion St
Bryant St
Peace Jordaan
BUITENGRACHT
Bree St
LOOP
LONG
WALE ST
Groote Kerk
Poyser Rd
Milner Rd
Military Rd
St. George's Cathedral
Parliament
Old Slave Lodge
Castle of Good Hope, Military Museum, W. Fehr Collection
Devonport Rd
Queens Rd
Brownlow Rd
Burnside
Leeuwenvoet
BUITENSINGLE STREET
Queen Victoria St
Ave
Parliament
PLEIN ST
City Hall
Albertus St
Barrack St
BUITENKANT STREET
DARLING ST
District Six Museum
Woodside
Gilmour Hills
Tamboerskloof
UPPER BUITENGRACHT
NEW CHURCH ST
PARK RD
ORANGE ST
South African Museum
Company's Gardens
Government
De Tuynhuys
National Art Gallery
ROELAND ST
CANTERBURY ST
Hanover Rd
Little Theatre
TAMBOERSKLOOF
Faure St
Rust-en-Vreugd
Oester Lane
Warren
Hastings
KLOOF NEK ROAD
Eaton Rd
Nicol
KLOOF
Wilkinson
ANNANDALE ST.
Bertram Hse. Mus.
Barnet St.
St.
Hatfield
Gordon
Glynnville
Hope
Wesley
BUITENKANT St.
Maynard
Upr. Canterbury St.
Glynn St.
McKenzie
STREET
DE VILLIERS ST
De Lorentz
Derwent Rd
Union St.
Camp St.
Scott
Wembley
MILL STREET
JUTLAND AVE.
Cape Town International Airport
De Waal Cres.

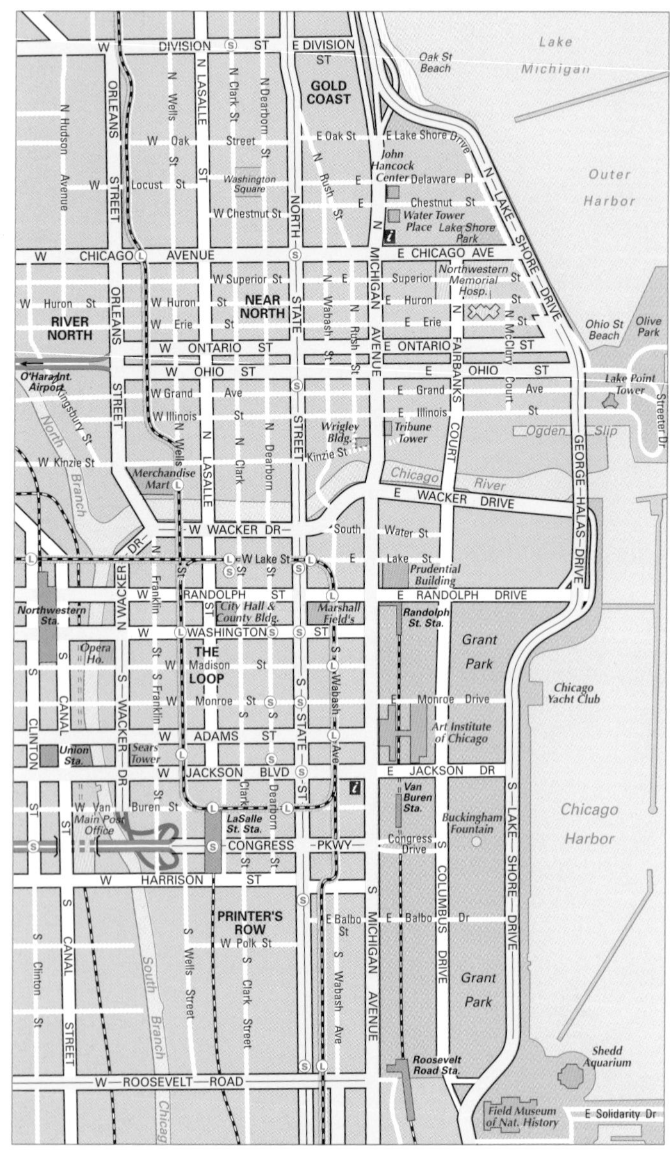
0 km 0.5
Lake Michigan
Oak St Beach
GOLD COAST
Outer Harbor
John Hancock Center
Water Tower Place
Lake Shore Park
Northwestern Memorial Hosp.
RIVER NORTH
NEAR NORTH
Ohio St Beach
Olive Park
Lake Point Tower
O'Hara Int. Airport
Ogden Slip
Wrigley Bldg.
Tribune Tower
Merchandise Mart
Chicago River
North Branch
Prudential Building
Northwestern Sta.
City Hall & County Bldg.
Marshall Field's
Randolph St. Sta.
Grant Park
Opera Ho.
THE LOOP
Chicago Yacht Club
Art Institute of Chicago
Union Sta.
Sears Tower
Van Buren Sta.
Buckingham Fountain
Main Post Office
LaSalle St. Sta.
Chicago Harbor
PRINTER'S ROW
South Branch
Roosevelt Road Sta.
Shedd Aquarium
Field Museum of Nat. History
Elevated rail lines
COPYRIGHT PHILIP'S

0 km 0.5

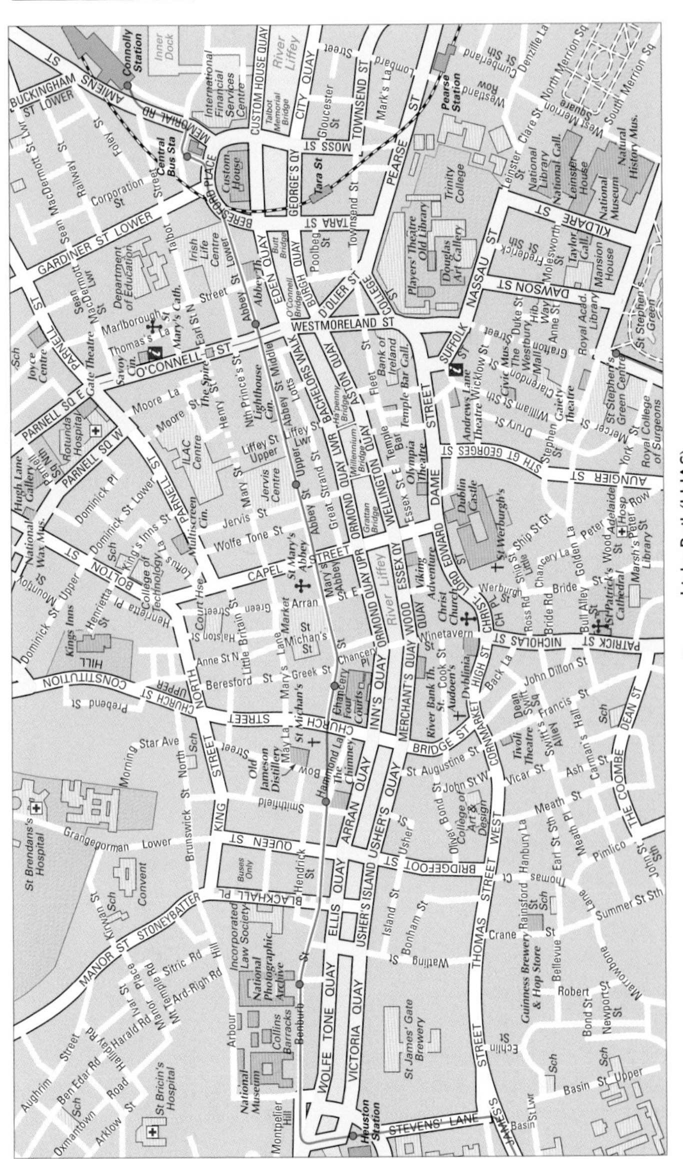
Connolly Station
Inner Dock
River Liffey
CUSTOM HOUSE QUAY
International Financial Services Centre
Talbot Memorial Bridge
CITY QUAY
Gloucester St
MOSS ST
TOWNSEND ST
Mark's La
Lombard Street
PEARSE ST
Pearse Station
Westland Row
Cumberland St Sth
Denzille La
North Merrion Sq
Merrion Square
West Merrion Sq
South Merrion Sq
Clare St
Leinster St
National Library
National Gall.
Leinster House
National Museum
Natural History Mus.
KILDARE ST
Trinity College
Players' Theatre
Old Library
Douglas Art Gallery
Tara St
TARA ST
GEORGE'S QY
Custom House
Central Bus Sta
MEMORIAL RD
AMIENS ST
BUCKINGHAM ST LOWER
BERESFORD PLACE
Foley St
Railway St
Sean MacDermott St Lwr
Corporation St
Talbot Street
GARDINER ST LOWER
Irish Life Centre
Department of Education
Sean MacDermott St Lwr
Marlborough St
St Mary's Cath.
Thomas's La
Earl St N
Abbey St Lower
Abbey Th.
EDEN QUAY
Butt Bridge
BURGH QUAY
O'Connell Bridge
Poolbeg St
Townsend St
D'OLIER ST
COLLEGE ST
WESTMORELAND ST
NASSAU ST
DAWSON ST
Frederick St Sth
Molesworth St
Taylor Gall.
Mansion House
Royal Acad. Library
St Stephen's Green
O'CONNELL ST
Savoy Cin.
Gate Theatre
PARNELL ST
Joyce Centre
Sch
The Spire
Henry St
Moore La
Moore St
Nth Prince's St
Lighthouse Cin.
Abbey St Middle
Lotts
BACHELORS WALK
ASTON QUAY
Fleet St
Bank of Ireland
Temple Bar Gall.
SUFFOLK ST
Grafton Street
Duke St
The Westbury Mall
Anne St
Civic Mus.
Clarendon St
Wicklow St
William St Sth
Gaiety Theatre
St Stephen's Green Centre
PARNELL SQ E
Rotunda Hospital
PARNELL SQ W
Parnell Sq N
Hugh Lane Gallery
ILAC Centre
Liffey St Upper
Liffey St Lwr
Abbey St Upper
Ha'penny Bridge
Millennium Bridge
QUAY LWR
Temple Bar
Olympia Theatre
Andrews Lane Theatre
Drury St
Mercer St
Royal College of Surgeons
York St
STH GT GEORGES ST
Stephen St
AUNGIER ST
DAME STREET
Dublin Castle
St Werburgh's
Dominick Pl
Dominick St Lower
PARNELL ST
Multiscreen Cin.
Jervis Centre
Mary St
Jervis St
Wolfe Tone St
Great Strand St
ORMOND QUAY
Grattan Bridge
WELLINGTON QUAY
Essex St E
National Wax Mus.
BOLTON ST
King's Inns St
College of Technology
Loftus La
CAPEL STREET
St Mary's Abbey
Mary's Abbey
ORMOND QUAY UPR
ESSEX QY
Viking Adventure
LORD EDWARD ST
Ship St Gt
Ship St Little
Chancery La
Golden La
Peter Row
Adelaide Hosp
Wood St
Marsh's Library
Peter St
Mountjoy St
Dominick St Upper
Henrietta Pl
Henrietta St
Court Hse.
Green Street
Arran St E
Bride St
Werburgh St
CHRIST CH PL
Bull Alley St
St Patrick's Cathedral
Kings Inns
HILL
Halston St
Little Britain St
Mary's Lane
Market
St Michan's St
Anne St N
Chancery Pl
WOOD QUAY
Christ Church
Winetavern St
Ross Rd
Bride Rd
NICHOLAS ST
PATRICK ST
CONSTITUTION
CHURCH ST UPPER
NORTH
Beresford St
Mary's La
Greek St
Chancery St
Four Courts
INN'S QUAY
MERCHANT'S QUAY
Cook St
HIGH ST
Back La
John Dillon St
Dean Swift Sq
Francis St
Swift's Alley
Sch
DEAN ST
Prebend St
CHURCH STREET
St Michan's
May La
Bow St
Hammond La
The Chimney
River Bank Th.
St Audoen's
Dvblinia
CORNMARKET
BRIDGE ST
Tivoli Theatre
Carman's Hall
Star Ave
Morning Star Ave
North King Street
Brunswick St North
Old Jameson Distillery
Smithfield
ARRAN QUAY
USHER'S QUAY
St Augustine St
John St W
College of Art & Design
Oliver Bond St
Vicar St
Ash St
Meath St
Meath Pl
Earl St Sth
Pimlico
THE COOMBE
John St Sth
St Brendan's Hospital
Grangegorman Lower
QUEEN ST
Buses Only
Hendrick St
Usher St
BRIDGEFOOT ST
THOMAS STREET WEST
Hanbury La
Thomas Ct
Summer St Sth
Convent
Kirwan St
Sch
STONEYBATTER
BLACKHALL PL
Incorporated Law Society
ELLIS QUAY
USHER'S ISLAND
Island St
Bonham St
Rainsford St
Crane St
Lane
MANOR ST
Sitric Rd
Hill
Ard-Righ Rd
Mt Temple Rd
Manor Place
Nth Temple Rd
Harald Rd
National Photographic Archive
Benburb St
WOLFE TONE QUAY
VICTORIA QUAY
Watling St
Guinness Brewery & Hop Store
Bellevue
Robert St
Marrowbone Lane
Newport St
Bond St
Halliday Rd
Aughrim Street
Ben Edar Rd
Road
Sch
Oxmantown
Arklow St
St Bricin's Hospital
Arbour Hill
Collins Barracks
National Museum
St James' Gate Brewery
Echlin St
Sch
Basin St Upper
Basin St Lwr
JAMES'S ST
STEVENS' LANE
Montpelier Hill
Heuston Station
Light Rail (LUAS)

The width of Victoria Harbour has been compressed so that the land area is better represented.

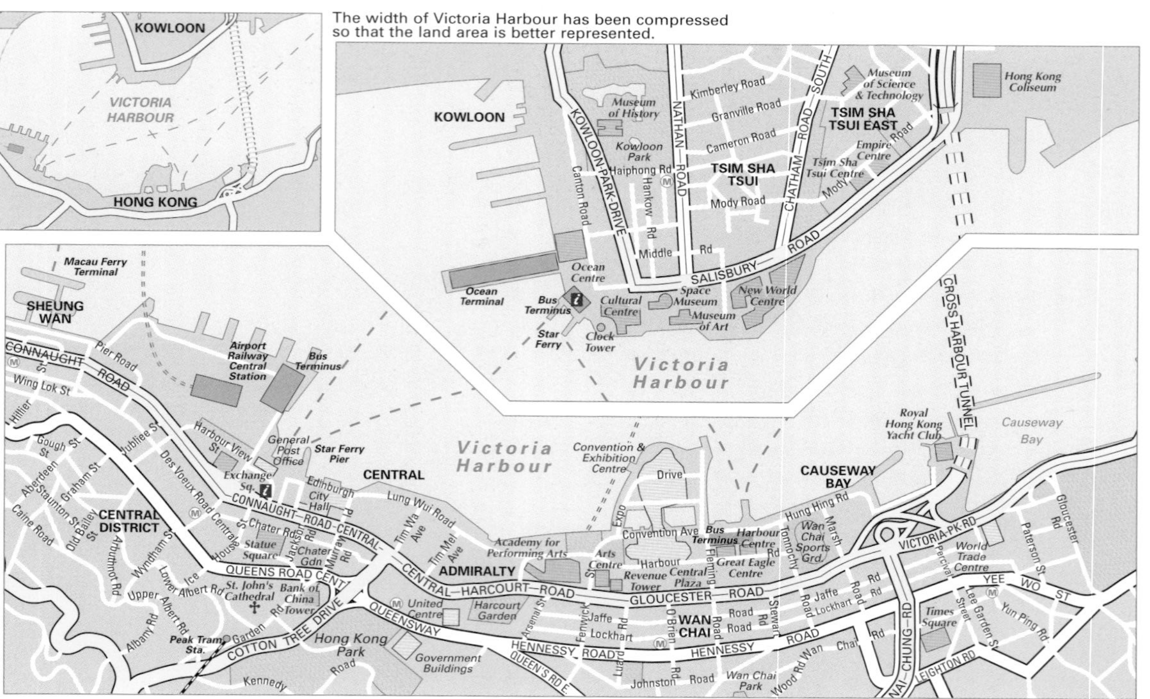

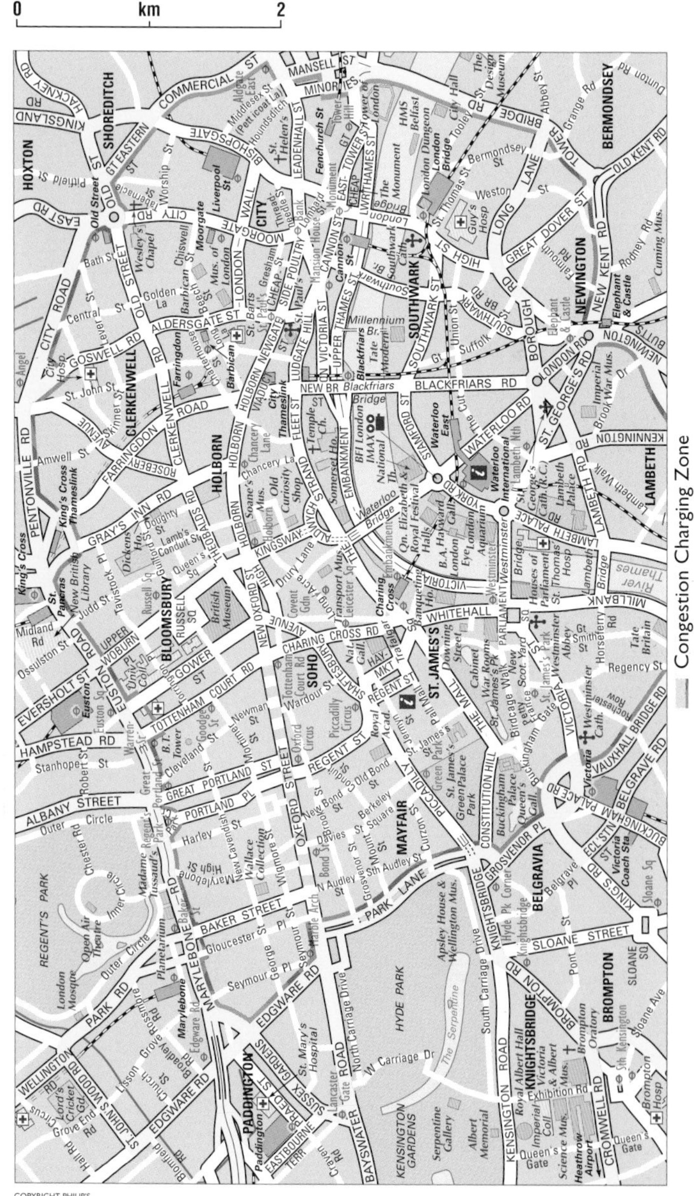

COPYRIGHT PHILIP'S

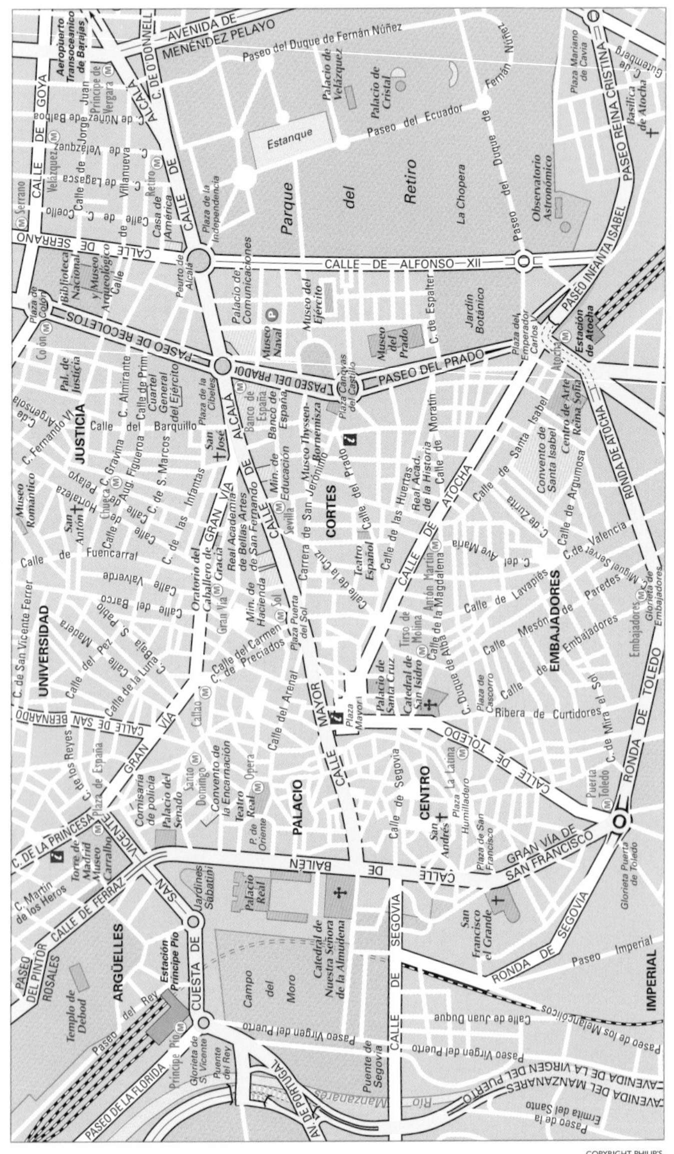
0
km
1
AVENIDA DE MENÉNDEZ PELAYO
Paseo del Duque de Fernán Núñez
Palacio de Velázquez
Palacio de Cristal
Estanque
Paseo del Ecuador
Parque del Retiro
La Chopera
Paseo del Duque de Fernán Núñez
Observatorio Astronómico
Plaza Mariano de Cavia
PASEO REINA CRISTINA
Basílica de Atocha
PASEO INFANTA ISABEL
CALLE DE ALFONSO XII
Plaza de la Independencia
Puerto de Alcalá
CALLE DE ALCALÁ
C. DE O'DONNELL
Aeropuerto Transoceánico de Barajas
Príncipe de Vergara
CALLE DE GOYA
CALLE DE SERRANO
C. de Núñez de Balboa
C. de Velázquez
C. de Lagasca
Calle de Claudio Coello
Villanueva
Casa de América
Retiro
Serrano
Biblioteca Nacional y Museo Arqueológico
Plaza de Colón
Colón
PASEO DE RECOLETOS
Palacio de Comunicaciones
Museo Naval
Museo del Ejército
Museo del Prado
C. de Espalter
Jardín Botánico
Plaza del Emperador Carlos V
Estación de Atocha
Atocha
PASEO DEL PRADO
Plaza de Cibeles
Plaza Cánovas del Castillo
Banco de España
Museo Thyssen-Bornemisza
Centro de Arte Reina Sofía
Convento de Santa Isabel
Calle de Santa Isabel
RONDA DE ATOCHA
CALLE DE ATOCHA
Pal. de Justicia
Cuartel General del Ejército
Calle del Barquillo
C. Almirante
JUSTICIA
San José
GRAN VÍA
Real Academia de Bellas Artes de San Fernando
Min. de Educación
Min. de Hacienda
CORTES
Carrera de San Jerónimo
Calle del Prado
Teatro Español
Calle de las Huertas
Real Acad. de la Historia
Calle de Moratín
Antón Martín
Calle de la Magdalena
Tirso de Molina
Calle de Lavapiés
Calle de Argumosa
C. de Valencia
C. del Ave María
EMBAJADORES
Calle Mesón de Paredes
Calle de Embajadores
Glorieta de Embajadores
Museo Romántico
San Antón
Chueca
Calle de Hortaleza
Calle de Fuencarral
Calle Valverde
Calle del Barco
Calle de las Infantas
Calle de Pelayo
Calle de S. Marcos
C. de Gravina
Calle de Aug. Figueroa
Calle de Fernando VI
C. de Argensola
Oratorio del Caballero de Gracia
Gran Vía
Sol
Plaza Puerta del Sol
Calle del Carmen
C. de Preciados
CALLE MAYOR
Calle de la Cruz
UNIVERSIDAD
C. de San Vicente Ferrer
Calle del Pez
Calle de la Luna
Calle de la Madera
CALLE DE SAN BERNARDO
Calle del Arenal
Callao
Plaza Mayor
Palacio de Santa Cruz
Catedral de San Isidro
C. Duque de Alba
Plaza de Cascorro
Ribera de Curtidores
C. de Mira el Sol
CALLE DE TOLEDO
RONDA DE TOLEDO
Puerta de Toledo
Glorieta Puerta de Toledo
Plaza de España
C. de los Reyes
Comisaría de policía
Palacio del Senado
Santo Domingo
Convento de la Encarnación
Teatro Real
Ópera
P. de Oriente
PALACIO
La Latina
CENTRO
Calle de Segovia
Plaza Humilladero
San Andrés
Plaza de San Francisco
C. DE LA PRINCESA
Torre de Madrid
Museo Cerralbo
Ventura Rodríguez
CALLE DE BAILÉN
GRAN VÍA DE SAN FRANCISCO
Jardines Sabatini
Palacio Real
Catedral de Nuestra Señora de la Almudena
CALLE DE SEGOVIA
San Francisco el Grande
RONDA DE SEGOVIA
Paseo Imperial
IMPERIAL
C. Martín de los Heros
CALLE DE FERRAZ
ARGÜELLES
PASEO DEL PINTOR ROSALES
Templo de Debod
Estación Príncipe Pío
CUESTA DE SAN VICENTE
Paseo del Rey
Campo del Moro
Paseo Virgen del Puerto
Calle de Juan Duque
Paseo de los Melancólicos
Puente de Segovia
Glorieta de S. Vicente
Puente del Rey
Príncipe Pío
PASEO DE LA FLORIDA
AV. DE PORTUGAL
Río Manzanares
AVENIDA DEL MANZANARES
AVENIDA DE LA VIRGEN DEL PUERTO
Paseo de la Ermita del Santo

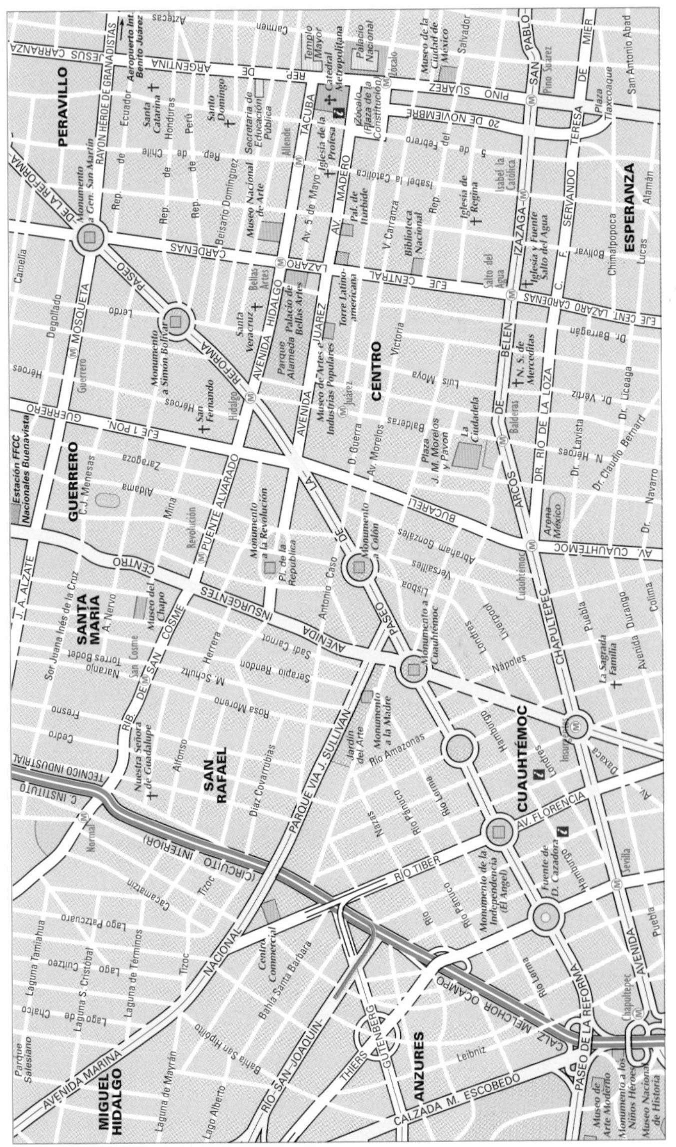
0 km 1
PERAVILLO
GUERRERO
SANTA MARÍA
SAN RAFAEL
MIGUEL HIDALGO
CENTRO
ESPERANZA
CUAUHTÉMOC
ANZURES
Monumento a Gen. San Martín
Monumento a Simón Bolívar
Monumento a la Revolución
Monumento a Colón
Monumento a Cuauhtémoc
Monumento a la Madre
Monumento de la Independencia (El Ángel)
Fuente de D. Cazadora
Templo Mayor
Catedral Metropolitana
Palacio Nacional
Zócalo (Plaza de la Constitución)
Museo de la Ciudad de México
Santo Domingo
Secretaría de Educación Pública
Museo Nacional de Arte
Palacio de Bellas Artes
Parque Alameda
Museo de Artes e Industrias Populares
Torre Latino-americana
Pal. de Iturbide
Biblioteca Nacional
Iglesia de Regina
Iglesia y Fuente Salto del Agua
La Ciudadela
Arena México
Estación FFCC Nacionales Buenavista
Museo del Chapo
Nuestra Señora de Guadalupe
Jardín del Arte
Centro Commercial
Aeropuerto Int. Benito Juárez
Museo de Arte Moderno
Monumento a los Niños Héroes
Museo Nacional de Historia
PASEO DE LA REFORMA
AVENIDA INSURGENTES
EJE CENTRAL LÁZARO CÁRDENAS
AVENIDA HIDALGO
AV. CHAPULTEPEC
AV. CUAUHTÉMOC
CIRCUITO INTERIOR
CALZ. MELCHOR OCAMPO
PARQUE VIA J. SULLIVAN
CALZADA M. ESCOBEDO
AVENIDA MARINA NACIONAL
RÍO TIBER
AV. FLORENCIA
COPYRIGHT PHILIP'S

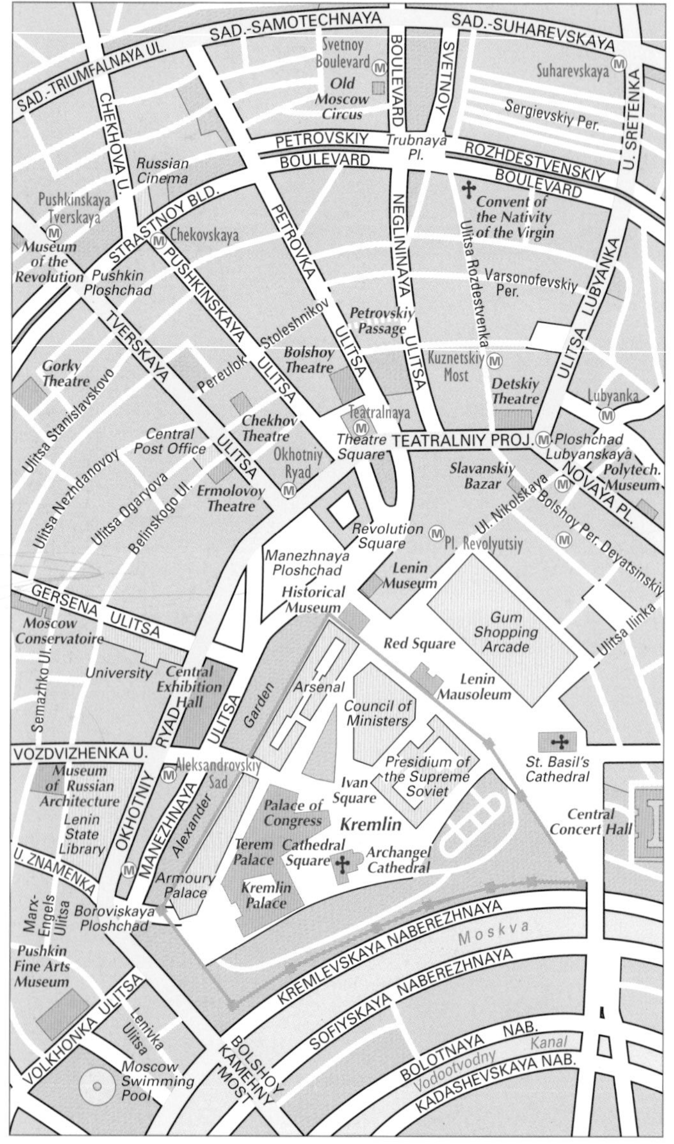
0 km 1
SAD.-SAMOTECHNAYA
SAD.-SUHAREVSKAYA
SAD.-TRIUMFALNAYA UL.
Svetnoy Boulevard
Old Moscow Circus
BOULEVARD
SVETNOY
Suharevskaya
Sergievskiy Per.
U. SRETENKA
CHEKHOVA U.
PETROVSKIY BOULEVARD
Trubnaya Pl.
ROZHDESTVENSKIY BOULEVARD
Russian Cinema
Pushkinskaya Tverskaya
Museum of the Revolution
STRASTNOY BLD.
Chekovskaya
PETROVKA
NEGLININAYA
Convent of the Nativity of the Virgin
Ulitsa Rozdestvenka
Pushkin Ploshchad
PUSHKINSKAYA
Varsonofevskiy Per.
ULITSA LUBYANKA
TVERSKAYA
Stoleshnikov
ULITSA
Petrovskiy Passage
ULITSA
Gorky Theatre
Pereulok
Bolshoy Theatre
Kuznetskiy Most
Detskiy Theatre
Ulitsa Stanislavskovo
ULITSA
Chekhov Theatre
Teatralnaya
Lubyanka
Central Post Office
Theatre Square
TEATRALNIY PROJ.
Ploshchad Lubyanskaya
Ulitsa Nezhdanovoy
ULITSA
Okhotniy Ryad
Slavanskiy Bazar
Polytech. Museum
Ulitsa Ogaryova
Belinskogo Ul.
Ermolovoy Theatre
Ul. Nikolskaya
NOVAYA PL.
Bolshoy Per. Deyatsinskiy
Revolution Square
Pl. Revolyutsiy
Manezhnaya Ploshchad
Lenin Museum
Historical Museum
Gum Shopping Arcade
GERSENA ULITSA
Moscow Conservatoire
Red Square
Ulitsa Ilinka
Semazhko Ul.
University
Central Exhibition Hall
Garden
Arsenal
Lenin Mausoleum
RYAD
ULITSA
Council of Ministers
VOZDVIZHENKA U.
Aleksandrovskiy Sad
Presidium of the Supreme Soviet
St. Basil's Cathedral
Museum of Russian Architecture
Ivan Square
OKHOTNIY
MANEZHNAYA
Alexander
Palace of Congress
Kremlin
Central Concert Hall
Lenin State Library
Terem Palace
Cathedral Square
Archangel Cathedral
U. ZNAMENKA
Armoury Palace
Kremlin Palace
Marx-Engels Ulitsa
Boroviskaya Ploshchad
KREMLEVSKAYA NABEREZHNAYA
Moskva
Pushkin Fine Arts Museum
SOFIYSKAYA NABEREZHNAYA
VOLKHONKA ULITSA
Lenivka Ulitsa
BOLOTNAYA NAB.
Kanal
Vodootvodny
Moscow Swimming Pool
BOLSHOY KAMENNY MOST
KADASHEVSKAYA NAB.

0 km 2

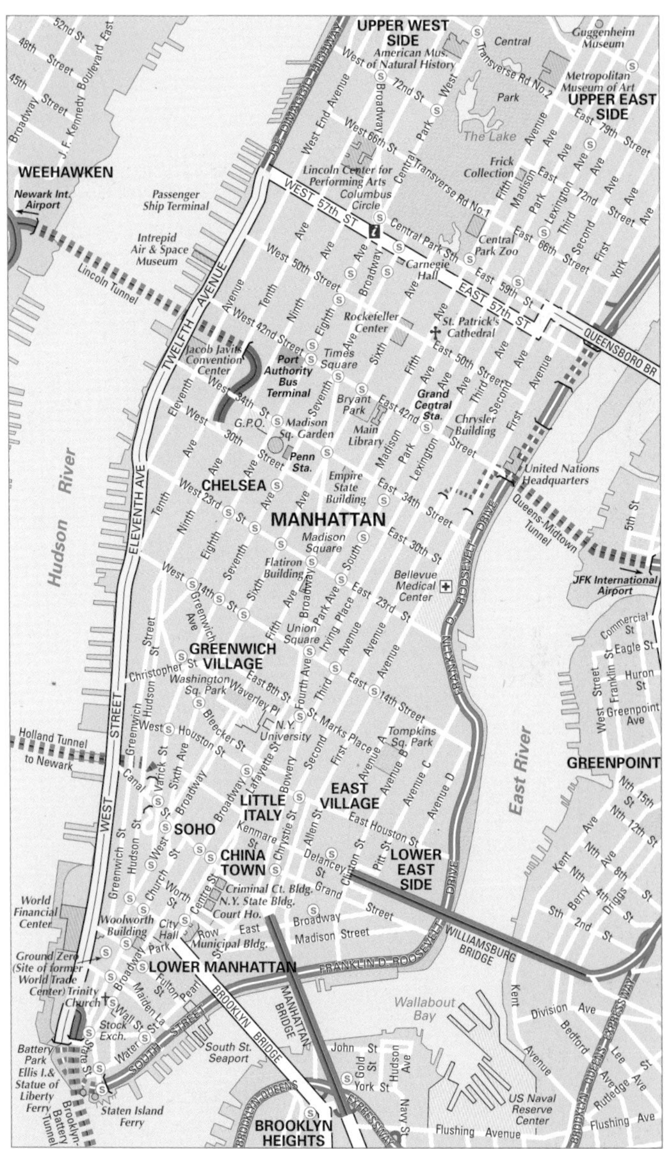
UPPER WEST SIDE
American Mus. of Natural History
Central Park
Guggenheim Museum
Metropolitan Museum of Art
UPPER EAST SIDE
Transverse Rd No.2
The Lake
Frick Collection
Lincoln Center for Performing Arts
Columbus Circle
Transverse Rd No.1
JOE DIMAGGIO HIGHWAY
West End Avenue
Broadway
72nd St
West 66th St
Central Park West
Fifth Avenue
Madison Ave
Park Ave
Lexington Ave
Third Ave
Second Ave
First Ave
York Ave
East 79th Street
East 72nd Street
East 66th Street
WEEHAWKEN
52nd St
48th Street
45th Street
Broadway
J.F. Kennedy Boulevard East
Newark Int. Airport
Passenger Ship Terminal
Intrepid Air & Space Museum
Lincoln Tunnel
WEST 57th ST
Central Park Sth
Central Park Zoo
Carnegie Hall
East 59th St
EAST 57th ST
QUEENSBORO BR
West 50th Street
TWELFTH AVENUE
Rockefeller Center
St. Patrick's Cathedral
East 50th Street
West 42nd Street
Jacob Javits Convention Center
Port Authority Bus Terminal
Times Square
Grand Central Sta.
Bryant Park
East 42nd Street
Chrysler Building
West 34th St
G.P.O.
Madison Sq. Garden
Main Library
Penn Sta.
Empire State Building
East 34th Street
United Nations Headquarters
Queens-Midtown Tunnel
West 30th Street
Hudson River
ELEVENTH AVE
CHELSEA
MANHATTAN
West 23rd St
Madison Square
East 30th St
Flatiron Building
Bellevue Medical Center
JFK International Airport
5th St
West 14th St
East 23rd St
Union Square
Irving Place
Commercial St
Eagle St
Huron St
Greenpoint Ave
West Street
Franklin St
GREENWICH VILLAGE
Christopher St
Washington Sq. Park
Waverley Pl
East 8th St
East 14th Street
FRANKLIN D. ROOSEVELT DRIVE
St. Marks Place
Tompkins Sq. Park
N.Y. University
Holland Tunnel to Newark
West Houston St
Bleecker St
WEST STREET
Canal St
Varick St
Sixth Ave
Lafayette St
Bowery
Avenue A
Avenue B
Avenue C
Avenue D
East River
GREENPOINT
LITTLE ITALY
EAST VILLAGE
SOHO
East Houston St
Kenmare St
Chrystie St
Allen St
Clinton St
Pitt St
LOWER EAST SIDE
Nth 15th St
Nth 12th St
CHINA TOWN
Delancey St
Kent Ave
Nth 8th St
Driggs Ave
Berry St
Sth 2nd St
Sth 4th St
World Financial Center
Criminal Ct. Bldg.
N.Y. State Bldg.
Court Ho.
Grand Street
Woolworth Building
City Hall Park
Row
Municipal Bldg.
East Broadway
Madison Street
WILLIAMSBURG BRIDGE
Ground Zero (Site of former World Trade Center)
Trinity Church
LOWER MANHATTAN
FRANKLIN D. ROOSEVELT DRIVE
Fulton St
Maiden La
Pearl St
Wall St
Stock Exch.
Water St
SOUTH STREET
BROOKLYN BRIDGE
MANHATTAN BRIDGE
Wallabout Bay
Division Ave
Bedford Avenue
BROOKLYN-QUEENS EXPRESSWAY
Lee Ave
Rutledge St
Battery Park
Ellis I. & Statue of Liberty Ferry
South St. Seaport
John St
Gold St
Hudson Ave
York St
Navy St
US Naval Reserve Center
Flushing Avenue
Brooklyn-Battery Tunnel
Staten Island Ferry
BROOKLYN HEIGHTS

0 km 1

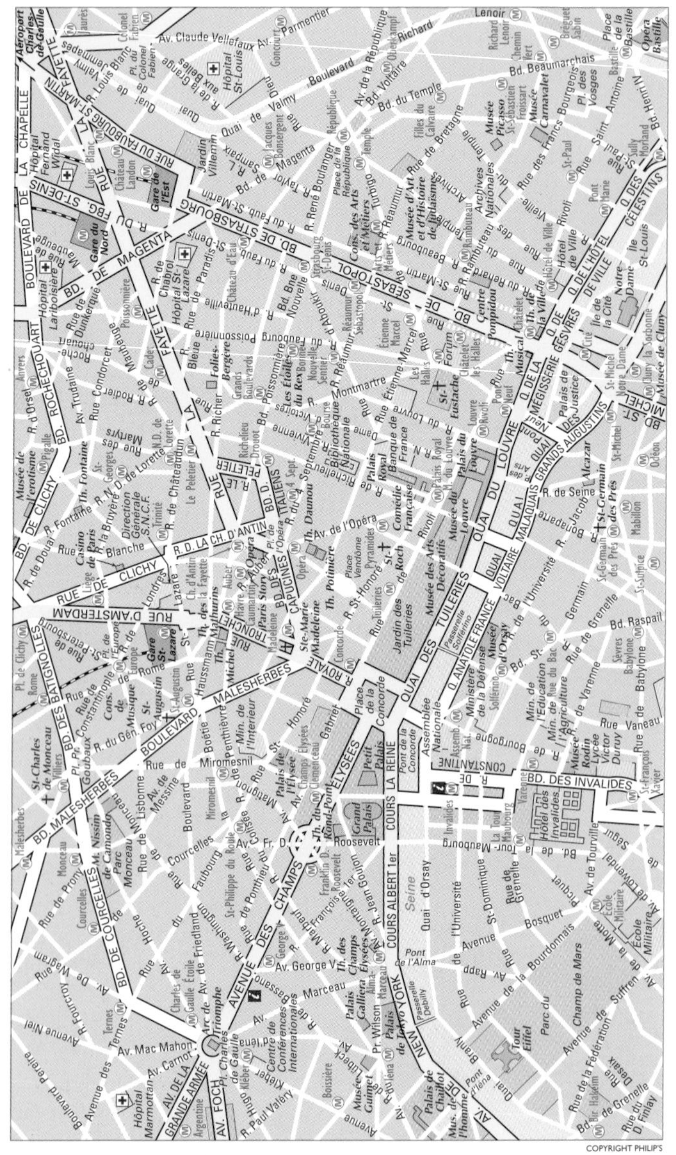

COPYRIGHT PHILIP'S

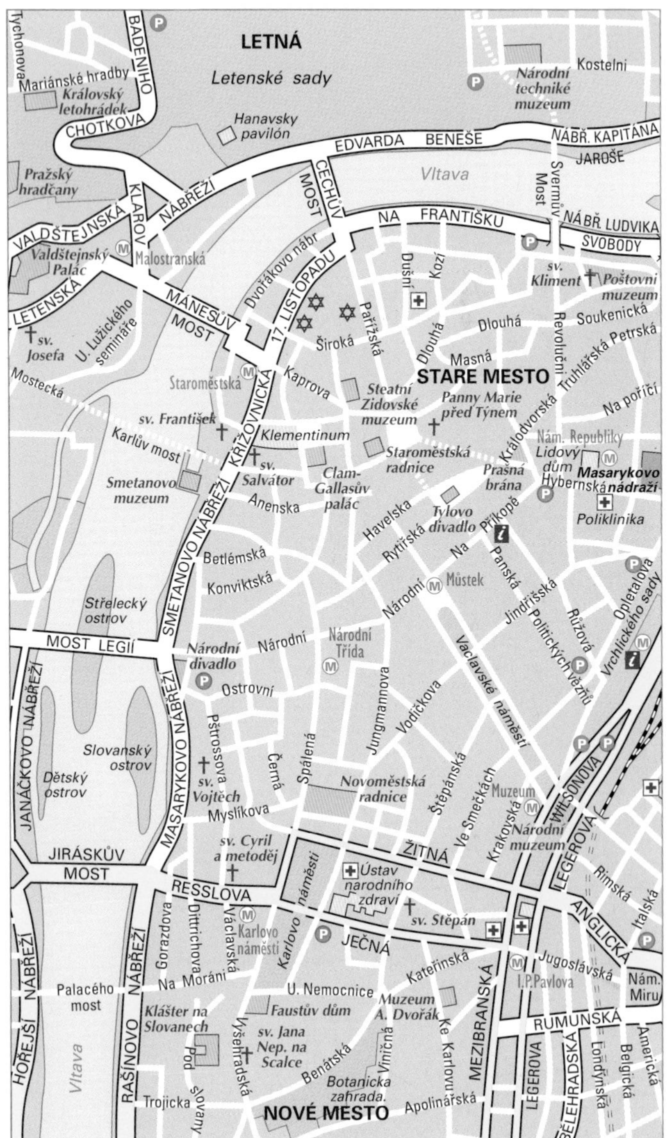
0 km 0.5
LETNÁ
Letenské sady
Hanavsky pavilón
Národní techniké muzeum
Kostelni
Mariánské hradby
Královský letohrádek
CHOTKOVA
BADENIHO
Tychonova
EDVARDA BENEŠE
NÁBŘ. KAPITÁNA JAROŠE
Vltava
Pražský hradčany
KLÁROV
NÁBŘEŽÍ
CECHŮV MOST
Svermův Most
NA FRANTIŠKU
NÁBŘ. LUDVIKA SVOBODY
VALDŠTEJNSKÁ
Valdštejnský Palác
Malostranská
LETENSKÁ
Dvořákovo nábr
17. LISTOPADU
Dušní
Kozí
sv. Kliment
Poštovni muzeum
MÁNESŮV MOST
Pařížská
Dlouhá
Soukenická
Revoluční
sv. Josefa
U. Lužického semináře
Široká
Masná
Petrská
Truhlářská
STARE MESTO
Mostecká
Staroměstská
Kaprova
Steatní Zidovské muzeum
Panny Marie před Týnem
Na poříčí
KŘIŽOVNICKÁ
sv. František
Klementinum
Králodvorská
Nám. Republiky
Karlův most
sv. Salvátor
Staroměstská radnice
Lidový dům
Masarykovo nádraží
Smetanovo muzeum
Clam-Gallasův palác
Prašná brána
Hybernská
Anenska
Havelska
Tylovo divadlo
Na Příkopě
Poliklinika
SMETANOVO NÁBŘEŽÍ
Rytířská
Betlémská
Panská
Konviktská
Můstek
Opletalova
Vrchlického sady
Střelecký ostrov
Národní
Jindřišská
Politických vězňů
Růžová
MOST LEGIÍ
Národní divadlo
Národní Třída
Vaclavské náměstí
Ostrovní
Jungmannova
Vodičkova
JANÁČKOVO NÁBŘEŽÍ
Pštrossova
Slovanský ostrov
Dětský ostrov
sv. Vojtěch
Černá
Spálená
Novoměstská radnice
Štěpánská
Ve Smečkách
Muzeum
WILSONOVA
MASARYKOVO NÁBŘEŽÍ
Myslíkova
Krakovská
Národní muzeum
LEGEROVA
JIRÁSKŮV MOST
sv. Cyril a metoděj
Karlovo náměstí
ŽITNÁ
Ústav narodního zdraví
Rimská
RESSLOVA
sv. Stěpán
ANGLICKÁ
Italská
Gorazdova
Dittrichova
Václavská
Karlovo náměstí
JEČNÁ
Jugoslávská
Palackého most
Na Moráni
Kateřinská
I.P.Pavlova
Nám. Miru
HOŘEJŠÍ NÁBŘEŽÍ
RAŠÍNOVO NÁBŘEŽÍ
U. Nemocnice
Faustův dům
Muzeum A. Dvořák
MEZIBRANSKÁ
RUMUNSKÁ
Klášter na Slovanech
sv. Jana Nep. na Scalce
Vyšehradská
Ke Karlovu
Viničná
Americká
Bělehradská
Londýnská
Belgická
Pod slovany
Benátská
Botanicka zahrada.
Trojicka
NOVÉ MESTO
Apolinářská
LEGEROVA

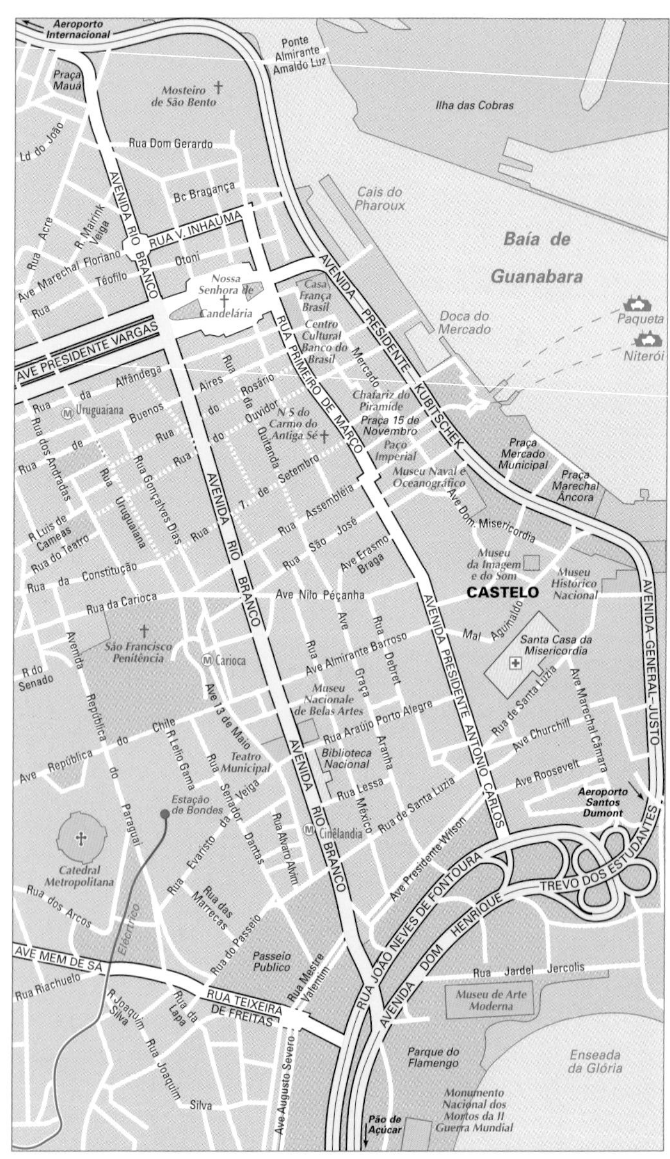
0 km 0.5
Aeroporto Internacional
Ponte Almirante Amaldo Luz
Praça Mauá
Mosteiro de São Bento
Ilha das Cobras
Rua Dom Gerardo
Ld do João
Cais do Pharoux
Bc Bragança
AVENIDA RIO BRANCO
RUA V. INHAUMA
Baía de Guanabara
Rua Acre
R. Mairink Veiga
Ave Marechal Floriano
Otoni
Teófilo
Nossa Senhora de Candelária
Casa França Brasil
AVENIDA PRESIDENTE KUBITSCHEK
Doca do Mercado
Paqueta
Niterói
Centro Cultural Banco do Brasil
AVE PRESIDENTE VARGAS
Rua da Alfândega
Rua Aires
Rua do Rosário
RUA PRIMEIRO DE MARÇO
Mercado
Chafariz do Piramide
Uruguaiana
Buenos
Rua do Ouvidor
Rua da Quitanda
N S do Carmo do Antiga Sé
Praça 15 de Novembro
Rua dos Andradas
Rua de Rua
Paço Imperial
Praça Mercado Municipal
Praça Marechal Âncora
Rua Uruguaiana
Rua Gonçalves Dias
7 de Setembro
Museu Naval e Oceanográfico
Rua Assembléia
Ave Dom Misericordia
R Luis de Cameas
Rua do Teatro
Rua São José
Ave Erasmo Braga
Museu da Imagem e do Som
Museu Histórico Nacional
Rua da Constitução
CASTELO
Rua da Carioca
Ave Nilo Péçanha
AVENIDA-GENERAL-JUSTO
AVENIDA PRESIDENTE ANTONIO CARLOS
Mal Aguinaldo
São Francisco Penitência
Santa Casa da Misericordia
Ave Graça
Rua Debret
Carioca
R do Senado
Ave Almirante Barroso
Avenida República do Paraguai
Museu Nacionale de Belas Artes
Ave 13 de Maio
Rua Araújo Porto Alegre
Rua de Santa Luzia
Ave Churchill
Ave Marechal Câmara
Chile
R Lelio Gama
Teatro Municipal
Biblioteca Nacional
Aranha
Ave República do Chile
Ave Roosevelt
Rua Senador Dantas
Rua Lessa
Aeroporto Santos Dumont
Estação de Bondes
Rua Evaristo da Veiga
Rua Alvaro Alvim
México
Rua de Santa Luzia
Cinêlandia
Ave Presidente Wilson
Catedral Metropolitana
Rua dos Arcos
Rua das Marrecas
RUA JOÃO NEVES DE FONTOURA
TREVO DOS ESTUDANTES
AVENIDA DOM HENRIQUE
Eléctrico
Rua do Passeio
Passeio Publico
AVE MEM DE SÁ
Rua Jardel Jercolis
Rua Riachuelo
Rua Mestre Valentim
R Joaquim Silva
Rua da Lapa
RUA TEIXEIRA DE FREITAS
Museu de Arte Moderna
Rua Joaquim Silva
Ave Augusto Severo
Parque do Flamengo
Enseada da Glória
Monumento Nacional dos Mortos da II Guerra Mundial
Pão de Açúcar

0 km 1

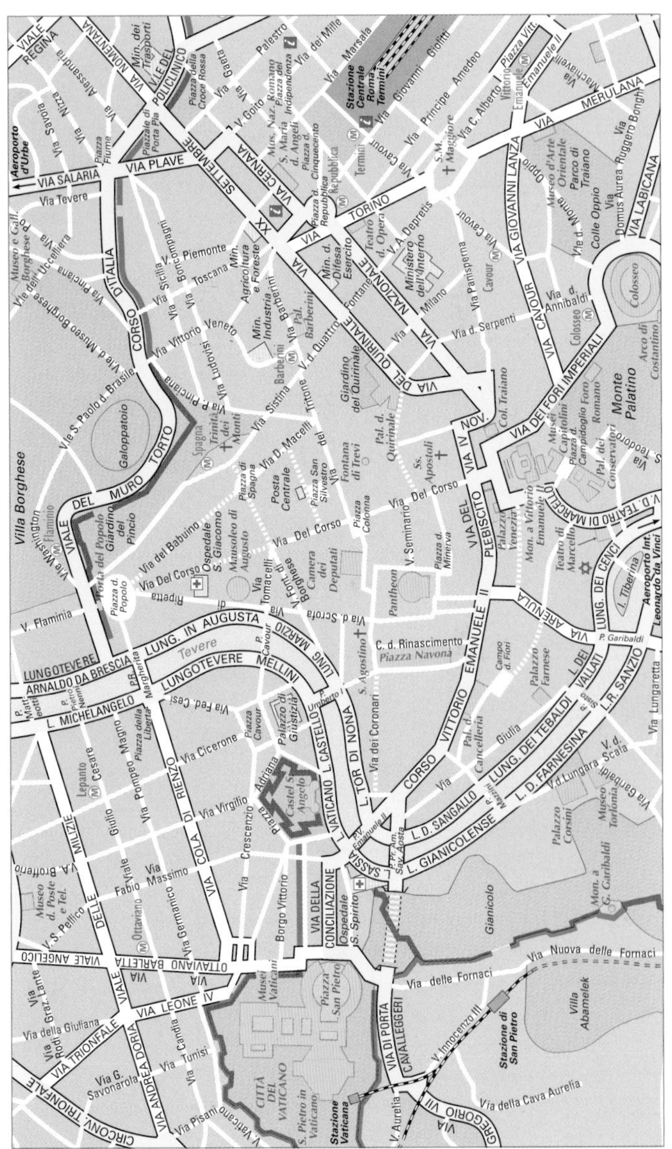
Villa Borghese
Galoppatoio
Museo e Gall. Borghese
Aeroporto d'Urbe
VIA SALARIA
VIA PLAVE
Piazza Fiume
Via Tevere
CORSO D'ITALIA
VIALE DEL MURO TORTO
Via Pinciana
Via Vittorio Veneto
Via Ludovisi
Via Boncompagni
V. Piemonte
Via Sicilia
Via Toscana
Min. Agricoltura e Foreste
Min. Industria e Commercio
Pal. Barberini
Barberini
Via Barberini
Via Sistina
Trinità dei Monti
Spagna
Piazza di Spagna
Via D. Macelli
V. d. Quattro Fontane
Tritone
VIA XX SETTEMBRE
VIA CERNAIA
Piazza della Repubblica
Repubblica
VIA TORINO
VIA NAZIONALE
Teatro d. Opera
Min. d. Difesa Esercito
Ministero dell'Interno
Via A. Depretis
Via Milano
Via Panisperna
Cavour
Via Cavour
VIA CAVOUR
Via d. Serpenti
Giardino del Quirinale
Pal. d. Quirinale
VIA DEL QUIRINALE
Fontana di Trevi
Piazza San Silvestro
Posta Centrale
Piazza Colonna
Via Del Corso
Ss. Apostoli
VIA IV NOV.
Col. Traiano
VIA DEI FORI IMPERIALI
Colosseo
Arco di Costantino
Monte Palatino
Via d. Annibaldi
VIA GIOVANNI LANZA
VIA LABICANA
Colle Oppio
Parco di Traiano
Museo d'Arte Orientale
VIA MERULANA
Piazza Vitt. Emanuele II
Vittorio Emanuele
Via C. Alberto
S.M. Maggiore
Via Principe Amedeo
Via Giovanni Giolitti
Stazione Centrale Roma Termini
Termini
Via Marsala
Via dei Mille
Piazza dei Cinquecento
S. Maria d. Angeli
Mus. Naz. Romano
Piazza del Indipendenza
V. Goito
Via Palestro
Via Gaeta
Piazza della Croce Rossa
VIALE DEL POLICLINICO
Piazzale di Porta Pia
Min. dei Trasporti
VIA NOMENTANA
VIALE REGINA
Via Alessandria
Via Nizza
Via Savoia
Piazza d. Popolo
Porta del Popolo
Giardino del Pincio
Flaminio
V. Flaminia
Via del Babuino
Via Del Corso
Via Ripetta
Ospedale S. Giacomo
Mausoleo di Augusto
Camera dei Deputati
Pantheon
Piazza d. Minerva
V. Seminario
Via d. Scrofa
S. Agostino
C. d. Rinascimento
Piazza Navona
Campo d. Fiori
Palazzo Farnese
Palazzo Venezia
VIA DEL PLEBISCITO
Mon. a Vittorio Emanuele II
Musei Capitolini
Piazza d. Campidoglio
Foro Romano
Pal. dei Conservatori
Teatro di Marcello
V. D. TEATRO DI MARCELLO
VIA D. CENCI
I. Tiberina
VIA ARENULA
P. Garibaldi
Aeroporto Int. Leonardo da Vinci
CORSO VITTORIO EMANUELE II
Via dei Coronari
Pal. d. Cancelleria
Via Giulia
LUNG. DEI TEBALDI
L. DEI VALLATI
L.R. SANZIO
Via Lungaretta
L. D. FARNESINA
Via Lungara
Palazzo Corsini
Museo Torlonia
Via Garibaldi
Mon. a G. Garibaldi
Gianicolo
Via Nuova delle Fornaci
Via delle Fornaci
Villa Abamelek
Stazione di San Pietro
Via della Cava Aurelia
VIA GREGORIO VII
V. Aurelia
VIA DI PORTA CAVALLEGGERI
Tevere
LUNG. IN AUGUSTA
LUNGOTEVERE MELLINI
LUNGOTEVERE ARNALDO DA BRESCIA
L. MICHELANGELO
Piazza Cavour
Palazzo di Giustizia
L. TOR DI NONA
L. CASTELLO
L. VATICANO
Castel S. Angelo
Piazza Adriana
Via Crescenzio
Via Cicerone
Via Virgilio
VIA COLA DI RIENZO
Via Pompeo Magno
Piazza della Libertà
Via Cesare
Lepanto
VIALE DELLE MILIZIE
Via Giulio
Viale Fabio Massimo
Via Germanico
Ottaviano
V.S. Pellico
Museo d. Poste e Tel.
VIALE ANGELICO
VIA OTTAVIANO
VIA BARLETTA
Borgo Vittorio
VIA DELLA CONCILIAZIONE
Ospedale S. Spirito
SASSIA
L. GIANICOLENSE
L. D. SANGALLO
Piazza San Pietro
Musei Vaticani
CITTÀ DEL VATICANO
S. Pietro in Vaticano
Stazione Vaticana
V. Vaticano
VIA LEONE IV
VIALE TRIONFALE
VIA ANDREA DORIA
Via della Giuliana
Via Candia
Via Tunisi
Via G. Savonarola
Via Pisani
CIRCONV. TRIONFALE
Via Rodi
Via Graz. Lante

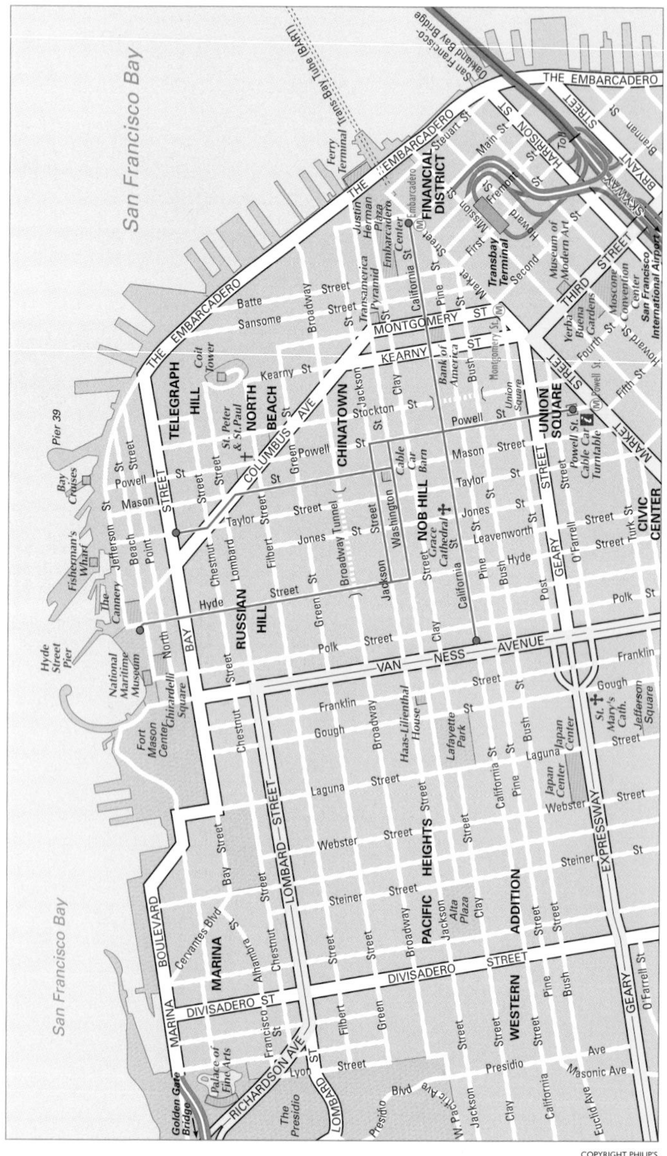
0 km 0.5
San Francisco Bay
San Francisco-Oakland Bay Bridge
San Francisco Trans Bay Tube (BART)
THE EMBARCADERO
Ferry Terminal
FINANCIAL DISTRICT
Justin Herman Plaza
Embarcadero Center
Transamerica Pyramid
Transbay Terminal
Museum of Modern Art
Yerba Buena Gardens
Moscone Convention Center
San Francisco International Airport
SKYWAY
Toll
MONTGOMERY ST
KEARNY ST
COLUMBUS AVE
TELEGRAPH HILL
Coit Tower
NORTH BEACH
St. Peter & St. Paul
CHINATOWN
Bank of America
Union Square
UNION SQUARE
Powell St. Cable Car Turntable
MARKET
THIRD STREET
Pier 39
Bay Cruises
Fisherman's Wharf
The Cannery
Hyde Street Pier
National Maritime Museum
Ghirardelli Square
Fort Mason Center
RUSSIAN HILL
Broadway Tunnel
Cable Car Barn
NOB HILL
Grace Cathedral
CIVIC CENTER
VAN NESS AVENUE
GEARY STREET
BAY STREET
Haas-Lilienthal House
Lafayette Park
Japan Center
St. Mary's Cath.
Jefferson Square
GEARY EXPRESSWAY
PACIFIC HEIGHTS
Alta Plaza
WESTERN ADDITION
LOMBARD STREET
DIVISADERO STREET
MARINA
MARINA BOULEVARD
DIVISADERO ST
RICHARDSON AVE
Palace of Fine Arts
The Presidio
Golden Gate Bridge
Presidio Blvd
Masonic Ave
Euclid Ave
COPYRIGHT PHILIP'S

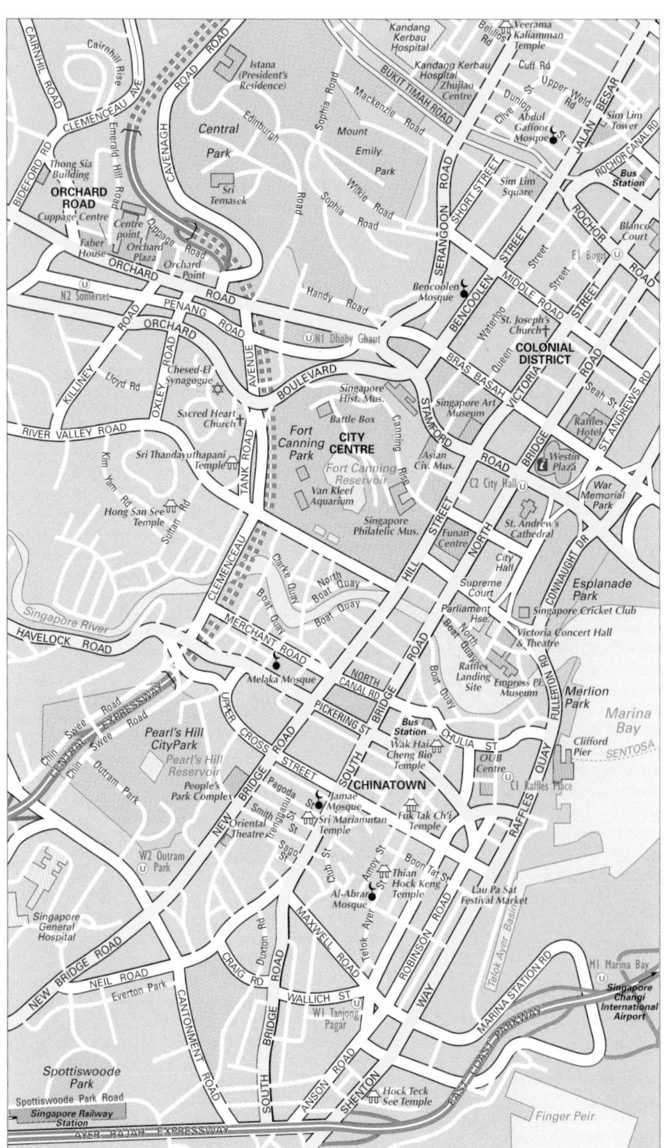
0 km 1
ORCHARD ROAD
CITY CENTRE
COLONIAL DISTRICT
CHINATOWN
Central Park
Fort Canning Park
Mount Emily Park
Esplanade Park
Merlion Park
Pearl's Hill CityPark
Spottiswoode Park
Marina Bay
Istana (President's Residence)
Kandang Kerbau Hospital
Veerama Kaliamman Temple
Abdul Gaffoor Mosque
Sim Lim Tower
Sim Lim Square
Bus Station
Blanco Court
Bencoolen Mosque
St. Joseph's Church
Singapore Hist. Mus.
Singapore Art Museum
Raffles Hotel
Westin Plaza
War Memorial Park
Asian Civ. Mus.
St. Andrew's Cathedral
City Hall
Supreme Court
Singapore Cricket Club
Victoria Concert Hall & Theatre
Parliament Hse.
Raffles Landing Site
Empress Pl. Museum
Clifford Pier
OUB Centre
Fuk Tak Ch'i Temple
Lau Pa Sat Festival Market
Thian Hock Keng Temple
Al-Abrar Mosque
Jamae Mosque
Sri Mariamman Temple
Oriental Theatre
People's Park Complex
Melaka Mosque
Wak Hai Cheng Bio Temple
Hock Teck See Temple
Singapore Railway Station
Singapore General Hospital
Singapore Changi International Airport
Chesed-El Synagogue
Sacred Heart Church
Sri Thandayuthapani Temple
Hong San See Temple
Thong Sia Building
Cuppage Centre
Centre point
Orchard Plaza
Orchard Point
Faber House
Van Kleef Aquarium
Singapore Philatelic Mus.
Funan Centre
Battle Box
Fort Canning Reservoir
Pearl's Hill Reservoir
Sri Temasek
Zhujiao Centre
N2 Somerset
N1 Dhoby Ghaut
E1 Bugis
C2 City Hall
C1 Raffles Place
W2 Outram Park
W1 Tanjong Pagar
M1 Marina Bay
SENTOSA
Finger Peir
Telok Ayer Basin
Singapore River
AYER RAJAH EXPRESSWAY
CENTRAL EXPRESSWAY
EAST COAST PARKWAY
ORCHARD ROAD
PENANG ROAD
RIVER VALLEY ROAD
HAVELOCK ROAD
NEW BRIDGE ROAD
SOUTH BRIDGE ROAD
NORTH BRIDGE ROAD
VICTORIA STREET
STAMFORD ROAD
BRAS BASAH ROAD
SHENTON WAY
ROBINSON ROAD
ANSON ROAD
CANTONMENT ROAD
MAXWELL ROAD
RAFFLES QUAY
MARINA STATION RD
BUKIT TIMAH ROAD
SERANGOON ROAD
BENCOOLEN STREET
JALAN BESAR
ROCHOR CANAL RD
ROCHOR ROAD
CAVENAGH ROAD
CLEMENCEAU AVE
CAIRNHILL ROAD
BIDEFORD RD
TANK ROAD
OXLEY ROAD
KILLINEY ROAD
NEIL ROAD
CRAIG RD
WALLICH ST
UPPER CROSS STREET
MERCHANT ROAD
PICKERING ST
CHULIA ST
NORTH CANAL RD
CONNAUGHT DR
FULLERTON RD
ST. ANDREWS RD
MIDDLE ROAD
BOULEVARD
HILL STREET
Spottiswoode Park Road
Everton Park
Duxton Rd
Club St
Telok Ayer St
Amoy St
Boon Tat St
Pagoda St
Smith St
Trengganu St
Sago St
Outram Park
Chin Swee Road
Clarke Quay
North Boat Quay
Boat Quay
Kim Yam Rd
Sultan Rd
Lloyd Rd
Handy Road
Sophia Road
Mackenzie Road
Wilkie Road
Edinburgh Road
Emerald Hill Road
Cuppage Road
Cairnhill Rise
Canning Rise
Waterloo Street
Queen Street
Seah St
Dunlop St
Clive St
Upper Weld Rd
Cuff Rd
Belilios Rd
Short Street

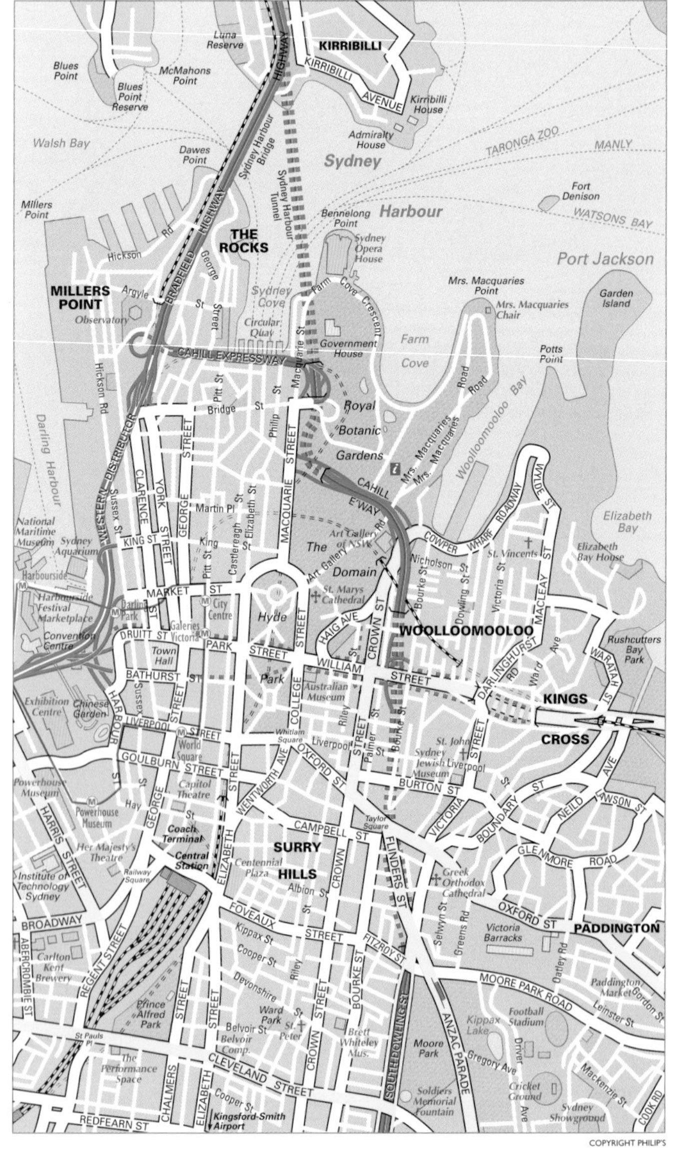
0 km 1
KIRRIBILLI
Kirribilli Avenue
Kirribilli House
Admiralty House
Luna Reserve
Blues Point
McMahons Point
Blues Point Reserve
Walsh Bay
Dawes Point
Sydney Harbour Bridge
Sydney Harbour Tunnel
Bradfield Highway
Sydney Harbour
Taronga Zoo
Manly
Fort Denison
Watsons Bay
Port Jackson
Garden Island
Millers Point
Bennelong Point
Sydney Opera House
THE ROCKS
MILLERS POINT
Observatory
Sydney Cove
Circular Quay
Government House
Farm Cove
Mrs. Macquaries Point
Mrs. Macquaries Chair
Potts Point
Cahill Expressway
Royal Botanic Gardens
Woolloomooloo Bay
Darling Harbour
National Maritime Museum
Sydney Aquarium
Harbourside
Harbourside Festival Marketplace
Convention Centre
Martin Pl
The Domain
Art Gallery of NSW
St. Marys Cathedral
Hyde Park
City Centre
Galeries Victoria
Town Hall
Elizabeth Bay
Elizabeth Bay House
St. Vincents
WOOLLOOMOOLOO
Rushcutters Bay Park
KINGS CROSS
Australian Museum
Exhibition Centre
Chinese Garden
World Square
Whitlam Square
St. John
Sydney Jewish Museum
Powerhouse Museum
Capitol Theatre
Coach Terminal
Central Station
Her Majesty's Theatre
Railway Square
Institute of Technology Sydney
SURRY HILLS
Centennial Plaza
Taylor Square
Greek Orthodox Cathedral
PADDINGTON
Victoria Barracks
Carlton Kent Brewery
Prince Alfred Park
Ward Park
St. Peter
Belvoir Comp.
Brett Whiteley Mus.
Moore Park
Kippax Lake
Football Stadium
Paddington Market
The Performance Space
Soldiers Memorial Fountain
Cricket Ground
Sydney Showground
Kingsford-Smith Airport
Cleveland Street
Redfearn St
Oxford St
Moore Park Road
Anzac Parade
South Dowling St
Flinders St
George Street
Elizabeth St
Macquarie Street
William Street
Park Street
Market St
King St
Bridge St
Broadway
Regent Street
Harris Street
Abercrombie St
Goulburn Street
Liverpool Street
Bathurst St
Campbell St
Foveaux Street
Crown Street
Bourke Street
Glenmore Road
Cowper Wharf Roadway
Darlinghurst Rd
Macleay St
Victoria St
COPYRIGHT PHILIP'S

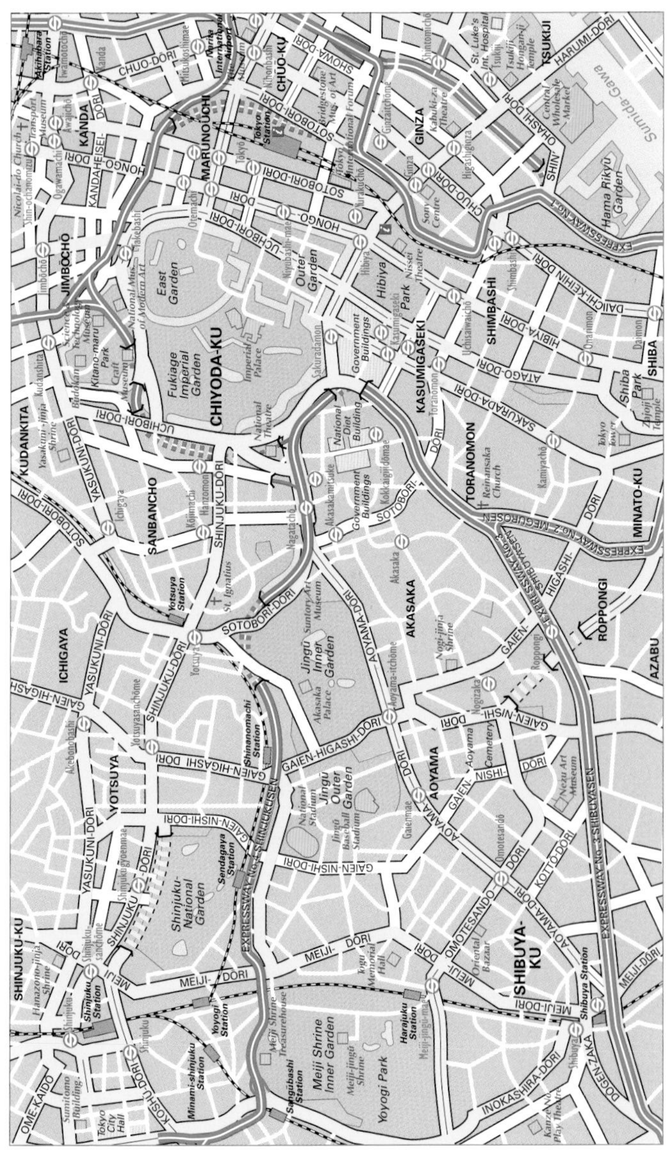

COPYRIGHT PHILIP'S

0 km 1

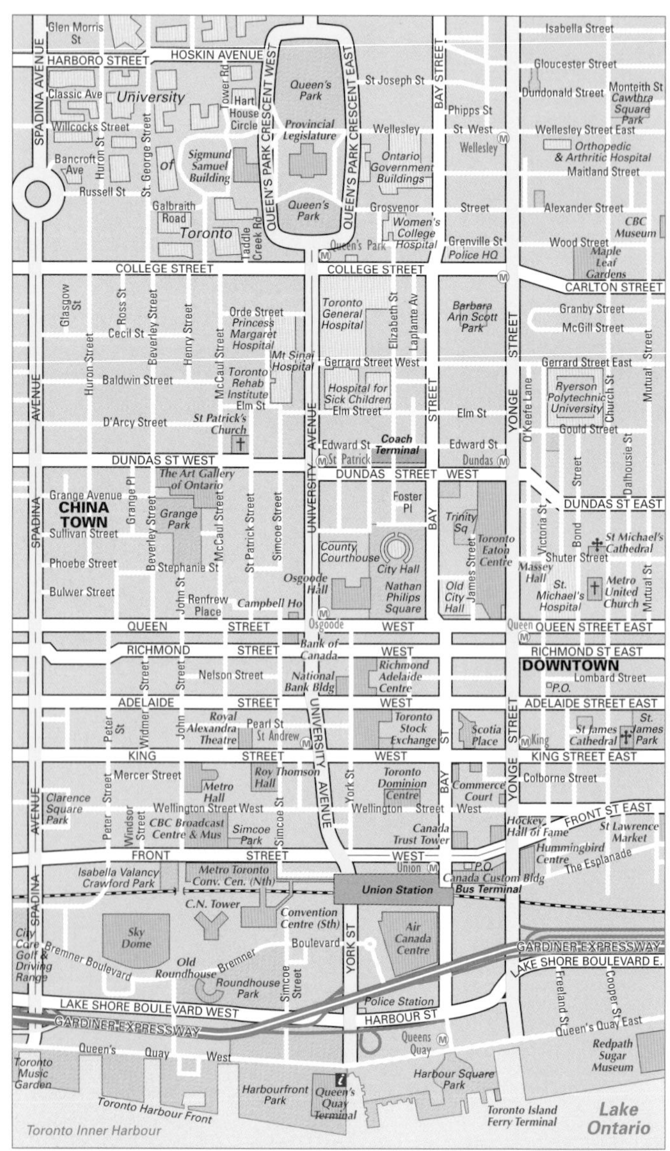

HARBORO STREET
HOSKIN AVENUE
SPADINA AVENUE
University of Toronto
Queen's Park
Provincial Legislature
QUEEN'S PARK CRESCENT WEST
QUEEN'S PARK CRESCENT EAST
BAY STREET
YONGE STREET
COLLEGE STREET
CARLTON STREET
DUNDAS ST WEST
DUNDAS STREET WEST
DUNDAS ST EAST
CHINA TOWN
UNIVERSITY AVENUE
QUEEN STREET WEST
QUEEN STREET EAST
RICHMOND STREET WEST
RICHMOND ST EAST
DOWNTOWN
ADELAIDE STREET WEST
ADELAIDE STREET EAST
KING STREET WEST
KING STREET EAST
FRONT STREET WEST
FRONT ST EAST
Union Station
Sky Dome
C.N. Tower
GARDINER EXPRESSWAY
LAKE SHORE BOULEVARD WEST
LAKE SHORE BOULEVARD E.
Queen's Quay West
Queen's Quay East
Toronto Inner Harbour
Lake Ontario

0 km 1

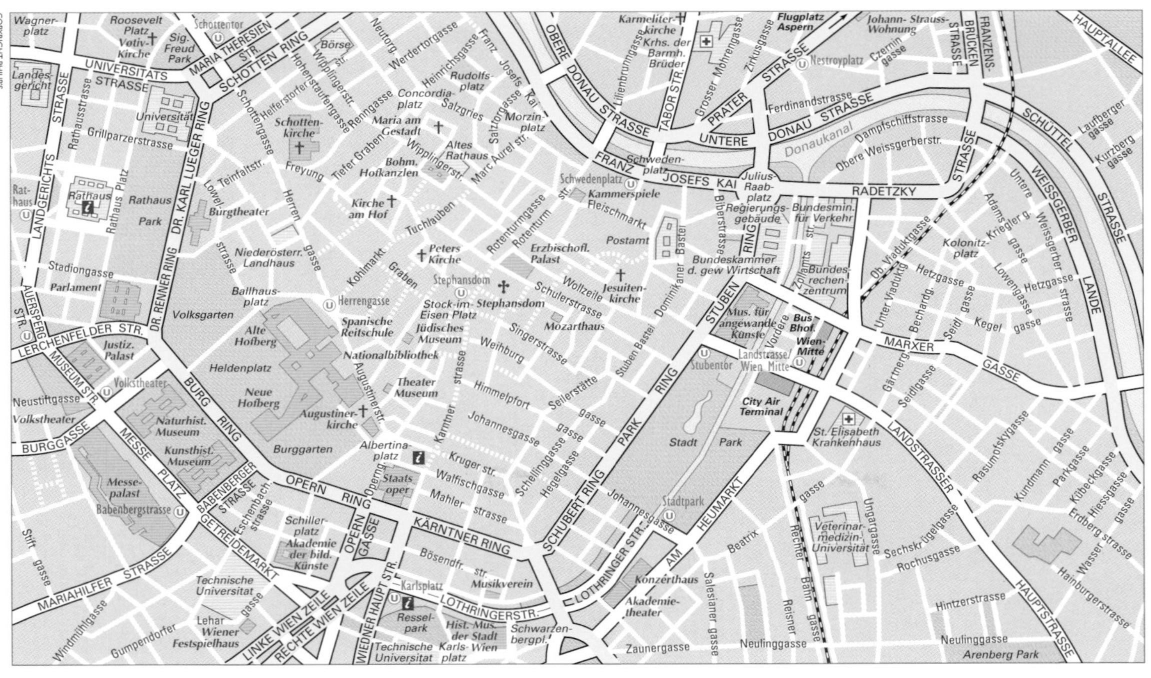
HAUPTALLEE
SCHÜTTEL STRASSE
WEISSGERBER LANDE
FRANZENS-BRÜCKEN STRASSE
RADETZKY STRASSE
MARXER GASSE
LANDSTRASSER HAUPTSTRASSE
Arenberg Park
Ungargasse
St. Elisabeth Krankenhaus
Veterinar-medizin-Universitat
Rechter Bahn gasse
Reisner
Neulinggasse
Salesianer gasse
Zaunergasse
Konzerthaus
Akademie-theater
AM HEUMARKT
Stadt Park
Stadtpark
City Air Terminal
Landstrasse/Wien Mitte
Wien-Mitte
Bus Bhof.
Mus. für angewande Künste
Stubentor
STUBEN RING
PARK RING
SCHUBERT RING
LOTHRINGER STR.
Johannesgasse
Schwarzenbergpl.
Musikverein
KÄRNTNER RING
Hist. Mus. der Stadt Wien
Karlsplatz
Ressel-park
Technische Universitat
Karls-platz
WIEDNER HAUPT STR.
LINKE WIEN ZEILE
RECHTE WIEN ZEILE
OPERN GASSE
OPERN RING
Staats oper
Albertina-platz
Akademie der bild. Künste
Schiller-platz
GETREIDEMARKT
Technische Universitat
Wiener Festspielhaus
Lehar
MARIAHILFER STRASSE
Windmühlgasse
Gumpendorfer
Stift gasse
Babenbergstrasse
Messe-palast
MESSE PLATZ
Kunsthist. Museum
Naturhist. Museum
BURG RING
Volkstheater
Neustiftgasse
BURGGASSE
MUSEUM STR.
LERCHENFELDER STR.
AUERSPERG STR.
Justiz. Palast
Parlament
Stadiongasse
DR. RENNER RING
DR. KARL LUEGER RING
Rathaus Park
Rathaus
Rathaus Platz
Grillparzerstrasse
Rathausstrasse
LANDGERICHTS STRASSE
Landes-gericht
Wagner-platz
UNIVERSITATS STRASSE
Roosevelt Platz
Votiv-Kirche
Sig. Freud Park
Universität
Schottentor
MARIA THERESIEN STR.
SCHOTTEN RING
Burgtheater
Volksgarten
Heldenplatz
Neue Hofberg
Alte Hofberg
Burggarten
Augustiner-kirche
Augustinerstr.
Nationalbibliothek
Spanische Reitschule
Herrengasse
Ballhaus-platz
Niederösterr. Landhaus
Schotten-kirche
Freyung
Börse
Hohenstaufengasse
Wipplingerstr.
Kirche am Hof
Bohm. Hofkanzlen
Maria am Gestadt
Altes Rathaus
Concordia-platz
Rudolfs-platz
Salzgries
Peters Kirche
Graben
Kohlmarkt
Tuchlauben
Stephansdom
Stock-im-Eisen Platz
Jüdisches Museum
Theater Museum
Kärntner strasse
Himmelpfort
Weihburg
Singerstrasse
Mozarthaus
Schulerstrasse
Wollzeile
Erzbischofl. Palast
Rotenturmstrasse
Jesuiten-kirche
Postamt
Fleischmarkt
Schwedenplatz
Kammerspiele
FRANZ JOSEFS KAI
OBERE DONAU STRASSE
UNTERE DONAU STRASSE
TABOR STR.
PRATER STRASSE
Karmeliter-kirche
Krhs. der Barmh. Brüder
Johann- Strauss-Wohnung
Nestroyplatz
Flugplatz Aspern
Julius-Raab-platz
Regierungs-gebäude
Bundesmin. für Verkehr
Bundes-rechen-zentrum
Bundeskammer d. gew Wirtschaft
Biberstrasse
Dominikaner Bastei
Donaukanal
Obere Weissgerberstr.
Dampfschiffstrasse
Kolonitz-platz
Kegel gasse
Lowengasse
Hetzgasse
Rasumofskygasse
Kundmann gasse
Erdberg strasse
Hainburgerstrasse
Rochusgasse
Hintzerstrasse

GAZETTEER OF NATIONS

AFGHANISTAN

GOVERNMENT Transitional
LANGUAGES Pashtu, Dari/Persian, Uzbek
CURRENCY Afghani = 100 puls
MEDICAL Visitors should protect against yellow fever, polio, typhoid, and malaria
TRAVEL Most governments currently advise against all travel to Afghanistan. The security situation remains serious, with danger away from main roads from mines and unexploded ordnance
WEATHER Jun to Aug very hot; Dec to Mar very cold; Jun to Sep scanty rainfall; mild at other times
BANKING 0800–1200 and 1300–1630 Sat to Wed; 0830–1330 Thu. However, at the time of writing, many banks are closed
EMERGENCY Unavailable
TIME ZONE GMT +4.30
INTERNATIONAL DIALING CODE Unavailable

ALBANIA

GOVERNMENT Multiparty republic
LANGUAGES Albanian (official)
CURRENCY Lek = 100 qindars
MEDICAL Water is untreated and not safe to drink. Medical facilities in the country are poor
TRAVEL Crime is high throughout parts of the country and visitors should remain vigilant at all times. It is advisable to dress down and avoid carrying expensive items. Street demonstrations against the government are common
WEATHER Jun to Sep warm and dry; Oct to May cool and wet
BANKING 0700–1500 Mon to Fri
EMERGENCY Police 24445; Fire 23333; Ambulance 22235
TIME ZONE GMT +1
INTERNATIONAL DIALING CODE 355

ALGERIA

GOVERNMENT Socialist republic
LANGUAGES Arabic and Berber (both official), French
CURRENCY Algerian dinar = 100 centimes
MEDICAL There is a risk of yellow fever, malaria, hepatitis A, typhoid, and polio
TRAVEL Most governments currently advise against all tourist and non-essential travel to Algeria. Travel by public transport should be avoided and only secure accommodation used
WEATHER Jun to Sep in the north is usually hot with high humidity along the coast; Oct to Feb wet and mild
BANKING 0900–1630 Sun to Thu
EMERGENCY Unavailable
TIME ZONE GMT +1
INTERNATIONAL DIALING CODE 213

AMERICAN SAMOA

GOVERNMENT US overseas territory
LANGUAGES Samoan, English
CURRENCY US dollar = 100 cents
MEDICAL Water is untreated and is unsafe to drink. Vaccination against polio and typhoid is recommended
TRAVEL Most visits to American Samoa are trouble-free and crime is low. Tourists should respect local culture and take usual precautions, especially in the towns
WEATHER Hot, tropical climate with heavy rainfall from Dec to Apr. The most comfortable time to visit is May to Sep
BANKING 0900–1500 Mon to Fri
EMERGENCY All services 911
TIME ZONE GMT –11
INTERNATIONAL DIALING CODE 1 684

ANDORRA

GOVERNMENT Parliamentary co-princedom
LANGUAGES Catalan, Spanish, French
CURRENCY Euro = 100 cents
MEDICAL There are no specific health risks
TRAVEL In Andorra, visitors will find some of the most stunning scenery and the best skiing in the Pyrenees. Shopping around, prices may often be up to 30% below those in France and Spain
WEATHER Jun to Sep warm and pleasant; Dec to Apr sunny but cold with abundant snow; rain falls throughout the year; snow often remains on the peaks of mountains until July
BANKING 0900–1300 and 1500–1700 Mon to Fri; 0900–1200 Sat
EMERGENCY Police 110; Fire/Ambulance 118
TIME ZONE GMT +1
INTERNATIONAL DIALING CODE 376

ANGOLA

GOVERNMENT Multiparty republic
LANGUAGES Portuguese (official), many others
CURRENCY Kwanza = 100 lwei
MEDICAL There is a risk of yellow fever, hepatitis A, polio, typhoid, and malaria
TRAVEL Most governments currently advise against tourist and non-essential travel to Angola due to the aftermath of civil war. Visitors should remain vigilant, particularly after dark. Crime levels are high and land mines are widely distributed and unmarked
WEATHER Warm to hot all year; Nov to Apr wet; cooler and wetter climate in the south
BANKING 0845–1600 Mon to Fri
EMERGENCY Unavailable
TIME ZONE GMT +1
INTERNATIONAL DIALING CODE 244

ANGUILLA

GOVERNMENT UK overseas territory
LANGUAGES English (official)
CURRENCY East Caribbean dollar = 100 cents
MEDICAL There are no specific health risks, but medical facilities are limited on the island
TRAVEL Most visits are trouble-free, but beachwear should be confined to resort areas. Travelers should take normal precautions, such as locking doors and securing valuables
WEATHER Tropical climate. Hurricane risk from Jun to Nov; Oct to Dec is the rainy season. Optimum diving conditions in summer months
BANKING 0800–1500 Mon to Thu; 0800–1700 Fri
EMERGENCY All services 911
TIME ZONE GMT –4
INTERNATIONAL DIALING CODE 1 264

ANTIGUA & BARBUDA

GOVERNMENT Constitutional monarchy
LANGUAGES English (official), English patois
CURRENCY East Caribbean dollar = 100 cents
MEDICAL Visitors should take normal precautions against mosquito bites. Vaccinations recommended against polio and typhoid
TRAVEL Generally trouble-free, but visitors should avoid isolated areas, including beaches, after dark
WEATHER Tropical with little variation between the seasons; rainfall is minimal. The islands are at risk from hurricanes from Jun to Nov
BANKING 0800–1400 Mon to Thu; 0800–1700 Fri
EMERGENCY All services 999/911
TIME ZONE GMT –4
INTERNATIONAL DIALING CODE 1 268

ARGENTINA

GOVERNMENT Federal republic
LANGUAGES Spanish (official)
CURRENCY Argentine peso = 10,000 australs
MEDICAL Cholera is a risk in the subtropical northern region
TRAVEL Occasional outbreaks of social unrest. It is inadvisable to walk in isolated, poorly-lit areas. Visitors should avoid carrying too much cash or wearing jewelry. Avoid military areas, which usually allow no stopping
WEATHER Jun to Aug cool in Buenos Aires area; Dec to Feb hot and humid; rain falls all year round
BANKING 1000–1500 Mon to Fri
EMERGENCY Police 101/107
TIME ZONE GMT –3
INTERNATIONAL DIALING CODE 54

ARMENIA

GOVERNMENT Multiparty republic
LANGUAGES Armenian (official)
CURRENCY Dram = 100 couma
MEDICAL Visitors should protect against hepatitis and bacterial infection
TRAVEL The border areas with Azerbaijan should be avoided at all times. Crime remains relatively low in Armenia, but occasional thefts from cars and pickpocketing may occur. The local standard of driving is poor, but most visits are generally trouble-free
WEATHER Apr to Oct hot and sunny; Jul to Sep little rainfall; Dec to Feb cold with heavy snow
BANKING 0930–1730 Mon to Fri
EMERGENCY Unavailable
TIME ZONE GMT +4
INTERNATIONAL DIALING CODE 374

ARUBA

GOVERNMENT Parliamentary democracy
LANGUAGES Dutch, English, Spanish, Papiamento
CURRENCY Aruba florin = 100 cents
MEDICAL Water is purified and should be safe; normal precautions should be taken with food
TRAVEL Beachwear should be confined to the beach. Travelers should take normal precautions, such as avoiding isolated areas after dark
WEATHER Tropical marine climate, warm and dry with average temperatures of 82°F [28°C]. Nov and Dec experience short showers
BANKING 0800–1200 and 1300–1600 Mon to Fri
EMERGENCY Police 11 000; Ambulance 74 300; Fire 115
TIME ZONE GMT –4
INTERNATIONAL DIALING CODE 297

AUSTRALIA

GOVERNMENT Federal constitutional monarchy
LANGUAGES English (official)
CURRENCY Australian dollar = 100 cents
MEDICAL No vaccinations required. There are few health hazards, but visitors should protect against sunburn, spider, and snake bites
TRAVEL Visitors should exercise caution in major urban areas, particularly after dark
WEATHER Tropical to temperate; Nov to Mar warm or hot in all areas; Jun to Aug mild in southeastern region; Sep to May warm to hot; rain falls all year round and is heaviest Mar to Jul
BANKING 0930–1600 Mon to Thu; 0930–1700 Fri, but hours vary throughout the country
EMERGENCY Emergency Services 000
TIME ZONE East GMT +10; Cen. +9.30; West +8
INTERNATIONAL DIALING CODE 61

AUSTRIA

GOVERNMENT Federal republic
LANGUAGES German (official)
CURRENCY Euro = 100 cents
MEDICAL There are no specific health risks in Austria
TRAVEL Visitors to the Alps should contact the Austrian Tourist Agency for advice on safety. Austria benefits all year round by providing summer sightseeing and winter sports
WEATHER Jun to Aug warm and pleasant; Oct to Apr cold; Mar to Aug higher rainfall
BANKING 0800–1230 and 1330–1500 Mon, Tue, Wed and Fri; Thu 0800–1230 and 1330–1730
EMERGENCY Emergency Services 112; Police 133; Ambulance 144
TIME ZONE GMT +1
INTERNATIONAL DIALING CODE 43

AZERBAIJAN

GOVERNMENT Federal multiparty republic
LANGUAGES Azerbaijani (official), Russian
CURRENCY Azerbaijani manat = 100 gopik
MEDICAL Visitors should protect against malaria, yellow fever, diptheria, tick-borne encephalitis, hepatitis, rabies, and typhoid fever
TRAVEL Travel to the western region of Nagorno-Karabakh and surrounding occupied area should be avoided. Passport photocopies should be carried at all times. Do not enter or leave the country via the land borders with Russia
WEATHER May to Sep sunny, warm and dry; Oct to Apr mild with some rain
BANKING 0930–1730 Mon to Fri
EMERGENCY Unavailable
TIME ZONE GMT +4
INTERNATIONAL DIALING CODE 994

AZORES

GOVERNMENT Portuguese autonomous region
LANGUAGES Portuguese
CURRENCY Euro = 100 cents
MEDICAL There are no specific health risks in the Azores
TRAVEL Most visits to the Azores are trouble-free. The nine large islands and numerous small ones are situated in the middle of the Atlantic Ocean and offer the traveler a wealth of stunning scenery
WEATHER Mild throughout the year; Jun to Sep sunny and warm; Jan to Apr changeable; Oct to Mar wet
BANKING Visitors should check at their hotel
EMERGENCY Unavailable
TIME ZONE GMT –1
INTERNATIONAL DIALING CODE Unavailable

BAHAMAS

GOVERNMENT Constitutional parliamentary democracy
LANGUAGES English (official), Creole
CURRENCY Bahamian dollar = 100 cents
MEDICAL Visitors should protect against dehydration, sunburn, tetanus, and jellyfish
TRAVEL Most visits are trouble-free, but crime exists in the cities of Nassau and Freeport. Keep valuables hidden and avoid walking alone
WEATHER Mild throughout the year; May to Oct warm and wet; Dec to Mar cooler and drier; Jun to Nov hurricanes occur
BANKING 0930–1500 Mon to Thu; 0930–1700 Fri, but hours on each island vary
EMERGENCY All Services 911
TIME ZONE GMT –5
INTERNATIONAL DIALING CODE 1 242

BAHRAIN

GOVERNMENT Monarchy (emirate) with a cabinet appointed by the Emir
LANGUAGES Arabic (official), English, Farsi, Urdu
CURRENCY Bahrain dinar = 1,000 fils
MEDICAL There are no specific health risks
TRAVEL Generally calm, but any increase in regional tension may affect travel advice. Visitors should avoid village areas, particularly after dark. Keep cash and valuables out of sight at all times
WEATHER Jun to Sep very hot; Nov to Mar milder and pleasant
BANKING 0800–1200 and 1600–1800 Sat to Wed; 0800–1100 Thu
EMERGENCY All Services 999
TIME ZONE GMT +3
INTERNATIONAL DIALING CODE 973

BANGLADESH

GOVERNMENT Multiparty republic
LANGUAGES Bengali (official), English
CURRENCY Taka = 100 paisas
MEDICAL Visitors should protect against cholera, dysentery, hepatitis, malaria, and meningitis
TRAVEL Avoid political gatherings. Driving conditions are very poor. Visitors should keep valuables hidden and avoid travel after dark
WEATHER Jun to Sep monsoon with heavy rain and very high humidity; Nov to Feb sunny and cool; Mar to Jun hot with thunderstorms
BANKING 0830–1430 Sun to Wed; 0830–1300 Thu. Closed Fri and Sat
EMERGENCY Police Dhaka 866 551–3; Fire and Ambulance Service Dhaka 9 555 555
TIME ZONE GMT +6
INTERNATIONAL DIALING CODE 880

BARBADOS

GOVERNMENT Parliamentary democracy
LANGUAGES English (local Bajan dialect also spoken)
CURRENCY Barbados dollar = 100 cents
MEDICAL The sun is intense and visitors should wear strong sunscreen at all times. Other health risks include dengue fever
TRAVEL Travel is generally risk-free, but visitors should avoid deserted beaches at night
WEATHER Warm all year round; Jun to Dec wet season; Feb to May cooler and drier
BANKING 0800–1500 Mon to Thu; 0800–1300 and 1500–1700 Fri
EMERGENCY Police 112; Ambulance 115; All Services 119
TIME ZONE GMT –4
INTERNATIONAL DIALING CODE 1 246

BELARUS

GOVERNMENT Multiparty republic
LANGUAGES Belarusian and Russian (both official)
CURRENCY Belarusian rouble = 100 kopecks
MEDICAL Visitors should avoid eating dairy produce, mushrooms, and fruits of the forests which can carry high levels of radiation. Other health risks include hepatitis A and B, and typhoid
TRAVEL Pickpocketing and theft from vehicles or hotel rooms is common. Visitors should avoid demonstrations and rallies, and remain vigilant at all times
WEATHER May to Aug mild; Oct to Apr cold; Jan to Mar snow cover; rain falls all year round
BANKING 0900–1730 Mon to Fri
EMERGENCY Police 02; Ambulance 03
TIME ZONE GMT +2
INTERNATIONAL DIALING CODE 375

BELGIUM

GOVERNMENT Federal constitutional monarchy
LANGUAGES Dutch, French, German (all official)
CURRENCY Euro = 100 cents
MEDICAL There are no specific health risks, but medical care is expensive
TRAVEL Most visits are trouble-free, but visitors should take sensible precautions to avoid the increasing threat of mugging, bag-snatching and pickpocketing, particularly in Brussels
WEATHER May to Sep mild; Nov to Mar cold; rain falls all year round, often as snow in winter
BANKING 0900–1200 and 1400–1600 Mon to Fri. Some banks open 0900–1200 Sat
EMERGENCY Police 101; Emergency Services 112 Fire/Ambulance 100 (112 from a mobile phone)
TIME ZONE GMT +1
INTERNATIONAL DIALING CODE 32

BELIZE

GOVERNMENT Constitutional monarchy
LANGUAGES English (official), Spanish, Creole
CURRENCY Belizean dollar = 100 cents
MEDICAL Precautions should be taken against polio, typhoid, and cholera. Malaria is present throughout the year, excluding urban areas
TRAVEL Nov to May is the best time to visit, but this is the busy tourist season when prices rise and hotels fill up. Belize has one of the longest barrier reefs in the world
WEATHER Hot and humid climate. Monsoon and hurricane season runs from Jun to Sep
BANKING 0800–1300 Mon to Thu; 0800–1200 and 1500–1800 Fri
EMERGENCY All services 911
TIME ZONE GMT –6
INTERNATIONAL DIALING CODE 501

BENIN

GOVERNMENT Multiparty republic
LANGUAGES French (official), Fon, Adja, Yoruba
CURRENCY CFA franc = 100 centimes
MEDICAL Visitors should protect against cholera and malaria. Yellow fever vaccination certificates are required for entry. Water is unsafe to drink
TRAVEL Travel is generally safe, but driving out of towns at night should be avoided due to poor street lighting. Occasional incidents of mugging and armed robberies occur in Cotonou
WEATHER Warm to hot all year round; Mar to Jul and Sep to Oct are rainy seasons in the south
BANKING 0800–1100 and 1500–1600 Mon to Fri
EMERGENCY Consult foreign embassy
TIME ZONE GMT +1
INTERNATIONAL DIALING CODE 229

BERMUDA

GOVERNMENT Self-governing British dependency
LANGUAGES English (some Portuguese is also spoken)
CURRENCY Bermuda dollar = 100 cents
MEDICAL There are no specific health risks
TRAVEL Most visits to Bermuda are trouble-free. Accommodation can be up to 40% cheaper between Nov and Mar, but events and entertainment are less plentiful at this time
WEATHER Jun to Sep very warm; Nov to Apr mild; rainfall is abundant and evenly distributed all year round
BANKING 0930–1500 Mon to Thu; 0930–1500 and 1630–1730 Fri
EMERGENCY All Services 911
TIME ZONE GMT –4
INTERNATIONAL DIALING CODE 1 441

BOLIVIA

GOVERNMENT Multiparty republic
LANGUAGES Spanish, Aymara, Quechua (official)
CURRENCY Boliviano = 100 centavos
MEDICAL Altitude sickness is common. Visitors should drink plenty of water and protect against cholera, hepatitis, malaria, polio, and tetanus
TRAVEL Pickpocketing is common and visitors are advised to remain vigilant at all times. The country is going through a period of unrest
WEATHER Average max. daily temperature of 62–66°F [17–19°C] all year round; low annual rainfall, most falling Dec to Mar
BANKING 0930–1500 Mon to Thu; 0930–1500 and 1630–1730 Fri
EMERGENCY All Services 911
TIME ZONE GMT –4
INTERNATIONAL DIALING CODE 591

BOSNIA-HERZEGOVINA

GOVERNMENT Federal republic
LANGUAGES Bosnian, Serbian, Croatian
CURRENCY Convertible marka = 100 convertible pfenniga
MEDICAL Medical facilities are limited. There is a risk of hepatitis and typhoid fever
TRAVEL Crime level is generally low, but isolated incidents of violence can flare up. Unexploded land mines and other ordnance still remain in certain areas
WEATHER Jun to Sep warm; Dec to Feb cold; spring and fall mild; rain falls all year round
BANKING 0730–1530 Mon to Fri
EMERGENCY Consult foreign office in country of residence before departure
TIME ZONE GMT +1
INTERNATIONAL DIALING CODE 387

BOTSWANA

GOVERNMENT Multiparty republic
LANGUAGES English (official), Setswana
CURRENCY Pula = 100 thebe
MEDICAL There are no specific health risks, but visitors should protect against malaria
TRAVEL Most visits are trouble-free, but there is an increasing incidence of crime. Prolonged rainfall may cause flooding and block roads from Dec to Apr
WEATHER In the east, May to Sep mild with little rainfall; Nov to Mar warm, rainy season but nights can be cold
BANKING 0900–1430 Mon, Tue, Thu and Fri; 0815–1200 Wed; 0815–1045 Sat
EMERGENCY Police 351161
TIME ZONE GMT +2
INTERNATIONAL DIALING CODE 267

BRAZIL

GOVERNMENT Federal republic
LANGUAGES Portuguese (official)
CURRENCY Real = 100 centavos
MEDICAL Visitors should take precautions against AIDS, malaria, meningitis, and yellow fever
TRAVEL High crime rate in major cities of Rio de Janeiro and São Paulo. Dress down and avoid wearing jewelry
WEATHER Jun to Sep pleasant in southeast; Dec to Mar hot and humid with high rainfall
BANKING 1000–1630 Mon to Fri
EMERGENCY All Services 0
TIME ZONE Eastern GMT –3; North East and East Pará –3; Western –4; Amapa and West Para –4; Acre State –5; Fernando de Noronha Archipelago –2
INTERNATIONAL DIALING CODE 55

BULGARIA

GOVERNMENT Multiparty republic
LANGUAGES Bulgarian (official), Turkish
CURRENCY Lev = 100 stotinki
MEDICAL There are no specific health risks
TRAVEL Most visits to Bulgaria are trouble-free, but there is a risk of robbery. Pickpockets operate in downtown Sofia and in the Black Sea resorts. Car theft is commonplace
WEATHER May to Sep warm with some rainfall; Nov to Mar cold with snow; rain falls frequently during spring and fall
BANKING 0800–1130 and 1400–1800 Mon to Fri; 0830–1130 Sat
EMERGENCY Police 166; Fire 160; Ambulance 150
TIME ZONE GMT +2
INTERNATIONAL DIALING CODE 359

BURMA (= MYANMAR)

GOVERNMENT Military regime
LANGUAGES Burmese (official); minority ethnic groups have their own languages
CURRENCY Kyat = 100 pyas
MEDICAL Visitors should protect against cholera, dysentery, hepatitis, malaria, rabies, and typhoid
TRAVEL Politically unsettled. Visitors should avoid large crowds and should not visit Aung San Suu Kyi without prior arrangement. Terrorist attacks have been reported in some areas
WEATHER Monsoon climate; Feb to May hot with very little rain; May to Oct wet; Nov to Feb cooler and drier
BANKING 1000–1400 Mon to Fri
EMERGENCY Unavailable
TIME ZONE GMT +6.30
INTERNATIONAL DIALING CODE 95

CAMBODIA

GOVERNMENT Constitutional monarchy
LANGUAGES Khmer (official), French, English
CURRENCY Riel = 100 sen
MEDICAL Visitors should protect against cholera, hepatitis, malaria, typhoid, and rabies
TRAVEL Visitors should seek advice before traveling. The greatest risks are from traffic accidents and armed robbery after dark. Land mines exist in certain rural areas
WEATHER Tropical monsoon climate; May to Oct monsoon; Dec to Jan lower humidity and little rainfall; Feb to Apr hot; temperatures are constant throughout the country
BANKING 0800–1500 Mon to Fri
EMERGENCY Unavailable
TIME ZONE GMT +7
INTERNATIONAL DIALING CODE 855

CANADA

GOVERNMENT Federal multiparty constitutional monarchy
LANGUAGES English and French (both official)
CURRENCY Canadian dollar = 100 cents
MEDICAL Medical treatment is expensive and it is essential that visitors have travel insurance. Blackfly and mosquitoes can cause problems in areas near water
TRAVEL Most visits to Canada are trouble-free
WEATHER Varies considerably; Jul to Aug tend to be warm all round the country; Nov to Mar very cold everywhere except west coast
BANKING 1000–1500 Mon to Fri
EMERGENCY Emergency Services 911 or 0
TIME ZONE Six zones exist from GMT –3.30 in Newfoundland to –8 on the Pacific coast
INTERNATIONAL DIALING CODE 1

CANARY ISLANDS

GOVERNMENT Spanish autonomous region
LANGUAGES Spanish
CURRENCY Euro = 100 cents
MEDICAL The Canary Islands are part of Spain and there are no specific health risks
TRAVEL The islands are volcanic and the landscape is varied. Many resorts suffer the effects of mass tourism, but beyond these areas there are stunning, peaceful regions to be enjoyed
WEATHER Subtropical climate; generally hot and sunny all year round, but Dec to Feb slightly cooler than rest of year
BANKING Visitors should enquire at hotel
EMERGENCY Unavailable
TIME ZONE GMT
INTERNATIONAL DIALING CODE 34

CAPE VERDE

GOVERNMENT Multiparty republic
LANGUAGES Portuguese, Creole
CURRENCY Cape Verde escudo = 100 centavos
MEDICAL Water is untreated and unsafe to drink. Avoid dairy products as they are unpasteurized. Polio and typhoid vaccinations are recommended; there is a risk of cholera and malaria
TRAVEL Most visits to Cape Verde are trouble-free. Visitors should avoid carrying valuables in pubilc and remain vigilant at all times
WEATHER Warm and temperate climate with a dry summer. The islands suffer periodically from drought
BANKING 0800–1400 Mon to Fri
EMERGENCY All services 87
TIME ZONE GMT –1
INTERNATIONAL DIALING CODE 238

CAYMAN ISLANDS

GOVERNMENT British crown colony
LANGUAGES English (local dialects also spoken)
CURRENCY Cayman Islands dollar = 100 cents
MEDICAL There is a risk of sunburn and poisonous plants are present
TRAVEL Most visits to the Cayman Islands are trouble-free. Car hire is a good way to move around the islands
WEATHER Warm tropical climate all year round; May to Oct wet season with usually brief showers
BANKING 0900–1600 Mon to Thu; 0900–1630 Fri
EMERGENCY Police 911; Ambulance 555; All Services 911
TIME ZONE GMT –5
INTERNATIONAL DIALING CODE 1 345

CHAD

GOVERNMENT Multiparty republic
LANGUAGES French and Arabic (both official)
CURRENCY CFA franc = 100 centimes
MEDICAL Visitors should be vaccinated against yellow fever, tetanus, cholera, and hepatitis A
TRAVEL Visitors to Chad should remain vigilant at all times especially in the southwest region along the border with Cameroon. Areas to avoid include the Aozou Strip and the Tibesti area on the border with Libya, where minefields exist
WEATHER Hot tropical climate; Mar to May very hot; May to Oct wet in south; Jun to Sep wet in central areas; little rain in northern regions
BANKING 0900–1400 Mon to Fri
EMERGENCY Unavailable
TIME ZONE GMT +1
INTERNATIONAL DIALING CODE 235

CHILE

GOVERNMENT Multiparty republic
LANGUAGES Spanish (official)
CURRENCY Chilean peso = 100 centavos
MEDICAL Visitors should protect themselves against cholera
TRAVEL Most visits are trouble-free, but visitors are advised to keep in groups and avoid walking alone, particularly after dark. Pickpockets and muggers are active in cities. Passport photocopies should be carried at all times
WEATHER Variable climate; Sep to Nov and Feb to Apr pleasant temperatures; Dec to Mar hotter; skiing is popular from Jun to Aug
BANKING 0900–1400 Mon to Fri
EMERGENCY Police 133; Fire 132
TIME ZONE GMT −4; Easter Island −6
INTERNATIONAL DIALING CODE 56

CHINA

GOVERNMENT Single-party Communist republic
LANGUAGES Mandarin Chinese (official)
CURRENCY Renminbi yuan = 10 jiao = 100 fen
MEDICAL Rabies is widespread. A virulent strain of viral pneumonia has emerged in the southeast and malaria is common in southern areas
TRAVEL Violent crimes are rare. Crime occurs in cities, and extra care should be taken around street markets and popular bar areas at night
WEATHER Climate varies; Apr to Sep humid and hot; Jan to Mar very cold; rainfall high in central areas; Jul to Sep typhoon season in the south
BANKING 0930–1200 and 1400–1700 Mon to Fri; 0900–1700 Sat
EMERGENCY Police 110; Fire 119
TIME ZONE GMT +8
INTERNATIONAL DIALING CODE 86

COLOMBIA

GOVERNMENT Multiparty republic
LANGUAGES Spanish (official)
CURRENCY Colombian peso = 100 centavos
MEDICAL Visitors should protect against altitude sickness, cholera, hepatitis A, B, and D, and malaria
TRAVEL Guerrilla and criminal attacks close to Bogota are increasing. Violence and kidnapping are serious problems in Colombia. The border area with Panama and the Uraba region of Antioquia are particularly dangerous
WEATHER Hot and humid; May to Nov rainy season; cooler in upland areas
BANKING 0900–1500 Mon to Fri
EMERGENCY All Services 112 (01 in smaller towns and rural areas)
TIME ZONE GMT −5
INTERNATIONAL DIALING CODE 57

COMOROS

GOVERNMENT Multiparty republic
LANGUAGES Arabic and French (both official)
CURRENCY CFA franc = 100 centimes
MEDICAL Strict food hygiene precautions are essential. Cholera and malaria are prevalant and medical facilities are basic and limited
TRAVEL Generally crime-free, but be aware of pickpockets. Visitors should not walk around town centers unaccompanied at night
WEATHER Tropical climate with average temperatures of 77°F [25°C]. Cyclone risk between Jan and Apr
BANKING 0730–1300 Mon to Thu; 0730–1100 Fri
EMERGENCY Unavailable
TIME ZONE GMT +3
INTERNATIONAL DIALING CODE 269

COSTA RICA

GOVERNMENT Multiparty republic
LANGUAGES Spanish (official), English
CURRENCY Costa Rican colón = 100 céntimos
MEDICAL Cases of dengue fever have been confirmed. Visitors should protect themselves against malaria, cholera, and hepatitis
TRAVEL Daylight muggings can occur. Do not wear jewelry or carry large amounts of cash. Riptides are very common on all beaches
WEATHER Coastal areas warmer than inland low-lying regions; Dec to Apr warm and dry; May to Nov rainy season; landslides can occur
BANKING 0900–1500 Mon to Fri
EMERGENCY Police 104; Fire 103; Ambulance 225/1436 and 228/2187
TIME ZONE GMT −7
INTERNATIONAL DIALING CODE 506

CROATIA

GOVERNMENT Multiparty republic
LANGUAGES Croatian
CURRENCY Kuna = 100 lipas
MEDICAL No specific health risks, although the health system is severely stretched at present
TRAVEL Exercise caution in the areas bordering Bosnia-Herzegovina and Serbia and Montenegro. There continue to be incidents of violence and many unexploded land mines remain undetected. It is inadvisable to use the Debelli Brijeg crossing-points into Montenegro
WEATHER Continental climate in the north and Mediterranean on the Adriatic Coast
BANKING 0700–1500 Mon to Fri
EMERGENCY Police 92; Fire 93; Ambulance 94
TIME ZONE GMT +1
INTERNATIONAL DIALING CODE 385

CUBA

Government Socialist republic
Languages Spanish (official)
Currency Cuban peso = 100 centavos
Medical Tap water is unsafe to drink, with a risk of contracting hepatitis A
Travel Street theft occurs, especially in Old Havana and major tourist sites. Do not carry large amounts of cash or jewelry. Do not travel with anyone other than your recognized tour operator. Avoid military zones
Weather May to Oct hot rainy season; Aug to Nov hurricane season; Dec to Apr cooler
Banking 0830–1200 and 1330–1500 Mon to Fri; 0830–1030 Sat
Emergency All Services 26811
Time zone GMT –4
International dialing code 53

CYPRUS

Government Multiparty republic
Languages Greek and Turkish (both official)
Currency Cypriot pound = 100 cents
Medical There are no specific health risks, but visitors should be protected against hepatitis
Travel Travel is generally trouble-free, but attempts to pass overland from the northern Turkish sector into the southern Greek region are not recommended
Weather Apr to May and Sep to Oct cool and pleasant; Jun to Aug hot and dry; Nov to Mar rainfall is heavier, but temperatures remain warm
Banking 0815–1230 in tourist areas; 1530–1730 in winter; 1630–1830 in summer
Emergency All Services 199
Time zone GMT +2
International dialing code 357

CZECH REPUBLIC

Government Multiparty republic
Languages Czech (official)
Currency Czech koruna = 100 haler
Medical Visitors to forested areas should seek advice about immunization against tick-borne encephalitis and lyme disease
Travel Most visits are trouble-free, but petty theft is a growing problem, particularly in Prague. Pickpocketing is very common at tourist attractions
Weather May to Sep mild; Apr and Oct much cooler
Banking 0800–1800 Mon to Fri
Emergency Police 158; Fire 150; Ambulance 155
Time zone GMT +1
International dialing code 42

DENMARK

Government Parliamentary monarchy
Languages Danish (official), English
Currency Danish krone = 100 øre
Medical There are no specific health risks in Denmark
Travel Visits to Denmark are generally trouble-free. Visitors will enjoy relatively low prices compared to other European countries
Weather Jun to Aug warm summer season; Oct to Mar cold and wet with chance of frost; spring and fall are usually mild and pleasant
Banking 0930–1700 Mon, Tue, Wed and Fri; 0930–1800 Thu. Some foreign exchange bureaux remain open until midnight
Emergency Emergency Services 112
Time zone GMT +1
International dialing code 45

DOMINICA

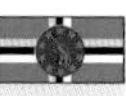

Government Parliamentary democracy
Languages English (official), Creole, French
Currency East Caribbean dollar = 100 cents
Medical Dengue fever is prevalent and visitors should guard against mosquito bites
Travel Most visits are trouble-free. Visitors are advised to take sensible precautions and be vigilant at all times
Weather Tropical climate with heavy rainfall, particularly in Jun to Oct, which is also the hottest period. Tropical storms and hurricanes can occur between Jun and Nov
Banking 0800–1500 Mon to Thu; 0800–1700 Fri
Emergency All services 999
Time zone GMT –4
International dialing code 1 767

DOMINICAN REPUBLIC

Government Multiparty republic
Languages Spanish (official)
Currency Dominican peso = 100 centavos
Medical Tourists should protect against polio and typhoid. There are occasional outbreaks of malaria and dengue fever; antimosquito skin repellants are recommended
Travel Border areas should be avoided while the political unrest in neighboring Haiti continues. Avoid any excursions that are not recommended by tour operators
Weather Hot tropical climate; Jun to Nov rainy season with the risk of hurricanes
Banking 0800–1600 Mon to Fri
Emergency Emergency Services 711
Time zone GMT –4
International dialing code 1 809

ECUADOR

GOVERNMENT Multiparty republic
LANGUAGES Spanish (official), Quechua
CURRENCY US dollar = 100 cents
MEDICAL There is a risk of dengue fever, hepatitis, malaria, typhoid, diptheria, and rabies
TRAVEL Street crimes such as muggings and pickpocketing are common in the cities. Visitors should avoid travel to the provinces bordering Colombia due to incidents of kidnapping
WEATHER Jan to Apr warm and rainy on mainland and Galapagos; Jun to Aug cold; Jun to Aug dry in Highlands; Aug to Feb dry in Oriente
BANKING 0900–1330 and 1430–1830 Mon to Fri
EMERGENCY Police 101; Ambulance 131
TIME ZONE GMT –5; Galapagos Islands –6
INTERNATIONAL DIALING CODE 593

EGYPT

GOVERNMENT Republic
LANGUAGES Arabic (official), French, English
CURRENCY Egyptian pound = 100 piastres
MEDICAL There are no specific health risks in Egypt
TRAVEL Due to continuing tensions, visitors should keep in touch with developments in the Middle East and remain vigilant at all times. Particular care should be taken when traveling in Luxor and beyond in the Nile Valley
WEATHER Jun to Aug very hot and dry; Sep to May dry and cooler; spring and fall months are pleasant; dusty Saharan winds during Apr
BANKING 0830–1400 Sun to Thu
EMERGENCY Unavailable
TIME ZONE GMT +2
INTERNATIONAL DIALING CODE 20

EL SALVADOR

GOVERNMENT Republic
LANGUAGES Spanish (official)
CURRENCY US dollar = 100 cents
MEDICAL Tourists should protect against cholera, hepatitis, malaria, rabies, and typhoid
TRAVEL El Salvador is more politically stable than ever, but has high levels of violent crime. Visitors traveling alone should be vigilant at all times
WEATHER Hot subtropical climate; Nov to Apr dry season; May to Oct rainy season with cooler evenings
BANKING 0900–1300 and 1345–1600 Mon to Fri
EMERGENCY All Services 123/121
TIME ZONE GMT –6
INTERNATIONAL DIALING CODE 503

ESTONIA

GOVERNMENT Multiparty republic
LANGUAGES Estonian (official), Russian
CURRENCY Estonian kroon = 100 senti
MEDICAL There are no specific health risks
TRAVEL Most visits are trouble-free. Despite independence in 1991, much tradition exists in Estonia. Skiing, skating, and ice fishing are popular during the winter months
WEATHER Large temperature variations; Apr to May warm and pleasant; Jun to Sep hot.; Dec to Mar very cold with heavy snowfall; rain falls all year round
BANKING 0930–1630 Mon to Fri
EMERGENCY Police 02; Fire 01; Ambulance 03 (dial an extra 0 first if in Tallinn)
TIME ZONE GMT +2
INTERNATIONAL DIALING CODE 372

ETHIOPIA

GOVERNMENT Federation of nine provinces
LANGUAGES Amharic (official), many others
CURRENCY Birr = 100 cents
MEDICAL Water-borne diseases and malaria are prevalent. Medical facilities outside the capital are extremely poor
TRAVEL Most governments advise against travel to the Gambella region and the Eritrean border. There is currently a high risk of terrorism throughout the country
WEATHER Lowlands are hot and humid, it is warm in the hills and cool in the upland areas
BANKING 0800–1200 and 1300–1700 Mon to Thu; 0830–1100 and 1300–1700 Fri
EMERGENCY Not available
TIME ZONE GMT +3
INTERNATIONAL DIALING CODE 251

FIJI ISLANDS

GOVERNMENT Transitional
LANGUAGES English (official), various Fijian dialects
CURRENCY Fijian dollar = 100 cents
MEDICAL Visitors should protect against dengue fever and should avoid mosquito bites
TRAVEL There has been an increase in petty crime due to the unsettled economic and political situations
WEATHER Tropical climate; Dec to Apr humid, rainy season with a risk of tropical cyclones; May to Oct cooler, dry season
BANKING 0930–1500 Mon to Thu; 0930–1600 Fri
EMERGENCY All Services 000
TIME ZONE GMT +12
INTERNATIONAL DIALING CODE 679

FINLAND

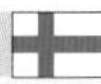

GOVERNMENT Multiparty republic
LANGUAGES Finnish and Swedish (both official)
CURRENCY Euro = 100 cents
MEDICAL There are no specific health risks, but if mushroom-picking/eating, seek advice on safety
TRAVEL Visits to Finland are generally trouble-free
WEATHER Temperate climate; May to Sep warm with midnight sun; Oct to Mar very cold; Nov to May snow cover in the north; skiing starts in Feb, the coldest month, and continues until Jun in Lapland
BANKING 0915–1615 Mon to Fri
EMERGENCY Police 002; Fire/Ambulance 000; Emergency Services 112; Doctor 008
TIME ZONE GMT +2
INTERNATIONAL DIALING CODE 358

FRANCE

GOVERNMENT Multiparty republic
LANGUAGES French (official)
CURRENCY Euro = 100 cents
MEDICAL There are no specific health risks
TRAVEL Most visits to France are trouble-free. There have been sporadic bomb attacks on the island of Corsica and care should be exercised
WEATHER Temperate climate in the north; rain falls all year round; Mediterranean climate in the south; mild in the west; May to Sep hot and sunny; Oct to Nov pleasant temperatures
BANKING 0900–1200 and 1400–1600 Mon to Fri. Some banks close on Mondays
EMERGENCY Police 17; Fire 18; Ambulance 15; Emergency Services 112
TIME ZONE GMT +1
INTERNATIONAL DIALING CODE 33

FRENCH POLYNESIA

GOVERNMENT French overseas territory
LANGUAGES French and Polynesian (both official)
CURRENCY French Pacific franc = 100 cents
MEDICAL Water is untreated and dairy foods are unpasteurized. Vaccinations against polio and typhoid are recommended
TRAVEL Most visits are trouble-free, but visitors should remain vigilant at al times. French Polynesia is made up of 130 islands, Tahiti being the most popular
WEATHER Tropical but moderate climate with occasional cyclonic storms in Jan. Cool and dry Mar to Nov
BANKING 0745–1530 Mon to Fri
EMERGENCY Dial operator
TIME ZONE GMT –9 to GMT –10
INTERNATIONAL DIALING CODE 689

GAMBIA, THE

GOVERNMENT Military regime
LANGUAGES English (official), Mandinka, Wolof
CURRENCY Dalasi = 100 butut
MEDICAL Water-borne diseases and malaria are common. Other health risks include yellow fever, hepatitis, rabies, and typhoid
TRAVEL Exercise caution when walking at night. Do not travel with valuables and dress modestly
WEATHER Nov to Mar dry and cool with winds from the Sahara; Jun to Oct rainy season; inland the cool season is shorter and temperatures are hot from Mar to Jun
BANKING 0800–1330 Mon to Thu; 0800–1100 Fri
EMERGENCY Consult foreign embassy
TIME ZONE GMT
INTERNATIONAL DIALING CODE 220

GEORGIA

GOVERNMENT Multiparty republic
LANGUAGES Georgian (official), Russian
CURRENCY Lari = 100 tetri
MEDICAL Diptheria and rabies cases have been reported. Tap water is unsafe to drink. Anthrax has been reported in the east. Medical care is poor and visitors should carry their own syringes
TRAVEL The regions of Abkhazia and South Ossetia should be avoided. Do not attempt access across the land borders with Russia
WEATHER Jul to Sep hot; Dec to Mar mild, especially in the southwest; low temperatures in alpine areas; rainfall heavy in southwest
BANKING 0930–1730 Mon to Fri
EMERGENCY Police 02; Fire 01; Ambulance 03
TIME ZONE GMT +4
INTERNATIONAL DIALING CODE 995

GERMANY

GOVERNMENT Federal multiparty republic
LANGUAGES German (official)
CURRENCY Euro = 100 cents
MEDICAL There are no specific health risks, but medical care is expensive
TRAVEL Visits to Germany are generally trouble-free. Travelers are able to enjoy a wealth of arts and culture, plus stunning natural scenery
WEATHER Very variable, temperate climate throughout the country; May to Oct warm; Nov to Apr cold; rain falls all year round
BANKING 0830–1300 and 1400/30–1600 Mon to Fri
EMERGENCY Police 110; Fire 112; Emergency Services 112
TIME ZONE GMT +1
INTERNATIONAL DIALING CODE 49

GIBRALTAR

GOVERNMENT UK overseas territory
LANGUAGES English and Spanish
CURRENCY Gibraltar pound = 100 pence
MEDICAL There are no specific health risks in Gibraltar
TRAVEL Most visits to Gibraltar are trouble-free. The country was recognized as a British possession in 1713, and despite Spanish claims, its population has consistently voted to retain its contacts with Britain
WEATHER Warm all year round; Jun to Sep hot and can be humid; Nov to Mar mild
BANKING 0900–1530 and 1630–1800 Mon to Fri
EMERGENCY All Services 999
TIME ZONE GMT +1
INTERNATIONAL DIALING CODE 350

GREECE

GOVERNMENT Multiparty republic
LANGUAGES Greek (official)
CURRENCY Euro = 100 cents
MEDICAL There is a risk of sunburn
TRAVEL Visitors should exercise normal precautions regarding safety and security. Tourists are strongly advised not to hire motorcycles, scooters, or mopeds
WEATHER Mediterranean climate; Aug to Nov pleasant temperatures; Nov to Mar heavy rainfall; Apr to Jun hot
BANKING 0800–1400 Mon to Fri
EMERGENCY Police 100; Fire 199; Ambulance 166; Emergency Services 112
TIME ZONE GMT +2
INTERNATIONAL DIALING CODE 30 + 1 for Athens; 31 Thessaloniki; 81 Heraklion; 661 Corfu

GRENADA

GOVERNMENT Constitutional monarchy
LANGUAGES English (official)
CURRENCY East Caribbean dollar = 100 cents
MEDICAL Tourists should protect against polio and typhoid. Antimosquito repellants are recommended
TRAVEL Trips are mostly trouble-free; however, tourists should remain vigilant at all times
WEATHER Tropical climate, rainy season is Jun to Sep when tropical storms and hurricanes occur. Jan to May is drier and less humid
BANKING 0800–1400 Mon to Thu; 0800–1300 and 1400–1700 Fri
EMERGENCY Police 112; Ambulance 434; Emergency services 911
TIME ZONE GMT –4
INTERNATIONAL DIALING CODE 1 473

GUADELOUPE

GOVERNMENT French overseas territory
LANGUAGES French (official), Creole
CURRENCY Euro = 100 cents
MEDICAL Polio and typhoid vaccinations are recommended. Water is untreated and unsafe to drink
TRAVEL Visits to Guadeloupe are generally trouble-free, and the French culture and influence is clearly evident. Soufriere de Guadeloupe is an active volcano
WEATHER Warm, humid weather all year round. Rainy season from Jun to Oct, when there is a risk of hurricanes
BANKING 0800–1600 Mon to Fri
EMERGENCY Police 17; Fire and Ambulance 18
TIME ZONE GMT –4
INTERNATIONAL DIALING CODE 590

HONG KONG

GOVERNMENT Special administrative region of China
LANGUAGES Chinese and English; Cantonese is most widely spoken
CURRENCY Hong Kong dollar = 100 cents
MEDICAL Visitors should protect against polio and typhoid. Slight risk of malaria in rural areas
TRAVEL Most visits are trouble-free
WEATHER Nov to Dec warm with pleasant breeze; Jan to Feb much cooler; Mar to Apr warmer; May to Sep very humid and uncomfortable, with a risk of cyclones in Sep
BANKING 0900–1630 Mon to Fri; 0900–1330 Sat
EMERGENCY All Services 999
TIME ZONE GMT +8
INTERNATIONAL DIALING CODE 852

HUNGARY

GOVERNMENT Multiparty republic
LANGUAGES Hungarian (official)
CURRENCY Forint = 100 fillér
MEDICAL There are no specific health risks in Hungary
TRAVEL Street theft is common in tourist areas, particularly in Budapest. It is illegal to drive having consumed alcohol. Passports to be carried at all times. Do not take photographs of anything connected with the military
WEATHER Jun to Aug very warm and sunny; spring and fall mild and pleasant; Jan to March very cold
BANKING 0900–1400 Mon to Fri
EMERGENCY Police 107; Fire/Ambulance 104
TIME ZONE GMT +1
INTERNATIONAL DIALING CODE 36

ICELAND

GOVERNMENT Multiparty republic
LANGUAGES Icelandic (official)
CURRENCY Icelandic króna = 100 aurar
MEDICAL There is a risk of hypothermia if trekking during the winter months
TRAVEL Visitors planning to travel off-road do so at their own risk and must contact the local authorities (Vegagerdin) prior to departure. Interior roads are closed in winter
WEATHER Weather is highly changeable all year round; May to Aug is mild with nearly 24 hours of daylight in Reykjavik; Sep to Apr is cold
BANKING 0915–1600 Mon to Fri
EMERGENCY Unavailable
TIME ZONE GMT
INTERNATIONAL DIALING CODE 354

INDIA

GOVERNMENT Multiparty federal republic
LANGUAGES Hindi, English, Telugu, Bengali, Marathi, Tamil, Urdu, Gujarati, Malayalam, Kannada, Oriya, Punjabi, Assamese, Kashmiri, Sindhi, and Sanskrit (all official)
CURRENCY Indian rupee = 100 paisa
MEDICAL There is a risk of malaria, AIDS, and intestinal problems. Precautions should be taken
TRAVEL Visitors are advised to avoid the Pakistan border areas, as well as Jammu and Kashmir
WEATHER Hot tropical climate that varies from region to region; Apr to Sep very hot with monsoon rains
BANKING 1000–1400 Mon to Fri
EMERGENCY Unavailable
TIME ZONE GMT +5.30
INTERNATIONAL DIALING CODE 91

INDONESIA

GOVERNMENT Multiparty republic
LANGUAGES Bahasa Indonesian (official)
CURRENCY Indonesian rupiah = 100 sen
MEDICAL There is a risk of polio, typhoid, hepatitis B, yellow fever, and TB. Unpasteurized dairy produce should be avoided
TRAVEL Non-essential travel to Indonesia is not recommended due to the risk of terrorism against Western interests
WEATHER Tropical, varying climate; May to Oct dry weather from eastern monsoon; Nov to Apr rains from western monsoon. In northern Sumatra this pattern is reversed
BANKING 0800–1500 Mon to Fri
EMERGENCY Police 110; Ambulance 118
TIME ZONE West GMT +7; Central +8; East +9
INTERNATIONAL DIALING CODE 62

IRAN

GOVERNMENT Islamic republic
LANGUAGES Persian, Turkic, Kurdish
CURRENCY Iranian rial = 100 dinars
MEDICAL There is a risk of polio, typhoid, malaria, and cholera
TRAVEL Visitors should monitor media reports before traveling. Any increase in regional tension will affect travel advice. Visitors should exercise caution and avoid carrying large sums of money since robbery and bag-snatching are common
WEATHER Dec to Mar very cold; Apr to Jun and Sep to Nov warm; Jun to Sep extremely hot
BANKING 0900–1600 Sat to Wed; 0900–1200 Thu. Closed on Fri
EMERGENCY Unavailable
TIME ZONE GMT +3.30
INTERNATIONAL DIALING CODE 98

IRELAND

GOVERNMENT Multiparty republic
LANGUAGES Irish (Gaelic) and English (both official)
CURRENCY Euro = 100 cents
MEDICAL There are no specific health risks
TRAVEL The Irish usually have close community bonds. Visitors should find people very friendly. Strong economic growth continues
WEATHER Rain falls all year round; Jul to Sep warm; Nov to Mar wet and cold; spring and fall mild
BANKING 1000–1600 Mon to Fri. Banks may open later in Dublin
EMERGENCY Emergency Services 112; All Services 999
TIME ZONE GMT
INTERNATIONAL DIALING CODE 353

ISRAEL

GOVERNMENT Multiparty republic
LANGUAGES Hebrew and Arabic (both official)
CURRENCY New Israeli shekel = 100 agorat
MEDICAL There are no specific health risks
TRAVEL Most governments currently strongly advise against travel to the West Bank, Gaza, and Jerusalem, or near their border areas with Israel. Visitors should keep car doors locked when traveling and avoid carrying large sums of cash
WEATHER Jul to Sep hot and windy; Dec to Mar cool in the north; spring and fall are warm and pleasant
BANKING 0830–1230 and 1600–1730 Mon, Tue and Thu; 0830–1230 Wed; 0830–1200 Fri
EMERGENCY Police/Fire100; Ambulance 101
TIME ZONE GMT +2
INTERNATIONAL DIALING CODE 972

ITALY

GOVERNMENT Multiparty republic
LANGUAGES Italian (official), German, French, Slovene
CURRENCY Euro = 100 cents
MEDICAL There are no specific health risks
TRAVEL Crime is rare, but visitors in tourist areas and city centers should remain vigilant after dark
WEATHER Apr to May and Oct to Nov warm and pleasant; Jun to Sep hot; Dec to Mar colder temperatures with heavy snow in mountain areas; warmer in the south
BANKING Generally 0830–1330 and 1530–1930 Mon to Fri
EMERGENCY Police 112; Fire 115; Ambulance 113; Emergency Services 112
TIME ZONE GMT +1
INTERNATIONAL DIALING CODE 39

JAMAICA

GOVERNMENT Constitutional monarchy
LANGUAGES English (official), patois English
CURRENCY Jamaican dollar = 100 cents
MEDICAL There are no specific health risks
TRAVEL Most visits are trouble-free, but violent crime does exist, mainly in Kingston. Visitors should avoid walking alone in isolated areas, and be particularly alert after dark and using public transport
WEATHER Tropical climate; temperatures remain high all year round; May to Oct rainy season, but showers can occur at any time
BANKING 0900–1400 Mon to Thu; 0900–1500 Fri
EMERGENCY Police 119; Fire/Ambulance 110
TIME ZONE GMT –5
INTERNATIONAL DIALING CODE 1 876

JAPAN

GOVERNMENT Constitutional monarchy
LANGUAGES Japanese (official)
CURRENCY Yen = 100 sen
MEDICAL Health and hygiene standards are high and visitors are not required to have vaccinations
TRAVEL Most visits remain trouble-free. There is a high risk of earthquakes and typhoons which often hit the country
WEATHER Sep to Nov typhoons and rain; Jun to Sep warm/very hot with rain in Jun; Mar to May pleasant; Dec to Feb cold winds and snow in western areas, but dry and clear on Pacific coast
BANKING 0900–1500 Mon to Fri
EMERGENCY Tokyo English Life Line 3403 7106; Japan Helpline 0120 461 997
TIME ZONE GMT +9
INTERNATIONAL DIALING CODE 81

JORDAN

GOVERNMENT Constitutional monarchy
LANGUAGES Arabic (official)
CURRENCY Jordan dinar = 1,000 fils
MEDICAL There are no specific health risks, but visitors should consider vaccination against hepatitis, polio, tetanus, typhoid, and diptheria
TRAVEL Before traveling, visitors should monitor media reports for any increase in regional tension. Crime is low, but visitors should dress modestly and respect local customs
WEATHER Jun to Sep hot and dry with cool evenings; Nov to Mar cooler with rainfall
BANKING 0830–1230 and 1530–1730 Sat to Thu; 0830–1000 during Ramadan
EMERGENCY Police 192; Fire/Ambulance 193
TIME ZONE GMT +2
INTERNATIONAL DIALING CODE 962

KENYA

GOVERNMENT Multiparty republic
LANGUAGES Kiswahili and English (both official)
CURRENCY Kenyan shilling = 100 cents
MEDICAL Malaria is endemic and AIDS is widespread. Water is unsafe to drink
TRAVEL Be alert at all times, particularly in Nairobi and Mombasa. Avoid traveling after dark and in isolated areas
WEATHER Complex and changeable; Jan to Feb hot and dry; Mar to May hot and wet; Jun to Oct warm and dry; Nov to Dec warm and wet; Cooler with rain at any time at higher altitudes
BANKING 0900–1500 Mon to Fri; 0900–1100 on first and last Sat of each month
EMERGENCY All Services 336886/501280
TIME ZONE GMT +3
INTERNATIONAL DIALING CODE 254

KOREA, SOUTH

GOVERNMENT Multiparty republic
LANGUAGES Korean (official)
CURRENCY South Korean won = 100 chon
MEDICAL There are no specific health risks, but medical and dental treatment can be expensive
TRAVEL Travel to South Korea is generally trouble-free, but some form of identification should be carried at all times
WEATHER Jul to Aug hot with heavy rainfall and a chance of typhoons; Sep to Nov and Apr to May mild and dry; Dec to Mar cold but dry, with good skiing
BANKING 0930–1630 Mon to Fri; 0930–1330 Sat
EMERGENCY Unavailable
TIME ZONE GMT +9
INTERNATIONAL DIALING CODE 82

KUWAIT

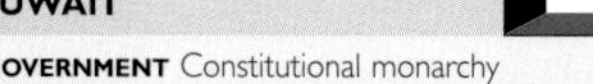

Government Constitutional monarchy
Languages Arabic (official), English
Currency Kuwaiti dinar = 1,000 fils
Medical Vaccinations against polio, typhoid and cholera are recommended
Travel Visitors should monitor media reports before traveling. Any increase in regional tension will affect travel advice. There is a danger from unexploded bombs and land mines on beaches and in rural areas. All Islamic laws should be respected. Photography permits are required
Weather Apr to Oct hot, humid with little rain; Nov to Mar cool and dry
Banking 0800–1200 Sun to Thu
Emergency Unavailable
Time zone GMT +3
International dialing code 965

LATVIA

Government Multiparty republic
Languages Latvian (official), Lithuanian, Russian
Currency Latvian lat = 10 santimi
Medical Visitors should protect themselves against tick-borne encephalitis, particularly if visiting forested areas
Travel Most visits are trouble-free, but tourists should exercise caution since muggings and pickpocketing have increased recently. Use guarded car parks and keep valuables hidden
Weather Temperate climate; Apr to Sep warm and clear; Nov to Mar extremely cold; spring and fall mild
Banking 1000–1800 Mon to Fri
Emergency Police 02; Fire 01; Ambulance 03
Time zone GMT +2
International dialing code 371

LEBANON

Government Multiparty republic
Languages Arabic (official), French, English
Currency Lebanese pound = 100 piastres
Medical Protection against polio and typhoid is recommended
Travel Visitors should remain alert to international developments in the Middle East. Most governments currently advise against travel to areas within the Israeli Occupied Zone
Weather Jun to Sep hot and dry, but humid along the coast; Dec to May high rainfall with snow in mountains; spring and fall pleasant
Banking 0830–1200 Mon to Sat
Emergency Police 386 440 425; Fire 310 105; Ambulance 386 675
Time zone GMT +2
International dialing code 961

LIBYA

Government Single-party socialist state
Languages Arabic (official), Berber
Currency Libyan dinar = 1,000 dirhams
Medical There is a slight risk of malaria, cholera and hepatitis
Travel Most visits to Libya are trouble-free, but any increase in regional tension will affect travel advice
Weather Warm all year round; Nov to Mar occasional rainfall; Apr to Sep can be very hot; May to Jun severe sandstorms from the south
Banking 0800–1200 Sat to Wed (during winter); 0800–1200 Sat to Thu; 1600–1700 Sat and Wed (during summer)
Emergency Unavailable
Time zone GMT +1
International dialing code 218

LIECHTENSTEIN

Government Hereditary constitutional monarchy
Languages German (official)
Currency Swiss franc = 100 centimes
Medical There is a risk of altitude sickness, sunburn and hypothermia in the Alps
Travel Most visits to Liechtenstein are trouble-free. The country is culturally and economically extremely similar to Switzerland. Winter sports are very popular in the Alps from Nov to Apr
Weather Temperate climate; Nov to Apr cool or cold; Jun to Sep warm with high rainfall
Banking 0800–1630 Mon to Fri
Emergency Police 117; Ambulance 144
Time zone GMT +1
International dialing code 41 75

LITHUANIA

Government Multiparty republic
Languages Lithuanian (official), Russian, Polish
Currency Litas = 100 centai
Medical Travelers to forested areas should seek advice about protection against rabies and tick-borne encephalitis
Travel There is a risk of pickpocketing, mugging and bag-snatching, particularly on public transport. Be alert at all times and avoid quiet areas after dark
Weather Temperate climate; May to Sep warm; Oct to Nov mild; Nov to Mar can be very cold with snowfall common
Banking 0900–1700 Mon to Fri
Emergency Police 02; Fire 01; Ambulance 03
Time zone GMT +2
International dialing code 370

LUXEMBOURG

GOVERNMENT Constitutional monarchy (Grand Duchy)
LANGUAGES Luxembourgish (official), French, German
CURRENCY Euro = 100 cents
MEDICAL There are no specific health risks
TRAVEL Most travel to Luxembourg is trouble-free. The country is prosperous with a very high quality of life. Visitors may find it expensive compared to other European countries
WEATHER May to Sep warm with rainfall; Oct to Apr cold with snow
BANKING Varies greatly but generally 0900–1200 and 1330–1630 Mon to Fri
EMERGENCY Police 113; Fire/Ambulance 112
TIME ZONE GMT +1
INTERNATIONAL DIALING CODE 352

MADAGASCAR

GOVERNMENT Republic
LANGUAGES Malagasy and French (both official)
CURRENCY Malagasy franc = 100 centimes
MEDICAL There is a risk of polio, typhoid, bilharzia, cholera, rabies, and hepatitis. Precautions should be taken. Water is unsafe to drink and unpasteurized dairy products should be avoided
TRAVEL Locals are very welcoming and have a relaxed attitude toward time. Local culture should be respected
WEATHER Generally hot and subtropical with varying temperatures. Inland is more temperate, and the south is dry and arid
BANKING 0800–1300 Mon to Fri
EMERGENCY Unavailable
TIME ZONE GMT +3
INTERNATIONAL DIALING CODE 261

MALAWI

GOVERNMENT Multiparty republic
LANGUAGES Chichewa and English (both official)
CURRENCY Malawian kwacha = 100 tambala
MEDICAL AIDS and malaria are very common. Outbreaks of cholera do occur, particularly during the rainy season
TRAVEL Be alert at all times, particularly after dark. Avoid travel out of town at night since the condition of roads is poor. Cases of muggings and bag-snatching are increasing. Do not resist demands since attacks can be very violent
WEATHER Apr to Oct hot and dry; May to Jul cool and cold at night; Nov to Apr rainy season
BANKING 0800–1300 Mon to Fri
EMERGENCY Unavailable
TIME ZONE GMT +2
INTERNATIONAL DIALING CODE 265

MALAYSIA

GOVERNMENT Federal constitutional monarchy
LANGUAGES Malay (official), Chinese, English
CURRENCY Ringgit (Malaysian dollar) = 100 cents
MEDICAL No vaccinations required, but visitors should be up-to-date with typhoid, tetanus, and hepatitis B. Also check malarial status of region
TRAVEL The penalty for all drug offences is harsh. There has been a recent increase in street crime in Kuala Lumpur
WEATHER Nov to Feb heavy rains in eastern areas; Apr to May and Oct thunderstorms in western areas; showers can occur all year round
BANKING 1000–1500 Mon to Fri
EMERGENCY All Services 999
TIME ZONE GMT +8
INTERNATIONAL DIALING CODE 60

MALDIVES

GOVERNMENT Republic
LANGUAGES Maldivian Dhivehi, English
CURRENCY Rufiyaa = 100 laari
MEDICAL There is a high risk of sunburn all year round
TRAVEL Travel to the Maldives is generally trouble-free, but visitors should be aware that there are very harsh penalties for drug offences. Visitors should respect the Islamic religion and act accordingly
WEATHER Hot, tropical climate; May to Oct warm, but humid and wet from the southwest monsoon; Nov to Apr hot and dry
EMERGENCY Police 119; Fire 118; Ambulance 102
TIME ZONE GMT +5
INTERNATIONAL DIALING CODE 960

MALTA

GOVERNMENT Multiparty republic
LANGUAGES Maltese and English (both official)
CURRENCY Maltese lira = 100 cents
MEDICAL There are no specific health risks
TRAVEL Most visits are trouble-free and crime is rare. However, bag-snatching and pickpocketing can occur. Caution should be exercised when traveling by car since many roads are poorly maintained. Visitors should dress modestly when visiting churches
WEATHER Jul to Sep hot with cool breezes; Feb to Jun mild; occasional sudden bursts of rain
BANKING 0800–1200 Mon to Thu; 0800–1200 and 1430–1600 Fri; 0800–1130 Sat
EMERGENCY Police 191; Ambulance 196
TIME ZONE GMT +1
INTERNATIONAL DIALING CODE 356

MARTINIQUE

Government Overseas department of France
Languages French, French Creole patois, English
Currency Euro = 100 cents
Medical There is a risk of sunburn and intestinal parasites. Bilharzia (schistosomiasis) may be present in fresh water
Travel Travel to Martinique is generally trouble-free
Weather Warm all year round; Sep can be very humid; Feb to May cooler and dry; Oct to Dec higher rainfall; upland areas are cooler than lowlands
Banking 0800–1600 Mon to Fri
Emergency Police 17; Fire/Ambulance 18
Time zone GMT –4
International dialing code 596

MAURITIUS

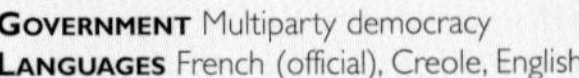

Government Multiparty democracy
Languages French (official), Creole, English
Currency Mauritian rupee = 100 cents
Medical Malaria exists in the northern rural areas and there is a risk of bilharzia
Travel Visitors should always respect local customs and traditions. Most visits are trouble-free, crime levels are low, but sensible precautions should be taken
Weather The weather is warm with a year-round sea breeze. Jan to May are the best months to visit. Tropical storms are likely to occur from Dec to Mar
Banking 0930–1430 Mon to Fri; 0930–1130 Sat
Emergency Unavailable
Time zone GMT +4
International dialing code 230

MEXICO

Government Federal republic
Languages Spanish (official)
Currency Mexican peso = 100 centavos
Medical Visitors should protect themselves against polio, tetanus, typhoid, and hepatitis A
Travel Most visits are trouble-free, but visitors should remain aware of incidents of armed robbery in urban areas, particularly Mexico City, and should dress down accordingly
Weather May to Oct humid, rainy season; Oct to May warm and dry; lowland areas are warmer and upland areas are cooler all year round
Banking 0900–1330 Mon to Fri
Emergency All Services 08
Time zone Spans three time zones from GMT –6 to –8
International dialing code 52

MONACO

Government Constitutional monarchy
Languages French, English, Italian, Monegasque
Currency Euro = 100 cents
Medical There are no specific health risks, but visitors should protect against hepatitis
Travel Most visits to Monaco are trouble-free. This is the country where Europe's wealthiest are to be found living a rich, glamorous lifestyle
Weather Mild climate throughout the country; Jun to Aug can be very hot; Jan to Feb cool with low rainfall; Apr to May and Sep to Oct warm and dry
Banking 0900–1200 and 1400–1630 Mon to Fri
Emergency Police 17; Fire/Ambulance 18
Time zone GMT +1
International dialing code 377

MONGOLIA

Government Multiparty republic
Languages Khalkha Mongolian (official), Turkic, Russian
Currency Tugrik = 100 möngös
Medical Visitors should protect against brucellosis, cholera, and meningitis
Travel Petty street crime is increasing. Visitors should avoid traveling alone after dark. In rural areas always carry a GPS and satellite phone
Weather May to Oct dry and mild; Nov to Apr bitterly cold. Note that between Oct and May sudden snowstorms can block roads and bring transport systems to a standstill
Banking 1000–1500 Mon to Fri
Emergency Unavailable
Time zone GMT +9
International dialing code 976

MOROCCO

Government Constitutional monarchy
Languages Arabic (official), Berber, French
Currency Moroccan dirham = 100 centimes
Medical There are no specific health risks, but malaria is present in northern coastal areas
Travel Visits are usually trouble-free, but visitors should only use authorized guides. Theft is increasing in major cities and valuables should be hidden at all times
Weather Winter cool and wet in north; Oct to Apr warm to hot in lowlands; Dec to Mar very cold in upland areas
Banking 0830–1130 and 1430–1700 Mon to Fri (winter); 0800–1530 Mon to Fri (summer)
Emergency Police 19; Fire/Ambulance 15
Time zone GMT
International dialing code 212

NAMIBIA

GOVERNMENT Multiparty republic
LANGUAGES English (official), Afrikaans, German
CURRENCY Namibian dollar = 100 cents
MEDICAL Malaria and bilharzia are endemic in the north and east respectively
TRAVEL Most visits are trouble-free. The Angola border should be avoided because of land mines left undetected after the civil war. Visitors should seek advice before traveling to townships
WEATHER Oct to Apr rain inland; May to Oct hot and dry; the coast is cool and relatively free of rain all year round
BANKING 0900–1530 Mon to Fri
EMERGENCY Police 1011; Fire 2032270; Ambulance 2032276
TIME ZONE GMT +2
INTERNATIONAL DIALING CODE 264

NEPAL

GOVERNMENT Constitutional monarchy
LANGUAGES Nepali (official), local languages
CURRENCY Nepalese rupee = 100 paisa
MEDICAL There is a risk of altitude sickness, hepatitis A, malaria (in lowland areas), and typhoid
TRAVEL There is now a cease-fire between the government and the Communist party. Trekkers should not venture out without a professional guide and should obtain up-to-date advice regarding the safety of their chosen route
WEATHER Oct to Nov clear and dry, and not too cold at higher altitudes; Dec to Jan cool; Feb to Apr warm; Jun to Sep monsoon season
BANKING 1000–1450 Sun to Thu; 1000–1230 Fri
EMERGENCY Unavailable
TIME ZONE GMT +5.45
INTERNATIONAL DIALING CODE 977

NETHERLANDS

GOVERNMENT Constitutional monarchy
LANGUAGES Dutch (official), Frisian
CURRENCY Euro = 100 cents
MEDICAL There are no specific health risks in the Netherlands
TRAVEL Most visits to the Netherlands are trouble-free. Attitudes here are very liberal. Locals are extremely welcoming and speak very good English
WEATHER Jun to Sep usually warm but changeable; Nov to Mar can be bitterly cold with some snow; rain falls all year round; Apr is best for daffodils and May is best for tulips
BANKING 0900–1600 Mon to Fri
EMERGENCY Emergency Services 112
TIME ZONE GMT +1
INTERNATIONAL DIALING CODE 31

NETHERLANDS ANTILLES

GOVERNMENT Parliamentary democracy
LANGUAGES Dutch (official), French, English, Spanish, many others
CURRENCY Netherlands Antillean gilder = 100 cents
MEDICAL Polio and typhoid vaccinations are recommended. Water is considered drinkable and normal precautions should be taken with food
TRAVEL Most visits to the Netherlands Antilles are trouble-free
WEATHER Hot and tropical climate with cool sea breezes
BANKING 0830–1530 Mon to Fri
EMERGENCY Police 599/5/22222; Ambulance 599/5/22111
TIME ZONE GMT –4
INTERNATIONAL DIALING CODE 599

NEW ZEALAND

GOVERNMENT Constitutional monarchy
LANGUAGES English and Maori (both official)
CURRENCY New Zealand dollar = 100 cents
MEDICAL There are no specific health risks
TRAVEL Most visits are trouble-free, but visitors should take precautions against street crime in urban areas after dark. Travel within the country is relatively cheap and efficient, and accommodation is varied and affordable
WEATHER Subtropical climate in North Island; no extremes of heat or cold, but Nov to Apr warmer; temperate in South Island with cool temperatures; rainfall occurs all year round
BANKING 0900–1630 Mon to Fri
EMERGENCY All Services 111
TIME ZONE GMT +12
INTERNATIONAL DIALING CODE 64

NIGERIA

GOVERNMENT Federal multiparty republic
LANGUAGES English (official), Hausa, Yoruba, Ibo
CURRENCY Naira = 100 kobo
MEDICAL Visitors must have a yellow fever vaccination and protect against cerebral malaria
TRAVEL Incidences of kidnapping are increasing. Violent street crime, armed robberies, and car theft are common throughout the country. Visitors should avoid using public transport and traveling after dark outside tourist areas
WEATHER Mar to Nov hot, humid, and wet; Apr to Sep wet; Dec to Mar dusty winds, but cooler
BANKING 0800–1500 Mon; 0800–1330 Tue to Fri
EMERGENCY Unavailable
TIME ZONE GMT +1
INTERNATIONAL DIALING CODE 234

NORWAY

Government Constitutional monarchy
Languages Norwegian (official)
Currency Norwegian krone = 100 ore
Medical There are no specific health risks in Norway
Travel Most visits to Norway remain trouble-free. The country offers beautiful mountain scenery and year-round skiing
Weather May to Sep sunny and warm with long daylight hours; Dec to Mar very cold and dark; midnight sun occurs from 13 May to 29 Jul, and from 28 May to 14 Jul in the Lofoten Islands
Banking 0900–1700 Mon to Thu; 0900–1530 Fri
Emergency Police (Oslo) 002; Ambulance 003
Time zone GMT +1
International dialing code 47

OMAN

Government Monarchy with consultative council
Languages Arabic (official), Baluchi, English
Currency Omani rial = 100 baizas
Medical Visitors should protect against malaria
Travel Most visits to Oman are trouble-free, but visitors should remain informed of developments in the Middle East. There are harsh penalties, including the death penalty, for drug offences. Driving conditions are hazardous
Weather Jun to Sep very hot; Oct to Mar pleasant; the rest of the year is cooler
Banking 0800–1200 Sat to Wed; 0800–1130 Thu
Emergency All Services 999
Time zone GMT +4
International dialing code 698

PAKISTAN

Government Military regime
Languages Urdu (official), many others
Currency Pakistan rupee = 100 paisa
Medical Visitors should protect against dengue fever, hepatitis A, and malaria. There is also a risk of encephalitis in rural regions
Travel Due to the threat from terrorism, most Western governments advise against all travel to Pakistan, except for their nationals of Pakistan origin
Weather Nov to Apr warm; Apr to Jul hot; Jul to Sep monsoon with high rainfall in upland areas
Banking 0900–1300 and 1500–2000 Sun to Thu; closed on Fri. Some banks open on Sat
Emergency Unavailable
Time zone GMT +5
International dialing code 92

PARAGUAY

Government Multiparty republic
Languages Spanish and Guaraní (both official)
Currency Guaraní = 100 céntimos
Medical There is a risk of cholera, hepatitis, hookworm, typhoid, malaria, and tuberculosis
Travel Most visits to Paraguay are trouble-free, but there is economic recession and some political instability. Attractions include several national parks, including the Chaco – South America's great wilderness
Weather Subtropical climate; Dec to Mar is the hottest and wettest season, but rain falls all year round
Banking 0845–1215 Mon to Fri
Emergency All Services 00
Time zone GMT +5
International dialing code 595

PERU

Government Transitional republic
Languages Spanish and Quechua (both official), Aymara
Currency New sol = 100 centavos
Medical Visitors should protect against altitude sickness, cholera, typhoid, hepatitis, and malaria
Travel Tourist areas are generally safe, but visitors should exercise caution, particularly in Lima and Cuzco, where crime has become a serious problem for foreign visitors
Weather Oct to Apr hot and dry in coastal areas, but much rainfall in highlands; May to Sep is dry and the best time to visit the highlands
Banking 0930–1600 Mon to Fri
Emergency All Services 011/5114
Time zone GMT –5
International dialing code 51

PHILIPPINES

Government Multiparty republic
Languages Filipino (Tagalog) and English (both official), Spanish, many others
Currency Philippine peso = 100 centavos
Medical Visitors should protect against cholera, malaria, rabies, and hepatitis
Travel Visitors should check developments before traveling. Bomb explosions and kidnapping by organized gangs or terrorists have occurred in Manila and Mindanao
Weather Tropical climate with sea breeze; Jun to Sep wet; Oct to Feb cool and dry; Mar to May hot and dry; Jun to Sep typhoons occur
Banking 0900–1600 Mon to Fri
Emergency Unavailable
Time zone GMT +8
International dialing code 63

POLAND

GOVERNMENT Multiparty republic
LANGUAGES Polish (official)
CURRENCY Zloty = 100 groszy
MEDICAL Medical care is generally poor, particularly in rural regions
TRAVEL Most visits to Poland are trouble-free, but there is a serious risk of robbery when using public transport. Locals are very hospitable and welcoming
WEATHER Temperate climate; May to Sep warm; Nov to Mar cold and dark; spring and fall are warm and pleasant; rain falls all year round
BANKING 0800–1800 Mon to Fri
EMERGENCY Police 997; Ambulance 999
TIME ZONE GMT +1
INTERNATIONAL DIALING CODE 48

PORTUGAL

GOVERNMENT Multiparty republic
LANGUAGES Portuguese (official)
CURRENCY Euro = 100 cents
MEDICAL Sunburn is a risk during summer
TRAVEL Most visits are trouble-free. Children under 18 years traveling to Portugal should be accompanied by parents/guardians, or someone in the country should be authorized to have responsibility for them
WEATHER Apr to Oct hot and sunny; Nov to Mar wetter, particularly in the north; summers are hotter and winters are longer in the north
BANKING 0830–1500 Mon to Fri
EMERGENCY Emergency Services 112; All Services 115
TIME ZONE GMT
INTERNATIONAL DIALING CODE 351

PUERTO RICO

GOVERNMENT Commonwealth of the United States
LANGUAGES Spanish and English (both official)
CURRENCY US dollar = 100 cents
MEDICAL There is a risk of sunburn and a slight risk of hepatitis and bilharzia
TRAVEL Most visits to Puerto Rico are trouble-free
WEATHER Tropical climate with little variation in temperature all year round; May to Nov hurricane season; cooler in upland regions
BANKING 0900–1430 Mon to Thu; 0900–1430 and 1530–1700 Fri
EMERGENCY Police 787 343 2020; Fire 787 343 2330; All Services 911
TIME ZONE GMT –4
INTERNATIONAL DIALING CODE 1 787

QATAR

GOVERNMENT Constitutional absolute monarchy
LANGUAGES Arabic (official), English,
CURRENCY Qatari riyal = 100 dirhams
MEDICAL There are no specific health risks
TRAVEL Visitors should keep informed of international developments before traveling. It is prohibited to bring drugs, alcohol, religious material or pork products into the country; videos may be censored. Visitors should dress modestly and respect local customs
WEATHER Jun to Sep very hot and dry; Apr to May and Dec to Feb frequent sandstorms; Nov and Feb to Mar warm with little wind
BANKING 0730–1130 Sat to Thu
EMERGENCY All Services 999
TIME ZONE GMT +3
INTERNATIONAL DIALING CODE 974

RÉUNION

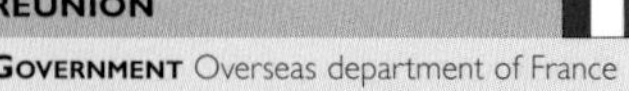

GOVERNMENT Overseas department of France
LANGUAGES French (official), Creole
CURRENCY Euro = 100 cents
MEDICAL Precautions should be taken against typhoid and rabies. Water is unsafe to drink and dairy products should be avoided as they are unpasteurized
TRAVEL Most trips to Réunion are trouble-free. Its society and culture are similar to Western Europe. Usual precautions should be taken
WEATHER Hot and tropical with cooler temperatures in the hills. Cool and dry from May to Nov; hot and wet from Dec to Apr
BANKING 0800–1600 Mon to Fri
EMERGENCY Police 17; Fire 18; Ambulance 15
TIME ZONE GMT +4
INTERNATIONAL DIALING CODE 262

ROMANIA

GOVERNMENT Multiparty republic
LANGUAGES Romanian (official), Hungarian
CURRENCY Leu = 100 bani
MEDICAL Visitors should protect against rabies, typhoid, and encephalitis
TRAVEL Petty theft is common in urban areas. It is illegal to exchange money on the street. Corruption is widespread. Roads are poorly maintained
WEATHER May to Oct warm, but coastal areas are cooled by sea breezes; Nov to Apr harsh winter with snow, but milder along the coast
BANKING 0900–1200 Mon to Fri; 1300–1500 Mon to Fri (currency exchange only)
EMERGENCY Police 955; Fire 981; Ambulance 961
TIME ZONE GMT +2
INTERNATIONAL DIALING CODE 40

RUSSIA

GOVERNMENT Federal multiparty republic
LANGUAGES Russian (official), many others
CURRENCY Russian ruble = 100 kopeks
MEDICAL Visitors should protect against diptheria, hepatitis A, typhoid, and encephalitis
TRAVEL Travel to the Chechen Republic and northern Caucasus is inadvisable. Visitors should keep all valuables out of sight
WEATHER Variable climate in north and central regions; Jul to Aug warm and wet; May to Jun and Sep to Oct dry; Nov to Apr very cold with snow
BANKING 0930–1730 Mon to Fri
EMERGENCY Police 02; Fire 01; Ambulance 03
TIME ZONE GMT +3 in Moscow and St Petersburg. Other areas vary
INTERNATIONAL DIALING CODE 7

ST KITTS & NEVIS

GOVERNMENT Constitutional monarchy
LANGUAGES English
CURRENCY East Caribbean dollar = 100 cents
MEDICAL Visitors should protect against mosquito bites as dengue fever is present. Water is untreated and is unsafe to drink
TRAVEL Most visits are trouble-free. The islands are now commercialized and tourists are welcomed. Usual precautions should be taken
WEATHER Hot and tropical with cooling sea breezes. There is little seasonal temperature variation. Hurricane season is Aug to Oct
BANKING 0800–1500 Mon to Thu; 0800-1500/1700 Fri; 0830–1100 Sat
EMERGENCY All Services 911
TIME ZONE GMT –4
INTERNATIONAL DIALING CODE 1 869

ST LUCIA

GOVERNMENT Parliamentary democracy
LANGUAGES English (official), French patois
CURRENCY East Caribbean dollar = 100 cents
MEDICAL Dengue fever is present; precautions should be taken against mosquito bites. Polio and typhoid vaccinations are recommended
TRAVEL Most trips to St Lucia are trouble-free, but sensible precautions should be taken. Beachwear should not be worn in towns
WEATHER Tropical climate moderated by trade winds. Temperatures are uniform at about 79°F [26°C]. St Lucia lies in the hurricane belt
BANKING 0800–1500 Mon to Thu; 0800–1700 Fri; 0800–1200 Sat
EMERGENCY All Services 999
TIME ZONE GMT –4
INTERNATIONAL DIALING CODE 1 758

ST VINCENT & THE GRENADINES

GOVERNMENT Parliamentary democracy
LANGUAGES English
CURRENCY East Caribbean dollar = 100 cents
MEDICAL Protection from polio, typhoid, and mosquito bites are recommended
TRAVEL Sensible precautions should be taken. There is a relaxed society and most visits are trouble-free. Excellent West Indian cuisine can be found on St Vincent
WEATHER Tropical climate with cooling trade winds. Hottest months are Jun and Jul. Tropical storms may occur from Jun to Nov
BANKING 0800–1500 Mon to Thu; 0800–1700 Fri
EMERGENCY All Services 999
TIME ZONE GMT –4
INTERNATIONAL DIALING CODE 1 809

SAMOA

GOVERNMENT Mix of parliamentary democracy and constitutional monarchy
LANGUAGES Samoan (Polynesian), English
CURRENCY Samoan dollar = 100 sene
MEDICAL Vaccination against polio and typhoid are recommended. Water is untreated and is unsafe to drink
TRAVEL Most visits are trouble-free, but traditional moral and religious codes are very important. Beachwear should not be worn outside resorts
WEATHER Tropical climate with cooler temperatures in the evenings. The rainy season is from Dec to Apr
BANKING 0900–1500 Mon to Fri; 0830–1130 Sat
EMERGENCY All services 999
TIME ZONE GMT –11
INTERNATIONAL DIALING CODE 685

SAUDI ARABIA

GOVERNMENT Absolute monarchy with consultative assembly
LANGUAGES Arabic (official)
CURRENCY Saudi riyal = 100 halalas
MEDICAL Cases of cerebral malaria have been reported in Jizan, southwest Saudi Arabia
TRAVEL Visitors should seek advice on recent developments. Islamic customs must be followed. Bombings have occurred in Riyadh and visitors should remain extremely vigilant
WEATHER Desert climate; extremely dry; May to Oct very hot; Nov to Feb mild
BANKING 0830–1200 and 1700–1900 Sat to Wed; 0830–1200 Thu
EMERGENCY Unavailable
TIME ZONE GMT +3
INTERNATIONAL DIALING CODE 966

SERBIA & MONTENEGRO

Government Federal republic
Languages Serbian (official), Albanian
Currency New dinar = 100 paras
Medical Visitors should protect themselves against hepatitis
Travel The situation in Serbia and Montenegro is calm at present, though visitors should seek advice on developments before traveling. Travel to Kosovo is still inadvisable
Weather Serbia has a continental climate; Nov to Mar very cold; Jun to Sep warm; Montenegro is similar with colder conditions in mountain regions
Banking 0900–1400 Mon to Fri
Emergency Police 107; Fire/Ambulance 104
Time zone GMT +1
International dialing code 36

SEYCHELLES

Government Democratic republic
Languages English, French, French Creole
Currency Seychelles rupee = 100 cents
Medical There are no specific health risks
Travel Crime is relatively rare, but incidents of theft do occur in tourist areas. Visitors, particularly women, should remain vigilant and avoid walking in quiet areas after dark. Roads often have sheer drops and no barriers
Weather Nov to Feb hot, humid monsoon; very warm temperatures all year round; May and Oct breezy at the start and finish of the trade winds
Banking 0830–1430 Mon to Fri
Emergency Unavailable
Time zone GMT +4
International dialing code 248

SINGAPORE

Government Multiparty republic
Languages Chinese, Malay, Tamil, and English (all official)
Currency Singapore dollar = 100 cents
Medical There are no specific health risks
Travel The crime rate is very low in Singapore and most visits remain trouble-free. There are harsh penalties, including the death penalty, for all drug offences. Smoking is illegal in public places
Weather Hot and humid all year round; Nov to Jan cool with most rainfall
Banking 1000–1500 Mon to Fri; 1100–1600 Sat
Emergency All Services 999
Time zone GMT +8
International dialing code 65

SLOVAK REPUBLIC

Government Multiparty republic
Languages Slovak (official), Hungarian
Currency Slovak koruna = 100 halierov
Medical There is risk from rabies and tick-borne encephalitis in forested areas during summer months
Travel Pickpockets operate around the main tourist areas, and foreigners are easily identified and targeted. Sensible precautions should be taken
Weather A temperate climate with cold winters and mild summers
Banking 0800–1700 Mon to Fri
Emergency Fire 150; Ambulance 155; Police 158
Time zone GMT +1 in winter; GMT +2 in summer
International dialing code 42

SLOVENIA

Government Multiparty republic
Languages Slovene (official), Serbo-Croatian
Currency Tolar = 100 stotin
Medical Summer visitors to forested areas should seek advice about protection against tick-borne encephalitis
Travel Harsh fines are given for traffic offences and jaywalking. Passports and international driving licences should be carried at all times
Weather Continental climate inland; Jun to Sep warm; Nov to Mar cold; Mediterranean climate in coastal areas; Sep is the best time for hiking and climbing
Banking 0800–1800 Mon to Fri
Emergency Police 92; Fire 93; Ambulance 94
Time zone GMT +1
International dialing code 386

SOUTH AFRICA

Government Multiparty republic
Languages Afrikaans, English, Ndebele, Pedi, Sotho, Swazi, Tsonga, Tswana, Venda, Xhosa, and Zulu (all official)
Currency Rand = 100 cents
Medical There is a high incidence of HIV/AIDS. Malaria is a risk in certain areas. Hygiene and water standards are high in tourist areas
Travel Violent crime is high in the townships. There is a risk of car-jacking and armed robbery. Visitors should hide valuables and seek advice about which areas to avoid
Weather Generally warm and sunny all year
Banking 0830–1530 Mon to Fri
Emergency Police 10111; Ambulance 10222
Time zone GMT +2
International dialing code 27

SPAIN

GOVERNMENT Constitutional monarchy
LANGUAGES Castilian Spanish (official), Catalan, Galician, Basque
CURRENCY Euro = 100 cents
MEDICAL There are no specific health risks in Spain
TRAVEL Most visits to Spain are trouble-free. The country is rich in arts and culture
WEATHER Temperate in north; Apr to Oct hot and dry, particularly in the south; central plateau can by very cold during winter
BANKING 0900–1400 Mon to Fri; 0900–1300 Sat (but not during summer)
EMERGENCY Police 091; Fire/Ambulance 085; Emergency Services 112
TIME ZONE GMT +1
INTERNATIONAL DIALING CODE 34

SRI LANKA

GOVERNMENT Multiparty republic
LANGUAGES Sinhala and Tamil (both official)
CURRENCY Sri Lankan rupee = 100 cents
MEDICAL There is a risk of cholera and malaria. Rabies is widespread
TRAVEL The northern region and the eastern coast remain heavily mined. A cease-fire between the Tamil Tigers and the government was signed in February 2002
WEATHER Tropical climate; May to Jul and Dec to Jan monsoon seasons; coastal regions are cool due to sea breezes
BANKING 0900–1300 Mon to Sat; 0900–1500 Tue to Fri
EMERGENCY All Services 1 691095/699935
TIME ZONE GMT +5.30
INTERNATIONAL DIALING CODE 94

SWEDEN

GOVERNMENT Constitutional monarchy
LANGUAGES Swedish (official), Finnish, Sami
CURRENCY Swedish krona = 100 öre
MEDICAL There are no specific health risks
TRAVEL Most visits to Sweden are generally trouble-free. Since devaluation of the Swedish currency, the country has become considerably more affordable
WEATHER May to Jul hot and dry, but Aug can be wet; the midnight sun can be seen from May to Jun above the Arctic Circle; Nov to Apr extremely cold, particularly in the north
BANKING 0930–1500 Mon to Fri
EMERGENCY Emergency Services 112; All Services 90 000/112
TIME ZONE GMT +1
INTERNATIONAL DIALING CODE 46

SWITZERLAND

GOVERNMENT Federal republic
LANGUAGES French, German, Italian, and Romansch (all official)
CURRENCY Swiss franc = 100 centimes
MEDICAL There is a risk of altitude sickness, sunburn, and hypothermia in the Alps
TRAVEL Most visits to Switzerland remain trouble-free
WEATHER Climate varies from region to region; Alpine regions have lower temperatures; Jun to Sep warm and sunny; Nov to Apr cold with snow which starts to melt in Apr
BANKING 0830–1630 Mon to Fri
EMERGENCY Police 117; Fire 118; Ambulance 144
TIME ZONE GMT +1
INTERNATIONAL DIALING CODE 41

SYRIA

GOVERNMENT Multiparty republic
LANGUAGES Arabic (official), Kurdish, Armenian
CURRENCY Syrian pound = 100 piastres
MEDICAL Visitors should vaccinate against polio, hepatitis A and B, and tetanus
TRAVEL Visitors should keep informed of developments in the Middle East. They should dress modestly and avoid driving out of main cities at night. Harsh penalties exist for drug offences
WEATHER Apr to Jun mild and dry; Jun to Sep hot; Dec to Mar very cold, particularly in coastal and upland regions
BANKING 0800–1400 Sat and Thu
EMERGENCY Contact hotel operator
TIME ZONE GMT +2
INTERNATIONAL DIALING CODE 963

TAIWAN

GOVERNMENT Unitary multiparty republic
LANGUAGES Mandarin Chinese (official)
CURRENCY New Taiwan dollar = 100 cents
MEDICAL There are no specific health risks, but visitors should be vaccinated against hepatitis
TRAVEL Most visits to Taiwan are trouble-free. Petty crime exists, but is not common. Some roads in central and southern areas may still be blocked by landslides following the 1999 earthquake
WEATHER Subtropical climate with moderate temperatures in the north; Jun to Sep very hot and humid; Jun to Oct typhoon season
BANKING 0900–1530 Mon to Fri; 0900–1230 Sat
EMERGENCY Police 110
TIME ZONE GMT +8
INTERNATIONAL DIALING CODE 886

TANZANIA

GOVERNMENT Multiparty republic
LANGUAGES Swahili and English (both official)
CURRENCY Tanzanian shilling = 100 cents
MEDICAL There is a risk of yellow fever, malaria, cholera, and hepatitis. AIDS is widespread
TRAVEL Most visits are trouble-free, but crime does occur, particularly on public transport and in tourist areas. There are increased risks in Zanzibar where bomb explosions have occurred
WEATHER Tropical climate; Mar to May rainy season in coastal areas; Jan to Feb hot and dry; Nov to Dec and Feb to May rainy season in highland areas
BANKING 0830–1600 Mon to Fri
EMERGENCY Unavailable
TIME ZONE GMT +3
INTERNATIONAL DIALING CODE 255

THAILAND

GOVERNMENT Constitutional monarchy
LANGUAGES Thai (official), English, local dialects
CURRENCY Baht = 100 satang
MEDICAL Visitors should protect against malaria, dengue fever, AIDS, and cholera
TRAVEL Harsh penalties exist for drug offences. Tourists should use licensed taxis with yellow number plates. Visitors should seek advice before traveling to border areas with Burma or Cambodia. Riptides occur off the coast of Phuket
WEATHER Jun to Oct hot and rainy monsoon; Nov to Feb dry and pleasant; Mar to May hot; temperatures are more consistent in the south
BANKING 0830–1530 Mon to Fri
EMERGENCY Unavailable
TIME ZONE GMT +7
INTERNATIONAL DIALING CODE 66

TRINIDAD & TOBAGO

GOVERNMENT Parliamentary democracy
LANGUAGES English (official), Spanish
CURRENCY Trinidad & Tobago dollar = 100 cents
MEDICAL Dengue fever has become a problem in recent years. Medical facilities are basic and limited
TRAVEL While most visits are trouble-free, attacks on travelers are on the increase. Visitors should remain viglant and alert at all times, and take sensible precautions
WEATHER Tropical climate with cooling trade winds. Hottest and wettest time is Jun to Nov
BANKING 0900–1400 Mon to Thu; 0900–1200 and 1500–1700 Fri
EMERGENCY Police 999; Ambulance/Fire 990
TIME ZONE GMT –4
INTERNATIONAL DIALING CODE 1 868

TUNISIA

GOVERNMENT Multiparty republic
LANGUAGES Arabic (official), French
CURRENCY Tunisian dinar = 1,000 millimes
MEDICAL There is a risk of yellow fever and malaria
TRAVEL Travel to Tunisia is generally trouble-free, but visitors to southern desert areas and to areas close to the Algerian border should exercise caution. Tunisian laws and customs should be respected. Drug offences carry harsh penalties
WEATHER Jun to Aug hot and humid; Jan to Feb. cooler; hotter inland; higher rainfall in winter
BANKING 0830–1200 and 1300–1700 Mon to Fri
EMERGENCY Unavailable
TIME ZONE GMT +1
INTERNATIONAL DIALING CODE 216

TURKEY

GOVERNMENT Multiparty republic
LANGUAGES Turkish (official), Kurdish, Arabic
CURRENCY New Turkish lira = 100 kurus
MEDICAL Contagious diseases are increasing and visitors should keep inoculations up-to-date
TRAVEL Most visits are trouble-free, but visitors should exercise caution, particularly in the tourist areas of Istanbul where street robbery is common, and seek recent advice before traveling
WEATHER Mediterranean climate; summers are hot and winters are mild
BANKING 0830–1200 and 1300–1700 Mon to Fri
EMERGENCY Police 155; Fire 111; Ambulance 112
TIME ZONE GMT +2
INTERNATIONAL DIALING CODE 90

UGANDA

GOVERNMENT Republic in transition
LANGUAGES English and Swahili (both official)
CURRENCY Ugandan shilling = 100 cents
MEDICAL There is a risk of AIDS, yellow fever, and malaria
TRAVEL Most visits to Uganda are trouble-free, but visitors should seek recent advice before traveling. It is inadvisable to travel to areas bordering the Democratic Republic of the Congo or Sudan, and visitors should remain cautious if traveling to areas bordering Rwanda
WEATHER Dec to Feb and Jun to Aug hot and dry; Mar to May and Oct to Nov heavy rain
BANKING 0830–1400 Mon to Fri
EMERGENCY Unavailable
TIME ZONE GMT +3
INTERNATIONAL DIALING CODE 256

UKRAINE

GOVERNMENT Multiparty republic
LANGUAGES Ukrainian (official), Russian
CURRENCY Hryvnia = 100 kopiykas
MEDICAL There is a risk of diptheria in western Ukraine. Tick-borne encephalitis is common in forested areas. Do not drink tap water without first boiling it
TRAVEL Crime in the Ukraine remains low, but visitors should remain vigilant and keep valuables out of sight, particularly in crowded areas where pickpocketing and bag-snatching can occur
WEATHER Jun to Aug warm; Oct to Nov sunny but cold; Dec to Mar cold with snowfall
BANKING 0900–1600 Mon to Fri
EMERGENCY Unavailable
TIME ZONE GMT +2
INTERNATIONAL DIALING CODE 380

UNITED ARAB EMIRATES

GOVERNMENT Federation of seven emirates, each with its own government
LANGUAGES Arabic (official), English
CURRENCY Dirham = 100 fils
MEDICAL There is a risk of hepatitis A and B
TRAVEL Visitors should remain informed of recent international developments before traveling. They should dress modestly and respect local customs. Penalties for all drug offences are harsh and can include the death penalty
WEATHER Jun to Sep very hot and dry; Oct to May cooler and is the best time to visit
BANKING 0800–1200 Sat to Wed and 0800–1100 Thu
EMERGENCY All Services 344 663
TIME ZONE GMT +4
INTERNATIONAL DIALING CODE 971

UNITED KINGDOM

GOVERNMENT Constitutional monarchy
LANGUAGES English (official), Welsh, Gaelic
CURRENCY Pound sterling = 100 pence
MEDICAL No vaccinations are required in the UK and citizens of all EU countries are entitled to free medical treatment at National Health Service hospitals
TRAVEL Most visits are trouble-free, but visitors should exercise caution in urban areas after dark
WEATHER May to Aug warm and wet; Sep to Apr mild and wet
BANKING 0900–1730 Mon to Fri. Some bank branches open on Saturday mornings
EMERGENCY Police/Fire/Ambulance 999; Emergency Services 112
TIME ZONE GMT
INTERNATIONAL DIALING CODE 44

UNITED STATES OF AMERICA

GOVERNMENT Federal republic
LANGUAGES English (official), Spanish, more than 30 others
CURRENCY US dollar = 100 cents
MEDICAL There are no specific health risks, but medical treatment is expensive
TRAVEL Most visits to the USA are trouble-free, but visitors should remain vigilant and avoid wearing valuable jewelry or walking through isolated urban areas after dark
WEATHER Varies considerably; check climate before traveling
BANKING 0900–1500 Mon to Fri
EMERGENCY Emergency Services 911
TIME ZONE USA has six time zones from GMT –5 on East coast to –10 in Hawai'i
INTERNATIONAL DIALING CODE 1

URUGUAY

GOVERNMENT Multiparty republic
LANGUAGES Spanish (official)
CURRENCY Uruguayan peso = 100 centésimos
MEDICAL There are no specific health risks, but medical treatment can be expensive
TRAVEL Most visits to Uruguay are trouble-free, but street crime exists in urban areas, including Montevideo. It is, however, less common than in other Latin American countries
WEATHER Dec to Mar hot, but nights can be cool; Apr to Nov mild
BANKING 1330–1730 Mon to Fri (summer); 1300–1700 Mon to Fri (winter)
EMERGENCY Police 109; Fire 104; Ambulance 105; All Services 999
TIME ZONE GMT –3
INTERNATIONAL DIALING CODE 598

VENEZUELA

GOVERNMENT Federal republic
LANGUAGES Spanish (official), local dialects
CURRENCY Bolívar = 100 céntimos
MEDICAL There is a risk of yellow fever, cholera, dengue fever, and hepatitis
TRAVEL The incidence of violent crime is high and the political situation is volatile. Visitors should take precautions. Terrorist and narcotic gangs are active in areas bordering Colombia, where there is the risk of kidnapping
WEATHER May to Dec rainy season; Jan to Apr pleasant temperatures
BANKING 0830–1130 and 1400–1630 Mon to Fri
EMERGENCY Doctor 02 483 7021; Ambulance 02 545 4545
TIME ZONE GMT –4
INTERNATIONAL DIALING CODE 58

VIETNAM

GOVERNMENT Socialist republic
LANGUAGES Vietnamese (official), English, Chinese
CURRENCY Dong = 10 hao = 100 xu
MEDICAL Malaria, dengue fever, and encephalitis are common throughout the country. Visitors should avoid mosquito bites. Typhoid is common in the Mekong Delta
TRAVEL Take care if traveling in border areas. Unexploded mines and bombs still exist in certain areas. Drug smuggling carries the death penalty. Serious flooding can occur in central areas
WEATHER May to Oct tropical monsoons; Nov to Apr hot and dry
BANKING 0800–1630 Mon to Fri
EMERGENCY Police 13; Fire 14; Ambulance 15
TIME ZONE GMT +7
INTERNATIONAL DIALING CODE 84

VIRGIN ISLANDS, BRITISH

GOVERNMENT UK overseas territory
LANGUAGES English (official)
CURRENCY US dollar = 100 cents
MEDICAL Medical facilities are limited. Precautions should be taken against polio, typhoid, and dengue fever
TRAVEL There is a low crime rate, but sensible precautions should be taken. Backpacking is discouraged throughout the 60 islands
WEATHER Subtropical and humid climate moderated by trade winds. Hurricanes are a risk from Jul to Oct
BANKING 0900–1500 Mon to Thu; 0900–1700 Fri
EMERGENCY Police 114; Ambulance 112
TIME ZONE GMT –4
INTERNATIONAL DIALING CODE 1 284

VIRGIN ISLANDS, US

GOVERNMENT US overseas territory
LANGUAGES English, Spanish, French, Creole
CURRENCY US dollar = 100 cents
MEDICAL Visitors should protect against typhoid and polio. Water is generally considered drinkable
TRAVEL Most visit are trouble-free and normal precautions should be taken. There is a large selection of hotel accommodation available
WEATHER Hot climate with cool winds. Low humidity with little seasonal temperature variation. The rainy season is Sep to Nov
BANKING 0900–1430 Mon to Thu; 0900–1400 and 1530–1700 Fri
EMERGENCY All services 911
TIME ZONE GMT –4
INTERNATIONAL DIALING CODE 1 340

YEMEN

GOVERNMENT Multiparty republic
LANGUAGES Arabic (official)
CURRENCY Yemeni rial = 100 fils
MEDICAL Visitors should protect against hepatitis A and B
TRAVEL Most governments currently strongly advise against travel to Yemen. Random armed kidnapping is common, and foreigners remain targets for crime and terrorism
WEATHER Varies with altitude; Oct to Mar nights can be very cold in upland regions; Apr to Sep very hot; Oct to Apr cool, dry and dusty
BANKING 0800–1200 Sat to Wed; 0800–1100 Thu. Closed on Fridays
EMERGENCY Unavailable
TIME ZONE GMT +3
INTERNATIONAL DIALING CODE 967

ZAMBIA

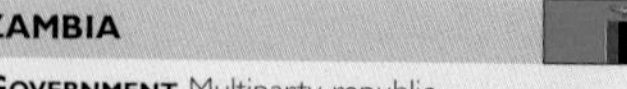

GOVERNMENT Multiparty republic
LANGUAGES English (official), Bemba, Nyanja
CURRENCY Zambian kwacha = 100 ngwee
MEDICAL Outbreaks of cholera and dysentery are common. Malaria is endemic, and cases of AIDS and tuberculosis are very high
TRAVEL Visitors should avoid traveling to areas bordering Angola and the Democratic Republic of the Congo. Armed robbery, bag-snatching and mugging are increasing, particularly in downtown areas. Keep valuables out of sight
WEATHER May to Sep very cool and dry; Oct to Nov hot and dry; Dec to Apr hot and wet
BANKING 0815–1430 Mon to Fri
EMERGENCY All Services 1 2 25067/254798
TIME ZONE GMT +2
INTERNATIONAL DIALING CODE 260

ZIMBABWE

GOVERNMENT Multiparty republic
LANGUAGES English (official), Shona, Ndebele
CURRENCY Zimbabwean dollar = 100 cents
MEDICAL There is a risk of bilharzia, cholera, malaria, yellow fever, and rabies. Incidences of HIV/AIDS are very high
TRAVEL There is currently political and social unrest throughout the country, in both rural and urban areas. Visitors should exercise caution and avoid large crowds and demonstrations
WEATHER May to Oct warm and dry, but cold at night; Nov to Apr wet and hot
BANKING 0800–1500 Mon, Tue, Thu and Fri. 0800–1300 Wed and 0800–1130 Sat
EMERGENCY Police 995; Ambulance 994
TIME ZONE GMT +2
INTERNATIONAL DIALING CODE 263

WORLD MAPS – GENERAL REFERENCE

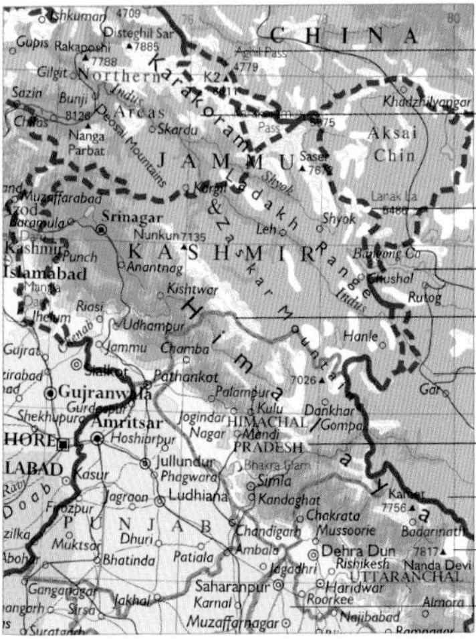

Pass

Permanent Ice and Glaciers

International Boundary (undefined or disputed)

Perennial Lake

Internal Boundary

Perennial Stream

Administrative Area Name

International Boundary

Elevation (m)

Railway

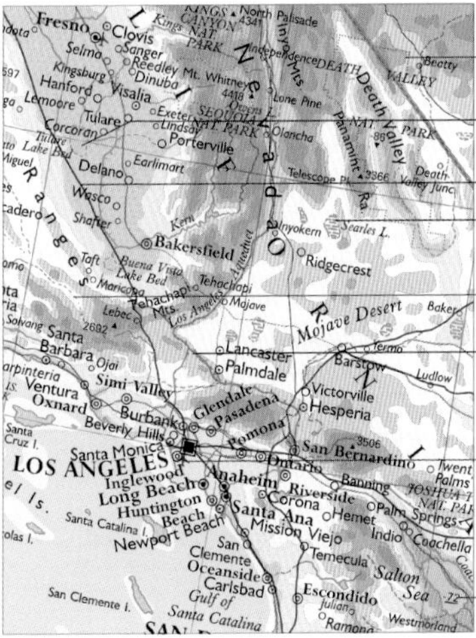

National Park Boundary

Seasonal or Dry Lake

Road

Salt Lake

Intermittent Stream

Canal or Aqueduct

Airport

Height of Lake Surface (m)

Settlements

Settlement symbols and type styles vary according to the scale of each map and indicate the importance of towns rather than speciific population figures.

2 NORTHERN HEMISPHERE

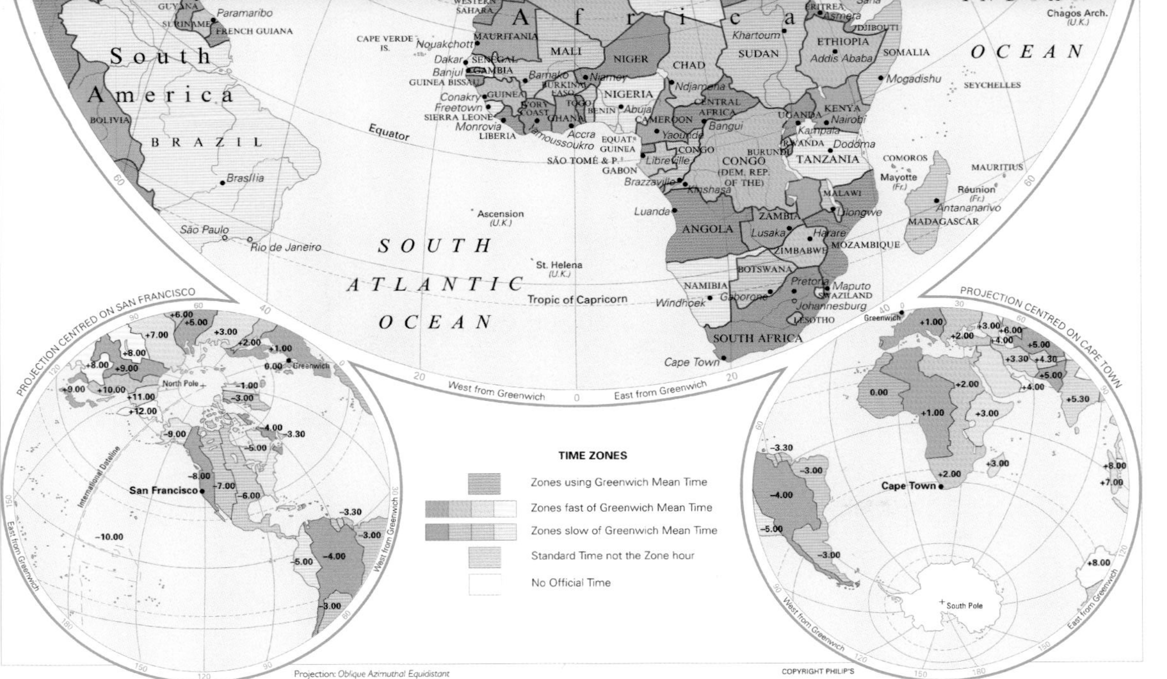
South America
Africa
SOUTH ATLANTIC OCEAN
OCEAN
GUYANA
SURINAME
FRENCH GUIANA
Paramaribo
BOLIVIA
BRAZIL
Brasília
São Paulo
Rio de Janeiro
Equator
CAPE VERDE IS.
WESTERN SAHARA
MAURITANIA
Nouakchott
Dakar
SENEGAL
Banjul
GAMBIA
GUINEA BISSAU
Conakry
GUINEA
Freetown
SIERRA LEONE
Monrovia
LIBERIA
MALI
Bamako
BURKINA FASO
IVORY COAST
Yamoussoukro
GHANA
Accra
TOGO
BENIN
NIGER
Niamey
NIGERIA
Abuja
CHAD
Ndjamena
CAMEROON
Yaoundé
CENTRAL AFRICA
Bangui
EQUAT. GUINEA
SÃO TOMÉ & P.
GABON
Libreville
CONGO
Brazzaville
Kinshasa
CONGO (DEM. REP. OF THE)
SUDAN
Khartoum
ERITREA
Asmera
DJIBOUTI
ETHIOPIA
Addis Ababa
SOMALIA
Mogadishu
UGANDA
Kampala
KENYA
Nairobi
RWANDA
BURUNDI
TANZANIA
Dodoma
ANGOLA
Luanda
ZAMBIA
Lusaka
MALAWI
Lilongwe
ZIMBABWE
Harare
MOZAMBIQUE
BOTSWANA
Gaborone
NAMIBIA
Windhoek
Pretoria
Johannesburg
Maputo
SWAZILAND
LESOTHO
SOUTH AFRICA
Cape Town
COMOROS
Mayotte (Fr.)
MADAGASCAR
Antananarivo
MAURITIUS
Réunion (Fr.)
SEYCHELLES
Chagos Arch. (U.K.)
Ascension (U.K.)
St. Helena (U.K.)
Tropic of Capricorn
West from Greenwich
East from Greenwich
PROJECTION CENTRED ON SAN FRANCISCO
North Pole
Greenwich
International Dateline
San Francisco
PROJECTION CENTRED ON CAPE TOWN
South Pole
Cape Town
TIME ZONES
Zones using Greenwich Mean Time
Zones fast of Greenwich Mean Time
Zones slow of Greenwich Mean Time
Standard Time not the Zone hour
No Official Time
Projection: Oblique Azimuthal Equidistant
COPYRIGHT PHILIP'S

All distances measured through the centre of the map are correct for scale
PROJECTION CENTRED ON THE ANTIPODES OF LONDON
• Capital cities
East from Greenwich
West from Greenwich
International Dateline
Tropic of Cancer
Equator
Tropic of Capricorn
Antarctic Circle
P A C I F I C
O C E A N
I N D I A N
O c e a n i a
A U S T R A L I A
Midway I. (U.S.A.)
Hawaiian Is. (U.S.A.)
Wake I. (U.S.A.)
MARSHALL IS.
Bonin Is. (Japan)
Northern Marianas (U.S.A.)
Guam (U.S.A.)
FED. STATES OF MICRONESIA
PALAU
PHILIPPINES
Manila
K I R I B A T I
TUVALU
SOLOMON IS.
PAPUA NEW GUINEA
Port Moresby
VANUATU
New Caledonia (Fr.)
FIJI
SAMOA
TONGA
Cook Is. (N.Z.)
Marquesas Is. (Fr.)
Tuamotu Arch. (Fr.)
Tahiti (Fr.)
FRENCH POLYNESIA
Pitcairn I. (U.K.)
Easter I. (Chile)
Galapagos Is. (Ecuador)
Kermadec Is. (N.Z.)
Auckland
NEW ZEALAND
Wellington
Chatham Is. (N.Z.)
Antipodes Is. (N.Z.)
Macquarie Is. (Austral.)
Auckland Is. (N.Z.)
Magnetic Pole
Victoria Land
Brisbane
Sydney
Canberra
Tasmania
Adelaide
Perth
EAST TIMOR
Ujung Pandang
Borneo
INDONESIA
Jakarta
SINGAPORE
Kuala Lumpur
MALAYSIA
BRUNEI
VIETNAM
Ho Chi Minh City
Cocos Is. (Austral.)

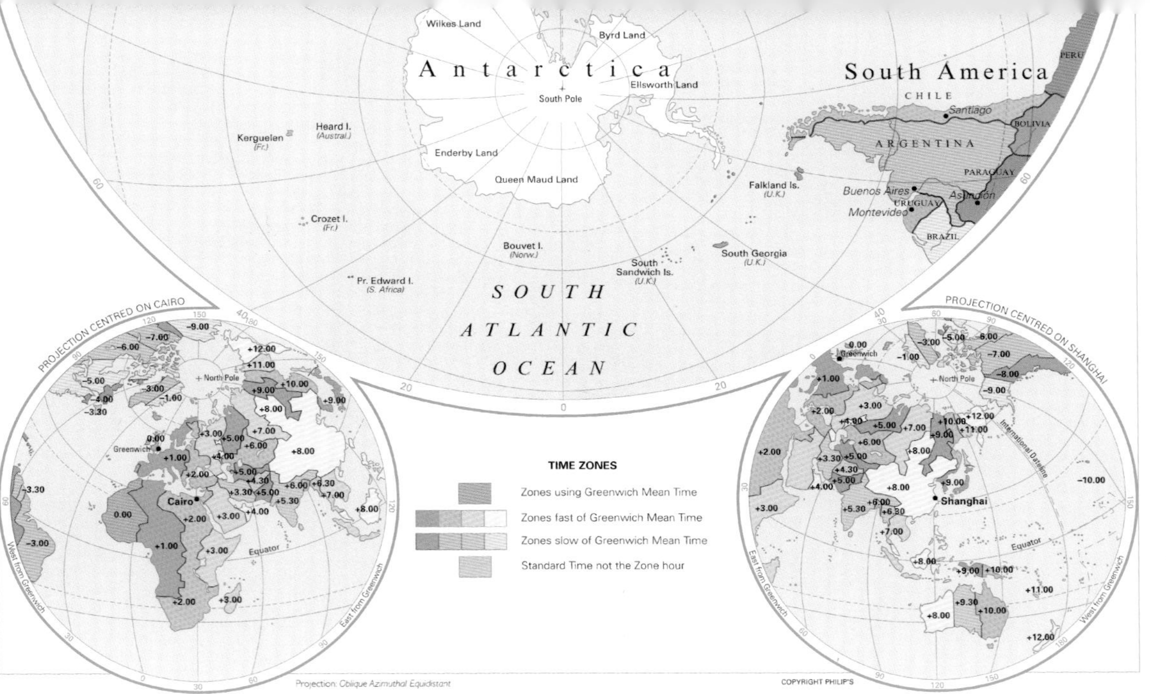

Projection: Oblique Azimuthal Equidistant

Arctic Circle
ICELAND
Reykjavík
Norwegian Sea
Tromsø
Faroe Is. (Den.)
SWEDEN
Trondheim
Shetland Is.
NORWAY
Bergen
ATLANTIC
UNITED KINGDOM
Hebrides
Orkney Is.
Gävle
Oslo
Stavanger
Uppsala
Örebro
Stockholm
SCOTLAND
Aberdeen
Glasgow
Dundee
Vänern
Vättern
Jönköping
Skagerrak
Kattegat
Gothenburg
N. IRELAND
Edinburgh
Ålborg
Belfast
North Sea
DENMARK
Århus
Gotland
IRELAND
Dublin
Newcastle-upon-Tyne
Copenhagen
Malmö
Manchester
Leeds
Liverpool
Cork
Sheffield
Baltic
Kiel
WALES
Birmingham
Cardiff
ENGLAND
Hamburg
Gdańsk
Bristol
Amsterdam
The Hague
Rotterdam
NETHERLANDS
Bremen
Elbe
Szczecin
Plymouth
Southampton
LONDON
Hannover
Berlin
Bydgoszcz
OCEAN
Antwerp
BELGIUM
Essen
Dortmund
GERMANY
Magdeburg
POLAND
Oder
Poznań
English Channel
Le Havre
Lille
Brussels
Cologne
Bonn
Halle
Leipzig
Łódź
Channel Is. (U.K.)
Brest
Rouen
Meuse
Wiesbaden
Chemnitz
Dresden
Wrocław
LUX.
Frankfurt am Main
Seine
PARIS
Luxembourg
Prague
Katowice
Ostrava
FRANCE
Strasbourg
Rhine
Nuremberg
CZECH REP.
Bay of Biscay
Nantes
Loire
Stuttgart
SLOVAKIA
Dijon
Munich
Vienna
Bratislava
Linz
Limoges
Zürich
LIECH.
Bern
Vaduz
Salzburg
AUSTRIA
Lyons
SWITZERLAND
Innsbruck
Budapest
Geneva
Graz
HUNGARY
La Coruña
Bordeaux
St-Étienne
Vigo
Garonne
Grenoble
Milan
SLOVENIA
Ljubljana
Zagreb
Porto
Douro
Bilbao
Toulouse
Rhône
Turin
Venice
Trieste
CROATIA
Genoa
Bologna
Valladolid
Ebro
ANDORRA
Andorra-la-Vella
Marseilles
Nice
MONACO
Florence
BOSNIA-HERZ.
PORTUGAL
Zaragoza
Toulon
SAN MARINO
Adriatic Sea
Split
Sarajevo
Lisbon
Tagus
Madrid
Tiber
SPAIN
Corsica
Ajaccio
ITALY
Guadiana
Barcelona
Valencia
Rome
Seville
Córdoba
Guadalquivir
Balearic Is.
Palma
Minorca
Sardinia
Tirana
Naples
Bari
Murcia
Ibiza
Majorca
Tyrrhenian Sea
Táranto
ALBANIA
Cádiz
Granada
Alicante
Str. of Gibraltar
Málaga
Gibraltar (U.K.)
Cagliari
Corfu
Tangier
Ceuta (Sp.)
Mediterranean Sea
Palermo
Messina
Ionian Sea
Algiers
Melilla (Sp.)
Annaba
Sicily
Catánia
Africa
MOROCCO
ALGERIA
Constantine
Tunis
TUNISIA
Pantelleria (Italy)
MALTA
Valletta

Projection: Bonne   West from Greenwich   East from Greenwich

■ LONDON Capital Cities

100 0 100 200 300 400 500 600 700 800 km
100 0 100 200 300 400 500 miles
FINLAND
ESTONIA
LATVIA
LITHUANIA
BELARUS
UKRAINE
MOLDOVA
ROMANIA
BULGARIA
MACEDONIA
GREECE
SERBIA & MONTENEGRO
RUSSIA
KAZAKHSTAN
GEORGIA
ARMENIA
AZERBAIJAN
TURKEY
SYRIA
IRAQ
IRAN
CYPRUS
ASIA
White Sea
Black Sea
Caspian Sea
Aegean Sea
Bothnia
Crete
Crimea
Bosporus
Hammerfest
Murmansk
Arkhangelsk
Kotlas
Luleå
Vaasa
Tampere
Turku
Helsinki
Vyborg
L. Ladoga
L. Onega
ST. PETERSBURG
Tallinn
L. Chudskoye
Riga
Kaunas
Vilnius
Kaliningrad
Vitebsk
Smolensk
Mogilev
Minsk
Gomel
Brest
Pripet
Białystok
Warsaw
Lublin
Kraków
Vistula
W. Dvina
N. Dvina
Vologda
Rybinsk Res.
Kostroma
Yaroslavl
Ivanovo
Nizhniy Novgorod
Kazan
Kirov
Perm
Nizhniy Tagil
Yekaterinburg
Chelyabinsk
Ufa
Magnitogorsk
Orenburg
Samara
Simbirsk
Penza
Volga
MOSCOW
Tula
Orel
Tambov
Voronezh
Kursk
Saratov
Uralsk
Ural
Atyrau
Volgograd
Astrakhan
Don
Ob
Chernigov
Kiev
Dnieper
Zhitomir
Kharkov
Lvov
Donetsk
Dnepropetrovsk
Taganrog
Rostov
Dniester
Bug
Krivoy Rog
Zaporozhye
Kherson
Nikolayev
Odessa
Kishinev
Stavropol
Krasnodar
Makhachkala
Miskolc
Debrecen
Cluj-Napoca
Timișoara
Brașov
Galați
Ploiești
Bucharest
Constanța
Sevastopol
Tbilisi
Baku
Yerevan
Araks
Tabriz
Belgrade
Danube
Niš
Sofia
Varna
Skopje
Plovdiv
Thessaloniki
ISTANBUL
Bursa
Samsun
Erzurum
Ankara
Kayseri
Diyarbakır
İzmir
Konya
Adana
Antalya
Aleppo
Euphrates
Tigris
Baghdad
Athens
Pátrai
Rhodes
Nicosia
COPYRIGHT PHILIP'S

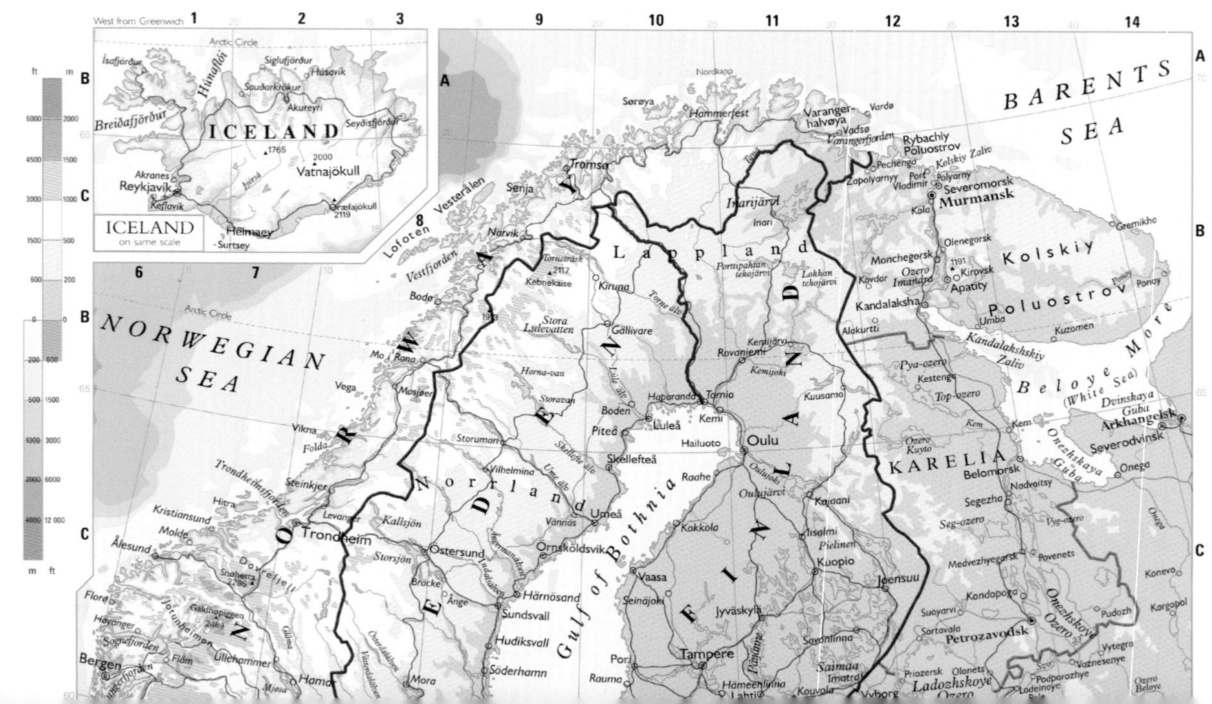
BARENTS SEA
NORWEGIAN SEA
Gulf of Bothnia
Beloye More (White Sea)
Kolskiy Poluostrov
KARELIA
Lappland
Norrland
FINLAND
SWEDEN
NORWAY
ICELAND
ICELAND on same scale
Arctic Circle
West from Greenwich
Murmansk
Severomorsk
Arkhangelsk
Severodvinsk
Kandalaksha
Apatity
Kirovsk
Monchegorsk
Belomorsk
Petrozavodsk
Onezhskoye Ozero
Ladozhskoye Ozero
Oulu
Kemi
Tornio
Rovaniemi
Kuopio
Joensuu
Jyväskylä
Tampere
Vaasa
Pori
Rauma
Luleå
Boden
Piteå
Skellefteå
Umeå
Örnsköldsvik
Härnösand
Sundsvall
Hudiksvall
Söderhamn
Östersund
Mora
Kiruna
Gällivare
Kebnekaise
Narvik
Tromsø
Hammerfest
Nordkapp
Vardø
Vadsø
Senja
Lofoten
Vesterålen
Bodø
Mo i Rana
Mosjøen
Trondheim
Steinkjer
Levanger
Kristiansund
Molde
Ålesund
Bergen
Lillehammer
Hamar
Jotunheimen
Dovrefjell
Reykjavík
Akureyri
Húsavík
Seyðisfjörður
Ísafjörður
Vatnajökull
Heimaey
Surtsey
Keflavík
Akranes

RUSSIA
ESTONIA
LATVIA
LITHUANIA
BELARUS
UKRAINE
POLAND
GERMANY
DENMARK
CZECH REP.
BALTIC SEA
Gulf of Finland
Gulf of Riga
Skagerrak
Kattegat
Svealand
Götaland
Jylland
STOCKHOLM
KØBENHAVN (Copenhagen)
SANKT-PETERBURG (St. Petersburg)
MOSKVA (Moscow)
MINSK
WARSZAWA (Warsaw)
BERLIN
HAMBURG
PRAHA (Prague)
KYYIV (Kiev)
Oslo
Helsinki
Tallinn
Riga
Vilnius
Kaliningrad (Russia)
Valdayskaya Vozvyshennost
Pripet Marshes
Projection: Conical with two standard parallels
East from Greenwich
COPYRIGHT PHILIP'S
50 0 100 200 300 400 km
50 0 50 100 150 200 250 miles
D
E
F
7
8
9
10
11
12

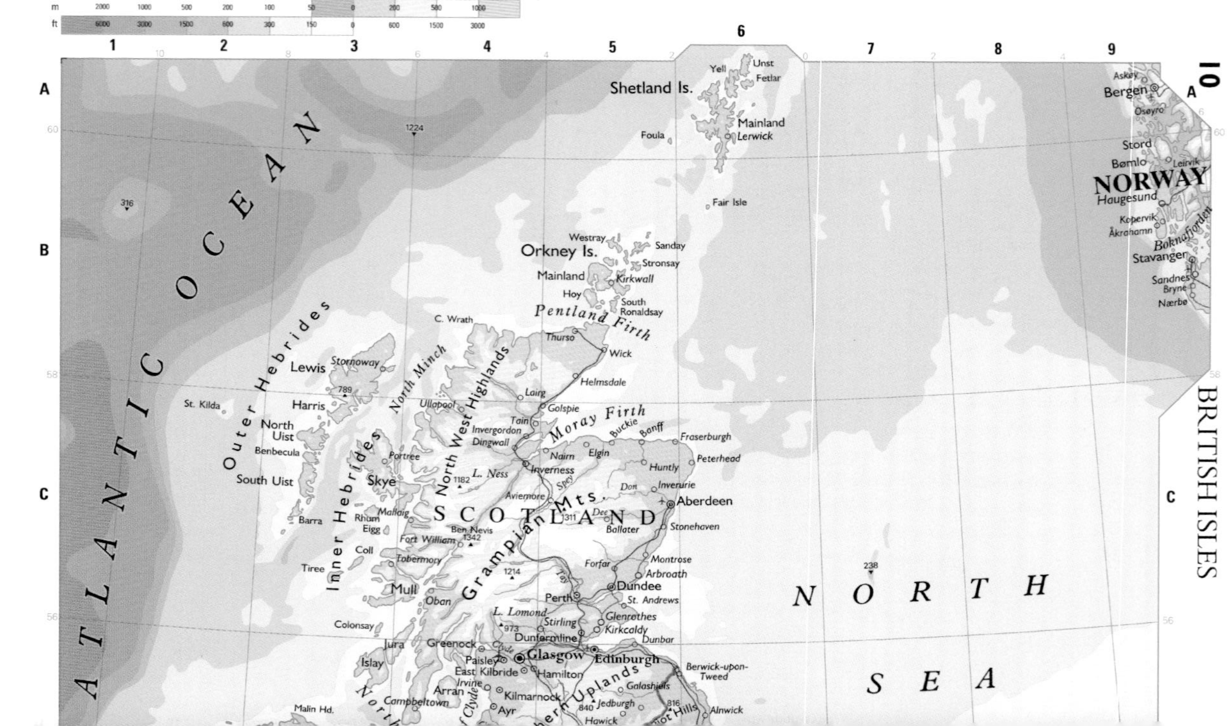

Shetland Is.
Yell
Unst
Fetlar
Mainland
Lerwick
Foula
Fair Isle
Orkney Is.
Westray
Sanday
Stronsay
Mainland
Kirkwall
Hoy
South Ronaldsay
Pentland Firth
C. Wrath
Thurso
Wick
Helmsdale
Lairg
Golspie
Tain
Invergordon
Dingwall
Ullapool
North Minch
North West Highlands
Moray Firth
Buckie
Banff
Fraserburgh
Peterhead
Nairn
Elgin
Huntly
Inverness
L. Ness
Spey
Don
Inverurie
Aberdeen
Aviemore
Grampian Mts.
SCOTLAND
Dee
Ballater
Stonehaven
Ben Nevis
1342
1311
1182
Fort William
Mallaig
Tobermory
1214
Forfar
Montrose
Arbroath
Dundee
Tay
Perth
St. Andrews
Oban
L. Lomond
973
Stirling
Glenrothes
Kirkcaldy
Dunfermline
Dunbar
Greenock
Clyde
Glasgow
Edinburgh
Paisley
East Kilbride
Hamilton
Irvine
Kilmarnock
Ayr
Arran
Campbeltown
Galashiels
Jedburgh
840
Hawick
816
Berwick-upon-Tweed
Alnwick
Lewis
Stornoway
789
Harris
St. Kilda
North Uist
Benbecula
South Uist
Barra
Outer Hebrides
Inner Hebrides
Skye
Portree
Rhum
Eigg
Coll
Tiree
Mull
Colonsay
Jura
Islay
Malin Hd.
ATLANTIC OCEAN
1224
316
NORTH SEA
238
NORWAY
Askøy
Bergen
Osøyro
Stord
Bømlo
Leirvik
Haugesund
Kopervik
Åkrahamn
Boknafjorden
Stavanger
Sandnes
Bryne
Nærbø
m 2000 1000 500 200 100 50 0 200 500 1000
ft 6000 3000 1500 600 300 150 0 600 1500 3000

UNITED KINGDOM
IRELAND
NORTHERN IRELAND
ENGLAND
WALES
NETHERLANDS
BELGIUM
FRANCE
IRISH SEA
CELTIC SEA
English Channel
Bristol Channel
St. George's Channel
Cardigan Bay
Str. of Dover
Galway B.
The Wash
Pennines
Cumbrian Mts.
Cambrian Mts.
Wicklow Mts.
Cotswold Hills
Exmoor
Dartmoor
Ulster
Connacht
Leinster
Munster
Flandre
Picardie
Pays de Caux
Cotentin
Dublin
Belfast
LONDON
BIRMINGHAM
Manchester
Liverpool
Leeds
Sheffield
Bradford
Newcastle-upon-Tyne
Sunderland
Middlesbrough
Kingston upon Hull
Nottingham
Leicester
Coventry
Wolverhampton
Stoke-on-Trent
Derby
Bristol
Cardiff
Swansea
Plymouth
Southampton
Portsmouth
Brighton
Bournemouth
Norwich
Ipswich
Cambridge
Oxford
Reading
Milton Keynes
Cork
Limerick
Waterford
Galway
Londonderry
BRUSSEL (Bruxelles)
's-Gravenhage (Den Haag)
ROTTERDAM
Antwerpen
Lille
Le Havre
Rouen
Caen
Cherbourg
Dunkerque
Calais
Boulogne-sur-Mer
Amiens
Channel Is. (U.K.)
Guernsey
Jersey
I. of Man
Isle of Wight
Isles of Scilly
Land's End
Projection: Conical with two standard parallels
West from Greenwich
East from Greenwich
COPYRIGHT PHILIP'S
125 miles
175 km

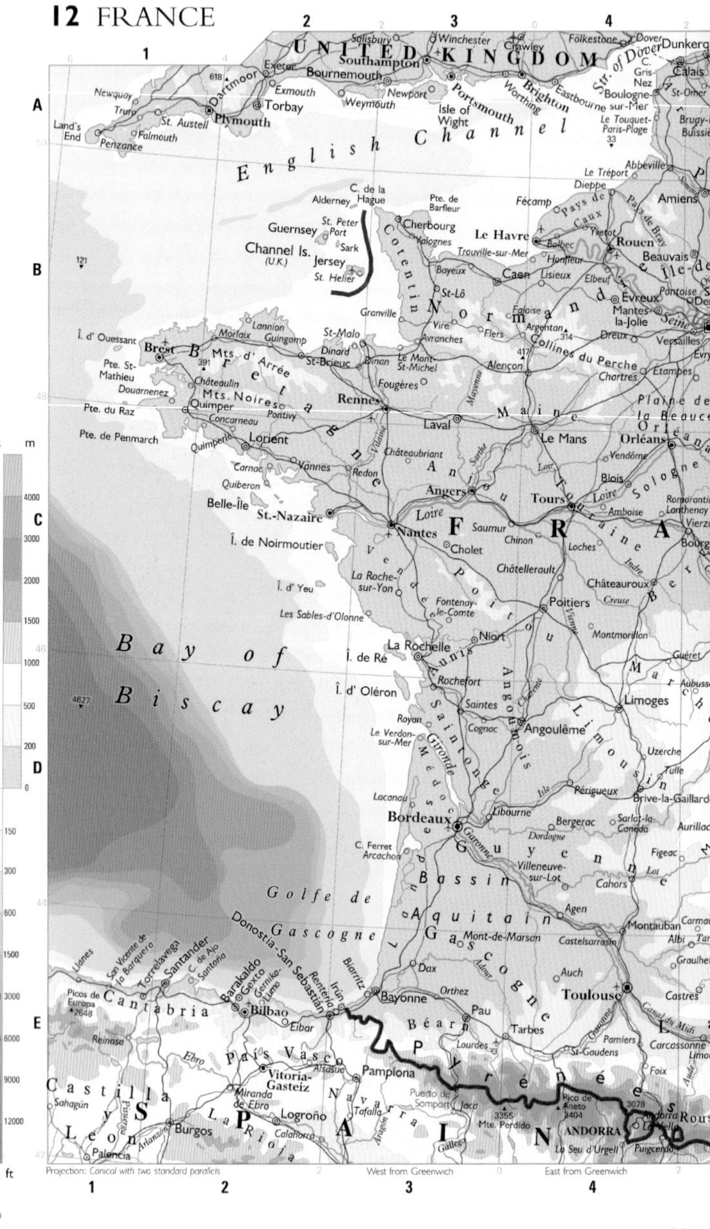

Projection: Conical with two standard parallels

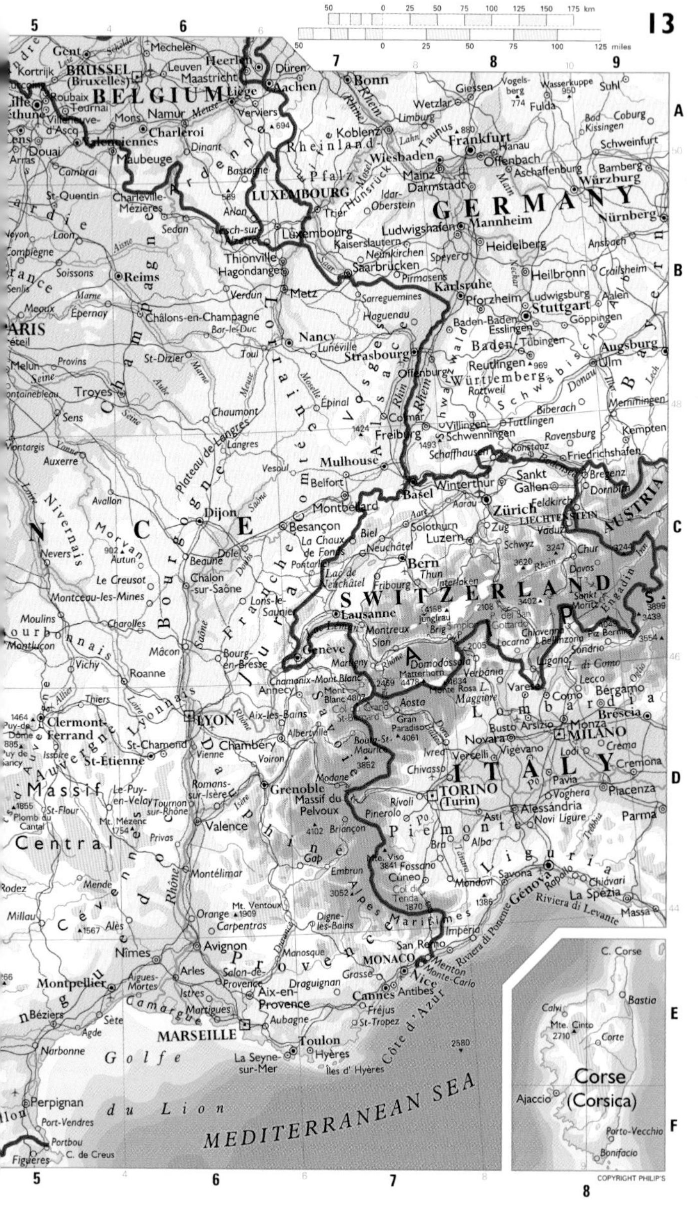
BELGIUM
LUXEMBOURG
GERMANY
SWITZERLAND
AUSTRIA
LIECHTENSTEIN
ITALY
MONACO
MEDITERRANEAN SEA
Golfe du Lion
Corse (Corsica)
BRUSSEL (Bruxelles)
LYON
MARSEILLE
TORINO (Turin)
MILANO
Genève
Lausanne
Bern
Zürich
Basel
Strasbourg
Frankfurt
Stuttgart
Dijon
Grenoble
Genova
Nice

14 GERMANY AND BENELUX

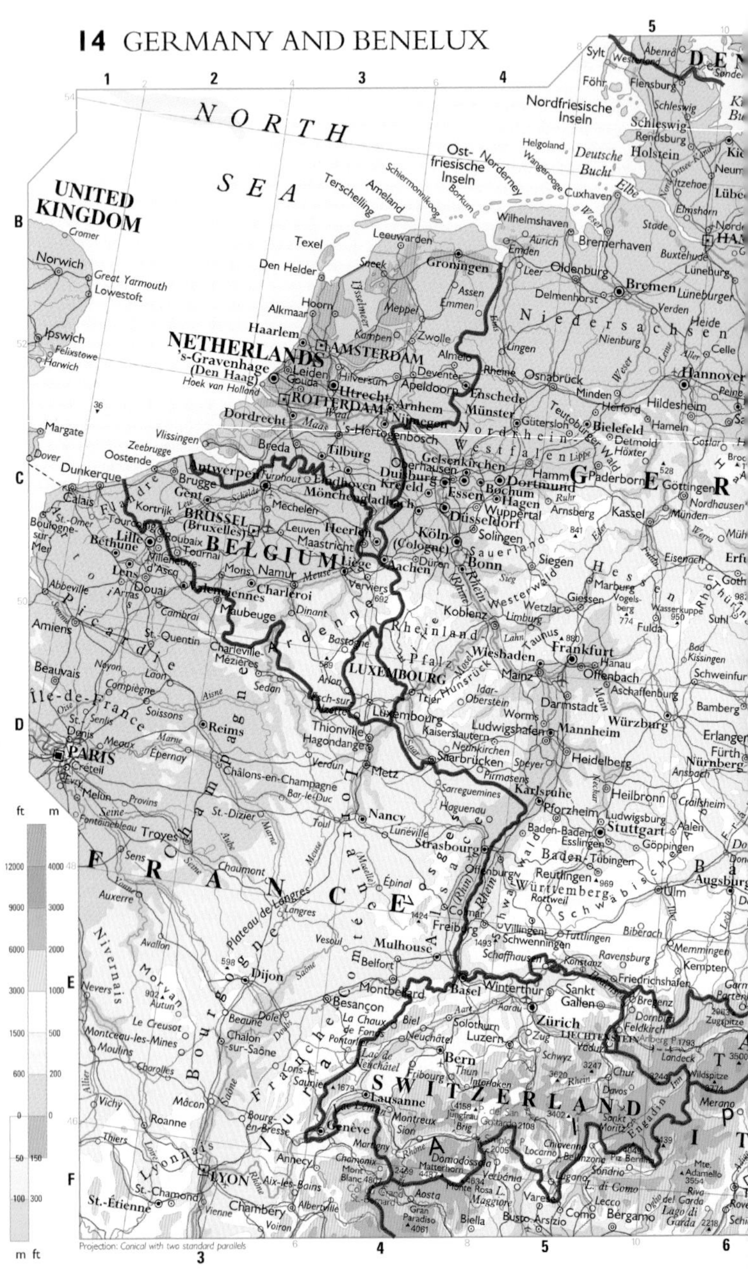

BALTIC SEA
Zatoka Gdańska
Zalew Wiślany
Rügen
Sassnitz
Stralsund
Greifswald
Rostock
Wismar
Travemünde
Mecklenburger Bucht
Fehmarn
Fehmarn Bælt
Lolland
Falster
Nykøbing
Rødbyhavn
Nakskov
Næstved
Svendborg
Møn
Gedser
Usedom
Wolin
Świnoujście
Stettiner Haff
Police
Goleniów
Szczecin
Stargard Szczeciński
Kołobrzeg
Białogard
Koszalin
Darłowo
Słupsk
Lębork
Wejherowo
Rumia
Gdynia
Sopot
Gdańsk
Tczew
Bytów
Elbląg
Malbork
Kwidzyn
Iława
Starogard Gdański
Pojezierze Pomorskie
Szczecinek
Chojnice
Świecie
Grudziądz
Chełmno
Brodnica
Wisła
Wałcz
Piła
Bydgoszcz
Toruń
Rypin
Wisła (Vistula)
Noteć
Inowrocław
Włocławek
Płock
Gniezno
Września
Kutno
Kolo
Łęczyca
Konin
Turek
Prosna
Łódź
Zduńska Wola
Pabianice
Sieradz
Kalisz
Piotrków Trybunalski
Radomsko
Wieluń
Warta
Częstochowa
Kluczbork
Myszków
Zawiercie
Opole
Tarnowskie Góry
Bytom
Zabrze
Gliwice
Katowice
Sosnowiec
Tychy
Oświęcim
Racibórz
Bielsko-Biała
Żywiec
Chorzów
Pyrzyce
Choszczno
Gorzów Wielkopolski
POLAND
Międzychód
Warta
Poznań
Nowy Tomyśl
Śrem
Kościan
Leszno
Krotoszyn
Ostrów Wielkopolski
Oleśnica
Wrocław
Oława
Świdnica
Dzierżoniów
Kłodzko
Nysa
Zielona Góra
Świebodzin
Frankfurt
Nowa Sól
Żagań
Żary
Głogów
Lubin
Legnica
Bolesławiec
Zgorzelec
Jelenia Góra
Wałbrzych
Śnieżka
Sudety
Odra
Oder
Neisse
Bóbr
Schwerin
Mecklenburg
Güstrow
Parchim
Müritz
Neubrandenburg
Neustrelitz
Brandenburg
Wittenberge
Neuruppin
Schwedt
Eberswalde-Finow
Oranienburg
Havel
Salzwedel
Stendal
Rathenow
BERLIN
Fürstenwalde
Potsdam
Wolfsburg
Braunschweig
Magdeburg
Spree
Luckenwalde
Sachsen-Anhalt
Dessau
Lutherstadt Wittenberg
Bernburg
Cottbus
GERMANY
Halle
Torgau
Lauchhammer
Leipzig
Merseburg
Sangerhausen
Riesa
Hoyerswerda
Naumburg
Bautzen
Elbe
Meissen
Dresden
Görlitz
Weimar
Zeitz
Jena
Gera
Sachsen
Chemnitz
Zwickau
Saalfeld
Greiz
Reichenbach
Plauen
Coburg
Hof
Erzgebirge
Bayreuth
Weiden
Amberg
Regensburg
Straubing
Deggendorf
Ingolstadt
Landshut
Passau
Freising
MÜNCHEN (Munich)
Rosenheim
Chiemsee
Kufstein
Innsbruck
Bayern
Böhmerwald
Donau (Danube)
Děčín
Ústí nad Labem
Teplice
Most
Chomutov
Litoměřice
Liberec
Jablonec
Mladá Boleslav
Trutnov
Hradec Králové
Pardubice
Karlovy Vary
Cheb
Kladno
PRAHA (Prague)
Beroun
Kolín
Plzeň
Příbram
CZECH REP.
Vltava
Tábor
Klatovy
Písek
České Budějovice
Jindřichuv Hradec
Českomoravská Vrchovina
Havlíčkův Brod
Jihlava
Třebíč
Znojmo
Brno
Vyškov
Prostějov
Olomouc
Šumperk
Přerov
Zlín
Opava
Ostrava
Havířov
Karviná
Frýdek-Místek
Cieszyn
Hodonín
Považská Bystrica
Žilina
Martin
Trenčín
Prievidza
Banská Bystrica
Biele Karpaty
Malé Karpaty
SLOVAK REP.
Trnava
Topoľčany
Zvolen
Nitra
Levice
Bratislava
Nové Zámky
Komárno
Dunaj
Gmünd
Horn
Zwettl
Freistadt
Krems
Stockerau
Linz
Wels
Ried
Braunau
Melk
Sankt Pölten
WIEN (Vienna)
Bruck an der Leitha
Amstetten
Steyr
Enns
Neusiedler See
Wiener Neustadt
Semmering P.
Mürzzuschlag
Salzburg
Gmunden
Bad Ischl
Eisenerz
Kapfenberg
Bruck an der Mur
Leoben
AUSTRIA
Steiermark
Graz
Badgastein
Grossglockner
Lienz
Kärnten
Wolfsberg
Villach
Klagenfurt
Karnische Alpen
Karawanken
Brenner P.
Bressanone
Bolzano
Sopron
Mosonmagyaróvár
Győr
Tatabánya
Esztergom
Vác
Dunakeszi
BUDAPEST
Pápa
Szombathely
Bakony
Ajka
Veszprém
Székesfehérvár
Dunaújváros
Siófok
Balaton
Zalaegerszeg
HUNGARY
Nagykanizsa
Kaposvár
Szekszárd
Kalocsa
Duna (Danube)
Baja
Pécs
Mohács
Maribor
Drava
Celje
Varaždin
Koprivnica
Virovitica
Bjelovar
Zagreb
Triglav
Kranj
Kobarid
Ljubljana
Sava
SLOVENIA
Kalce
Udine
Gorizia
Pordenone
Conegliano
Vittorio Veneto
Belluno
ITALY
Dolomiti
East from Greenwich
A
B
C
D
E
F
6
7
8
9
10
0 25 50 75 100 125 150 175 km
0 25 50 75 100 125 miles

CENTRAL EUROPE

Projection: *Conical with two standard parallels*

17
50 0 25 50 75 100 125 150 175 km
50 0 25 50 75 100 125 miles
6
7
8
9
10
Marijampolė
Alytus
Suwałki
Druskininkai
Augustów
Lida
Hrodna
BELARUS
MINSK
346
Dzyarzhynsk
Hrodzyanka
Bykhaw
Slawharad
Drut
Sozh
323
Navahrudak
Stowbtsy
Nyasvizh
Asipovichy
Babruysk
Ragachow
Zhlobin
B
Sokółka
(Nyoman)
Dzyatlava
Masty
Vawkavysk
Slonim
Baranavichy
Klyetsk
Slutsk
Białystok
Svislach
Lyakhavichy
Salihorsk
Glusk
Ptsich
Aktsyabrski
Byarezina
Svyetlahorsk
Homyel
Hajnówka
Hantsavichy
Ivatsevichy
Rechytsa
Bielsk Podlaski
Pruzhany
Byaroza
Tsyelyakhany
Vasilevichi
Yaselda
Luninyets
(Pripyats)
Pyetrikaw
Kalinkavichy
52
Kobryn
Dragichyn
Ivanava
(Pripet)
Mazyr
Loyew
Khoyniki
Zhabinka
Pinsk
Horyn
Davyd Haradok
Biała Podlaska
Siedlce
Brest
Stolin
Ubort
Yelsk
Pripet Marshes
Międzyrzec Podlaski
D
Malaryta
316
Ovruch
Prypyat
Chornobyl
Kamin-Kashyrskyy
Dubrovytsya
C
Włodawa
Wieprz
Olevsk
Uzh
Oster
Belokorovichi
Kyyivske Vdskh.
Lyuboml
Kovel
Staryy Chartoriysk
Sluch
Korosten
Dymer
Lublin
Chełm
Malyn
Teterev
Irpin
Świdnik
Kostopil
Novohrad-Volynskyy
KYYIV (Kiev)
Kraśnik
Novovolynsk
Rozhyshche
Kivertsi
Volodymyr-Volynskyy
Oleksandriya
Korets
Radomyshl
Lutsk
Rivne
Zdolbuniv
Zamość
Korostyshev
Vasylkiv
Stalowa Wola
Horokhiv
Sokal
Dubno
341
Ostroh
Slavuta
Zhytomyr
Pershotravensk
Fastiv
50
Chervonohrad
Berestechko
Kremenets
Shepetivka
Polonne
Rava-Ruska
Radekhiv
Izyaslav
Berdychiv
Bila Tserkva
San
390
Kamyanka-Buzka
Brody
UKRAINE
Skvyra
Tarashcha
Nesterov
Kozyatyn
Rzeszów
Yavoriv
Khemelnik
Jarosław
Starokonstyantyniv
Przemyśl
Mostyska
Lviv (Lvov)
Zolochiv
Zbarazh
Tetiyev
Horodok
Ternopil
Khmelnytskyy
Lipovets
Zhashkiv
D
Sanok
Skalat
384
Vinnytsya
Sambir
Khodoriv
Berezhany
Hrymayliv
Drohobych
Rogatyn
Terebovlya
Kopychyntsi
Horodok
Bar
Zhmerynka
Boryslav
327
Haysyn
Truskavets
Stryy
Buchach
Chortkiv
Skala-Podilska
Tulchyn
270
Uman
1346
Skole
Kalush
Dnister
Podilska vysochyna
Bolekhiv
Kamyanets-Podilskyy
Vapnyarka
Haivoron
Ivano-Frankivsk
Horodenka
(Dniester)
Zalishchyky
Mohyliv-Podilskyy
Bershad
Michalovce
Nadvirna
Kolomyya
Khotyn
Ocnița
Balta
Uzhhorod
Volovets
Pechenizhyn
Snyatyn
Novoselytsya
Lipcani
Yampil
48
Chop
Mukacheve
1881
Yaremcha
Chernivtsi
Drochia
Soroca
Berehove
Yasinya
Storozhynets
Hlyboka
Edineț
Florești
Ananyiv
Khust
Rakhiv
Dorohoi
Bălți
Râbnița
Kotovsk
Vynohradiv
Tyachiv
Siret
Fălești
Dubăsari Vdkhr.
Nyíregyháza
Sighetu-Marmatiei
Rădăuți
MOLDOVA
Satu Mare
Suceava
Botoșani
Cornești
Dubăsari
1565
Baia Mare
Borșa
Fălticeni
Orhei
Carei
2303
Pietrosul
Pașcani
Ungheni
Chișinău
E
Someș
Iași
Tiraspol
Vatra-Dornei
Bisztrița
2100
1804
Roman
418
Tighina
Dnister (Nistru)
Bistrița
Pietrosul
Zalău
Dej
Huși
Oradea
Piatra Neamț
Vaslui
Leova
Cimișlia
Mureș
Bilhorod-Dnistrovskyy
Reghin
1777
Basarabeasca
Salonta
Cluj-Napoca
Târgu Mureș
Bacău
Comrat
1836
Turda
Miercurea Ciuc
Siret
Bârlad
Prut
Artsyz
46
Munții Bihor
1848
Odorheiu Secuiesc
Onești
Ciadâr-Lunga
Crișul Alb
Abrud
Aiud
Târnăveni
Sighișoara
Cahul
Tatarbunary
Transylvania
Brad
Alba-Iulia
Mediaș
Sfântu Gheorghe
Tecuci
Vulcanești
Bolhrad
Ozero Sasyk
Mureș
Olt
1783
Focșani
Kiliya
Vylkove
Deva
Sibiu
Făgăraș
Brașov
Reni
Izmayil
ROMANIA
Simeria
Galați
1380
Săcele
Râmnicu Sărat
Sulina
F
Lugoj
Hunedoara
Carpații Meridionali
P. Tumu Roșu
2543
Moldoveanu
Brăila
Tulcea
Petroșani
Câmpulung
2507
Vf. Omul
Câmpina
Caransebeș
Vf. Peleaga 2509
Vulcan
2518
Paringul Mare
Curtea de Argeș
Buzău
Buzău
Babadag
Dunărea (Danube)
1445
22
24
26
6
East from Greenwich
7
8
9
COPYRIGHT PHILIP'S

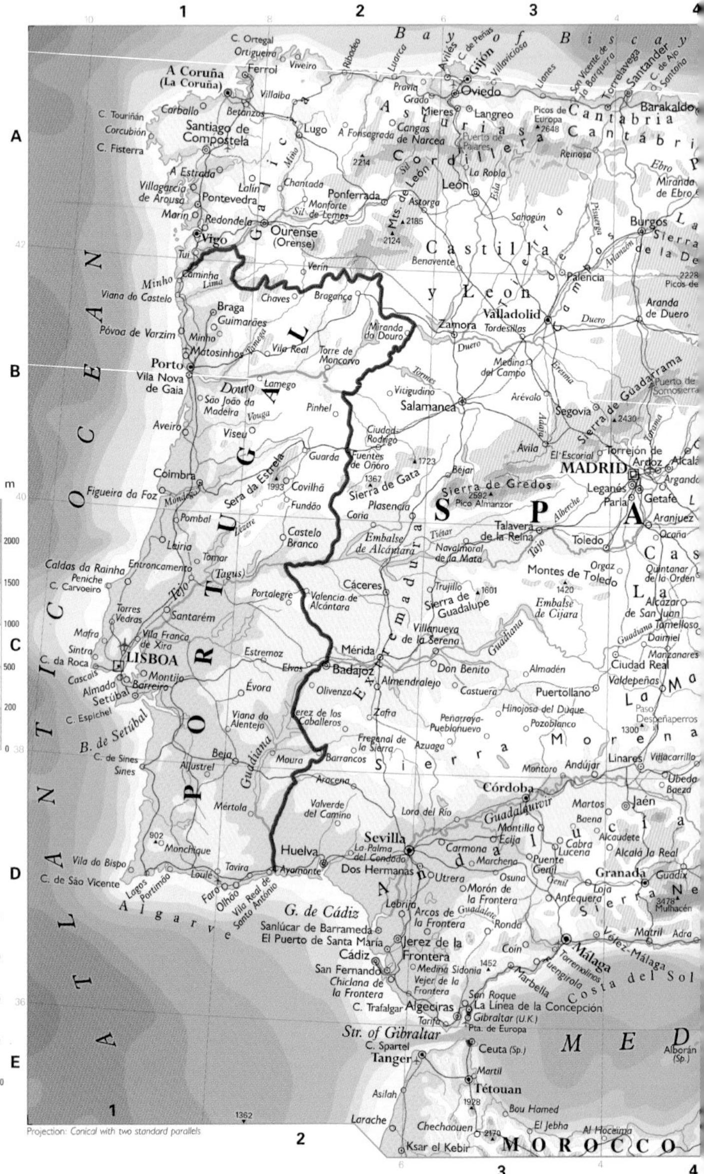
Bay of Biscay
ATLANTIC OCEAN
PORTUGAL
SPAIN
MOROCCO
A Coruña (La Coruña)
Santiago de Compostela
Vigo
Ourense (Orense)
Lugo
Oviedo
Gijón
Santander
León
Burgos
Valladolid
Salamanca
Porto
Vila Nova de Gaia
Coimbra
LISBOA
Setúbal
Évora
Badajoz
Mérida
Cáceres
MADRID
Toledo
Córdoba
Sevilla
Huelva
Cádiz
Jerez de la Frontera
Granada
Málaga
Gibraltar (U.K.)
Str. of Gibraltar
Ceuta (Sp.)
Tanger
Tétouan
Cordillera Cantábrica
Castilla y León
Extremadura
Andalucía
Sierra Morena
Sierra Nevada
Sierra de Gredos
Sierra de Guadarrama
Algarve
Costa del Sol
G. de Cádiz
B. de Setúbal
Douro
Tejo (Tagus)
Guadiana
Guadalquivir
Projection: Conical with two standard parallels

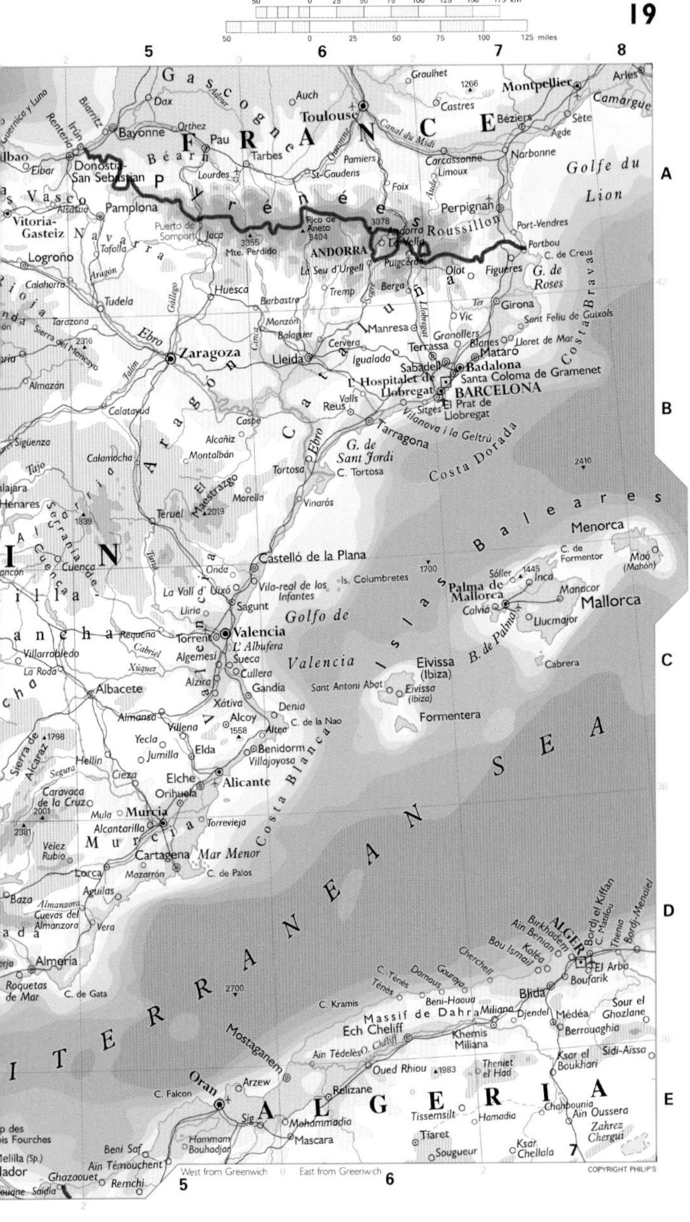
FRANCE
Gascogne
Toulouse
Montpellier
Arles
Camargue
Béziers
Sète
Agde
Narbonne
Golfe du Lion
Carcassonne
Limoux
Perpignan
Roussillon
Port-Vendres
Portbou
C. de Creus
Pyrénées
ANDORRA
Andorra La Vella
Pamplona
Bayonne
Pau
Tarbes
Lourdes
Donostia-San Sebastián
Bilbao
Vitoria-Gasteiz
Logroño
Zaragoza
Huesca
Lleida
Barcelona
Badalona
Santa Coloma de Gramenet
L'Hospitalet de Llobregat
El Prat de Llobregat
Sabadell
Terrassa
Mataró
Girona
Figueres
Costa Brava
Tarragona
Costa Dorada
Tortosa
Teruel
Aragón
Cataluña
Castelló de la Plana
Valencia
Golfo de Valencia
Islas Baleares
Menorca
Mallorca
Palma de Mallorca
Eivissa (Ibiza)
Formentera
Cabrera
Alicante
Murcia
Cartagena
Mar Menor
Almería
Costa Blanca
MEDITERRANEAN SEA
ALGERIA
ALGER
Oran
Blida
Médéa
Mostaganem
Relizane
Tiaret
West from Greenwich
East from Greenwich
COPYRIGHT PHILIP'S

20

AUSTRIA
SWITZERLAND
HUNGARY
SLOVENIA
CROATIA
BOSNIA-HERZEGOVINA
FRANCE
MONACO
SAN MARINO
VATICAN CITY
ITALY
ADRIATIC SEA
LIGURIAN SEA
Golfo di Venézia
Golfo di Génova
Corse (Corsica)
Elba
MILANO
TORINO (Turin)
ROMA
Venézia (Venice)
Firenze (Florence)
Génova
Bologna
Trieste
Ljubljana
Zagreb
Sarajevo
Graz
Klagenfurt
Pécs
Osijek
Banja Luka
Mostar
Split
Zadar
Rijeka
Pula
Ancona
Pescara
Rímini
Ravenna
Pádova
Verona
Vicenza
Trento
Bolzano
Brescia
Bergamo
Parma
Modena
Ferrara
Piacenza
Alessándria
Pisa
Livorno
Perúgia
Siena
Grenoble
Nice
Cannes
Bastia
Ajaccio
Dolomiti
Alpes Maritimes
Karnische Alpen
Velebit Planina
Dinara Planina
Dalmacija
Istra
Po
Drava
Sava
Drina
Bosna

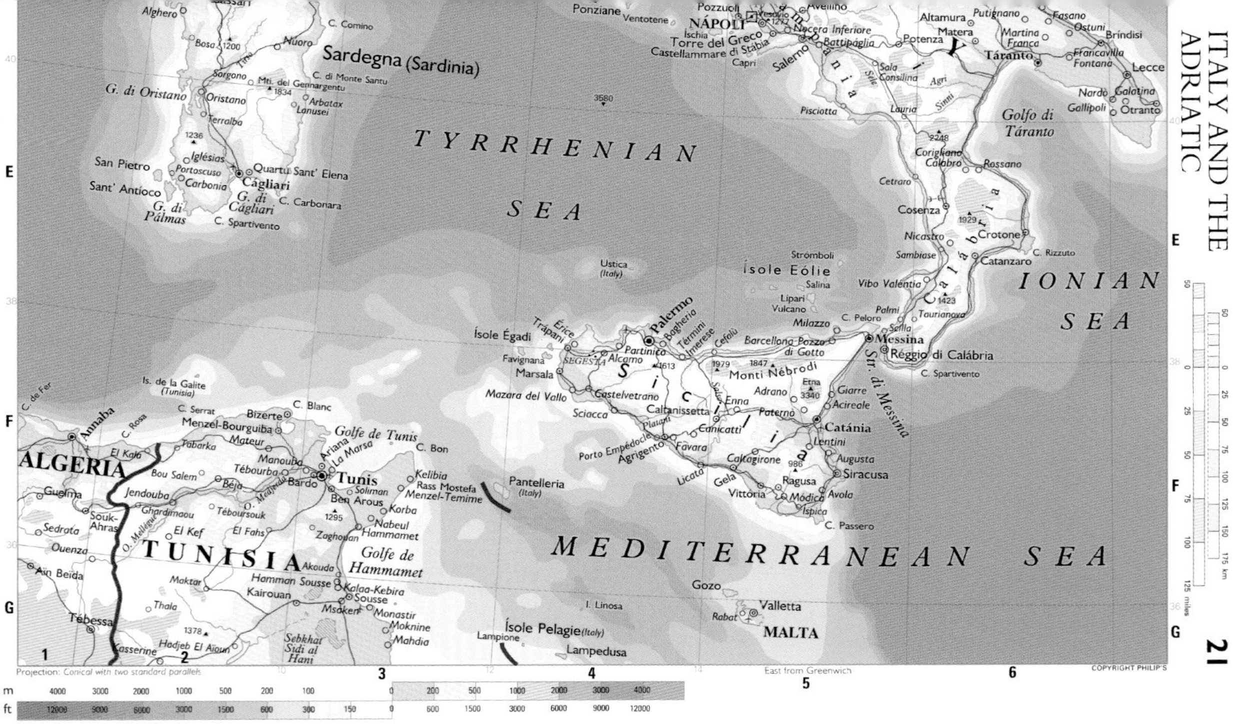
TYRRHENIAN SEA
IONIAN SEA
MEDITERRANEAN SEA
Sardegna (Sardinia)
ALGERIA
TUNISIA
MALTA
Alghero
C. Comino
Bosa
Nuoro
Sorgono
Mti. del Gennargentu
C. di Monte Santu
Arbatax
Lanusei
G. di Oristano
Oristano
Terralba
Iglésias
Portoscuso
Carbonia
San Pietro
Sant' Antíoco
Quartu Sant' Elena
Cágliari
G. di Cágliari
C. Carbonara
G. di Pálmas
C. Spartivento
Ponziane
Ventotene
Pozzuoli
NÁPOLI
Ischia
Torre del Greco
Castellammare di Stábia
Capri
Salerno
Avellino
Nocera Inferiore
Battipáglia
Sala Consilina
Pisciotta
Lauria
Potenza
Altamura
Matera
Putignano
Martina Franca
Táranto
Fasano
Ostuni
Brindisi
Francavilla Fontana
Lecce
Nardò
Galatina
Gallipoli
Otranto
Golfo di Táranto
Corigliano Cálabro
Rossano
Cetraro
Cosenza
Nicastro
Crotone
Sambiase
Catanzaro
C. Rizzuto
Vibo Valéntia
Palmi
Taurianova
Scilla
Messina
Réggio di Calábria
C. Spartivento
Str. di Messina
Ustica (Italy)
Strómboli
Ísole Eólie
Salina
Lipari
Vulcano
Milazzo
C. Peloro
Barcellona Pozzo di Gotto
Ísole Égadi
Érice
Trápani
Palermo
Bagheria
Termini Imerese
Cefalù
Favignana
SEGESTA
Alcamo
Partinico
Marsala
Monti Nébrodi
Etna
3340
Adrano
Mazara del Vallo
Castelvetrano
Caltanissetta
Enna
Paternò
Giarre
Acireale
Catánia
Sciacca
Canicattì
Lentini
Porto Empédocle
Agrigento
Favara
Licata
Caltagirone
Augusta
Siracusa
Gela
Ragusa
Vittória
Módica
Avola
Íspica
C. Passero
Is. de la Galite (Tunisia)
C. de Fer
C. Serrat
Bizerte
C. Blanc
Annaba
C. Rosa
Menzel-Bourguiba
Mateur
Golfe de Tunis
El Kala
Tabarka
Manouba
Ariana
La Marsa
C. Bon
Tébourba
Tunis
Kelibia
Rass Mostefa
Menzel-Temime
Bou Salem
Béja
Bardo
Soliman
Ben Arous
Guelma
Jendouba
Ghardimaou
Téboursouk
Korba
Souk-Ahras
Nabeul
Hammamet
Sedrata
El Kef
El Fahs
Zaghouan
Golfe de Hammamet
Ouenza
Akouda
Aïn Beïda
Maktar
Hamman Sousse
Kalaa-Kebira
Kairouan
Sousse
Thala
Msaken
Monastir
Moknine
Mahdia
Tébessa
Sebkhat Sidi al Hani
Hadjeb El Aïoun
Kasserine
Pantelleria (Italy)
I. Linosa
Ísole Pelagie (Italy)
Lampione
Lampedusa
Gozo
Rabat
Valletta
Projection: Conical with two standard parallels
East from Greenwich
COPYRIGHT PHILIP'S
m 4000 3000 2000 1000 500 200 100 0 200 500 1000 2000 3000 4000
ft 12000 9000 6000 3000 1500 600 300 150 0 600 1500 3000 6000 9000 12000
50 0 25 50 75 100 125 150 175 km
50 0 25 50 75 100 125 miles

UKRAINE
ROMANIA
HUNGARY
CROATIA
BOSNIA-HERZEGOVINA
SERBIA AND MONTENEGRO
SERBIA
MONTENEGRO
KOSOVO
BULGARIA
MACEDONIA (F.Y.R.O.M.)
BLACK SEA
ADRIATIC SEA
BUCUREŞTI (Bucharest)
BEOGRAD (Belgrade)
SOFIYA
ISTANBUL
Sarajevo
Skopje
Tiranë
Podgorica
Constanţa
Varna
Burgas
Ruse
Plovdiv
Craiova
Timişoara
Novi Sad
Niš
Transilvania
Carpaţii Meridionali
Valahia
Dobruja
Vojvodina
Stara Planina
Rhodopi Planina
Dunărea (Danube)
Marmara

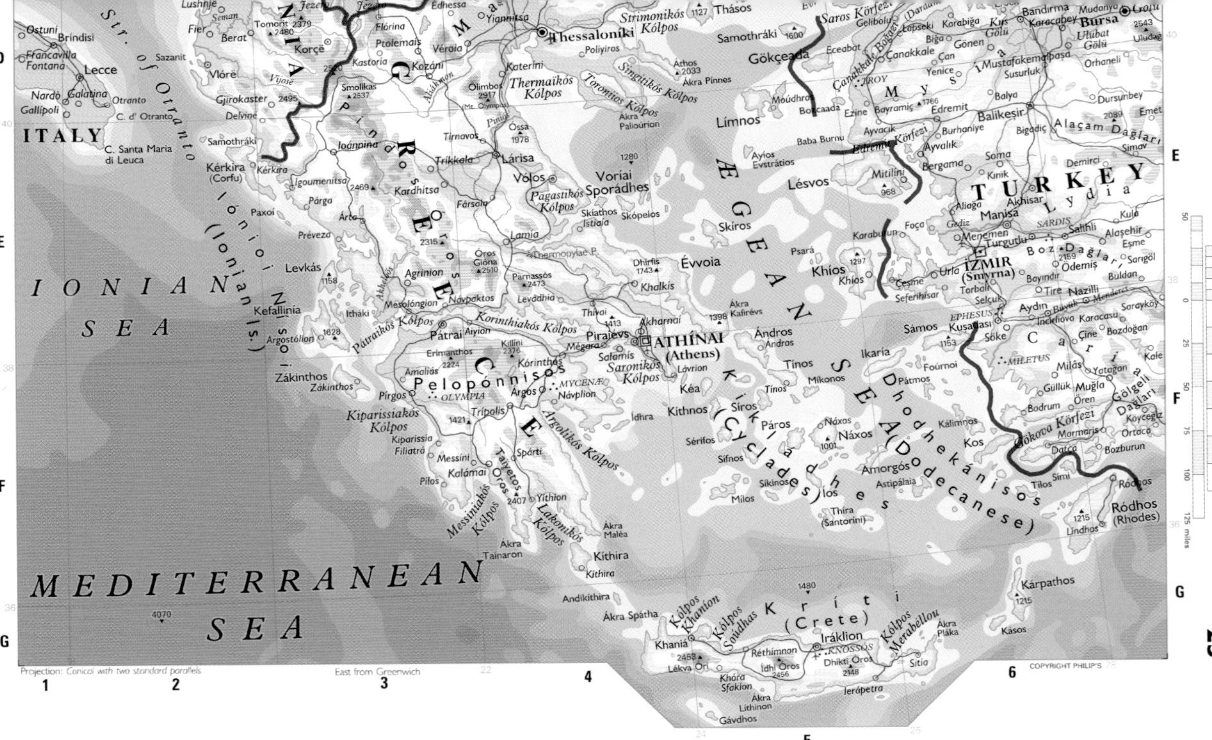
50 0 25 50 75 100 125 150 175 km
50 0 25 50 75 100 125 miles
ITALY
Brindisi
Ostuni
Francavilla Fontana
Lecce
Nardò
Galatina
Gallipoli
Otranto
C. d' Otranto
C. Santa Maria di Leuca
Sazanit
Str. of Otranto
IONIAN SEA
MEDITERRANEAN SEA
4070
Lushnjë
Fier
Seman
Berat
Vlorë
Tomorit 2379
2480
Korçë
Vijosë
Gjirokaster
2495
Delvinë
Samothráki
Kérkira (Corfu)
Kérkira
Paxoí
Igoumenitsa
Párga
Préveza
Levkás
1158
Itháki
Kefallinía
Argostólion
1628
Zákinthos
Iónioi Nísoi (Ionian Is.)
GREECE
Pindos Óros
Edhessa
Flórina
Ptolemaïs
Véroia
Kastoria
Kozáni
Smolikas 2637
2520
Aliákmon
Ioánnina
2469
Árta
Kardhítsa
Trikkala
Tirnavos
Lárisa
Fársala
Pinios
Ólimbos 2917 (Mt. Olympus)
Óssa 1978
Katerini
Yiannitsa
Thessaloníki
Thermaïkós Kólpos
Poliyiros
Toronaíos Kólpos
Singitikós Kólpos
Strimonikós Kólpos
Áthos 2033
Ákra Pínnes
Ákra Paliouríon
Vólos
Pagasitikós Kólpos
Lamía
Thermopylae P.
Agrinion
2315
Óros Gióna 2510
Parnassós 2473
Levádhia
Akhelóos
Mesolóngion
Návpaktos
Pátrai
Patraïkós Kólpos
Aíyion
Korinthiakós Kólpos
Thívai
1413
Khalkís
Dhirfis 1743
Évvoia
Voríai Sporádhes
Skíathos
Istiaía
Skópelos
1280
Skíros
Piraiévs
ATHÍNAI (Athens)
Akharnaí
Mégara
Salamís
Saronikós Kólpos
Lávrion
Kórinthos
Killíni 2376
Erímanthos 2224
Amaliás
Pelopónnisos
Pírgos
OLYMPIA
Árgos
MYCENÆ
Návplion
Trípolis
1421
Kiparissiakós Kólpos
Kiparissía
Filiatrá
Messíni
Kalámai
Pílos
Messiniakós Kólpos
Taíyetos Óros 2407
Spárti
Yíthion
Lakonikós Kólpos
Argolikós Kólpos
Ákra Taínaron
Ákra Maléa
Kíthira
Andikíthira
Ídhra
Kéa
Kíthnos
Sérifos
Sífnos
Mílos
Síros
Páros
Náxos
1001
Íos
Síkinos
Thíra (Santoríni)
Kikládhes (Cyclades)
Ándros
1398
Ákra Kafirévs
Tínos
Míkonos
Ikaría
Sámos
1153
Foúrnoi
Pátmos
Kálimnos
Kos
Amorgós
Astipálaia
Dhodhekánisos (Dodecanese)
Tílos
Sími
Ródhos
Ródhos (Rhodes)
1215
Líndhos
Kárpathos
1215
Kásos
Kríti (Crete)
Khaniá
Kólpos Khanion
Kólpos Soúdhas
2453
Lévka Óri
Khóra Sfakíon
Ákra Líthinon
Gávdhos
Réthimnon
Ídhi Óros 2456
1480
Iráklion
KNOSSOS
Dhíkti Óros 2148
Ierápetra
Kólpos Merabéllou
Sitía
Ákra Pláka
Ákra Spátha
ÆGEAN SEA
Thásos
1127
Samothráki
1600
Gökçeada
Límnos
Moúdhros
Áyios Evstrátios
Lésvos
Mitilíni
968
Psará
Khíos
1297
Baba Burnu
Bozcaada
Saros Körfezi
Gelibolu
Çanakkale Boğazı (Dardanelles)
Eceabat
Çanakkale
TROY
Lapseki
Biga
Karabiğa
Çan
Ezine
Bayramiç
1766
Edremit Körfezi
Edremit
Ayvacık
Ayvalık
Burhaniye
Bergama
Yenice
Gönen
Kuş Gölü
Bandırma
Mudanya
Karacabey
Bursa
Ulubat Gölü
Uludağ
2543
Mustafakemalpaşa
Susurluk
Orhaneli
Balya
Balıkesir
Dursunbey
Alaçam Dağları
2089
Emet
Bigadiç
Simav
Mysia
TURKEY
Lydia
Soma
Kınık
Demirci
Akhisar
Manisa
Aliağa
Gediz
Foça
Karaburun
Menemen
Turgutlu
SARDIS
Salihli
Alaşehir
Kula
Eşme
İZMİR (Smyrna)
Urla
Çeşme
Seferihisar
Torbalı
Bayındır
Boz Dağları
2159
Ödemiş
Sarıgöl
Tire
Nazilli
Buldan
Selçuk
EPHESUS
Aydın
Büyük Menderes
Kuşadası
Söke
Incirliova
Karacasu
Sarayköy
Çine
Bozdoğan
MILETUS
Caria
Milâs
Yatağan
Kale
Güllük
Muğla
Bodrum
Ören
Gölgeli Dağları
Gökova Körfezi
Köyceğiz
Marmaris
Ortaca
Datça
Bozburun
Projection: Conical with two standard parallels
East from Greenwich
1 2 3 4 5 6
D E F G
COPYRIGHT PHILIP'S

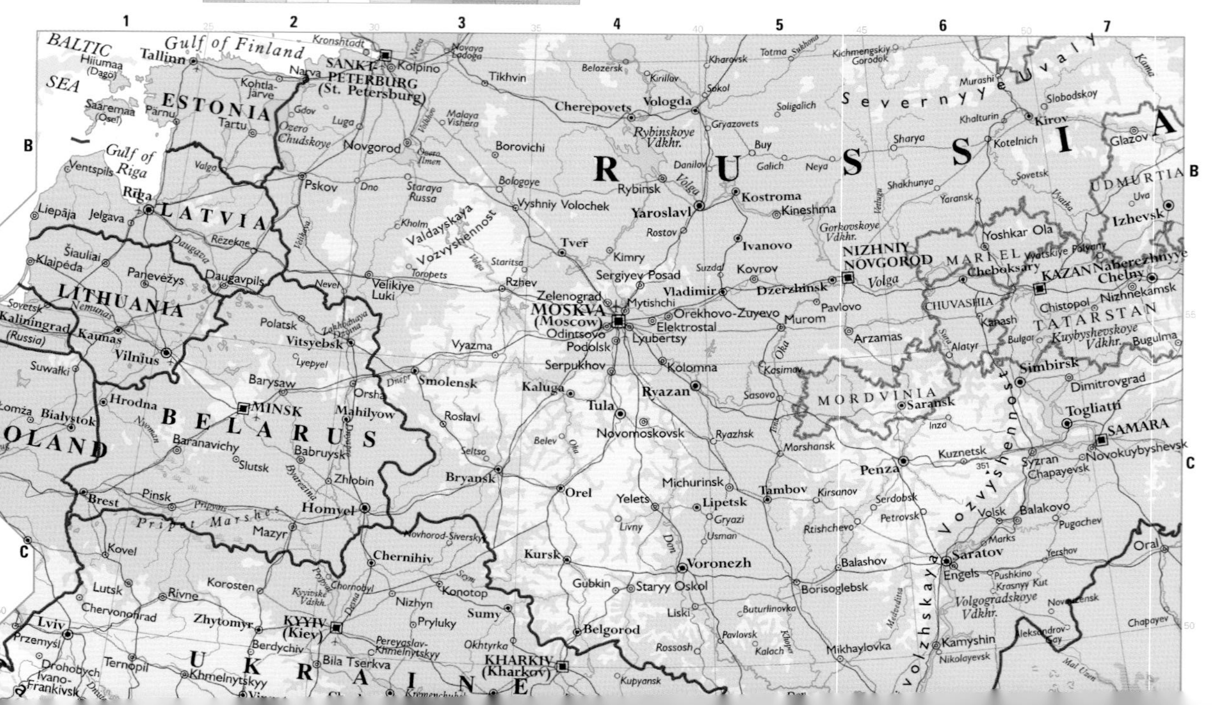
RUSSIA
ESTONIA
LATVIA
LITHUANIA
BELARUS
POLAND
UKRAINE
UDMURTIA
TATARSTAN
CHUVASHIA
MARI EL
MORDVINIA
BALTIC SEA
Gulf of Finland
Gulf of Riga
Severnyye Uvaly
Valdayskaya Vozvyshennost
Privolzhskaya Vozvyshennost
Pripet Marshes
MOSKVA (Moscow)
SANKT-PETERBURG (St. Petersburg)
MINSK
KYYIV (Kiev)
KHARKIV (Kharkov)
NIZHNIY NOVGOROD
KAZAN
SAMARA
Tallinn
Riga
Vilnius
Kaliningrad (Russia)
Kaunas
Klaipėda
Liepāja
Šiauliai
Panevėžys
Daugavpils
Tartu
Pärnu
Narva
Pskov
Novgorod
Tver
Yaroslavl
Vologda
Cherepovets
Kostroma
Ivanovo
Vladimir
Ryazan
Tula
Kaluga
Smolensk
Bryansk
Orel
Kursk
Belgorod
Voronezh
Lipetsk
Tambov
Penza
Saratov
Syzran
Togliatti
Simbirsk
Izhevsk
Kirov
Cheboksary
Yoshkar Ola
Saransk
Vitsyebsk
Mahilyow
Homyel
Hrodna
Brest
Pinsk
Babruysk
Chernihiv
Zhytomyr
Rivne
Lutsk
Lviv
Ternopil
Khmelnytskyy
Sumy
Kama
Volga
Oka
Don
Dnepr
Nyoman
Daugava

BLACK SEA
CASPIAN SEA
Sea of Azov
Caucasus Mountains
Caspian Depression
Kuzey Anadolu Dağları
Anadolu
ROMANIA
MOLDOVA
BULGARIA
TURKEY
GEORGIA
ARMENIA
AZERBAIJAN
IRAN
KAZAKHSTAN
KALMYKIA
CRIMEA
DAGESTAN
CHECHENIA
ABKHAZIA
AJARIA
ADYGEA
KARACHEY-CHERKESSIA
KABARDINO-BALKARIA
NORTH OSSETIA
South Ossetia
BUCUREȘTI (Bucharest)
İSTANBUL
ANKARA
İZMIR (Smyrna)
BURSA
TBILISI
YEREVAN
BAKI (Baku)
TABRĪZ
ODESA
DNIPROPETROVSK
DONETSK
ROSTOV
VOLGOGRAD
Chișinău
Kryvyy Rih
Zaporizhzhya
Mariupol
Mykolayiv
Kherson
Simferopol
Sevastopol
Yalta
Kerch
Feodosiya
Krasnodar
Novorossiysk
Stavropol
Astrakhan
Elista
Makhachkala
Groznyy
Vladikavkaz
Nalchik
Sochi
Sokhumi
Batumi
Kutaisi
Trabzon
Samsun
Erzurum
Kayseri
Sivas
Eskişehir
Konstanța
Varna
Burgas
Elbrus 5642
Van Gölü
Tuz Gölü
Projection: Conical with two standard parallels
East from Greenwich
COPYRIGHT PHILIP'S
D
E
F
2
3
4
5
6
0 50 100 150 200 250 miles
0 100 200 300 400 km

C
B
A
D
E
F
G
H
J
K
L
ATLANTIC OCEAN
ARCTIC
GREENLAND
ICELAND
Arctic Circle
Svalbard
Barents Sea
Novaya Zemlya
Kara Sea
UNITED KINGDOM
NORWAY
North Sea
LONDON
SWEDEN
FINLAND
Murmansk
White Sea
Arkhangelsk
Vorkuta
Salekhard
Ob
Yenisei
PARIS
FRANCE
GERMANY
Berlin
Europe
ST.PETERSBURG
R U
Prague
Warsaw
Vienna
Nizhniy Novgorod
MOSCOW
Kazan
Perm
Yekaterinburg
Irtysh
Toms
ITALY
Rome
UKRAINE
Ufa
Chelyabinsk
Volga
Samara
Omsk
Novosibirs
Belgrade
Odessa
Danube
Don
Volgograd
Rostov
Astrakhan
Astana
Pavlodar
Qaraghandy
KAZAKHSTAN
Black Sea
Athens
ISTANBUL
Bursa
Ankara
İzmir
Konya
TURKEY
GEORGIA
Yerevan
Tbilisi
ARMENIA
AZERBAIJAN
Baku
Caspian Sea
Aral Sea
L. Balkhash
Syrdarya
UZBEKISTAN
Tashkent
Bishkek
Almaty
KYRGYZSTAN
Mediterranean Sea
Nicosia
CYPRUS
Adana
Beirut
LEBANON
Aleppo
SYRIA
Euphrates
Mosul
Tabriz
TURKMENISTAN
Samarkand
Ashkhabad
TAJIKISTAN
Dushanbe
Kashi
Alexandria
ISRAEL
Damascus
Jerusalem
'Ammān
JORDAN
LIBYA
CAIRO
Suez
EGYPT
Nile
Aswân
Baghdād
IRAQ
Tigris
Basra
Kuwait
KUWAIT
TEHRĀN
IRAN
Mashhad
Eşfahān
Herāt
Kābul
AFGHANISTAN
Qandahār
Islamabad
JAMMU & KASHMIR
Hotan
Faisalabad
Lahore
Shīrāz
Zāhedān
Persian Gulf
Red Sea
SAUDI ARABIA
Medina
Riyadh
BAHRAIN
Al Manāmah
Doha
QATAR
Jedda
Mecca
UNITED ARAB EMIRATES
Abu Dhabi
G. of Oman
Muscat
PAKISTAN
Indus
KARACHI
DELHI
New Delhi
Jaipur
Lucknow
Kanpur
Varanasi
Port Sudan
SUDAN
Khartoum
ERITREA
INDIA
Ahmadabad
Vadodara
Indore
Bhopal
Surat
Nagpur
MUMBAI (Bombay)
Pune
Hyderaba
OMAN
Sana'
YEMEN
Aden
G. of Aden
DJIBOUTI
Arabian Sea
Socotra (Yemen)
Addis Ababa
ETHIOPIA
SOMALI REP.
Africa
Bangalore
CHENNA (Madras)
Lakshadweep Is. (India)
Madurai
UGANDA
L. Victoria
KENYA
Mogadishu
Equator
Colombo
MALDIVES
Male
INDIAN OC
Nairobi
CONGO (DEM. REP. OF THE)
Dodoma
TANZANIA
Mombasa
Dar es Salaam
SEYCHELLES
Victoria
ZAMBIA
MALAWI
Aldabra Is. (Seychelles)
Amirante Is. (Seychelles)
Chagos Arch. (U.K.)
Projection: Bonne
East from Greenwich
Hanoi ● Capital Cities
6
7
8
9
10
11

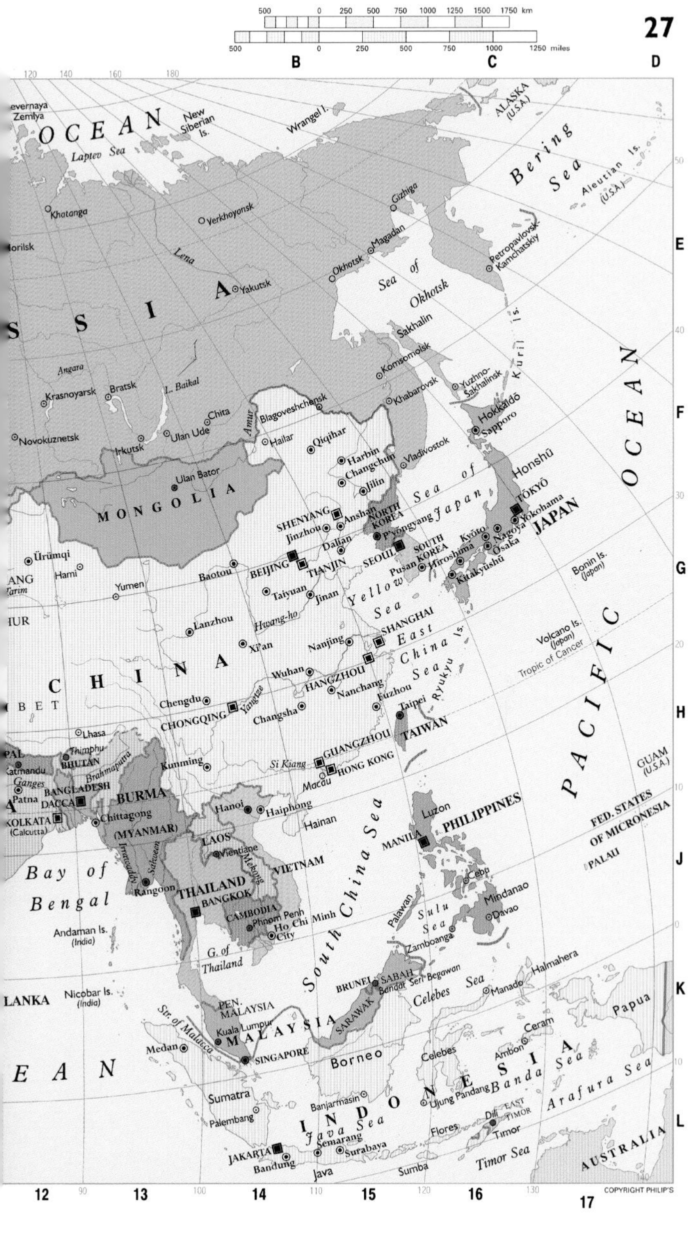

OCEAN
Laptev Sea
New Siberian Is.
Wrangel I.
ALASKA (U.S.A.)
Bering Sea
Aleutian Is. (U.S.A.)
Khatanga
Verkhoyansk
Gizhiga
Lena
Magadan
Okhotsk
Sea of Okhotsk
Petropavlovsk-Kamchatskiy
Yakutsk
ASIA
Sakhalin
Kuril Is.
Komsomolsk
Angara
Krasnoyarsk
Bratsk
L. Baikal
Yuzhno-Sakhalinsk
Khabarovsk
Blagoveshchensk
Chita
Amur
Hokkaidō
Sapporo
Novokuznetsk
Irkutsk
Ulan Ude
Hailar
Qiqihar
Harbin
Changchun
Vladivostok
Ulan Bator
MONGOLIA
Jilin
Sea of Japan
Honshū
TOKYO
Yokohama
JAPAN
SHENYANG
Anshan
NORTH KOREA
P'yongyang
Jinzhou
Dalian
Kyōto
Nagoya
Ōsaka
SEOUL
SOUTH KOREA
Pusan
Hiroshima
Kitakyūshū
BEIJING
TIANJIN
Ürümqi
Hami
Baotou
Bonin Is. (Japan)
Yumen
Taiyuan
Jinan
Yellow Sea
Lanzhou
Hwang-ho
SHANGHAI
Xi'an
Nanjing
East China Sea
Volcano Is. (Japan)
Tropic of Cancer
CHINA
Wuhan
HANGZHOU
Nanchang
Ryukyu Is.
PACIFIC
OCEAN
Chengdu
CHONGQING
Yangtze
Changsha
Fuzhou
Taipei
TAIWAN
Lhasa
Thimphu
BHUTAN
Brahmaputra
Kunming
GUANGZHOU
Si Kiang
HONG KONG
Macau
GUAM (U.S.A.)
Katmandu
Ganges
Patna
BANGLADESH
DACCA
BURMA
KOLKATA (Calcutta)
Chittagong
(MYANMAR)
Hanoi
Haiphong
Hainan
South China Sea
Luzon
PHILIPPINES
MANILA
FED. STATES OF MICRONESIA
PALAU
LAOS
Vientiane
Mekong
VIETNAM
Irrawaddy
Salween
Bay of Bengal
Rangoon
THAILAND
BANGKOK
CAMBODIA
Phnom Penh
Ho Chi Minh City
Cebu
Mindanao
Davao
Palawan
Sulu Sea
Zamboanga
Andaman Is. (India)
G. of Thailand
Halmahera
BRUNEI
SABAH
Bandar Seri Begawan
Celebes Sea
Manado
LANKA
Nicobar Is. (India)
PEN. MALAYSIA
SARAWAK
Papua
Str. of Malacca
Kuala Lumpur
MALAYSIA
Ceram
Medan
SINGAPORE
Borneo
Celebes
Ambon
INDONESIA
Banda Sea
Sumatra
Banjarmasin
Ujung Pandang
Arafura Sea
Palembang
Java Sea
Dili
EAST TIMOR
Timor
Flores
Semarang
Surabaya
JAKARTA
Bandung
Java
Sumba
Timor Sea
AUSTRALIA
B
C
D
E
F
G
H
J
K
L
12
13
14
15
16
17
500 0 250 500 750 1000 1250 1500 1750 km
500 0 250 500 750 1000 1250 miles
COPYRIGHT PHILIP'S

WESTERN RUSSIA AND CENTRAL ASIA

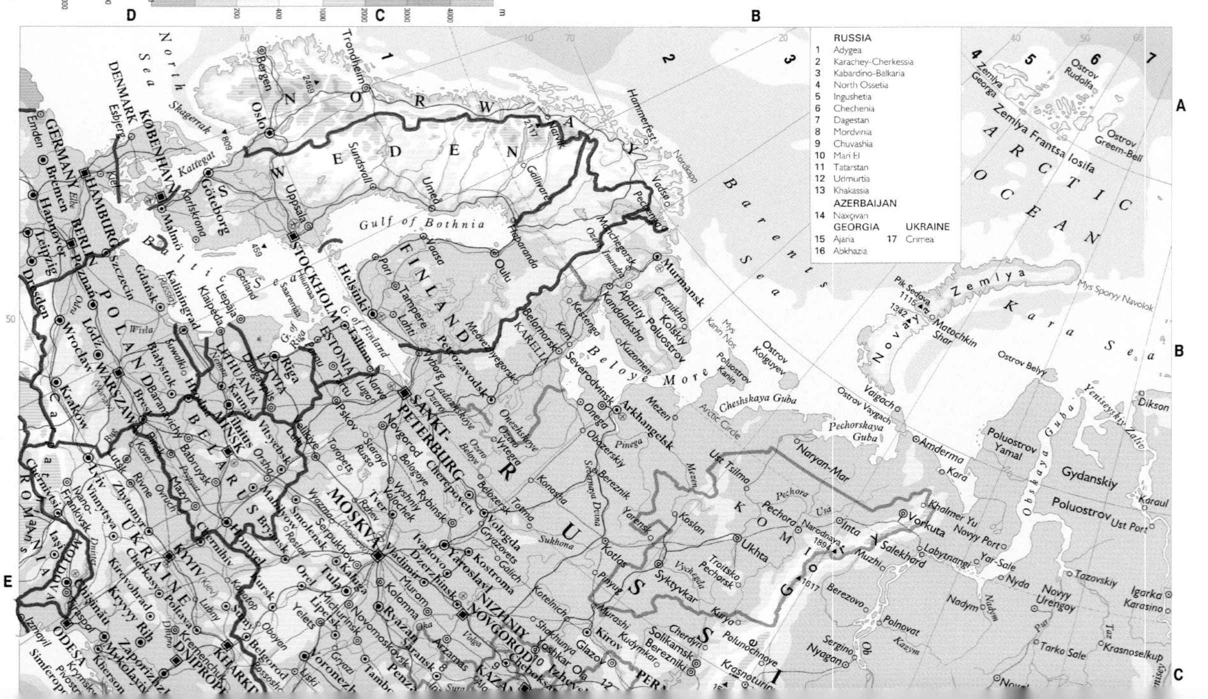

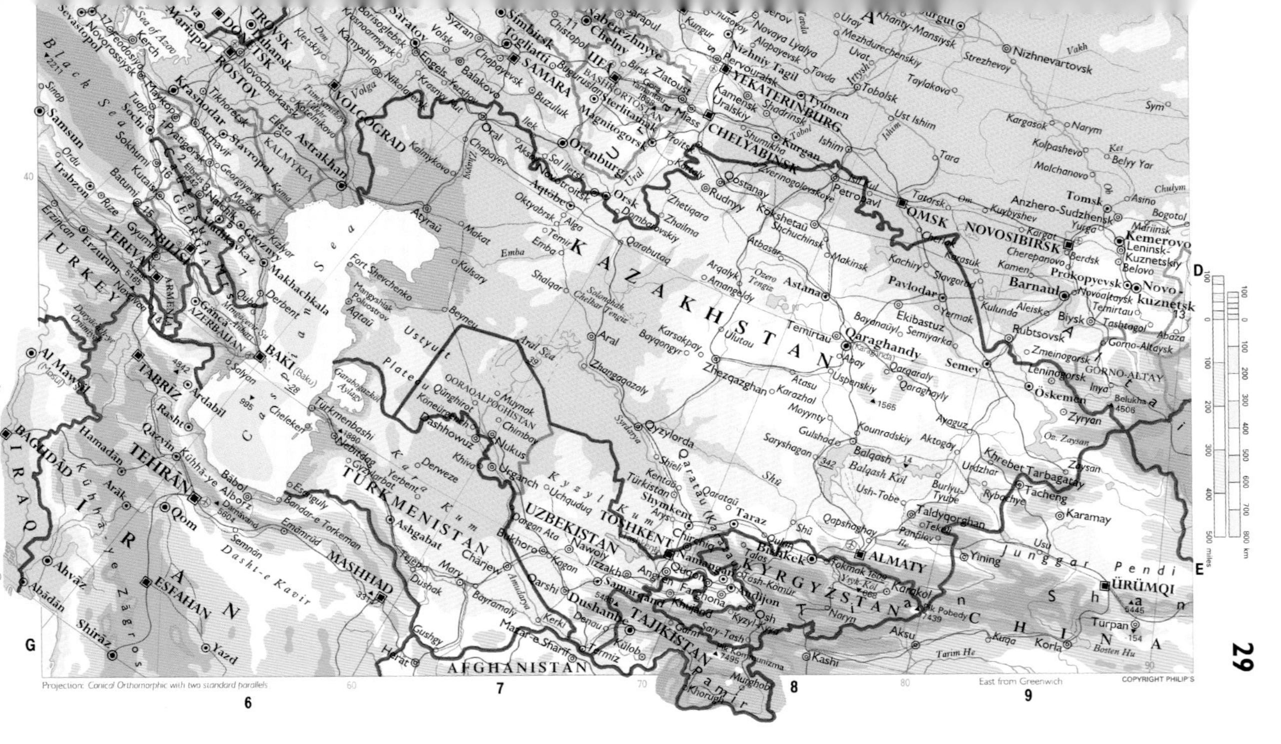
KAZAKHSTAN
UZBEKISTAN
TURKMENISTAN
KYRGYZSTAN
TAJIKISTAN
AFGHANISTAN
IRAN
IRAQ
TURKEY
GEORGIA
ARMENIA
AZERBAIJAN
CHINA
Black Sea
Sea of Azov
Caspian Sea
Aral Sea
Kyzyl Kum
Kara Kum
Ustyurt Plateau
Qaratau
Pamir
Junggar Pendi
Dasht-e Kavir
Kühhä-ye Zägros
Kühhä-ye Alborz
ALMATY
TOSHKENT
Bishkek
Dushanbe
Ashgabat
TEHRAN
BAKI
TBILISI
YEREVAN
BAGHDAD
ÜRÜMQI
NOVOSIBIRSK
OMSK
CHELYABINSK
YEKATERINBURG
SAMARA
VOLGOGRAD
ROSTOV
DONETSK
MASHHAD
ESFAHAN
TABRIZ
Astana
Qaraghandy
Pavlodar
Semey
Öskemen
Barnaul
Tomsk
Kemerovo
Novokuznetsk
Orenburg
Orsk
Aqtöbe
Oral
Atyraū
Aqtaū
Astrakhan
Makhachkala
Türkmenbashi
Nukus
Urganch
Bukhoro
Samarqand
Qyzylorda
Shymkent
Taraz
Aral
Zhezqazghan
Qostanay
Petropavl
Kökshetaū
Tyumen
Kurgan
Saratov
Krasnodar
Stavropol
Grozny
Derbent
Rasht
Qom
Hamadän
Shiräz
Ahväz
Abädän
Al Mawsil
Erzurum
Trabzon
Samsun
Sochi
Batumi
Kutaisi
Kashi
Aksu
Korla
Turpan
Yining
Karamay
Zaysan
Tacheng
Ekibastuz
Balqash
Balqash Köl
Ysyk-Köl
Termiz
Qarshi
Mary
Chärjew
Dashhowuz
Herät
Yazd
D
E
F
G
6
7
8
9
40
60
70
80
90
30
100 0 100 200 300 400 500 600 700 800 km
100 0 100 200 300 400 500 miles
Projection: Conical Orthomorphic with two standard parallels
East from Greenwich
COPYRIGHT PHILIP'S

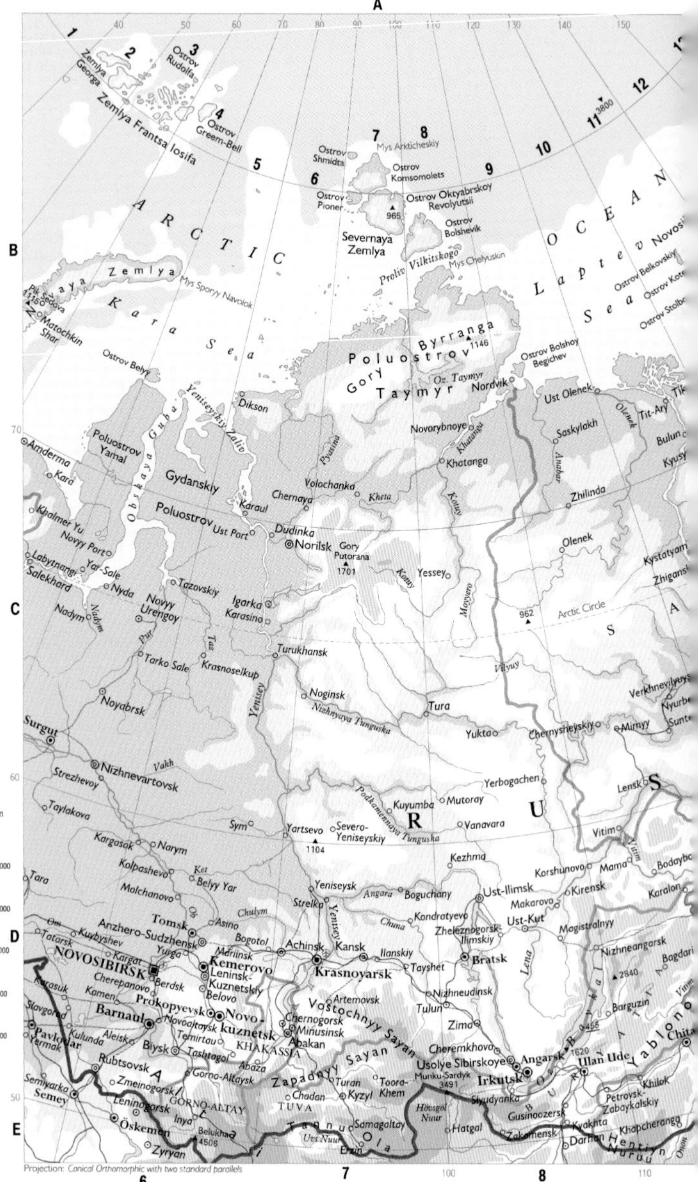

Projection: Conical Orthomorphic with two standard parallels

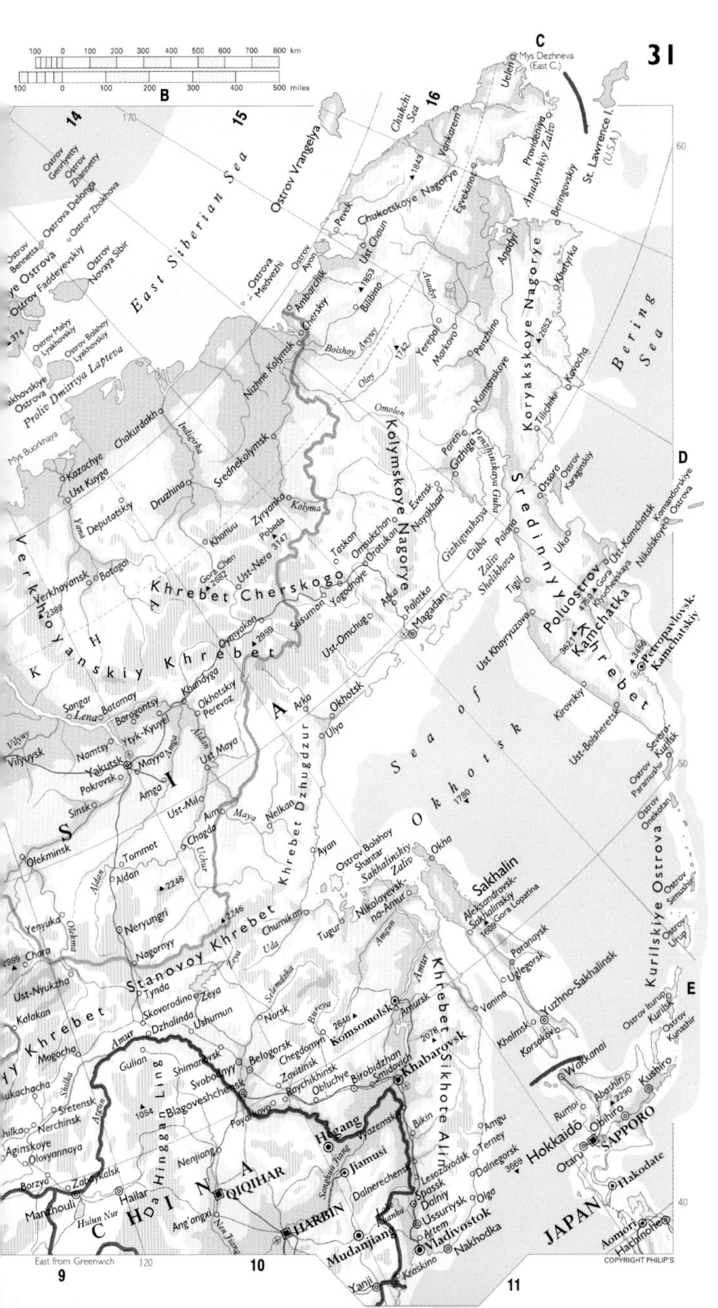
100 0 100 200 300 400 500 600 700 800 km
100 0 100 200 300 400 500 miles
B
C
D
E
14
15
16
9
10
11
170
60
50
40
120
East from Greenwich
Mys Dezhneva (East C.)
Uelen
St. Lawrence I. (U.S.A.)
Provideniya
Anadyrskiy Zaliv
Chukchi Sea
Vankarem
Ostrov Vrangelya
East Siberian Sea
Ostrov Genriyetty
Ostrov Zhannetty
Ostrova Delonga
Ostrov Zhokhova
Ostrov Bennetta
Ostrov Faddeyevskiy
Ostrov Novaya Sibir
Ostrov Malyy Lyakhovskiy
Ostrov Bolshoy Lyakhovskiy
Proliv Dmitriya Lapteva
Mys Buorkhaya
Ostrova Medvezhi
Ostrov Ayon
Pevek
Chukotskoye Nagorye
Egvekinot
Beringovskiy
Ust Chaun
Bilibino
Ambarchik
Cherskiy
Nizhne Kolymsk
Bolshoy Anyuy
Anadyr
Yerepol
Markovo
Penzhino
Koryakskoye Nagorye
Khatyrka
Bering Sea
Kavacha
Tilichiki
Kamenskoye
Oloy
Omolon
Kolymskoye Nagorye
Paren
Gizhiga
Penzhinskaya Guba
Chokurdakh
Indigirka
Srednekolymsk
Kazachye
Ust Kuyga
Druzhina
Yana
Deputatskiy
Zyryanka
Kolyma
Evensk
Nayakhan
Ossora
Ostrov Karaginskiy
Sredinnyy Khrebet
Komandorskiye Ostrova
Ostrov Nikolskoye
Ust-Kamchatsk
Uka
Palana
Gizhiginskaya Guba
Khonuu
Pobeda 3147
Taskan
Omsukchan
Orotukan
Verkhoyansk
Batagai
Gora Chen 2682
Ust-Nera
Khrebet Cherskogo
Yagodnoye
Atka
Palatka
Zaliv Shelikhova
Tigil
Poluostrov Kamchatka
Gora Klyuchevskaya 4750
2389
Verkhoyanskiy Khrebet
Oymyakon
2959
Susuman
Ust-Omchug
Magadan
Ust Khayryuzovo
3621
3456
Petropavlovsk-Kamchatskiy
Khandyga
Okhotskiy Perevoz
Sangar
Lena
Batamay
Borogontsy
Ytyk-Kyuyel
Amga
Aldan
Arka
Okhotsk
Ulya
Kirovskiy
Ust-Bolsheretsk
Severo-Kurilsk
Vilyuy
Vilyuysk
Namtsy
Yakutsk
Mayya
Ust Maya
Pokrovsk
Sea of Okhotsk
Ostrov Paramushir
Ostrov Onekotan
1780
Sinsk
Ust-Mil
Aim
Maya
Nelkan
Khrebet Dzhugdzur
Olekminsk
Tommot
Chagda
Uchur
Ayan
Ostrov Bolshoy Shantar
Sakhalinskiy Zaliv
Okha
Sakhalin
Kurilskiye Ostrova
Ostrov Simushir
Ostrov Urup
Aldan
2246
Nikolayevsk-na-Amur
Aleksandrovsk-Sakhalinskiy
1609 Gora Lopatina
Yenyuka
Olekma
Neryungri
Chumikan
Tugur
Amgun
Poronaysk
2999
Chara
Nagornyy
Stanovoy Khrebet
Uda
Uglegorsk
Ust-Nyukzha
Tynda
Zeya
Selemdzha
Amur
Khrebet Sikhote Alin
Vanino
Yuzhno-Sakhalinsk
Kalakan
Skovorodino
Dzhalinda
Ushumun
Norsk
Bureya
2640
Komsomolsk
Amursk
Kholmsk
Korsakov
Ostrov Iturup
Kurilsk
Ostrov Kunashir
Mogocha
Gulian
Shimanovsk
Belogorsk
Chegdomyn
2078
Khabarovsk
Wakkanai
Svobodnyy
Zavitinsk
Raychikhinsk
Obluchye
Birobidzhan
Smidovich
Abashiri
2290
Kushiro
Bukachacha
Shilka
Sretensk
Argun
Da Hinggan Ling
1054
Blagoveshchensk
Poyarkovo
Hegang
Vyazemskiy
Bikin
Amgu
Rumoi
Obihiro
Shilka
Nerchinsk
Aginskoye
Olovyannaya
Nenjiang
Jiamusi
Songhua Jiang
Terney
Hokkaido
Otaru
SAPPORO
Lesozavodsk
Dalnegorsk
3669
Dalnerechensk
Spassk Dalniy
Hakodate
Borzya
Zabaykalsk
Hailar
QIQIHAR
Olga
Ussuriysk
Manzhouli
Hulun Nur
CHINA
Ang'angxi
Nen Jiang
HARBIN
Lake Khanka
Artem
Vladivostok
Nakhodka
JAPAN
Aomori
Hachinohe
Mudanjiang
Kraskino
Yanji

CHINA
RUSSIA
NORTH KOREA
SEA OF JAPAN
(EAST SEA)
Hokkaidō
L. Khanka
Zaliv Petra Velikogo
Khrebet Sikhote Alin
Tsugaru Strait
Ishikari-Wan
Uchiura-Wan
Mutsu-Wan
Sendai-Wan
Abashiri-Wan
Teshio-Gawa
Ishikari-Gawa
Mogami-Gawa
Towada-Ko
Sikotu-Ko
Toya-Ko
Linkou
Suifenhe
Novokachalinsk
Kamen-Rybolov
Lipovcy
Manzovka
Ussuriysk
Spassk Dalniy
Lesozavodsk
Kirovskiy
Gornyy
Rakitnoye
Ariadnoye
Yakovlevka
Arsenev
Kavalerovo
Dalnegorsk
Plastun
Terney
Margaritovo
Preobrazheniye
Lazo
Nakhodka
Artem
Vladivostok
Slavyanka
Trudovoye
Khasan
Najin
Chŏngjin
1498
1855
Wakkanai
Rebun-Tō
Rishiri-Tō
Teshio
Embetsu
Haboro
Esashi
Otoineppu
Ōmu
Mombetsu
Yūbetsu
Abashiri
Shari
Nakashibetsu
Shibecha
Nemuro
Akkeshi
Kushiro
Honbetsu
Rausu-Dake
1661
Ostrov Kunashir
Nayoro
Shibetsu
Engaru
Kitami
Asahigawa
Daisetsu-Zan
2290
2077
Rumoi
Takikawa
Bibai
Iwamizawa
Ebetsu
Atsuta
Kamui-Misaki
Otaru
SAPPORO
Iwanai
Suttsu
Tomakomai
Muroran
Obihiro
Poroshiri-Dake
2052
Samani
Hiroo
Erimo-misaki
Setana
Okushiri-Tō
Yakumo
Esashi
Hakodate
Esan-Misaki
Matsumae
Shiragami-Misaki
Ohata
Mutsu
Shiriya-Zaki
Kanagi
Aomori
Towada
Hachinohe
Goshogawara
Hirosaki
Odate
Kuji
Henashi-Misaki
Noshiro
Oga
Oga-Hantō
Akita
Iwate-San
2041
Morioka
1914
Miyako
Iwaizumi
Kamaishi
Omagari
Hanamaki
Kesennuma
Ichinoseki
Furukawa
Ishinomaki
Sendai
Honjō
2230
Sakata
Tsuruoka
1980
Yamagata
Sado
Ryōtsu

JAPAN
Honshū
PACIFIC OCEAN
SOUTH KOREA
Pohang
Ullŭng-do (S. Korea)
Tok-do
Oki-Shotō (Japan)
Korea Strait
Tsushima (Japan)
Iki
Gotō-Rettō
Fukue-Shima
Koshikijima-Rettō
Amakusa-Shotō
Kyūshū
Shikoku
Chūgoku-Sanchi
Bungo Channel
Kii Channel
Tosa-Wan
Ise-Wan
Suruga-Wan
Toyama-Wan
Wakasa-Wan
Biwa-Ko
Kiso-Gawa
Izu-Shotō
Nanpō-Shotō
Ō-Shima
Nii-Jima
Miyake-Jima
Hachijō-Jima
Aoga-Shima
TŌKYŌ
YOKOHAMA
KAWASAKI
NAGOYA
KYŌTO
ŌSAKA
KOBE
HIROSHIMA
KITAKYŪSHŪ
FUKUOKA
Chiba
Ichihara
Funabashi
Kawaguchi
Kawagoe
Tsuchiura
Mito
Hitachi
Kitaibaraki
Iwaki
Kōriyama
Aizuwakamatsu
Niitsu
Sanjo
Nagaoka
Tōkamachi
Takada
Nagano
Maebashi
Takasaki
Kumagaya
Matsumoto
Kōfu
Ina
Iida
Fuji
Fuji-San 3776
Shizuoka
Numazu
Itō
Odawara
Yokosuka
Tateyama
Hamamatsu
Iwata
Toyohashi
Okazaki
Toyota
Ichinomiya
Gifu
Ōgaki
Yokkaichi
Matsusaka
Owase
Shingū
Kushimoto
Tanabe
Wakayama
Izumi-Sano
Higashiōsaka
Amagasaki
Ōtsu
Tsuruga
Takefu
Fukui
Komatsu
Kanazawa
Takaoka
Toyama
Himi
Nanao
Wajima
Suzu
Suzu-Misaki
Takayama
Hodaka-Dake 3190
Maizuru
Ayabe
Toyooka
Fukuchiyama
Tottori
Himeji
Tsuyama
Okayama
Yonago
Matsue
Izumo
Ōda
Hamada
Masuda
Hagi
Yamaguchi
Ube
Hōfu
Tokuyama
Iwakuni
Kure
Fukuyama
Fuchū
Imabari
Matsuyama
Takamatsu
Naruto
Awaji-Shima
Tokushima
Anan
Mugi
Muroto
Ikeda
Kōchi
Nakamura
Sukumo
Uwajima
Yawatahama
Marugame
Shimonoseki
Nōgata
Buzen
Beppu
Ōita
Saiki
Nobeoka
Hyūga
Miyazaki
Miyakonojō
Nichinan
Kanoya
Ibusuki
Kagoshima
Makurazaki
Sendai
Minamata
Yatsushiro
Kumamoto
Ōmuta
Kurume
Saga
Karatsu
Imari
Sasebo
Isahaya
Nagasaki
Ushibuka
Sata-Misaki
Ashizuri-Zaki
Muroto-Misaki
Shio-no-Misaki
Daiō-Misaki
Irō-Zaki
Nojima-Zaki
Kyō-ga-Saki
Utsunomiya
Oyama
Kiryū
Tajima
Tanakura
Sukagawa
3192
3063
2782
2578
2024
1915
1955
1712
1787
8412
9076
0 25 50 75 100 125 150 175 km
0 25 50 75 100 125 miles
Projection: Conical with two standard parallels
East from Greenwich
COPYRIGHT PHILIP'S

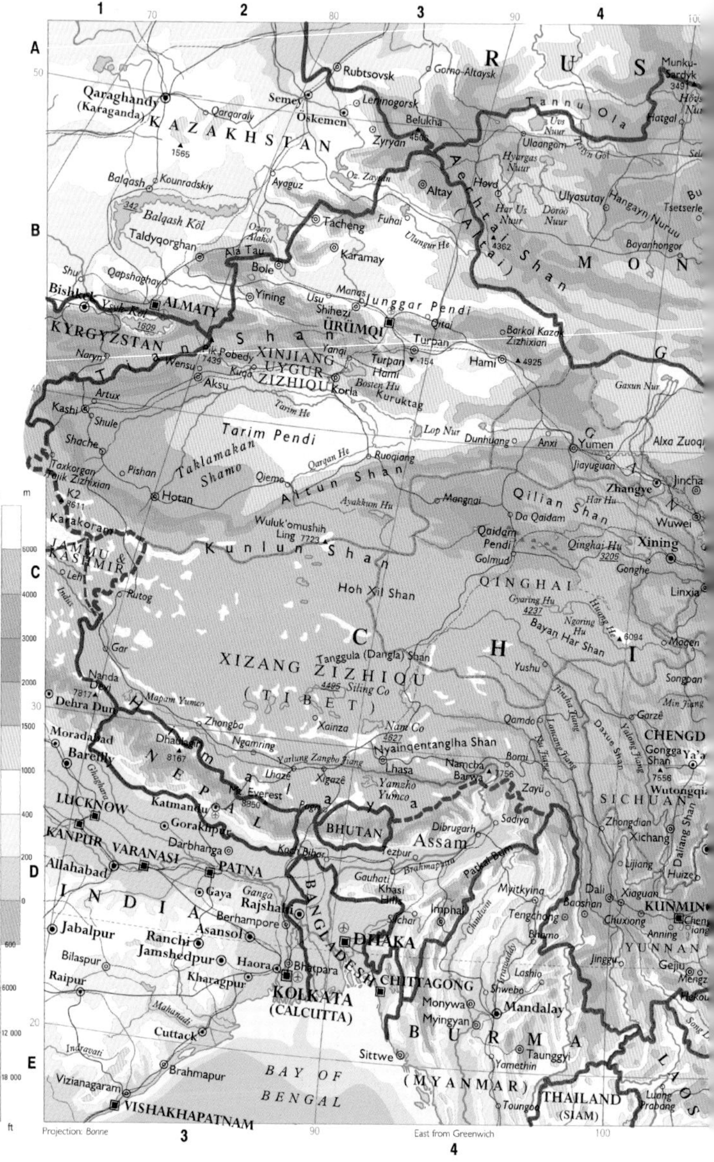

RUSSIA
KAZAKHSTAN
KYRGYZSTAN
XINJIANG UYGUR ZIZHIQU
MONGOLIA
CHINA
QINGHAI
XIZANG ZIZHIQU (TIBET)
SICHUAN
YUNNAN
NEPAL
BHUTAN
BANGLADESH
INDIA
BURMA (MYANMAR)
THAILAND (SIAM)
LAOS
JAMMU & KASHMIR
Assam
BAY OF BENGAL
Qaraghandy (Karaganda)
Rubtsovsk
Gorno-Altaysk
Semey
Öskemen
Leninogorsk
Belukha 4506
Zyryan
Balqash
Kounradskiy
Ayaguz
Balqash Köl
Taldyqorghan
Ala Tau
Tacheng
Karamay
Bole
Altay
Hovd
Ulaangom
Uliastay
Bayanhongor
Tannu Ola
Altun Shan
Kunlun Shan
Tian Shan
Qilian Shan
Junggar Pendi
Tarim Pendi
Taklamakan Shamo
Qaidam Pendi
Bishkek
ALMATY
ÜRÜMQI
Yining
Shihezi
Turpan
Hami
Aksu
Korla
Kashi
Shule
Shache
Hotan
Pishan
Qiemo
Ruoqiang
Lop Nur
Dunhuang
Anxi
Yumen
Jiayuguan
Zhangye
Wuwei
Xining
Golmud
Qinghai Hu
Pik Pobedy 7439
K2 8611
Karakoram
Leh
Rutog
Gar
Nanda Devi 7817
Dehra Dun
Moradabad
Bareilly
LUCKNOW
KANPUR
VARANASI
Allahabad
PATNA
Gaya
Rajshahi
Jabalpur
Ranchi
Jamshedpur
Asansol
Haora
KOLKATA (CALCUTTA)
DHAKA
CHITTAGONG
Mandalay
Monywa
Sittwe
Taunggyi
Raipur
Bilaspur
Cuttack
Brahmapur
Vizianagaram
VISHAKHAPATNAM
Katmandu
Everest 8850
Dhaulagiri 8167
Gorakhpur
Darbhanga
Lhasa
Xigazê
Nam Co
Nyainqentanglha Shan
Tanggula (Dangla) Shan
Hoh Xil Shan
Bayan Har Shan
Yushu
Qamdo
Namcha Barwa 7756
Dibrugarh
Sadiya
Imphal
Myitkyina
Dali
Lijiang
Xichang
KUNMING
Gejiu
CHENGDU
Gongga Shan 7556
Linxia
Projection: Bonne
East from Greenwich

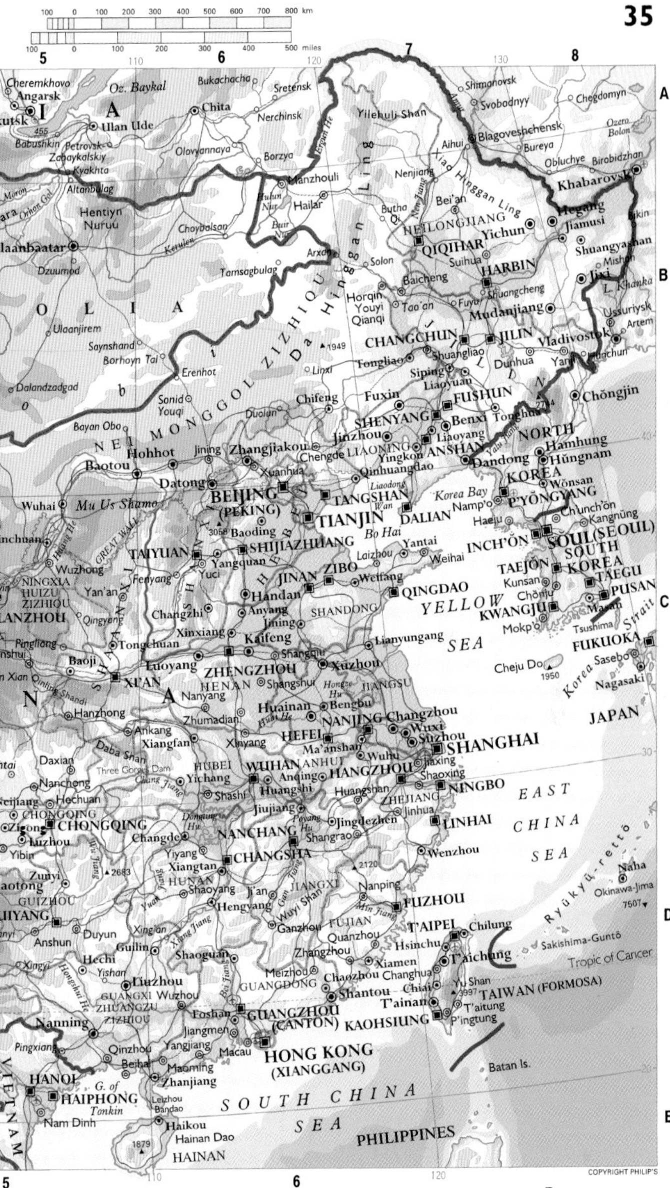
100 0 100 200 300 400 500 600 700 800 km
100 0 100 200 300 400 500 miles
5
6
7
8
110
120
130
A
B
C
D
E
Cheremkhovo
Angarsk
Oz. Baykal
Bukachacha
Sretensk
Shimanovsk
Svobodnyy
Chegdomyn
Chita
Nerchinsk
Yilehuli Shan
Ulan Ude
Babushkin
Petrovsk-Zabaykalskiy
Olovyannaya
Borzya
Kyakhta
Altanbulag
Ergun He
Amur
Blagoveshchensk
Bureya
Aihui
Ozero Bolon
Obluchye
Birobidzhan
Khabarovsk
Manzhouli
Nenjiang
Xiao Hinggan Ling
Hulun Nur
Hailar
Hentiyn Nuruu
Bei'an
Bikin
Hegang
Jiamusi
Butha Qi
HEILONGJIANG
Yichun
Shuangyashan
Choybalsan
Kerulen
Buir Nur
Ulaanbaatar
QIQIHAR
Suihua
Mishan
Arxan
Solon
HARBIN
Jixi
Dzuunmod
Tamsagbulag
Da Hinggan Ling
Baicheng
L. Khanka
Shuangcheng
Horqin Youyi Qianqi
Tao'an
Fuyu
Mudanjiang
Ussuriysk
Artem
Ulaanjirem
JILIN
Vladivostok
CHANGCHUN
Saynshand
▲1949
Shuangliao
Dunhua
Hunchun
Borhoyn Tal
Tongliao
Yanji
Erenhot
Linxi
Siping
Liaoyuan
Dalandzadgad
NEI MONGGOL ZIZHIQU
FUSHUN
Chŏngjin
Sonid Youqi
Chifeng
Fuxin
2744
Duolun
SHENYANG
Benxi
Tonghua
Bayan Obo
Liaoyang
NORTH
Jinzhou
Yalu Jiang
Hamhung
Hohhot
Jining
Zhangjiakou
Chengde
LIAONING
Yingkou
ANSHAN
Dandong
Hŭngnam
Baotou
Xuanhua
Qinhuangdao
KOREA
Datong
Liaodong Wan
Wŏnsan
BEIJING (PEKING)
TANGSHAN
Korea Bay
Wuhai
Mu Us Shamo
Nampo
P'YŎNGYANG
TIANJIN
DALIAN
Ch'unch'ŏn
3058
Baoding
Bo Hai
Haeju
Kangnŭng
Yinchuan
GREAT WALL
SHIJIAZHUANG
INCH'ŎN
SOUL (SEOUL)
TAIYUAN
Yantai
SOUTH
Huang He
Yangquan
Laizhou
Weihai
KOREA
Wuzhong
Yuci
TAEJŎN
TAEGU
NINGXIA HUIZU ZIZHIQU
Fenyang
JINAN
ZIBO
Weifang
Kunsan
Yan'an
Handan
QINGDAO
Chŏnju
PUSAN
LANZHOU
Qingyang
Changzhi
Anyang
SHANDONG
YELLOW
KWANGJU
Masan
Jining
Mokp'o
Tsushima
Strait
Pingliang
Xinxiang
Kaifeng
Lianyungang
SEA
FUKUOKA
Tianshui
Tongchuan
Shangqiu
Baoji
Luoyang
Korea
Cheju Do
Sasebo
ZHENGZHOU
Xuzhou
1950
Nagasaki
Tin Xian
XI'AN
HENAN
Shangshui
Hongze Hu
JIANGSU
Qinling Shandi
Nanyang
Huainan
Bengbu
Hanzhong
Zhumadian
Huai He
NANJING
Changzhou
JAPAN
Ankang
Wuxi
Xiangfan
Xinyang
HEFEI
Suzhou
Daba Shan
Ma'anshan
SHANGHAI
Wuhu
Daxian
Three Gorges Dam
HUBEI
WUHAN
ANHUI
Jiaxing
Nanchong
Chang Jiang
Yichang
Anqing
HANGZHOU
Shaoxing
Neijiang
Hechuan
Shashi
Huangshi
Huangshan
NINGBO
EAST
CHONGQING
ZHEJIANG
Jiujiang
Jinhua
Zigong
Dongting Hu
Poyang Hu
Jingdezhen
LINHAI
CHINA
Luzhou
Changde
NANCHANG
Shangrao
Yibin
Wu Jiang
SEA
Yiyang
CHANGSHA
Wenzhou
▲2683
Xiangtan
2120
Naha
Zunyi
HUNAN
Ryūkyū-rettō
Zhaotong
Shaoyang
Ji'an
JIANGXI
Nanping
Okinawa-Jima
GUIZHOU
Hengyang
Gan Jiang
Wuyi Shan
Min Jiang
FUZHOU
7507
GUIYANG
Yuan Jiang
FUJIAN
Duyun
Xing'an
Ganzhou
T'AIPEI
Chilung
Anshun
Quanzhou
Xiang Jiang
Hsinchu
Guilin
Shaoguan
Zhangzhou
T'aichung
Sakishima-Guntō
Hechi
Xiamen
Tropic of Cancer
Yishan
Meizhou
Chaozhou
Changhua
Liuzhou
GUANGDONG
Yu Shan
Chiai
Hongshui He
GUANGXI ZHUANGZU ZIZHIQU
Wuzhou
Shantou
3997
TAIWAN (FORMOSA)
Bei Jiang
T'ainan
T'aitung
Foshan
GUANGZHOU (CANTON)
KAOHSIUNG
P'ingtung
Nanning
Jiangmen
Pingxiang
Qinzhou
Yangjiang
Macau
HONG KONG (XIANGGANG)
Beihai
Maoming
Batan Is.
HANOI
G. of Tonkin
Zhanjiang
HAIPHONG
Leizhou Bandao
SOUTH CHINA
VIETNAM
Nam Dinh
Haikou
SEA
Hainan Dao
PHILIPPINES
1879
HAINAN

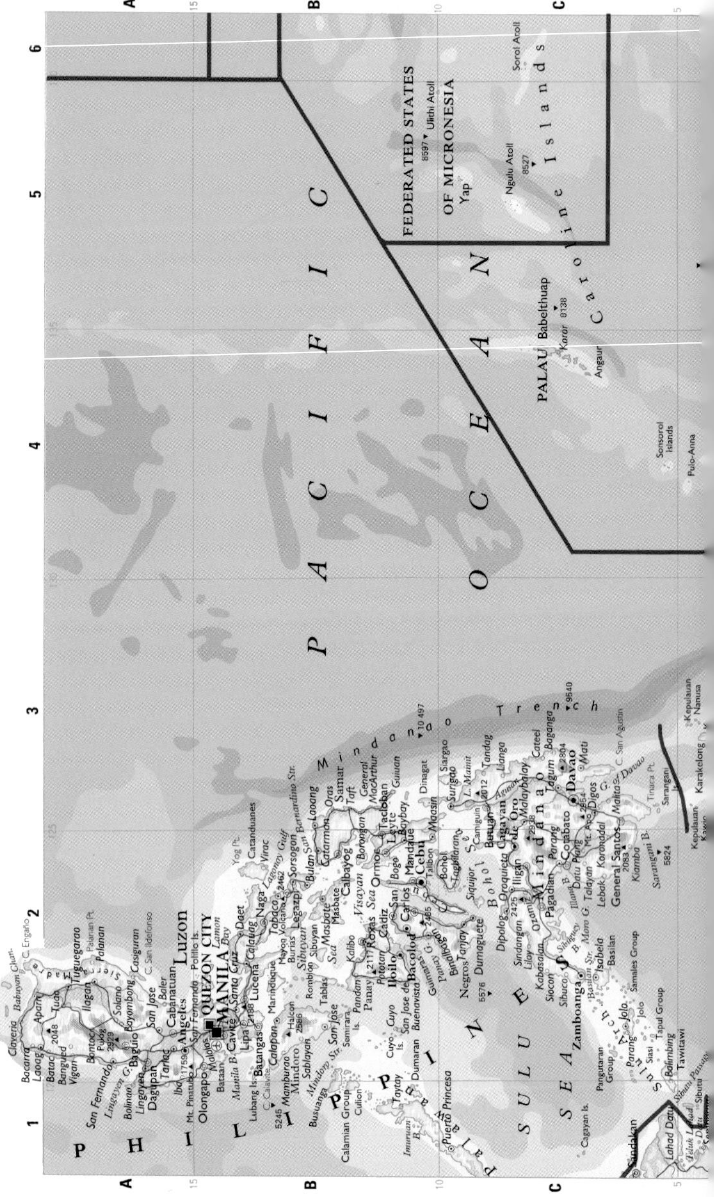
PACIFIC OCEAN
FEDERATED STATES OF MICRONESIA
Yap
Ulithi Atoll
Ngulu Atoll
Sorol Atoll
Caroline Islands
PALAU
Babelthuap
Koror
Angaur
Sonsorol Islands
Pulo-Anna
PHILIPPINES
Luzon
QUEZON CITY
MANILA
Mindoro
Panay
Negros
Samar
Leyte
Cebu
Bohol
Mindanao
Davao
Zamboanga
Iloilo
Bacolod
Palawan
Puerto Princesa
SULU SEA
Mindanao Trench
Sandakan
Kepulauan Nanusa

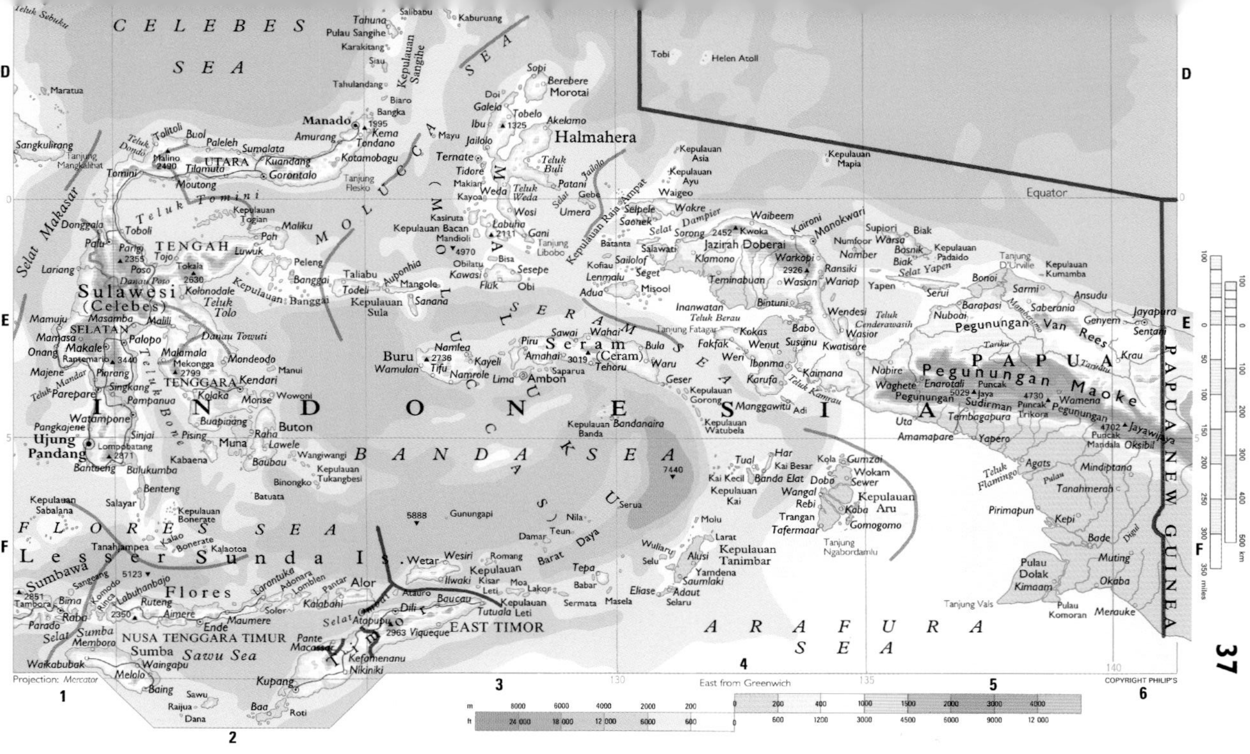
CELEBES SEA
MOLUCCA SEA
SERAM SEA
BANDA SEA
FLORES SEA
ARAFURA SEA
Sawu Sea
INDONESIA
PAPUA NEW GUINEA
PAPUA
Equator
Halmahera
Morotai
Ternate
Tidore
Manado
Gorontalo
UTARA
TENGAH
SELATAN
TENGGARA
Sulawesi (Celebes)
Selat Makasar
Teluk Tomini
Teluk Bone
Teluk Tolo
Palu
Ujung Pandang
Kendari
Buton
Muna
Kepulauan Banggai
Kepulauan Sula
Kepulauan Sangihe
Kepulauan Bacan
Kepulauan Raja Ampat
Kepulauan Asia
Kepulauan Ayu
Kepulauan Mapia
Kepulauan Padaido
Kepulauan Kumamba
Kepulauan Watubela
Kepulauan Gorong
Kepulauan Banda
Kepulauan Kai
Kepulauan Aru
Kepulauan Tanimbar
Kepulauan Tukangbesi
Kepulauan Bonerate
Kepulauan Sabalana
Kepulauan Togian
Kepulauan Leti
Waigeo
Misool
Salawati
Obi
Buru
Seram (Ceram)
Ambon
Sorong
Jazirah Doberai
Manokwari
Biak
Yapen
Teluk Cenderawasih
Fakfak
Kaimana
Pegunungan Van Rees
Pegunungan Maoke
Pegunungan Sudirman
Puncak Jaya 5029
Puncak Trikora 4730
Puncak Mandala 4702
Jayapura
Merauke
Pulau Dolak
Tual
Dobo
Saumlaki
Lesser Sunda Is.
Sumbawa
Flores
Sumba
Alor
Wetar
Timor
Kupang
Dili
EAST TIMOR
NUSA TENGGARA TIMUR
Roti
Sawu
Tobi
Helen Atoll
7440
5888
5123
3440
3019
2963
2926
2871
2851
2799
2736
2630
2490
2452
2355
2350
2131
1995
1325
4970
Projection: Mercator
East from Greenwich
COPYRIGHT PHILIP'S
1 2 3 4 5 6
D E F

BURMA
RANGOON (YANGON)
(MYANMAR)
THAILAND
BANGKOK
LAOS
Vientiane (Viangchan)
CAMBODIA
Phnom Penh (Phnum Penh)
VIETNAM
THANH PHO HO CHI MINH (Ho Chi Minh City)
SOUTH CHINA SEA
ANDAMAN SEA
Gulf of Thailand
Malay Pen.
PENINSULAR MALAYSIA
MALAYSIA
PHILIPPINES
Palawan
SABAH
BRUNEI
Strait of Malacca
Paracel Is.
Spratly Is.
Da Nang
Hue
Nha Trang
Kota Kinabalu
George Town
Phuket

INDIAN OCEAN
INDONESIA
Borneo
KALIMANTAN
Sumatera
Greater Sunda Islands
JAVA SEA
Jawa (Java)
Java Trench
Selat Karimata
Selat Makasar
Selat Bangka
Selat Sunda
Selat Berhala
Kepulauan Mentawai
UTARA
BARAT
RIAU
JAMBI
SELATAN
BENGKULU
LAMPUNG
SARAWAK
TIMUR
TENGAH
BALI
NUSA TENGGARA BARAT
MEDAN
KUALA LUMPUR
SINGAPORE
PALEMBANG
JAKARTA
BANDUNG
SEMARANG
SURABAYA
Kuching
Pontianak
Banjarmasin
Balikpapan
Samarinda
Padang
Pekanbaru
Jambi
Bengkulu
Tanjungkarang Telukbetung
Bogor
Cirebon
Surakarta
Yogyakarta
Malang
Denpasar
Mataram
Kuantan
Seremban
Melaka
Johor Baharu
Kepulauan Riau
Kepulauan Lingga
Kepulauan Anambas
Kepulauan Natuna Selatan
Kepulauan Karimunjawa
Madura
Bangka
Belitung
Nias
Simeulue
Siberut
Enggano
Lombok
Sumbawa
Projection: Mercator
East from Greenwich
COPYRIGHT PHILIP'S
100 0 100 200 300 400 500 km
100 0 50 100 150 200 250 300 350 miles
m 8000 6000 4000 2000 200 0 200 400 1000 1500 2000 3000 4000
ft 24 000 18 000 12 000 6000 600 0 600 1200 3000 4500 6000 9000 12 000
1 2 3 4 5
D E F

XIZANG
(TIBET)
Nganglong Kangri
Gangdisê Shan
NEPAL
Siwalik Range
INDIA
UTTAR PRADESH
MADHYA PRADESH
BIHAR
JHARKHAND
CHHATTISGARH
ORISSA
ANDHRA PRADESH
HIMACHAL PRADESH
UTTARANCHAL
HARYANA
WEST BENGAL
BAY
INDIAN
DELHI
New Delhi
HYDERABAD
Chamba
Hanle
Nganglong Kangri 7315
Gar
Shiquan He
Ombu
Tangra Yumco
Gyaring Co
Xainza
Coqên
Palampur
Kulu
Jogindar Nagar
Mandi
Dankhar Gompa
Hoshiarpur
Bhakra Dam
Simla
Kandaghat
Ludhiana
Kamet 7756
Mapam Yumco
La'nga Co
(Sutlej)
Chakrata
Mussoorie
Chandigarh
Badarinath
Patiala
Ambala
Dehra Dun
Rishikesh
Nanda Devi 7817
Jagadhri
Saharanpur
Haridwar
Karnal
Roorkee
Muzaffarnagar
Najibabad
Bijnor
Almora
Ramnagar
Simikot
Mugu
Namse Shankou 4944
Baitadi
Dandeldhura
Silgarhi Doti
Jumla
7059
Zhongba
Saga
Maquan
Mustang
Maquan He
Lhazê
Hansi
Sonipat
Meerut
Amroha
Moradabad
Haldwani
Karnali
Muktinath
Gyala Shankou 5602
Bhiwani
Hapur
Rampur
Dhangarhi
Dhaulagiri 8172
Xixabangma Feng 8013
Nyalam
Ghaziabad
Sambhal
Pilibhit
Bulandshahr
Bareilly
Sarda
Nepalganj
Nuwakot
Gurkha
Nawakot
Mt. Everest 8850
Rewari
Faridabad
Shahjahanpur
Lakhimpur
Katmandu
Bhaktapur
Kanchenjunga 8598
Aligarh
Hathras
Jarwa
Nautanwa
Ramechhap
Alwar
Mathura
Fatehgarh
Hardoi
Sitapur
Bahraich
Balrampur
Chisapani Garhi
Sun Kosi
Bharatpur
Mainpuri
Kannauj
Gonda
Birganj
Dhankuta
Agra
Firozabad
Basti
Bettiah
Raxaul
Udaipur Garhi
Dholpur
Etawah
Lucknow
Faizabad
Gorakhpur
Motihari
Jaynagar
Shiliguri
Chambal
Bhind
Kanpur
Unnao
Rae Bareli
Deoria
Gandak
Darbhanga
Nirmali
Kishanganj
Gwalior
Ganga
Ghaghara
Sultanpur
Azamgarh
Siwan
Muzaffarpur
Supaul
Sawai Madhopur
Orai
Fatehpur
Chhapra
Purnia
Sheopur
Konch
Hamirpur
Bela
Jaunpur
Ara
Bankipore
Behariganj
Datia
Mau Ranipur
Banda
Yamuna
Varanasi
Ghazipur
Patna
Mokama
Munger
Katihar
Shivpuri
Jhansi
Allahabad
Bihar
Jamalpur
Bhagalpur
Baran
521
Jahanabad
Gaya
Tinpahar
Chhatarpur
Manikpur
Mirzapur
Sasaram
Guna
Lalitpur
Tikamgarh
Panna
Satna
Mauganj
Aurangabad
Deoghar
Jhalawar
Rewa
Rampur Hat
Rajgarh
Sironj
Bina-Etawah
Banda
690
Dudhi
Hazaribag
Barhi
Giridih
Siuri
Murwara
Gomoh
Dhanbad
Sagar
Damoh
1366
Raniganj
Vidisha
Umaria
Bharatpur
Lohardaga
Ramgarh
Asansol
Durgapur
Shajapur
Bhanrer Range
Chirmiri
1225
Ranchi
Purulia
Bankura
Barddhaman
Vindhya Range
Bhopal
Shahdol
Ambikapur
Sehore
Narsimhapur
Jabalpur
Anuppur
Jamshedpur
Hoshangabad
Mandla
1127
Chakradharpur
Medinipur
Haora
Kannod
Gadarwara
Shrirampur
Satpura Range
1353
Nainpur
Birmitrapur
Raurkela
Gua
Chaibasa
Kharagpur
Diamond Harbour
Makrai
Chhindwara
Maikala Range
Bilaspur
Sundargarh
Badampahar
Haldia
Khandwa
Balaghat
Kawardha
Raigarh
Jharsuguda
Contai
Burhanpur
Betul
Tirodi
Katangi
Hirakud Dam
Sambalpur
Keonjhargarh
Baleshwar
Subarnarekha
Hugli
Gawilgarh Hills
Ramtek
Gondia
Khairagarh
Sarangarh
1187
Achalpur
Nagpur
Raipur
Bhadrakh
Amravati
Bhandara
Raj Nandgaon
Durg
Sonepur
Talcher
Brahmani
Balangir
Mahanadi
Dhenkanal
Kendrapara
Akola
Wardha
Bramhapuri
Dhamtari
Cuttack
Paradip
Yavatmal
Wainganga
Hinganghat
Kanker
Bhubaneshwar
Washim
Darwha
1001
Titlagarh
Russellkonda
Wani
Penganga
Ghugus
Chandrapur
Bhawanipatna
Puri
Hingoli
Adilabad
Satmala Hills
Chilka L.
Asifabad
Ahiri
Brahmapur
Parbhani
Pranhita
Bhamragarh
Bastar
Rayagada
Chatrapur
Nanded
Nirmal
Indravati
Ichchapuram
1501
Palam
Bijapur
Jagdalpur
Jeypore
Godavari
Jagtial
Parvatipuram
Bodhan
1240
Salur
Bobbili
Tekkali
Latur
Nizamabad
Manthani
Udgir
Karimnagar
Venkatapuram
1680
Srikakulam
Manjra
Vizianagaram
Siddipet
Warangal
Konta
Northern Circars
Anakapalle
Bidar
Kottagudem
Vishakhapatnam
Gulbarga
Secunderabad
Eastern Ghats
Nalgonda
Suriapet
Rajahmundry
Pithapuram
Godavari Point
Kakinada
Narayanpet
Yadgir
Krishna
Mahbubnagar
Eluru
Vijayawada
Narasapur
Raichur
Gadwal
Tenali
Machilipatnam
917
Nallamalai Hills
Tungabhadra
Kurnool
Chirala
Bapatla
Adoni
Erramala Hills
Cumbum
Ongole
Hospet
Nandyal
Velikonda Range
Guntakal
Bellary
1100
Projection: Conical with two standard parallels
East from Greenwich

50 0 100 200 300 400 km
50 0 50 100 150 200 250 miles
C H I N A
Baqên
Nangqên
Gamtog
Garzê
Siling Co
Nagqu
Dêngqên
Qamdo
Baiyü
Xinlong
Nu Jiang
S I C H U A N
Yajiang
Nam Co
Lhorong
(Salween)
Yidun
Litang
Lhari
Zhaxizê
Ningjing
Gongbo'gyamda
Lhinzub
Goqên
(Mekong)
Lancang Jiang
Jinsha Jiang
Riga
Lhasa
(Brahmaputra)
Jido
Muli Zangzu Zizhixian
(Tsangpo)
Yarlung Zangbo Jiang
Mainkung
Xigazê
Gyangzê
Nang Xian
Nizamghat
Dibang
Hkakabo Razi (Thala L.)
Zhongdian
Subansiri
Minutang
Zizhixian
Lhunzê
Comai
Cona
A R U N A C H A L P R A D E S H
Murkongselek
Hpungan Pass
Putao
Weixi
Kangto
Saikhoa Ghat
Dum Duma
Konglu
Lijiang
Punakha
Thunkar
Towang
Dibrugarh
Tinsukia
Tipongpani
Chaukan Pass
Tongsa Dzong
Rupa
North Lakhimpur
Sibsagar
Patkai Bum
Kawngtim
Jianchuan
Thimphu
B H U T A N
Gangtok
Taga Dzong
Bumhpa Bum
Hukawng Valley
Lawng Pit
Balipara
Dergaon
Jorhat
Jayanti
Tezpur
Maingkwan
K A C H I N
Manas
Rangia
Silghat
A S S A M
Yunlong
W. BENGAL
Alipur Duar
Barpeta
Mairabari
Nowgong
Mokokchung
Kumon Bum
Mali
Nmai
Y U N N A N
Koch Bihar
Goalpara
Guwahati
NAGALAND
Singkaling Hkamti
Kohima
Brahmaputra
Myitkyina
Sadon
Baoshan
Saidpur
Dhuburi
Chindwin
Mogaung
Kurigram
Shillong
Tengchong
Rangpur
Barail Range
Haflong
Ukhrul
Homalin
Tura
MEGHALAYA
Cherrapunji
Longling
Changning
Barakhola
Tamenglong
Phulchari
Jamalpur
Mohanganj
Sylhet
Silchar
Imphal
Bhamo
SYLHET
MANIPUR
Bogra
Mymensingh
Churachandpur
Thaungdut
Katha
Shwegu
Sirajganj
Indaw
Tamu
Wuntho
Bengal
Lalaghat
Tigyaing
Tropic of Cancer
East
DHAKA
Kalni
Kolosib
Kunlong
Salween
Pabna
Brahmanbaria
SAGAING
Man Na
Hsenwi
Pang-Long
Dhaka
TRIPURA
Sairang
Mawlaik
Agartala
Aizawl
Kushtia
Amarpur
Tiddim
Kyunhla
Bawdwin
Namtu
Kawnro
MIZORAM
Kennedy
Kalewa
Krishnanagar
Narayanganj
Comilla
Dighinala
Taungdeik
Lashio
Mogok
Munar
Chandpur
Ranaghat
Jessore
Madaripur
Belonia
Lunglei
Mingin
Shwebo
Mong Yai
Falam
Khulna
Bhola
Maijdi
Kaptai L.
Budalin
Madaya
Gokteik
Pang-Yang
Mong Hsu
Mong Pawk
Bhatpara
Barakpur
Alon
Monywa
Barisal
Gangaw
KOLKATA (CALCUTTA)
Chittagong
Mandalay
Hatia
Yinmabin
Mong Kung
Mong Wa
Dohazari
CHIN
Sagaing
Kyaukse
S H A N
Port Canning
Patuakhali
The Sundarbans
BARISAL
Keng Tung
Lakshmikantapur
Pauk
Myingyan
Haringhata
Pakokku
Ganges
Mt. Victoria
Pondaung
Kaladan
Mouths of the Ganges
Cox's Bazar
Paletwa
Kanpetlet
Meiktila
Taunggyi
Keng Tawng
B U R M A (M Y A N M A R)
Thazi
Heho
Inle L.
Mong Nai
Mong Ton
Kyaukpadaung
Yamethin
Yenangyaung
Mawk Mai
Mong Pan
Muang Chiang Rai
Magwe
Taungdwingyi
Loi-kaw
Minbu
MAGWE
Sittwe (Akyab)
Pyinmana
ARAKAN
KAYAH
Mae Hong Son
Thayetmyo
Chiang Mai
Bawlake
THAILAND
Kyaukpyu
Toungoo
Letpan
Irrawaddy
Muang Lamphun
Ramree I.
Prome
Lampang
Taungup
Arakan Coast
Arakan Yoma
Pegu Yoma
Cheduba I.
Pyu
Papun
BAY OF BENGAL
Sandoway
Myanaung
Madauk
Sittang Myit
Dawna Range
Letpadan
Tharrawaddy
Gwa
Henzada
Tak
Kyonpyaw
Pegu
Thaton
Yandoon
PEGU
Pa-an
Martaban
Insein
RANGOON (YANGON)
Bassein
Ma-ubin
Moulmein
Myaungmya
IRRAWADDY
Pyapon
MON
Rangoon
G. of Martaban
Amherst
Kalegauk
Lamaing
Maudin Sun
Mouths of the Irrawaddy
Sangkhla Buri
Mae Klong
Ye
Natkyizin
Preparis North Channel
OCEAN
Sangkhla
Nam Tok
Pariparit Kyun (Burma)
Preparis South Channel
Moscos Is.
Maungmagan Is.
Yebyu
Tavoy
Koko Kyunzu (Burma)
Launglon Bok
7088
7756
5881
7314
7554
7089
3072
2432
3411
5500
3824
2424
1412
1961
2704
2299
2693
3053
2519
2256
2163
2576
2620
2080
B
C
D
E
F
G
H
J
K
7 8 9 10 11 12 13
88 90 92 94 96 98 100
30 28 26 24 22 20 18 16 14

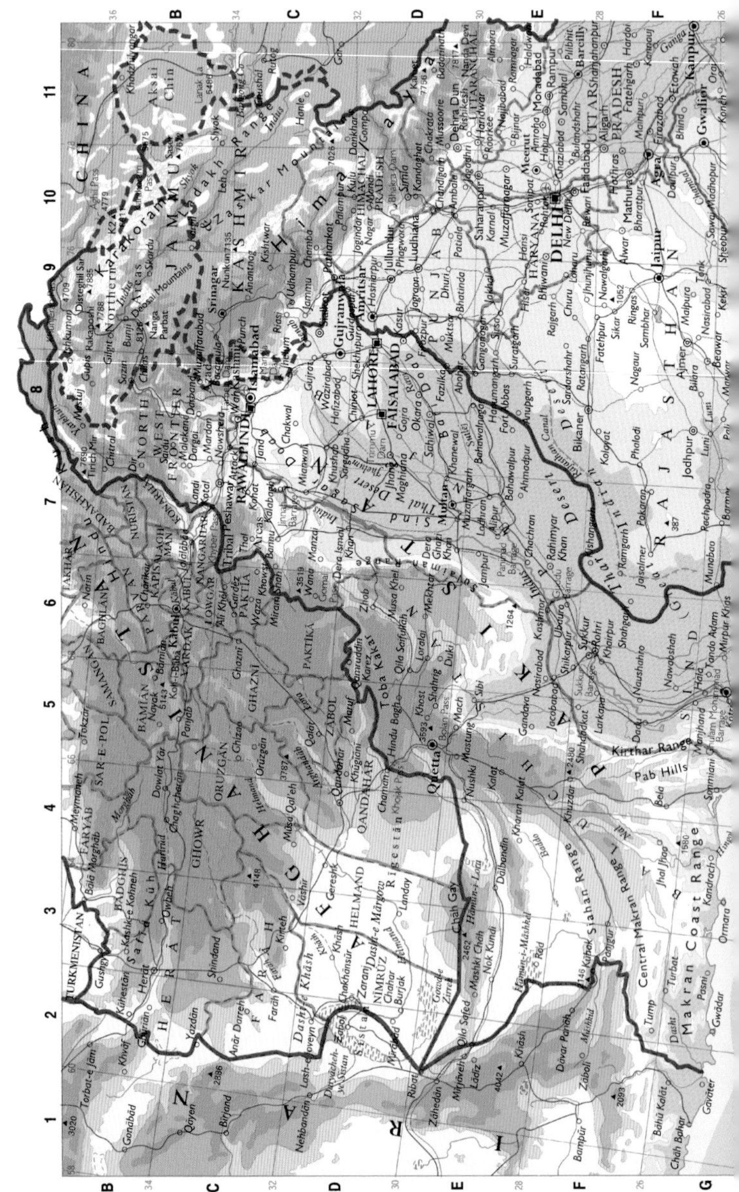
CHINA
Aksai Chin
Karakoram
JAMMU
KASHMIR
Ladakh
Northern Areas
Deosai Mountains
Srinagar
Islamabad
RAWALPINDI
Peshawar
LAHORE
FAISALABAD
Gujranwala
Amritsar
Jullundur
Ludhiana
Simla
Chandigarh
Dehra Dun
HIMACHAL PRADESH
UTTARANCHAL
UTTAR PRADESH
PUNJAB
HARYANA
DELHI
New Delhi
Meerut
Moradabad
Bareilly
Agra
Gwalior
Kanpur
Jaipur
Ajmer
Jodhpur
Bikaner
RAJASTHAN
Thar Desert
Multan
Bahawalpur
Quetta
Kabul
Herat
Kandahar
Sukkur
Kirthar Range
Pab Hills
Central Makran Range
Makran Coast Range
Siahan Range
Toba Kakar
Sulaiman Range
NORTH WEST FRONTIER
HELMAND
NIMRUZ
GHAZNI
ZABOL
ORUZGAN
GHOWR
BAMIAN
BADGHIS
FARYAB
SAR-E-POL
PAKTIKA
PAKTIA
TURKMENISTAN
BADAKHSHAN
NURISTAN
Dasht-e Margow
Registan
Chah Gay
Zahedan
Gwadar
Pasni
Ormara
Turbat

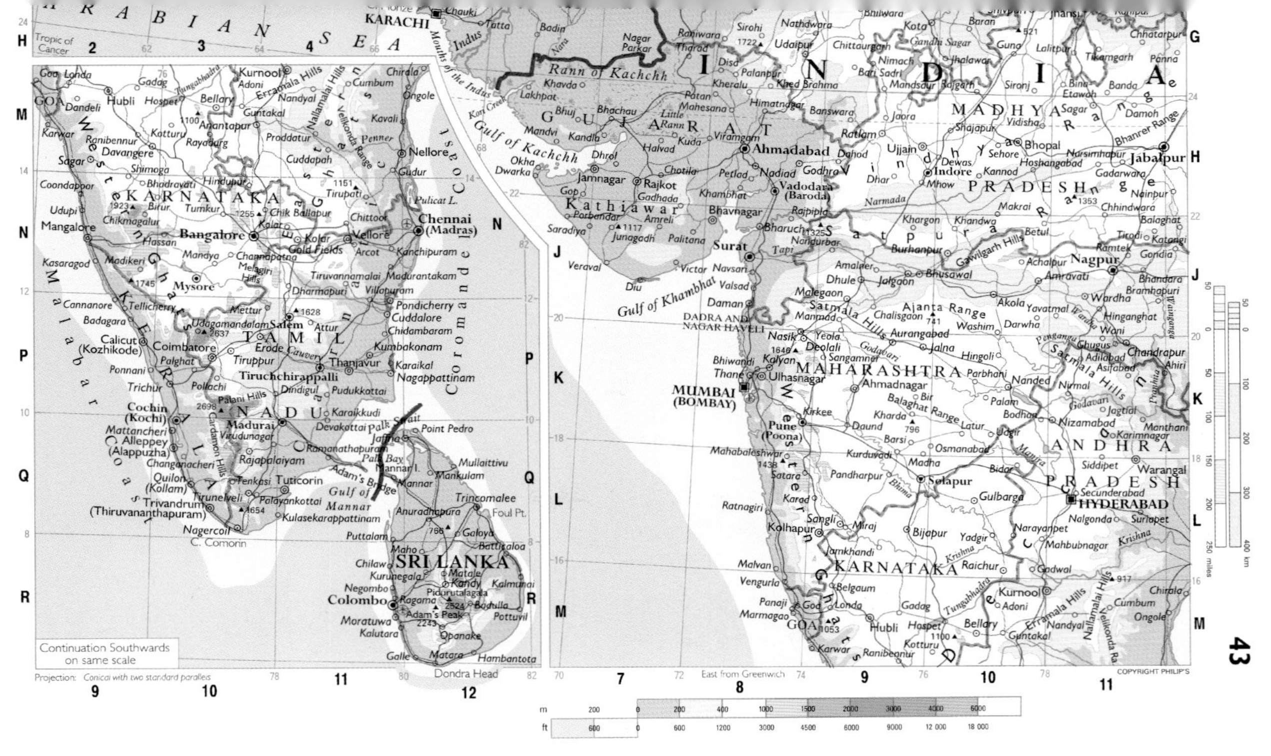

ARABIAN SEA
INDIA
MADHYA PRADESH
GUJARAT
MAHARASHTRA
ANDHRA PRADESH
KARNATAKA
TAMIL NADU
KERALA
SRI LANKA
GOA
DADRA AND NAGAR HAVELI
KARACHI
Ahmadabad
Vadodara (Baroda)
Surat
Rajkot
Bhavnagar
MUMBAI (BOMBAY)
Thane
Pune (Poona)
Nasik
Nagpur
Jabalpur
Bhopal
Indore
Ujjain
HYDERABAD
Secunderabad
Solapur
Kolhapur
Belgaum
Hubli
Bangalore
Mysore
Mangalore
Calicut (Kozhikode)
Cochin (Kochi)
Coimbatore
Madurai
Tiruchchirappalli
Salem
Vellore
Chennai (Madras)
Pondicherry
Trivandrum (Thiruvananthapuram)
Quilon (Kollam)
Nagercoil
Tuticorin
Colombo
Kandy
Jaffna
Trincomalee
Galle
Rann of Kachchh
Gulf of Kachchh
Kathiawar
Gulf of Khambhat
Gulf of Mannar
Palk Strait
Adam's Bridge
Mouths of the Indus
Western Ghats
Eastern Ghats
Coromandel Coast
Malabar Coast
Vindhya Range
Satpura Range
Ajanta Range
Satmala Hills
Nallamalai Hills
Velikonda Range
Cardamon Hills
Adam's Peak
Dondra Head
C. Comorin
Tropic of Cancer
Continuation Southwards on same scale
Projection: Conical with two standard parallels
East from Greenwich
COPYRIGHT PHILIP'S
50 0 100 200 300 400 km
50 0 50 100 150 200 250 miles
m 200 0 200 400 1000 1500 2000 3000 4000 6000
ft 600 0 600 1200 3000 4500 6000 9000 12 000 18 000

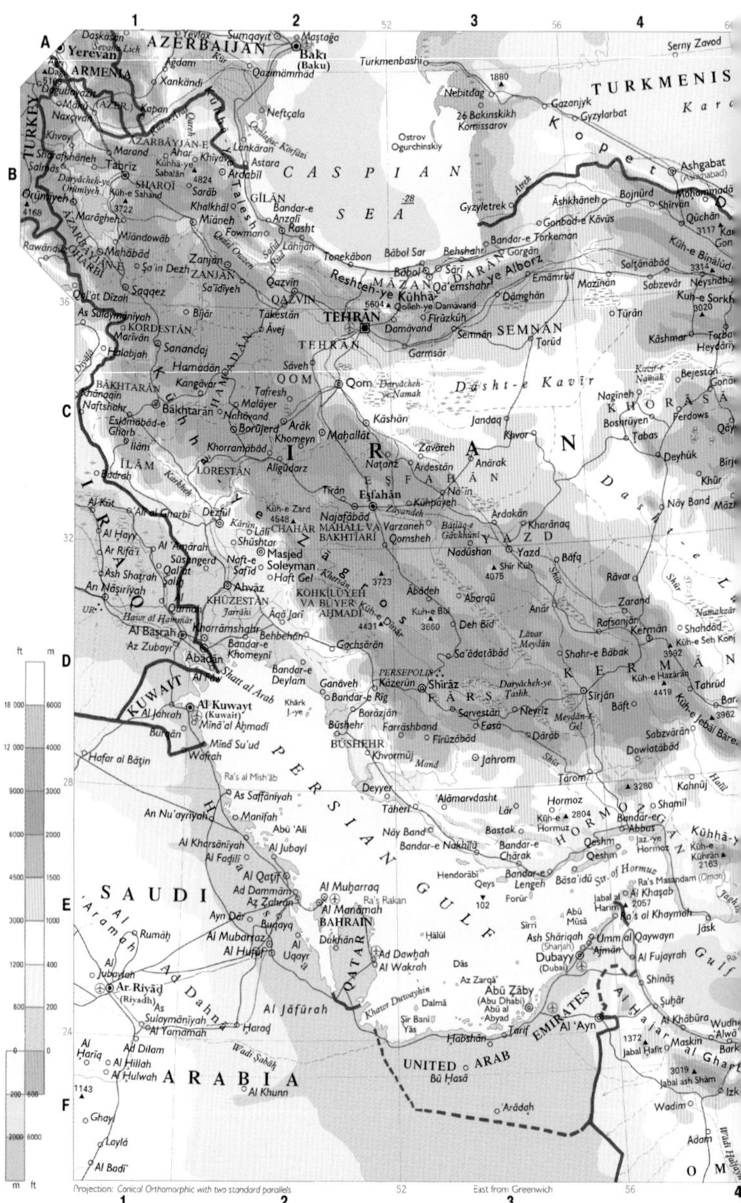
AZERBAIJAN
ARMENIA
TURKEY
TURKMENISTAN
CASPIAN SEA
IRAN
IRAQ
KUWAIT
PERSIAN GULF
SAUDI ARABIA
BAHRAIN
QATAR
UNITED ARAB EMIRATES
TEHRĀN
Eşfahān
Shīrāz
Dasht-e Kavīr
Projection: Conical Orthomorphic with two standard parallels
East from Greenwich

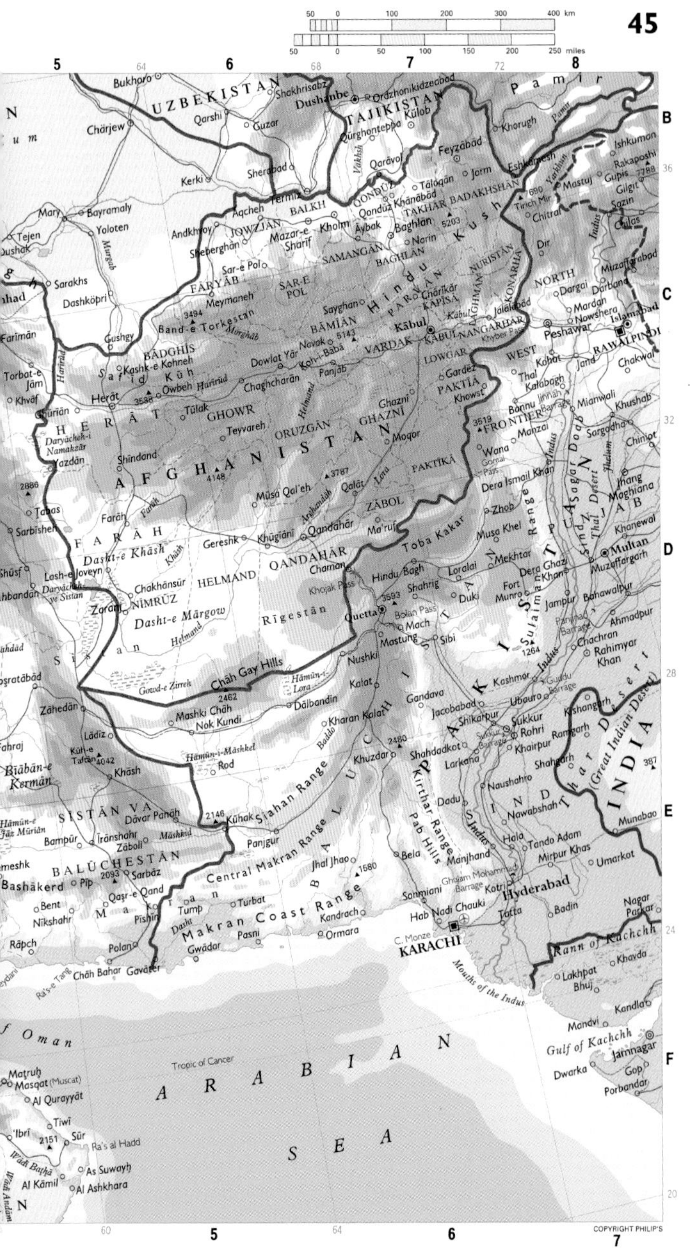

50 0 100 200 300 400 km
50 0 50 100 150 200 250 miles
5
6
7
8
64
68
72
B
C
D
E
F
36
32
28
24
20
60
64
UZBEKISTAN
TAJIKISTAN
AFGHANISTAN
PAKISTAN
INDIA
Bukhoro
Qarshi
Guzar
Shakhrisabz
Dushanbe
Ordzhonikidzeabad
Kŭlob
Qŭrghonteppa
Vakhsh
Qarāvol
Sherabad
Termiz
Chārjew
Kerki
Mary
Bayramaly
Yoloten
Murgab
Tejen
Dushak
Sarakhs
Dashkōpri
Gushgy
Pamir
Khorugh
Feyzābād
Eshkamesh
Jorm
Tāloqān
Qondūz
Khānābād
TAKHĀR
BADAKHSHĀN
BALKH
Āqcheh
Andkhvoy
JOWZJĀN
Mazār-e Sharīf
Kholm
Āybak
Baghlān
5203
Narin
Sheberghān
Sar-e Pol
SAMANGĀN
BAGHLĀN
FĀRYĀB
SAR-E POL
Meymaneh
3494
Band-e Torkestān
Morghāb
Sayghan
BĀMĪĀN
Hindu Kush
PARVĀN
Chārīkār
KAPĪSĀ
NŪRISTĀN
KONARHA
LAGHMĀN
Jalālābād
NANGARHĀR
Kābul
KĀBUL
Khyber Pass
VARDAK
Navak
5143
Koh-i-Bābā
Dowlat Yār
Panjāb
LOWGAR
Gardēz
PAKTIĀ
Khowst
BĀDGHĪS
Kashk-e Kohneh
Safīd Kūh
Owbeh
Harīrūd
Chaghcharān
Herāt
3538
Tūlak
GHOWR
Helmand
Ghaznī
GHAZNĪ
Teyvareh
ORUZGĀN
Moqor
HERĀT
Ghūriān
Daryācheh-i Namakzār
Yazdān
Shīndand
4148
3787
Mūsā Qal'eh
Qalāt
PAKTĪKĀ
ZĀBOL
2886
Tabas
Farāh
Farah
FARĀH
Sarbīsheh
Dasht-e Khāsh
Khāsh
Gereshk
Khūgīānī
Qandahār
Ma'ruf
Arghandāb
Lora
QANDAHĀR
Chaman
HELMAND
Shūsf
Losh-e Joveyn
Daryācheh-ye Sīstan
Chakhānsūr
NĪMRŪZ
Zaranj
Dasht-e Mārgow
Rīgestān
Khojak Pass
Quetta
Bolan Pass
Mach
Mastung
Sibi
Hindu Bagh
Shahrig
3593
Loralai
Duki
Fort Munro
Toba Kakar
Sīstān
Nushki
Hāmūn-i-Lora
Chāh Gay Hills
2462
Gowd-e Zirreh
Dālbandīn
Kalat
Mashki Chāh
Nok Kundi
Kharan Kalat
Baddo
Zāhedān
Lādīz
Kūh-e Taftān
4042
Khāsh
Hāmūn-i-Māshkel
Rod
2480
Khuzdar
Siahan Range
BALUCHISTAN
Kirthar Range
Pab Hills
Bīābān-e Kermān
SĪSTĀN VA BALŪCHESTĀN
Dāvar Panāh
2146
Kūhak
Māshkīd
Hāmūn-e Jāz Mūriān
Bampūr
Īrānshahr
Zāboli
Panjgur
Central Makran Range
Jhal Jhao
1580
Bela
Sarbāz
2093
Pīp
Bashākerd
Qasr-e Qand
Tump
Turbat
Makran Coast Range
Kandrach
Ormara
Pasni
Gwādar
Dasht
Bent
Nīkshahr
Pishin
Rāpch
Polān
Chāh Bahār
Gavāter
Ra's-e Tang
Gulf of Oman
Sonmiani
Hab
Nadi Chauki
C. Monze
KARACHI
Mouths of the Indus
Tatta
Kotri
Hyderabad
Ghulam Mohammad Barrage
Manjhand
Hala
Tando Adam
Mirpur Khas
Umarkot
Badin
Nagar Parkar
Rann of Kachchh
Khavda
Lakhpat
Bhuj
Kandla
Mandvi
Gulf of Kachchh
Jamnagar
Dwarka
Gop
Porbandar
Nawabshah
SIND
Dadu
Naushahro
Larkana
Shahdadkot
Khairpur
Rohri
Sukkur
Sukkur Barrage
Shikarpur
Jacobabad
Gandava
Ubauro
Kashmor
Guddu Barrage
Indus
Sulaiman Range
1264
Rahimyar Khan
Chachran
Panjnad Barrage
Ahmadpur
Bahawalpur
Jampur
Dera Ghazi Khan
Muzaffargarh
Multan
Khanewal
Mekhtar
Musa Khel
Zhob
Dera Ismail Khan
Gomal Pass
Wana
Manzai
3519
NORTH-WEST FRONTIER
Bannu
Jinnah Barrage
Kalabagh
Thal
Kohat
Mianwali
Khushab
Sargodha
Chiniot
Jhang Maghiana
Sind Sagar Doab
Thal Desert
Jhelum
PUNJAB
Kishangarh
Ramgarh
Shahgarh
Thar Desert (Great Indian Desert)
387
Munabao
Peshawar
Mardan
Nowshera
Islamabad
RAWALPINDI
Jand
Chakwal
Dargai
Darband
Muzaffarabad
Dir
Chitral
Tirich Mir
7690
Mastuj
Yarkhun
Gupis
Gilgit
Rakaposhi
7788
Ishkuman
Sazin
Chilas
ARABIAN SEA
Tropic of Cancer
Matruh
Masqat (Muscat)
Al Qurayyāt
Tīwī
Sūr
'Ibrī
2151
Ra's al Hadd
Wādī Bathā
As Suwayh
Al Kāmil
Al Ashkhara
Wādī Andam
Torbat-e Jām
Khvāf
Farīmān
Harīrud
Kūh-e Bazmān
Fahraj
Zahdad
Nosratābād
Jāsk

5
6
7

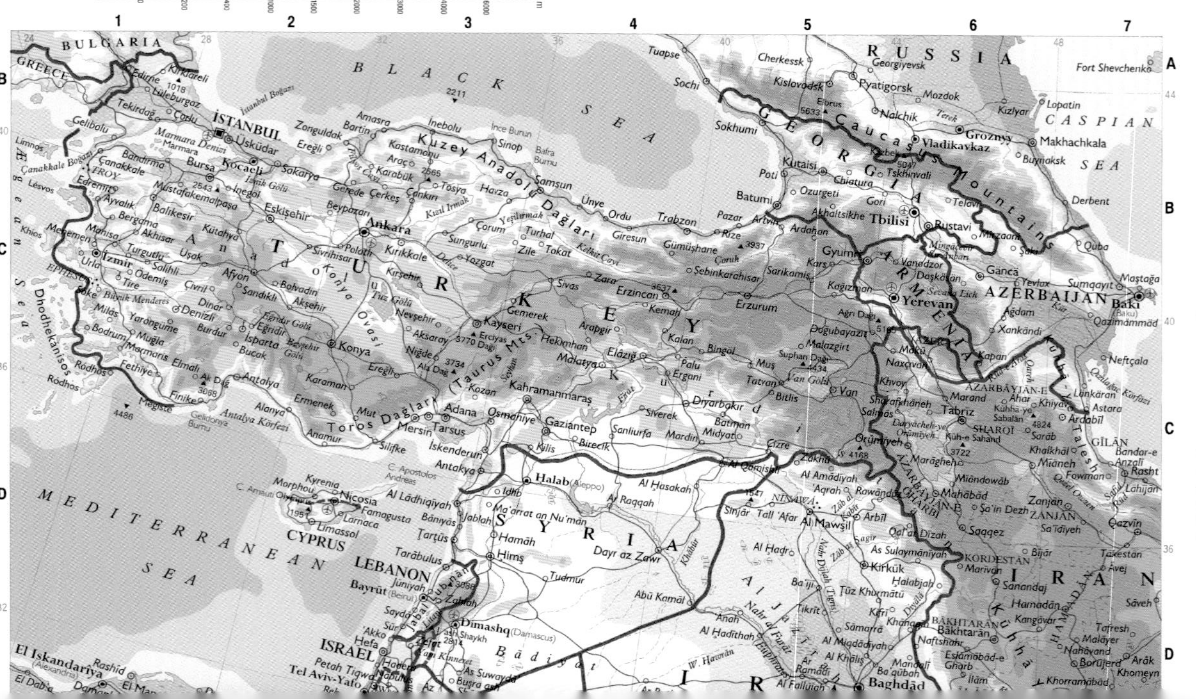
BLACK SEA
CASPIAN SEA
MEDITERRANEAN SEA
RUSSIA
GEORGIA
ARMENIA
AZERBAIJAN
TURKEY
SYRIA
IRAQ
IRAN
CYPRUS
LEBANON
ISRAEL
BULGARIA
GREECE
Caucasus Mountains
Kuzey Anadolu Dağları
Toros Dağları
Konya Ovası
Dhodhekánisos
İSTANBUL
Ankara
Tbilisi
Yerevan
Baki
Nicosia
Bayrūt
Dimashq (Damascus)
Halab (Aleppo)
Baghdād
Tabrīz
İzmir
Bursa
Konya
Adana
Kayseri
Erzurum
Trabzon
Samsun
Sinop
Antalya
Gaziantep
Diyarbakır
Van
Van Gölü
Tuz Gölü
Nahr Dijlah (Tigris)
Nahr al Furāt (Euphrates)
ft
m
18 000
12 000
9000
6000
4500
3000
1200
600
0
200
2000
6000
4000
3000
2000
1500
1000
400
200
0
200
600

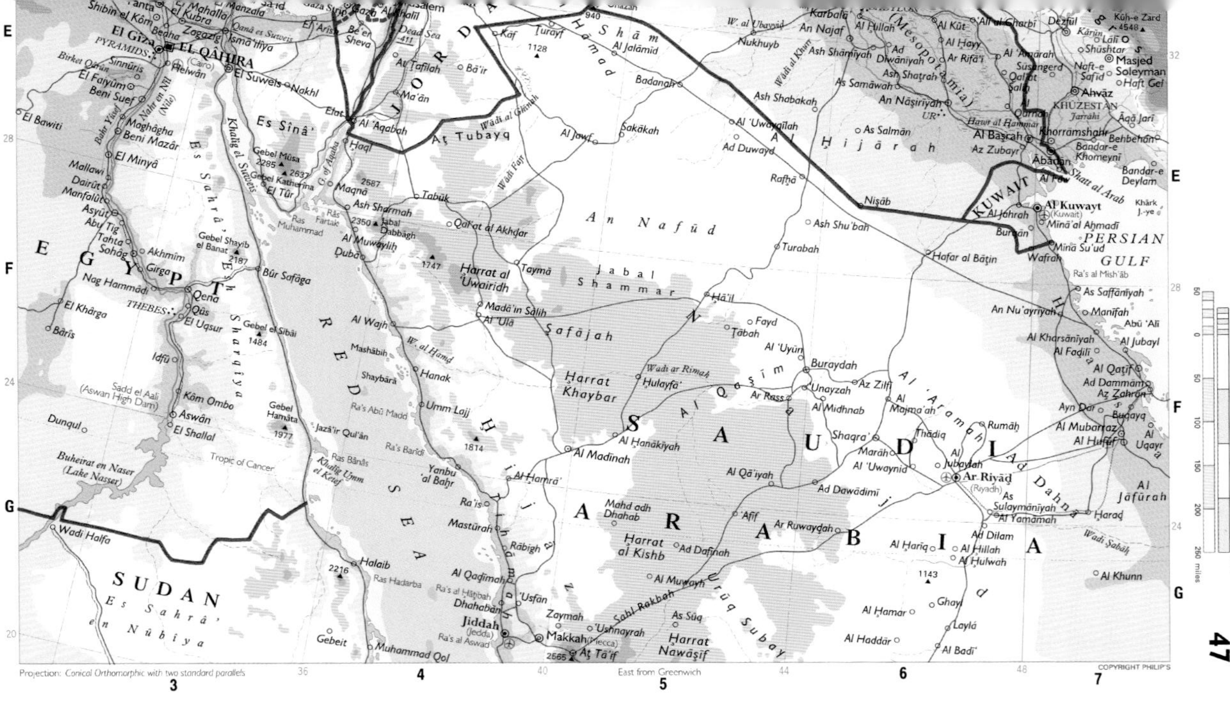
50 0 100 200 300 400 km
50 0 50 100 150 200 250 miles
E
F
G
32
28
24
20
48
44
40
36
3
4
5
6
7
COPYRIGHT PHILIP'S
East from Greenwich
Projection: Conical Orthomorphic with two standard parallels
PERSIAN GULF
RED SEA
EGYPT
SUDAN
SAUDI ARABIA
KUWAIT
JORDAN
Al Kuwayt
(Kuwait)
Ar Riyāḍ
(Riyadh)
EL QÂHIRA
(Cairo)
El Gîza
PYRAMIDS
Makkah
(Mecca)
Jiddah
(Jedda)
Al Madīnah
Al Başrah
Ahvāz
Abādān
Khorramshahr
Shaţţ al Arab
KHŪZESTĀN
(Mesopotamia)
UR
An Nafūd
Al Ḩijārah
Jabal Shammar
Ḩarrat Khaybar
Ḩarrat al 'Uwairidh
Ḩarrat al Kishb
Ḩarrat Nawāşif
Ad Dahnā
Al 'Aramah
Al Qaşīm
Al Jāfūrah
'Urūq Subay'
Ḩamad
Ash Shām
Aţ Ţubayq
Şafājah
Es Sînâ'
Khalig el Suweis
G. of Aqaba
Es Sahrâ' esh Sharqîya
Es Sahrâ' en Nûbîya
Tropic of Cancer
Buheirat en Naser
(Lake Nasser)
Sadd el Aali
(Aswan High Dam)
Nahr en Nîl
(Nile)
THEBES
Dead Sea
Wadi Halfa
Aswân
Kôm Ombo
Qena
Asyût
El Minyâ
Beni Suef
El Faiyûm
El Bawiti
El Khârga
Bûr Safâga
El Suweis
El Tûr
Gebel Mûsa
2285
Gebel Katherîna
2637
Halaib
Gebeit
2216
Tabūk
Al 'Aqabah
Ma'ān
Al Jawf
Sakākah
Ţurayf
Ḩā'il
Taymā
Al 'Ulā
Madā'in Şāliḩ
Al Wajh
Yanbu 'al Baḩr
Buraydah
'Unayzah
Ar Rass
Az Zilfī
Al Hufūf
Al Mubarraz
Ad Dammām
Az Zahrān
Al Qaţīf
Al Jubayl
Ra's al Mish'āb
Ḩafar al Bāţin
Nişāb
An Najaf
Karbalā'
As Samāwah
An Nāşirīyah
Al Kūt
Aţ Ţā'if
1128
1143
1747
1814
1977
1484
2187
2350
2587
2565
940

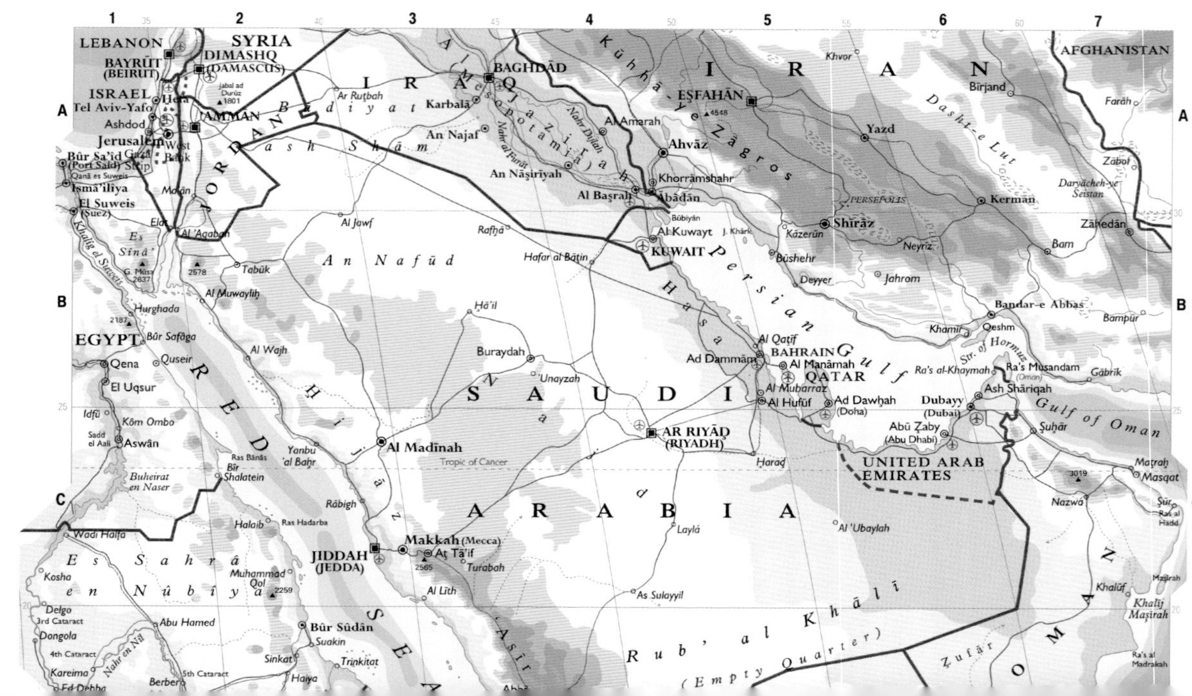
LEBANON
BAYRŪT (BEIRUT)
SYRIA
DIMASHQ (DAMASCUS)
ISRAEL
Tel Aviv-Yafo
Ashdod
Jerusalem
West Bank
Gaza Strip
'AMMAN
JORDAN
Bûr Sa'îd (Port Said)
Ismâ'ilîya
El Suweis (Suez)
Es Sînâ'
Elat
Al 'Aqabah
EGYPT
Hurghada
Bûr Safâga
Quseir
Qena
El Uqsur
Idfû
Kôm Ombo
Aswân
Buheirat en Naser
Wadi Halfa
Es Sahrâ en Nûbîya
Kosha
Delgo
Dongola
Kareima
Abu Hamed
Bûr Sûdân
Suakin
Sinkat
Trinkitat
Haiya
Berber
Halaib
Bîr Shalatein
RED SEA
IRAQ
BAGHDĀD
Karbalā'
An Najaf
An Nāşirīyah
Al 'Amārah
Al Başrah
Al Jazīrah (Mesopotamia)
Nahr Dijlah
Nahr al Furāt
Bādiyat ash Shām
Ar Ruţbah
Al Jawf
Rafḩā
An Nafūd
Tabūk
Al Muwayliḩ
Al Wajh
Ḩā'il
Buraydah
'Unayzah
Hafar al Bāţin
IRAN
AFGHANISTAN
Kūhhā-ye Zāgros
EŞFAHĀN
Yazd
Shīrāz
Kerman
Birjand
Farāh
Zābol
Dasht-e Lut
Zāhedān
Bam
Bandar-e Abbās
Ahvāz
Khorramshahr
Ābādān
Būshehr
KUWAIT
Al Kuwayt
Persian Gulf
Al Hasa
BAHRAIN
Al Manāmah
QATAR
Ad Dawḩah (Doha)
Ad Dammām
Al Hufūf
SAUDI ARABIA
AR RIYĀḐ (RIYADH)
Al Madīnah
Makkah (Mecca)
JIDDAH (JEDDA)
Aţ Ţā'if
Ḩijāz
Tropic of Cancer
Rub' al Khālī (Empty Quarter)
UNITED ARAB EMIRATES
Abū Zaby (Abu Dhabi)
Dubayy (Dubai)
Ash Shāriqah
Str. of Hormuz
Gulf of Oman
Masqat
Şuḩār
Nazwá
OMAN
Zufār

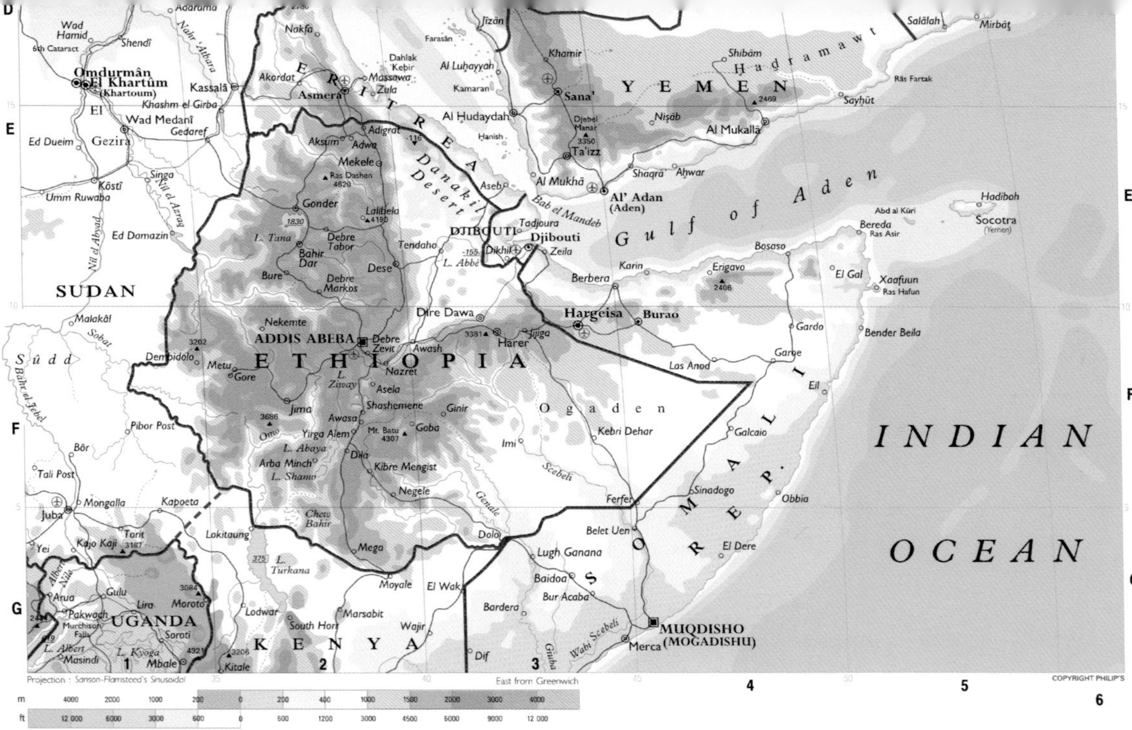

SUDAN
ETHIOPIA
ERITREA
DJIBOUTI
YEMEN
SOMALI REP.
KENYA
UGANDA
INDIAN OCEAN
Gulf of Aden
Hadramawt
Danakil Desert
Ogaden
Sûdd

Wad Hamid
6th Cataract
Shendî
Omdurmân
El Khartûm (Khartoum)
Kassalâ
Khashm el Girba
Wad Medanî
Gedaref
El Gezira
Ed Dueim
Kôstî
Umm Ruwaba
Singa
Nîl el Azraq
Nîl el Abyad
Ed Damazin
Nahr 'Atbara
Malakâl
Sobat
Bahr el Jebel
Pibor Post
Bôr
Tali Post
Juba
Mongalla
Kapoeta
Torit
Kajo Kaji
3187
Yei
Nakfa
Akordat
Asmera
Massawa
Dahlak Kebir
Zula
Farasân
Jîzân
Al Luhayyah
Kamaran
Al Hudaydah
Hanish
Khamir
Sana'
Djebel Manar
3350
Ta'izz
Al Mukhā
Al' Adan (Aden)
Bab el Mandeb
Shaqrā'
Ahwar
Nisāb
Shibām
2469
Al Mukallā
Sayhūt
Rās Fartak
Salālah
Mirbāṭ
Hadiboh
Socotra (Yemen)
Abd al Kūri
Bereda
Ras Asir
Xaafuun
Ras Hafun
El Gal
Bosaso
Erigavo
2406
Karin
Berbera
Hargeisa
Burao
Gardo
Bender Beila
Garoe
Las Anod
Eil
Galcaio
Obbia
Sinadogo
El Dere
Ferfer
Belet Uen
Lugh Ganana
Baidoa
Bur Acaba
Bardera
Dif
Giuba
Wabi Scebeli
Merca
MUQDISHO (MOGADISHU)
Adigrat
Aksum
Adwa
Mekele
Ras Dashen 4620
Gonder
Lalibela
4190
1830
L. Tana
Debre Tabor
Bahir Dar
Bure
Debre Markos
Dese
Tendaho
-116
-155
L. Abbé
Aseb
Tadjoura
Djibouti
Dikhil
Zeila
Dire Dawa
3381
Harer
Jijiga
Nekemte
ADDIS ABEBA
Debre Zevit
Awash
Nazret
L. Ziway
Asela
Shashemene
Ginir
Goba
Mt. Batu 4307
Awasa
Yirga Alem
Dila
Kibre Mengist
Negele
Imi
Scebeli
Genale
Kebri Dehar
Dolo
Mega
Moyale
El Wak
Wajir
Marsabit
South Horr
Lodwar
Lokitaung
375
L. Turkana
Chew Bahir
L. Abaya
Arba Minch
L. Shamo
Omo
3686
Jima
Metu
Gore
Dembidolo
3202
Kitale
3206
Mbale
4321
Soroti
Moroto
3084
Lira
Gulu
Arua
Pakwach
Murchison Falls
L. Kyoga
L. Albert
Masindi
Albert Nile
619
2484

D
E
F
G
1
2
3
4
5
6
15
10
5
35
40
45
50

Projection : Sanson-Flamsteed's Sinusoidal

East from Greenwich

m	4000	2000	1000	200	0	200	400	1000	1500	2000	3000	4000
ft	12 000	6000	3000	600	0	600	1200	3000	4500	6000	9000	12 000

100 0 100 200 300 400 500 600 km
100 0 100 200 300 400 miles

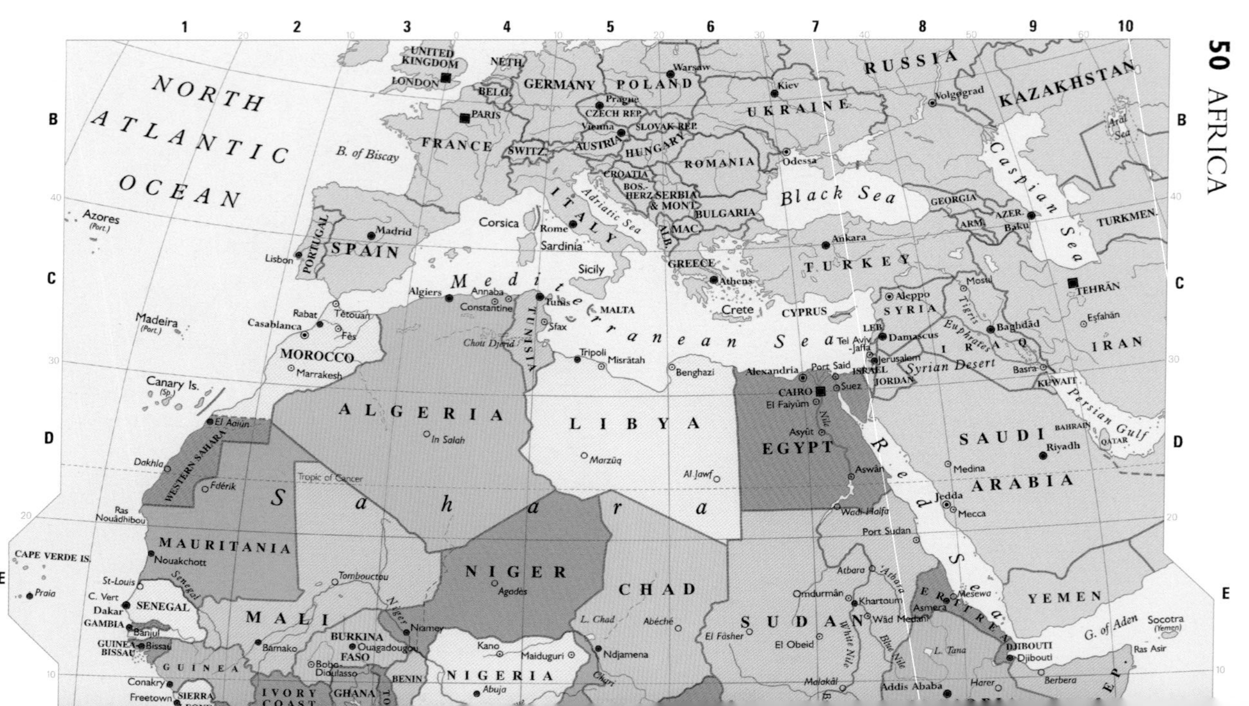
NORTH ATLANTIC OCEAN
Azores (Port.)
Madeira (Port.)
Canary Is. (Sp.)
CAPE VERDE IS.
Praia
B. of Biscay
UNITED KINGDOM
LONDON
PARIS
FRANCE
SPAIN
Madrid
PORTUGAL
Lisbon
MOROCCO
Rabat
Casablanca
Marrakesh
Fès
Tétouan
WESTERN SAHARA
El Aaiún
Dakhla
MAURITANIA
Nouakchott
Fdérik
Ras Nouâdhibou
SENEGAL
Dakar
C. Vert
St-Louis
Senegal
GAMBIA
Banjul
GUINEA-BISSAU
Bissau
GUINEA
Conakry
Freetown
MALI
Bamako
Tombouctou
Niger
BURKINA FASO
Ouagadougou
Bobo-Dioulasso
IVORY COAST
GHANA
BENIN
NIGER
Niamey
Agades
NIGERIA
Kano
Abuja
Maiduguri
CHAD
Ndjamena
L. Chad
Abéché
Chari
ALGERIA
Algiers
Annaba
Constantine
In Salah
Chott Djerid
Tropic of Cancer
Sahara
TUNISIA
Tunis
Sfax
LIBYA
Tripoli
Misrātah
Benghazi
Marzūq
Al Jawf
EGYPT
CAIRO
Alexandria
Port Said
Suez
El Faiyûm
Asyût
Aswân
Wadi Halfa
Nile
SUDAN
Khartoum
Omdurmân
Port Sudan
Atbara
El Obeid
El Fasher
Wad Medani
Malakâl
White Nile
Blue Nile
ERITREA
Asmera
Mesewa
DJIBOUTI
Djibouti
Addis Ababa
Harer
Berbera
L. Tana
YEMEN
G. of Aden
Socotra (Yemen)
Ras Asir
SAUDI ARABIA
Riyadh
Medina
Mecca
Jedda
Red Sea
Persian Gulf
QATAR
BAHRAIN
KUWAIT
IRAN
TEHRĀN
Eşfahān
IRAQ
Baghdād
Basra
Mosul
Tigris
Euphrates
Syrian Desert
SYRIA
Damascus
Aleppo
LEB.
ISRAEL
JORDAN
Jerusalem
Tel Aviv-Jaffa
CYPRUS
TURKEY
Ankara
Crete
Athens
GREECE
Mediterranean Sea
MALTA
Sicily
Sardinia
Corsica
ITALY
Rome
Adriatic Sea
ALB.
MAC.
SERBIA & MONT.
BOS.-HERZ.
CROATIA
BULGARIA
ROMANIA
HUNGARY
SLOVAK REP.
AUSTRIA
Vienna
CZECH REP.
Prague
SWITZ.
GERMANY
NETH.
BELG.
POLAND
Warsaw
UKRAINE
Kiev
Odessa
Black Sea
GEORGIA
ARM.
AZER.
Baku
Caspian Sea
RUSSIA
Volgograd
KAZAKHSTAN
Aral Sea
TURKMEN.

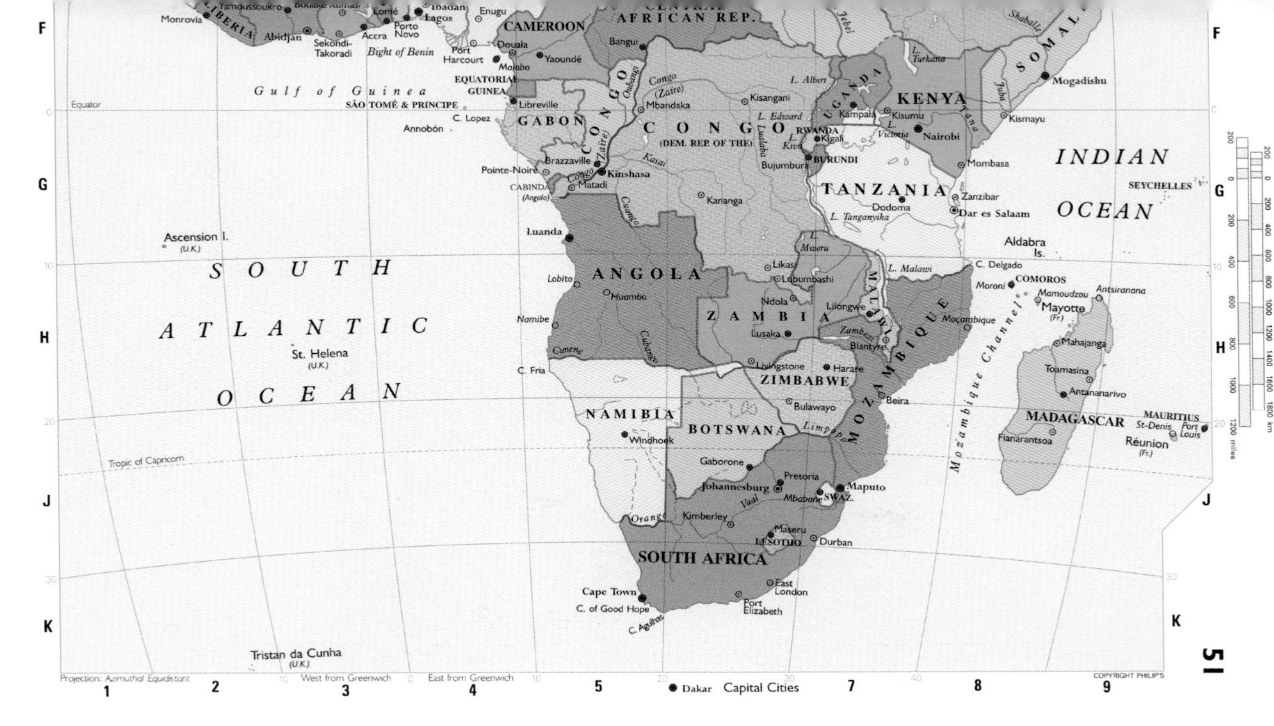

SOUTH ATLANTIC OCEAN
INDIAN OCEAN
Gulf of Guinea
Bight of Benin
Mozambique Channel
Equator
Tropic of Capricorn
LIBERIA
Monrovia
Yamoussoukro
Abidjan
Sekondi-Takoradi
Accra
Lomé
Porto Novo
Lagos
Ibadan
Enugu
Port Harcourt
CAMEROON
Douala
Yaoundé
Malabo
EQUATORIAL GUINEA
SÃO TOMÉ & PRINCIPE
Annobón
C. Lopez
GABON
Libreville
CENTRAL AFRICAN REP.
Bangui
CONGO
Brazzaville
Pointe-Noire
CABINDA (Angola)
CONGO (DEM. REP. OF THE)
Kinshasa
Matadi
Mbandaka
Kisangani
Kananga
Lubumbashi
Likasi
Congo (Zaïre)
Oubangui
Kasai
Cuango
Lualaba
L. Albert
L. Edward
L. Kivu
L. Mweru
L. Tanganyika
L. Victoria
L. Turkana
L. Malawi
UGANDA
Kampala
RWANDA
Kigali
BURUNDI
Bujumbura
KENYA
Kisumu
Nairobi
Mombasa
Tana
Jebel
SOMALIA
Mogadishu
Kismayu
Shaballe
Juba
TANZANIA
Dodoma
Zanzibar
Dar es Salaam
SEYCHELLES
Aldabra Is.
C. Delgado
COMOROS
Moroni
Mamoudzou
Mayotte (Fr.)
ANGOLA
Luanda
Lobito
Huambo
Namibe
Cubango
Cunene
C. Fria
ZAMBIA
Lusaka
Ndola
Livingstone
MALAWI
Lilongwe
Blantyre
Zambezi
MOZAMBIQUE
Moçambique
Beira
Maputo
ZIMBABWE
Harare
Bulawayo
Limpopo
NAMIBIA
Windhoek
BOTSWANA
Gaborone
SOUTH AFRICA
Pretoria
Johannesburg
Kimberley
Vaal
Orange
Durban
East London
Port Elizabeth
Cape Town
C. of Good Hope
C. Agulhas
SWAZ.
Mbabane
LESOTHO
Maseru
MADAGASCAR
Antsiranana
Mahajanga
Toamasina
Antananarivo
Fianarantsoa
MAURITIUS
Port Louis
St-Denis
Réunion (Fr.)
Ascension I. (U.K.)
St. Helena (U.K.)
Tristan da Cunha (U.K.)
Projection: Azimuthal Equidistant
West from Greenwich
East from Greenwich
Dakar Capital Cities
COPYRIGHT PHILIP'S
km
miles

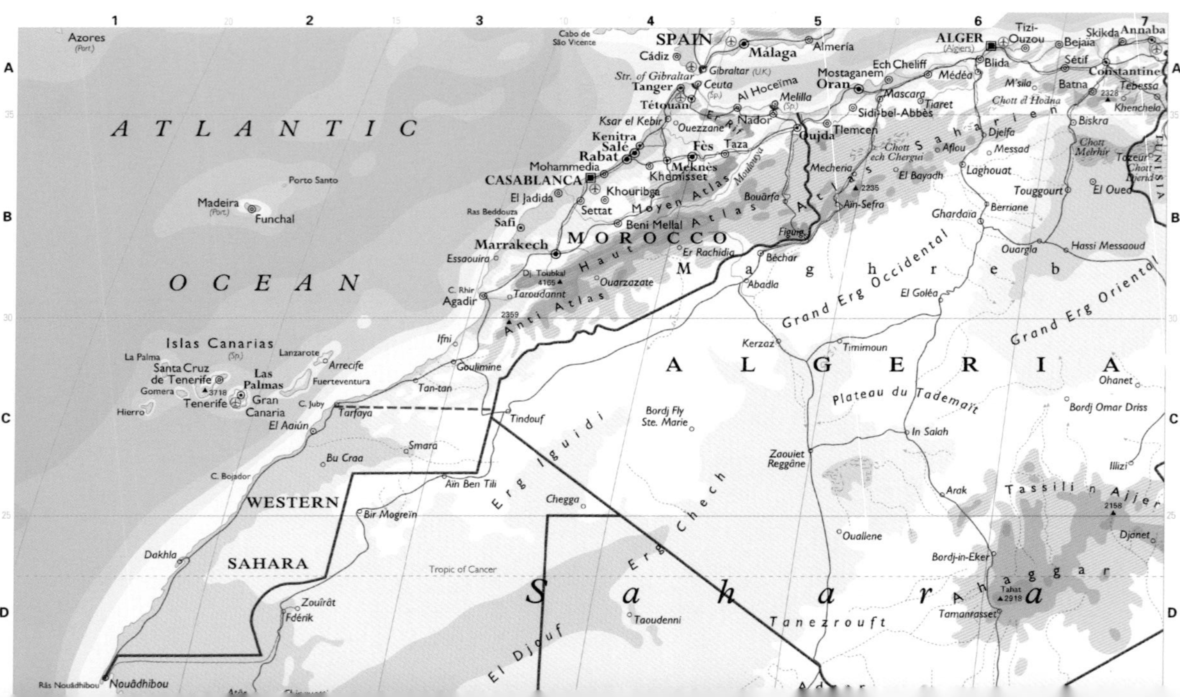

ATLANTIC
OCEAN
ALGERIA
MOROCCO
WESTERN
SAHARA
SPAIN
TUNISIA
Sahara
Azores (Port.)
Madeira (Port.)
Funchal
Porto Santo
Islas Canarias (Sp.)
La Palma
Hierro
Gomera
Santa Cruz de Tenerife
Tenerife
3718
Las Palmas
Gran Canaria
Lanzarote
Fuerteventura
Arrecife
C. Juby
C. Bojador
Dakhla
Nouâdhibou
Râs Nouâdhibou
El Aaiún
Tarfaya
Bu Craa
Smara
Tan-tan
Ifni
Goulimine
Agadir
C. Rhir
Essaouira
Ras Beddouza
Safi
El Jadida
Marrakech
CASABLANCA
Mohammedia
Rabat
Salé
Kenitra
Ksar el Kebir
Settat
Khouribga
Beni Mellal
Ouarzazate
Taroudannt
Dj. Toubkal 4165
2359
Haut Atlas
Anti Atlas
Moyen Atlas
Er Rif
Moulouya
Tanger
Tétouan
Ceuta (Sp.)
Gibraltar (U.K.)
Str. of Gibraltar
Cádiz
Málaga
Almería
Cabo de São Vicente
Ouezzane
Fès
Meknès
Khemisset
Taza
Al Hoceima
Nador
Melilla (Sp.)
Oujda
Er Rachidia
Béchar
Abadla
Figuig
Bouârfa
Oran
Mostaganem
Ech Cheliff
Tlemcen
Sidi-bel-Abbès
Mascara
Tiaret
Médéa
ALGER (Algiers)
Blida
Tizi-Ouzou
Bejaïa
Sétif
Skikda
Constantine
Annaba
Batna
Tébessa
Khenchela
2328
Biskra
M'sila
Chott el Hodna
Chott Melrhir
Chott Djerid
Tozeur
Djelfa
Messad
Laghouat
Aflou
El Bayadh
Chott ech Chergui
Atlas Saharien
Aïn-Sefra
2235
Mecheria
Ghardaïa
Berriane
Ouargla
Touggourt
El Oued
Hassi Messaoud
El Goléa
Maghreb
Grand Erg Occidental
Grand Erg Oriental
Timimoun
Kerzaz
Zaouiet Reggâne
In Salah
Plateau du Tademaït
Arak
Bordj-in-Eker
Tamanrasset
Tahat 2918
Ahaggar
Tassili n Ajjer
2158
Illizi
Djanet
Bordj Omar Driss
Ohanet
Ouallene
Tanezrouft
Bordj Fly Ste. Marie
Erg Chech
Erg Iguidi
Tindouf
Chegga
Taoudenni
Aïn Ben Tili
Bir Mogreïn
Zouîrât
Fdérik
El Djouf
Tropic of Cancer

MAURITANIA
Akjoujt
Râs Timirist
Nouakchott
Rachid
Tidjikja
Aoukâr
Aleg
Rosso
Kaédi
Kiffa
'Ayoûn el 'Atroûs
Néma
St. Louis
Dagana
Senegal
Matam
Louga
Linguère
Mboro
C. Vert
Thiès
Tivaouane
DAKAR
SENEGAL
Sélibabi
Bakel
Kayes
Kaolack
Banjul
GAMBIA
Tambacounda
Gambia
Sédhiou
Ziguinchor
GUINEA-BISSAU
Bissau
Arq. dos Bijagós
Bafoulabé
Kita
Nioro du Sahel
Nara
Didiéni
Diafarabé
Mopti
MALI
Tombouctou
Niger
Bourem
Gao
Hombori
Ménaka
Ansongo
Kidal
Adrar des Iforas
Ténéré
Arlit
Iférouâne
Aïr
1900
NIGER
Agadez
I-n-Gall
Sahel
Famalé
Filingué
Tahoua
Tanout
Zinder
Birni Nkonni
Niamey
Dosso
Maradi
Katsina
Gumel
Hadejia
Azare
Sokoto
Birnin Kebbi
Jega
Gusau
Kano
Funtua
Zaria
Dori
Tougan
Kaya
BURKINA FASO
Ouagadougou
Koudougou
Fada-n-Gourma
Botou
Gaya
Ségou
San
Bamako
Bougouni
Sikasso
Satadougou
Fouta Djalon
Siguiri
Bafing
Labé
Gaoual
GUINEA
Dalaba
Dabola
Mamou
Faranah
Kankan
Kindia
C. Verga
Dubréka
Conakry
Fabala
Kabala
1948
SIERRA LEONE
Port Loko
Yonibana
Freetown
Kissidougou
Kenema
Pendembu
Bo
Sherbro I.
Bonthe
Sulima
Monrovia
LIBERIA
Sanniquellie
Ganta
1752
Nzérékoré
Tapeta
Buchanan
River Cess
Harper
C. Palmas
Grain Coast
Bobo-Dioulasso
Gaoua
Tingrela
Odienné
Korhogo
Boundiali
Ferkéssédougou
Kong
Koro
Bouna
IVORY COAST
Séguéla
Katiola
Bouaké
Bondoukou
Man
L. de Kossou
Bouaflé
Danané
Daloa
Yamoussoukro
Gagnoa
Lakota
Divo
Adzopé
Agboville
Sassandra
ABIDJAN
Grand Bassam
San Pédro
Tabou
Ivory Coast
Berekum
Abengourou
Tumu
Black Volta
Bawku
Savelugu
Tamale
Salaga
GHANA
Wenchi
Lake Volta
Kloutu
Kumasi
Obuasi
Asamankese
Tarkwa
Axim
Sekondi-Takoradi
C. Three Points
Cape Coast
Accra
Tema
Koforidua
Gold Coast
Dapaong
Mango
TOGO
Sokodé
Savalou
Lomé
Slave Coast
Natitingou
BENIN
Kandi
Bembèrèkè
Parakou
Abomey
Cotonou
Porto-Novo
Bight of Benin
Shanga
Kontagora
Kainji Res.
NIGERIA
Kaduna
Bauchi
Jos
Bena
Minna
Kafanchan
Abuja
Shendam
Bida
Keffi
Lafia
Baro
Shaki
Ilorin
Ogbomosho
Offa
Oyo
Oshogbo
Ikare
Lokoja
Benue
Iwo
Ilesha
Owo
Makurdi
Wukari
IBADAN
Ife
Akure
Abeokuta
Ijebu-Ode
Benin City
Enugu
Oturkpo
LAGOS
Sapele
Warri
Onitsha
Burutu
Aba
Uyo
Port Harcourt
Calabar
Bamenda
CAMEROON
Bafoussam
Nkongsamba
Kumba
Mt. Cameroun
4010
Limbe
Douala
Rey Malabo
Bioko
2850
Projection : Sanson-Flamsteed's Sinusoidal
West from Greenwich
East from Greenwich
COPYRIGHT PHILIP'S
m
ft
km
miles

MEDITERRANEAN SEA
TUNISIA
LIBYA
EGYPT
GREECE
TURKEY
CYPRUS
LEBANON
ISRAEL
SYRIA
IRAQ
JORDAN
SAUDI ARABIA
RED SEA
Sahara
Bizerte
Ariana
CARTHAGE
TUNIS
Béja
Nabeul
Sousse
Kairouan
Mahdia
Sfax
Gafsa
Golfe de Gabès
Gabès
Île de Djerba
Zarzis
Médenine
Tatahouine
Dehibat
Sicilia
MALTA
Valletta
Zuwārah
Tarābulus (Tripoli)
Az Zāwiyah
Al Khums
Misrātah
Gharyān
968
Mizdah
Tripolitania
Daraj
Ghudāmis
Hūn
Surt
Khalīj Surt
Banghāzī
Suluq
Zāwiyat al Bayḍā
Al Marj
Darnah
Tubruq
Bardīyah
Ajdābiyā
Cyrenaica
Awjilah
Al Jaghbūb
Zillah
Idehan Awbārī
Brach
Sabhah
Awbārī
1200
Marzūq
Fezzan
Ghat
Wāw al Kabīr
Al Qaṭrūn
Sahrâ' Rebiana
Al Jawf
Al Kufrah
Toummo
Madama
Chirfa
Aozou
Bardai
Pic Toussidé 3265
3150 Tarso Emissi
Tibesti
Ma'ṭan as Sarra
J. Uweinat 1893
1082
Salûm
Marsâ Matrûh
El Alamein
EL ISKANDARÎYA (Alexandria)
El Mahalla el Kubra
Damanhûr
Tanta
Zagazig
Dumyât
El Mansûra
Bûr Sa'îd
Qanâ es Suweis
Ismâ'iliya
EL GÎZA
EL QÂHIRA (Cairo)
El Suweis
Helwân
El Faiyûm
Beni Suef
Maghâgha
El Minyâ
Mallawi
Manfalût
Asyût
Tahta
Sohâg
Girga
THEBES
KARNAK
Qena
El Uqsur
Idfû
Kom Ombo
Aswân
Sadd el Aali
Buheirat en Naser
ABU SIMBEL
Wadi Halfa
Kosha
Siwa
-133
Munkhafed el Qattâra
Sahrâ' Lîbîya
Qasr Farâfra
El Wâhât el-Dakhla
Mût
El Khârga
El Wâhât el-Khârga
El Wâhât el Selîma
Es Sahrâ Esh Sharqîya
Nahr en Nîl
Khalig el Suweis
Es Sinâ'
G. Mûsa 2837
2187
Hurghada
Bûr Safâga
Quseir
Bîr Shalatein
Ras Bânâs
Halaib
Ras Hadarba
Muhammad
Antalya
ADANA
Rôdhos
Irâklion
Kriti
Antakya
HALAB
Nahr al Furāt
Al Lādhiqiyah
Nicosia
Tarābulus
Ḥimş
BAYRŪT (Beirut)
DIMASHQ (Damascus)
Jabal ad Durūz 1801
Tel Aviv-Yafo
Ashdod
Hefa
Jerusalem
West Bank
'AMMĀN
Ma'ān
Elat
Al 'Aqabah
Ar Ruṭbah
Al Jawf
2578
Tabūk
Al Muwayliḥ
Al Wajh
Hijaz
Yanbu 'al Baḥr
Rābigh

SUDAN
ETHIOPIA
ERITREA
CENTRAL AFRICAN REPUBLIC
CAMEROON
El Khartûm (Khartoum)
Omdurmân
Bûr Sûdân
Kassalâ
Wâd Medanî
Gezira
Kôstî
El Obeid
Ndjamena
Maiduguri
Bangui
Yaoundé
Juba
Wâw
Lac Tchad
L. Tana
Nîl el Abyad
Nîl el Azraq
Nahr 'Atbara
Bahr el Ghazâl
Bahr el Jebel
Bahr el Arab
Oubangi
Chari
Dârfûr
Kordofân
Sûdd
El Istiwâ'iya
Jebel Marra 3088
East from Greenwich
Projection : Sanson-Flamsteed's Sinusoidal
COPYRIGHT PHILIP'S

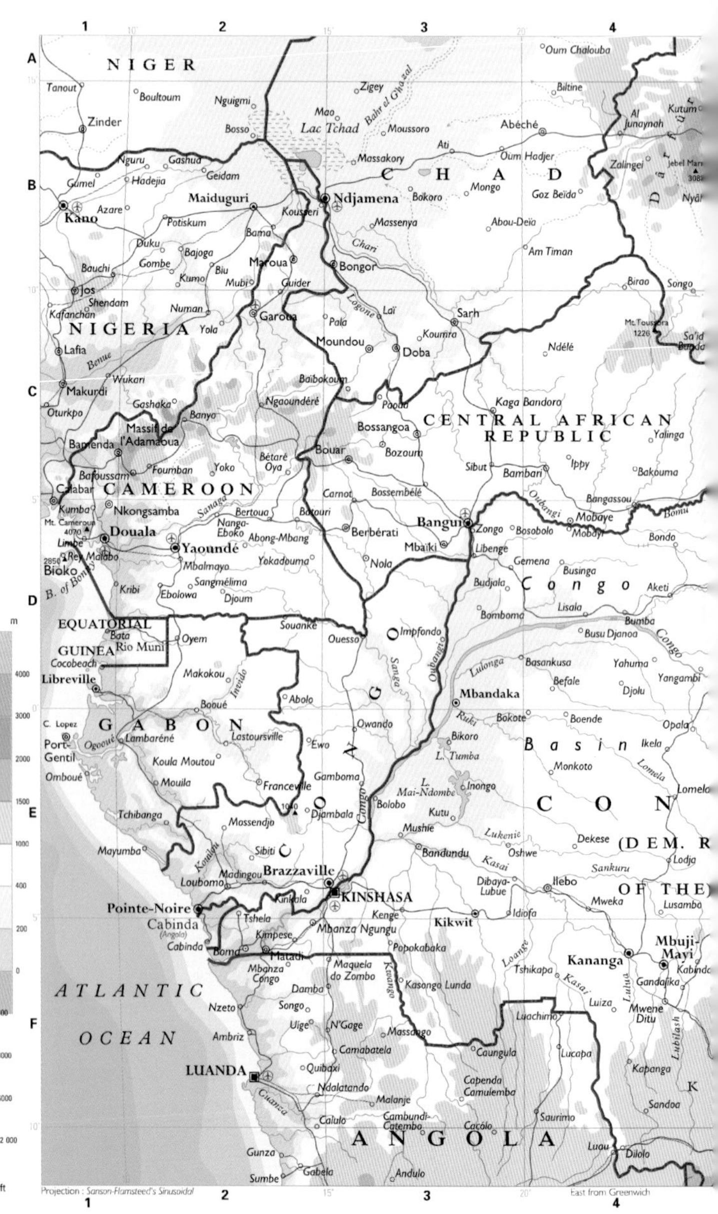

1
2
3
4
10°
15°
20°
A
B
C
D
E
F
NIGER
Oum Chalouba
Tanout
Boultoum
Zigey
Bahr el Ghazal
Biltine
Nguigmi
Mao
Zinder
Bosso
Lac Tchad
Moussoro
Abéché
Al Junaynah
Kutum
Ati
Oum Hadjer
Nguru
Gashua
Massakory
Zalingei
Jebel Marra 3088
Gumel
Hadejia
Geidam
C H A D
Mongo
Goz Beïda
Maiduguri
Ndjamena
Bokoro
Nyala
Kano
Azare
Kousseri
Potiskum
Massenya
Abou-Deïa
Dār Fūr
Bama
Duku
Chari
Bajoga
Am Timan
Gombe
Maroua
Bauchi
Biu
Bongor
Kumo
Mubi
Guider
Birao
Songo
Jos
Shendam
Logone
Laï
Numan
Garoua
Pala
Sarh
Kafanchan
NIGERIA
Yola
Mt. Toussoro 1226
Koumra
Sa'id Bundas
Moundou
Ndélé
Lafia
Doba
Benue
Wukari
Baïbokoum
Makurdi
Gashaka
Ngaoundéré
Paoua
Kaga Bandoro
Oturkpo
Banyo
CENTRAL AFRICAN REPUBLIC
Massif de l'Adamaoua
Bossangoa
Yalinga
Bamenda
Bozoum
Bétaré Oya
Bouar
Ippy
Bafoussam
Foumban
Yoko
Sibut
Bambari
Bakouma
Calabar
CAMEROON
Carnot
Bossembélé
Bangassou
Kumba
Nkongsamba
Sanaga
Bertoua
Batouri
Oubangi
Mobaye
Bomu
Mt. Cameroun 4070
Nanga-Eboko
Bangui
Zongo
Bosobolo
Mobayi
Bondo
Douala
Abong-Mbang
Berbérati
Limbe
Yaoundé
Mbaïki
Libenge
Rey Malabo
Yokadouma
Nola
Gemena
2850
Bioko
Mbalmayo
Busingo
Sangmélima
Budjala
Congo
Aketi
B. of Bonny
Kribi
Ebolowa
Djoum
Lisala
Bomboma
Bumba
EQUATORIAL GUINEA
Souanké
Impfondo
Bata
Oyem
Ouesso
Busu Djanoa
Congo
Rio Muni
Cocobeach
Lulonga
Basankusa
Yahuma
Makokou
Sanga
Oubangui
Libreville
Ivindo
Befale
Yangambi
Mbandaka
Djolu
Abolo
Booué
Ruki
Bokote
Boende
C. Lopez
GABON
Owando
Opala
Lastoursville
Bikoro
Port-Gentil
Ogooué
Lambaréné
Ewo
Basin
Ikela
L. Tumba
Koula Moutou
Monkoto
Lomela
Omboué
Mouila
Gamboma
Franceville
L. Mai-Ndombe
Inongo
Lomela
Bolobo
1040
Djambala
Kutu
CON
Tchibanga
Mossendjo
Congo
Mushie
Lukenie
Dekese
(DEM. R
Mayumba
Sibiti
Bandundu
Kasai
Oshwe
Kouilou
Lodja
Madingou
Brazzaville
Sankuru
Loubomo
Dibaya-Lubue
Ilebo
OF THE
Pointe-Noire
Kinkala
KINSHASA
Mweka
Lusambo
Cabinda (Angola)
Tshela
Kenge
Kikwit
Idiofa
Kimpese
Mbanza Ngungu
Mbuji-Mayi
Cabinda
Boma
Matadi
Popokabaka
Loange
Kananga
Kabinda
Mbanza Congo
Maquela do Zombo
Kwango
Tshikapa
Kasai
Gandajika
ATLANTIC
Damba
Kasongo Lunda
Luiza
Mwene Ditu
Nzeto
Songo
Lulua
Luachimo
Uige
N'Gage
Lubilash
Ambriz
Massango
OCEAN
Camabatela
Caungula
Lucapa
LUANDA
Quibaxi
Kapanga
Ndalatando
Capenda Camulemba
K
Cuanza
Malanje
Sandoa
Calulo
Cambundi-Catembo
Cacólo
Saurimo
ANGOLA
Luau
Dilolo
Gunza
Gabela
Andulo
Sumbe
ft
m
12 000
4000
9000
3000
6000
2000
4500
1500
3000
1000
1200
400
600
200
0
0
200
600
1000
3000
2000
6000
4000
12 000
m
ft
Projection : Sanson-Flamsteed's Sinusoidal
East from Greenwich

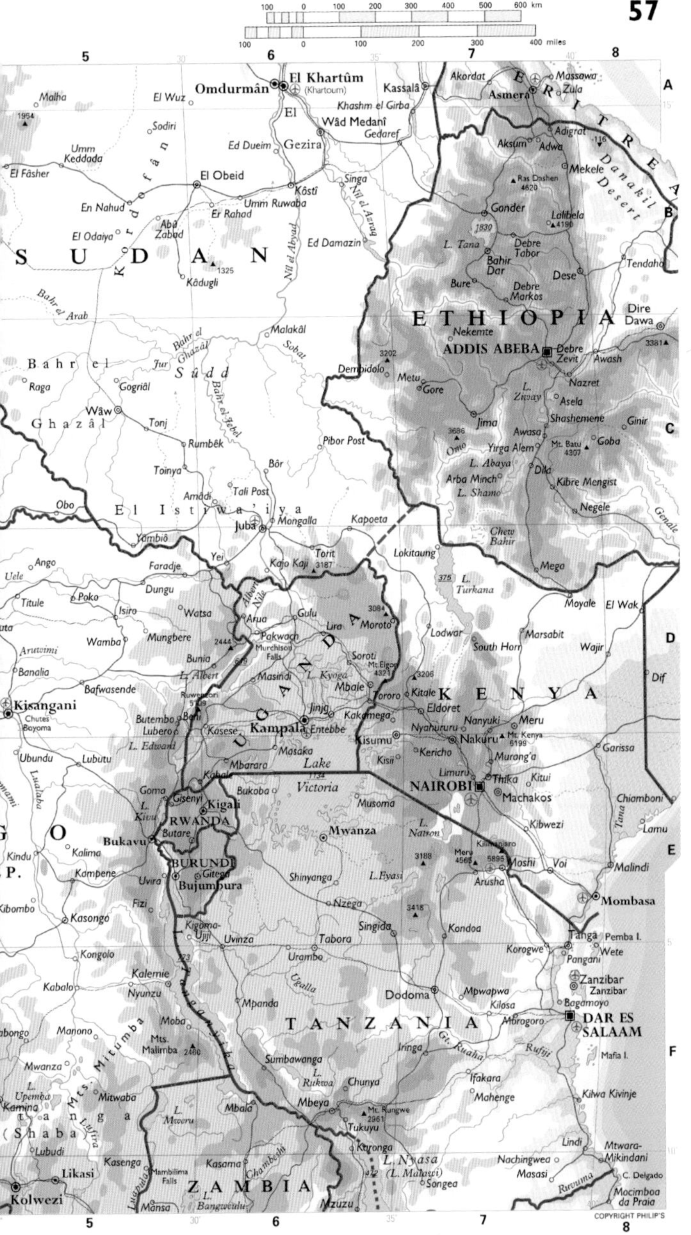

El Khartûm
Omdurmân
Kassalâ
Asmera
Massawa
Zula
ERITREA
Wâd Medanî
Gedaref
Gezira
El Obeid
Kôstî
El Fâsher
Umm Keddada
En Nahud
Kordofân
SUDAN
Ed Damazin
Kâdugli
Gonder
Lalibela
Ras Dashen 4620
Mekele
Aksum
Adwa
Adigrat
Danakil Desert
L. Tana
Bahir Dar
Debre Tabor
Dese
Debre Markos
Tendaho
ETHIOPIA
Dire Dawa
ADDIS ABEBA
Nekemte
Awash
Nazret
Asela
Shashemene
Jima
Gore
Metu
Dembidolo
Malakâl
Sobat
Bahr el Arab
Bahr el Ghazâl
Sûdd
Raga
Gogriâl
Wâw
Tonj
Rumbêk
Bahr el Jebel
Pibor Post
Bôr
Tali Post
Juba
Mongalla
Kapoeta
El Istywa'iya
Yambiô
Yei
Torit
Kajo Kaji
Lokitaung
L. Turkana
Chew Bahir
Mega
Moyale
El Wak
Marsabit
Wajir
Lodwar
South Horr
KENYA
Kitale
Eldoret
Nanyuki
Meru
Mt. Kenya 5199
Nakuru
Nyahururu
Kisumu
Kericho
Kisii
Murang'a
Thika
Kitui
NAIROBI
Machakos
Garissa
Kibwezi
Voi
Malindi
Mombasa
Kilimanjaro 5895
Moshi
Arusha
UGANDA
Gulu
Lira
Moroto
Arua
Pakwach
Murchison Falls
Soroti
Mt. Elgon 4321
Mbale
Tororo
Jinja
Kakamega
Kampala
Entebbe
Masindi
L. Kyoga
L. Albert
Bunia
Ruwenzori 5109
Beni
Butembo
Lubero
Kasese
L. Edward
Mbarara
Masaka
Kabale
Lake Victoria
Bukoba
Musoma
Mwanza
RWANDA
Kigali
Gisenyi
Goma
L. Kivu
Butare
Bukavu
BURUNDI
Gitega
Bujumbura
Uvira
Kisangani
Chutes Boyoma
Ubundu
Lubutu
Kindu
Kalima
Kampene
Kasongo
Kongolo
Kabalo
Kalemie
Nyunzu
Kigoma-Ujiji
Uvinza
Tabora
Urambo
Shinyanga
Nzega
Singida
Kondoa
Dodoma
Mpwapwa
Kilosa
Morogoro
DAR ES SALAAM
Bagamoyo
Zanzibar
Pemba I.
Wete
Pangani
Tanga
Korogwe
TANZANIA
Mpanda
Sumbawanga
L. Rukwa
Chunya
Mbeya
Iringa
Ifakara
Mahenge
Kilwa Kivinje
Mafia I.
Lindi
Mtwara-Mikindani
Nachingwea
Masasi
C. Delgado
Mocimboa da Praia
Tukuyu
Mt. Rungwe 2961
Karonga
L. Nyasa (L. Malawi)
Songea
Mzuzu
ZAMBIA
Kasama
Mansa
L. Bangweulu
Mambilima Falls
Kasenga
Likasi
Kolwezi
Lubudi
Shaba
Mitwaba
L. Mweru
Mbala
Mts. Mitumba
Mts. Malimba 2460
Moba
Manono
Kabongo
Mwanza
L. Upemba
Kamina
Kibombo
Fizi
Isiro
Watsa
Dungu
Faradje
Poko
Titule
Ango
Uele
Wamba
Mungbere
Banalia
Aruwimi
Bafwasende
Obo
Malha
El Wuz
Sodiri
Ed Dueim
Singa
Nil el Azraq
Nil el Abyad
Er Rahad
Umm Ruwaba
Abu Zabad
El Odaiya
Khashm el Girba
Akordat
Awasa
Yirga Alem
Dila
L. Abaya
Arba Minch
L. Shamo
Kibre Mengist
Negele
Goba
Ginir
Mt. Batu 4307
Genale
Tana
Chiamboni
Lamu
Dif
L. Natron
Meru 4565
L. Eyasi
Ugalla
Gt. Ruaha
Rufiji
Ruvuma
Chambeshi
Luapula
Lufira
Lualaba
COPYRIGHT PHILIP'S

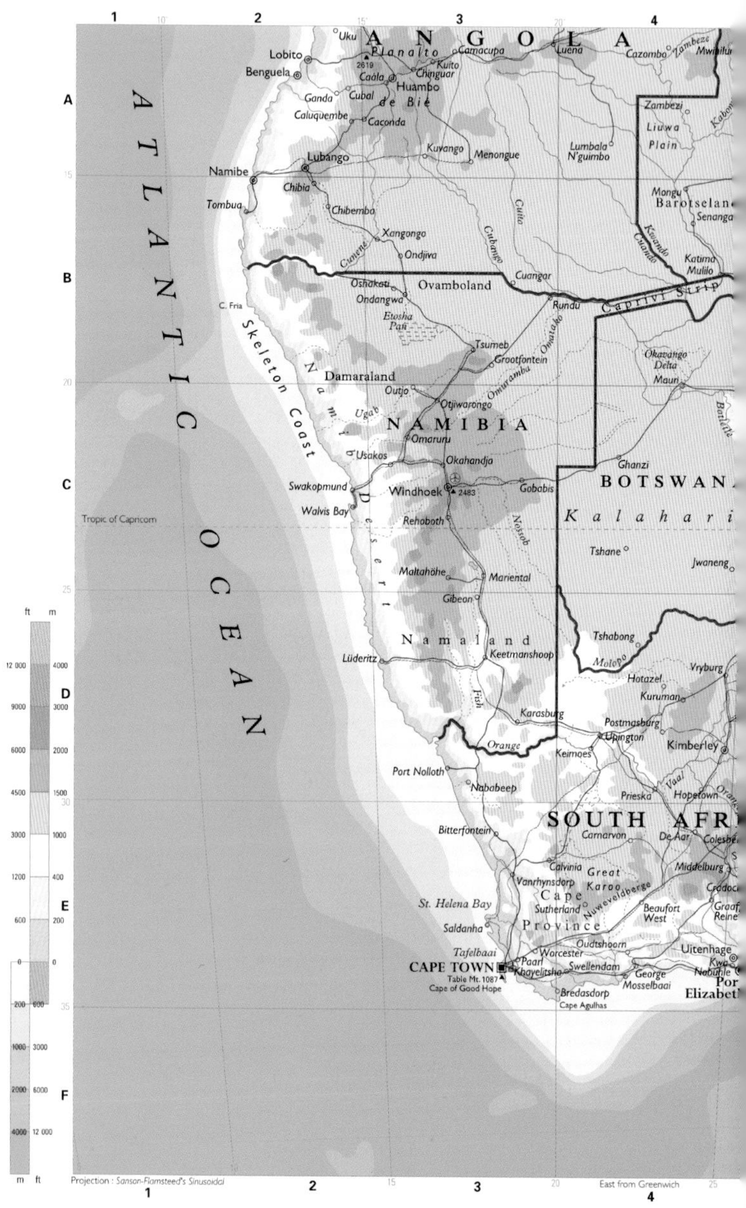
ANGOLA
Lobito
Benguela
Planalto
Camacupa
Luena
Cazombo
Zambeze
Kuito
Caála
Chinguar
Huambo
de Bié
Ganda
Cubal
Caluquembe
Caconda
Kuvango
Menongue
Lumbala N'guimbo
Zambezi
Liuwa Plain
Lubango
Namibe
Chibia
Tombua
Chibembo
Mongu
Senanga
Xangongo
Ondjiva
Cunene
Cubango
Cuito
Kwando
Cuando
Katima Mulilo
Oshakati
Ondangwa
Ovamboland
Cuangar
Rundu
Caprivi Strip
C. Fria
Etosha Pan
Skeleton Coast
Tsumeb
Grootfontein
Omatako
Omuramba
Okavango Delta
Maun
Damaraland
Outjo
Otjiwarongo
Ugab
NAMIBIA
Omaruru
Usakos
Okahandja
Ghanzi
BOTSWANA
Swakopmund
Windhoek
2483
Gobabis
Walvis Bay
Rehoboth
Tropic of Capricorn
Kalahari
Tshane
Nossob
Jwaneng
Namib Desert
Maltahöhe
Mariental
Gibeon
ATLANTIC OCEAN
Namaland
Tshabong
Lüderitz
Keetmanshoop
Molopo
Vryburg
Hotazel
Kuruman
Fish
Karasburg
Postmasburg
Upington
Kimberley
Orange
Keimoes
Port Nolloth
Nababeep
Vaal
Prieska
Hopetown
SOUTH AFR
Bitterfontein
Carnarvon
De Aar
Calvinia
Great Karoo
Middelburg
Vanrhynsdorp
Cape Province
Nuweveldberge
St. Helena Bay
Sutherland
Beaufort West
Saldanha
Oudtshoorn
Tafelbaai
Worcester
Uitenhage
CAPE TOWN
Paarl
Swellendam
Khayelitsha
George
Mosselbaai
Table Mt. 1087
Cape of Good Hope
Bredasdorp
Cape Agulhas
ft
m
12 000
4000
9000
3000
6000
2000
4500
1500
1000
1200
400
600
200
0
3000
Projection : Sanson-Flamsteed's Sinusoidal
East from Greenwich

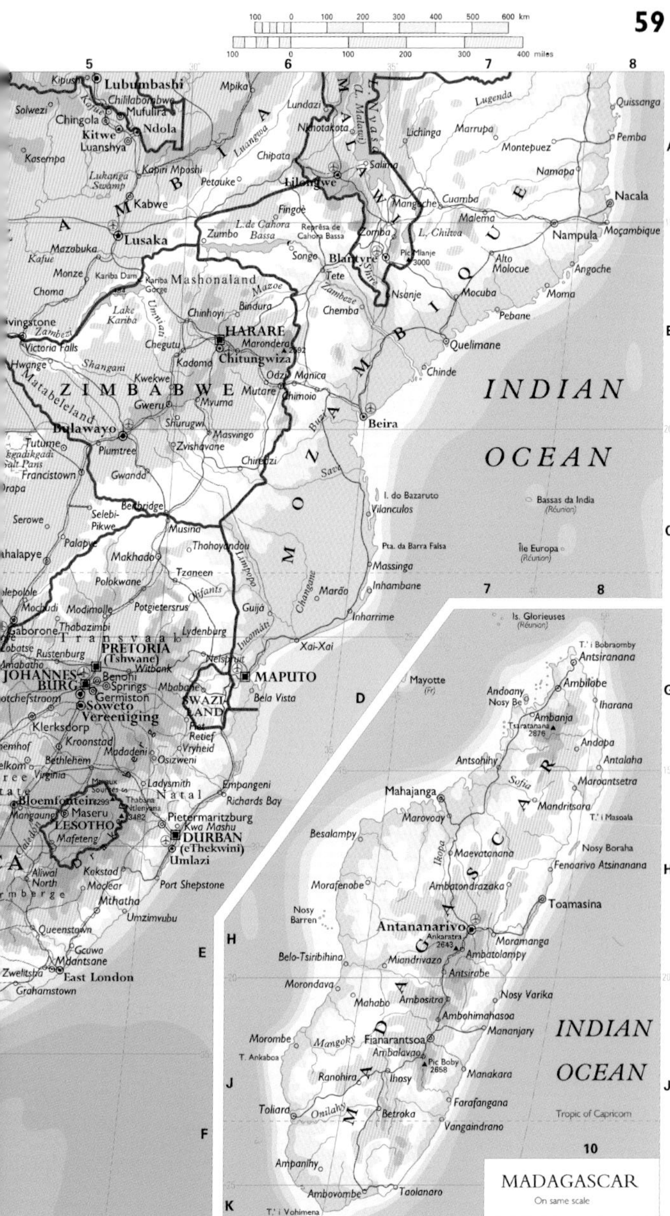
INDIAN OCEAN
ZIMBABWE
MOZAMBIQUE
MALAWI
ZAMBIA
LESOTHO
SWAZILAND
MADAGASCAR
Lubumbashi
Ndola
Kitwe
Lusaka
HARARE
Bulawayo
Lilongwe
Blantyre
Nampula
Beira
Quelimane
MAPUTO
PRETORIA (Tshwane)
JOHANNESBURG
DURBAN (eThekwini)
Pietermaritzburg
East London
Maseru
Antananarivo
Toamasina
Mahajanga
Fianarantsoa
Toliara
Antsiranana
Tropic of Capricorn
MADAGASCAR
On same scale
COPYRIGHT PHILIP'S

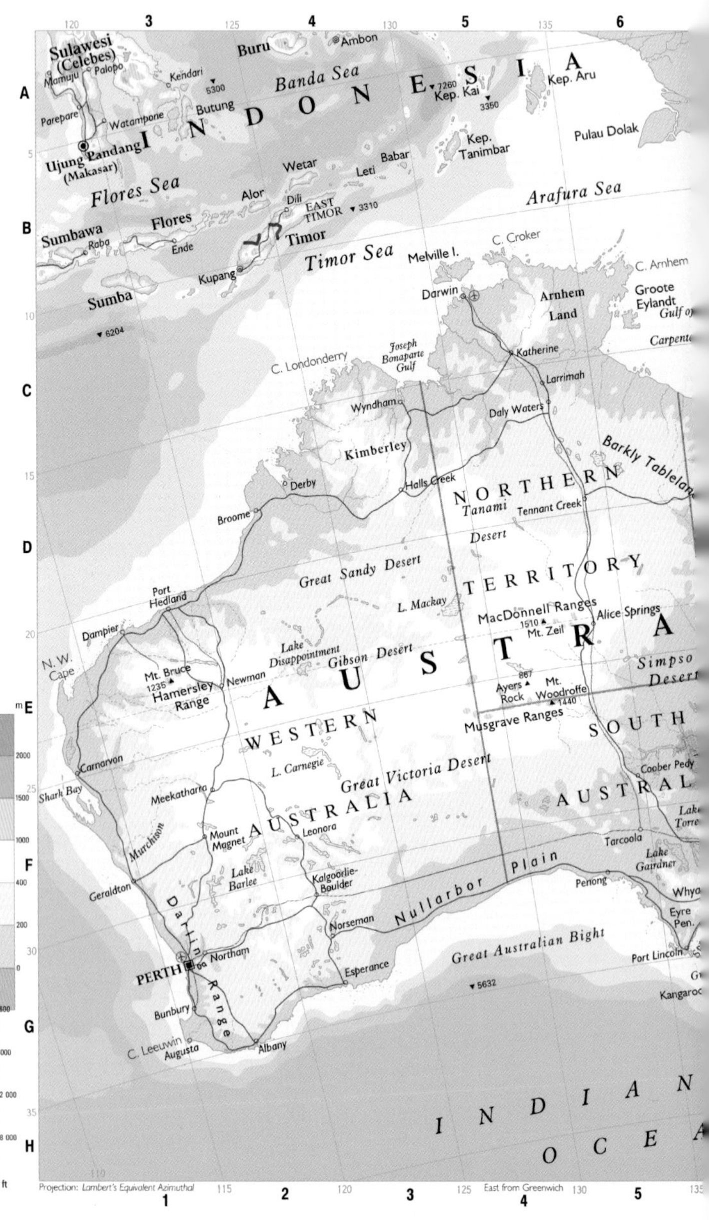
Sulawesi (Celebes)
Mamuju
Palopo
Parepare
Watampone
Ujung Pandang (Makasar)
Kendari
Butung
Buru
Ambon
Banda Sea
INDONESIA
Kep. Kai
Kep. Aru
Kep. Tanimbar
Pulau Dolak
Flores Sea
Wetar
Leti
Babar
Alor
Dili
EAST TIMOR
Arafura Sea
Sumbawa
Raba
Flores
Ende
Timor
Timor Sea
Kupang
Sumba
Melville I.
C. Croker
C. Arnhem
Darwin
Arnhem Land
Groote Eylandt
Gulf of Carpentaria
Joseph Bonaparte Gulf
C. Londonderry
Katherine
Larrimah
Wyndham
Daly Waters
Kimberley
Barkly Tableland
Derby
Halls Creek
NORTHERN TERRITORY
Tanami Desert
Tennant Creek
Broome
Great Sandy Desert
Port Hedland
L. Mackay
MacDonnell Ranges
Alice Springs
Mt. Zeil
Dampier
N. W. Cape
Lake Disappointment
Gibson Desert
AUSTRALIA
Simpson Desert
Mt. Bruce
Hamersley Range
Newman
Ayers Rock
Mt. Woodroffe
Musgrave Ranges
WESTERN AUSTRALIA
SOUTH AUSTRALIA
L. Carnegie
Carnarvon
Great Victoria Desert
Coober Pedy
Shark Bay
Meekatharra
Lake Torrens
Murchison
Mount Magnet
Leonora
Tarcoola
Lake Gairdner
Lake Barlee
Kalgoorlie-Boulder
Nullarbor Plain
Penong
Geraldton
Whyalla
Eyre Pen.
Darling Range
Norseman
Great Australian Bight
Northam
PERTH
Esperance
Port Lincoln
Kangaroo
Bunbury
C. Leeuwin
Augusta
Albany
INDIAN OCEAN
Projection: Lambert's Equivalent Azimuthal
East from Greenwich

PAPUA NEW GUINEA
New Guinea
Mount Hagen
Mt. Wilhelm
Lae
New Britain
Solomon Sea
Bougainville
Mt. Balbi
SOLOMON ISLANDS
Choiseul
Santa Isabel
New Georgia
Malaita
Honiara
Guadalcanal
San Cristóbal
Rennell
Fly
Gulf of Papua
Owen Stanley Range
Port Moresby
D'Entrecasteaux Islands
Louisiade Archipelago
Torres Strait
C. York
Weipa
Cape York Peninsula
Great Barrier Reef
Coral Sea
PACIFIC OCEAN
CORAL SEA ISLANDS TERRITORY
Îles D'Entrecasteaux
Îles Chesterfield
Tropic of Capricorn
Cooktown
Wellesley Is.
Mitchell
Cairns
Normanton
Forsayth
Flinders
Townsville
Charters Towers
Mackay
Cloncurry
Hughenden
Dajarra
Winton
Great Dividing Range
QUEENSLAND
Emerald
Rockhampton
Gladstone
Longreach
AUSTRALIA
Bundaberg
Yaraka
Diamantina
Maryborough
Gympie
Charleville
Roma
Grey Range
Quilpie
BRISBANE
Toowoomba
Ipswich
Gold Coast
Cooper Creek
Cunnamulla
Thargomindah
Dirranbandi
Lismore
Lake Eyre
Moree
Grafton
Walgett
Bourke
Marree
Tamworth
Round Mt.
Port Macquarie
Flinders Ranges
NEW SOUTH WALES
Taree
Lord Howe I. (Austral.)
Broken Hill
Cobar
Dubbo
Darling
Port Augusta
Newcastle
Bathurst
Orange
SYDNEY
Port Pirie
Murray
Mildura
Griffith
Wollongong
Hay
Goulburn
ADELAIDE
Wagga Wagga
Canberra
A.C.T.
Tasman Sea
Swan Hill
Mt. Kosciuszko
Shepparton
Albury-Wodonga
Snowy Mts.
Bendigo
Bombala
Encounter B.
Horsham
VICTORIA
C. Howe
Ballarat
MELBOURNE
Sale
Mount Gambier
Geelong
Warrnambool
Bass Strait
King I.
Furneaux Group
Burnie
Launceston
Mt. Ossa
TASMANIA
Hobart
S.E.Cape

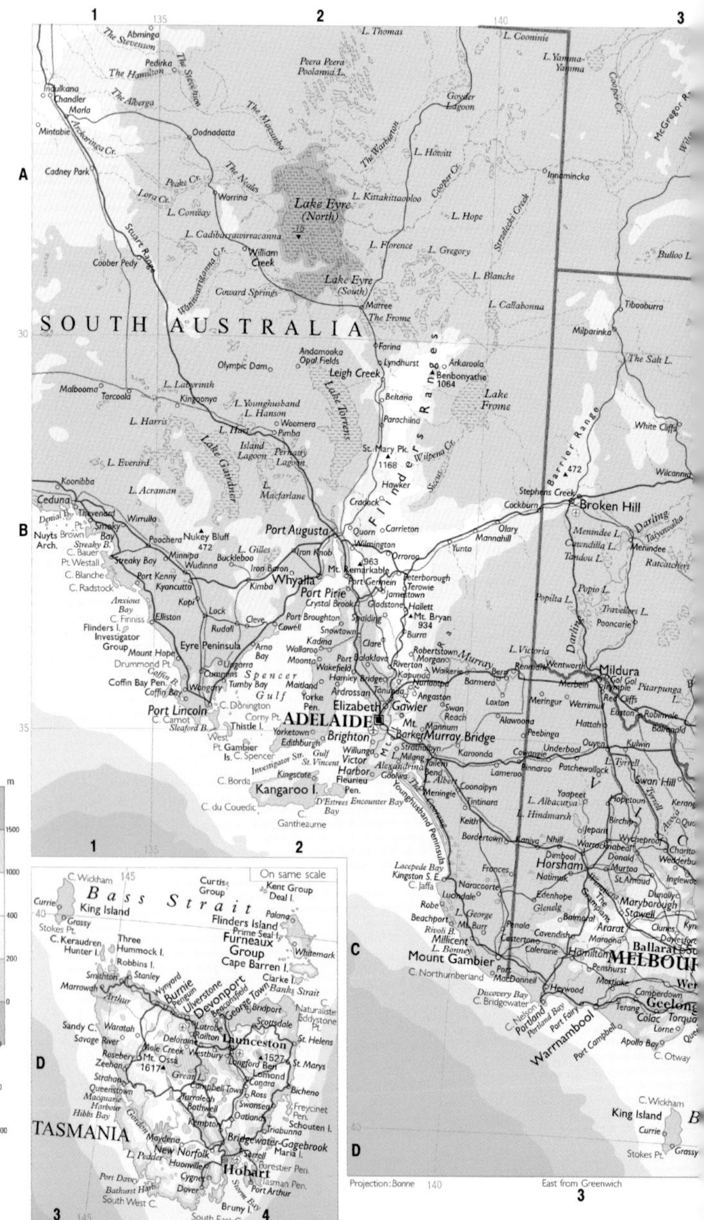
SOUTH AUSTRALIA
Abminga
The Stevenson
Pedirka
The Hamilton
Indulkana
Chandler
Marla
The Alberga
Mintabie
Oodnadatta
The Macumba
Arckaringa Cr.
Cadney Park
Peake Cr.
The Neales
Warrina
Lake Eyre (North)
Lora Cr.
L. Conway
L. Cadibarrawirracanna
William Creek
Coober Pedy
Stuart Range
Coward Springs
Lake Eyre (South)
L. Thomas
Peera Peera Poolanna L.
Goyder Lagoon
The Warburton
L. Howitt
Cooper Cr.
Innamincka
L. Kittakittaooloo
L. Hope
Strzelecki Creek
L. Florence
L. Gregory
L. Blanche
L. Callabonna
Marree
The Frome
L. Coonnie
L. Yamma-Yamma
Cooper Cr.
McGregor R.
Bulloo L.
Tibooburra
Milparinka
The Salt L.
Farina
Lyndhurst
Arkaroola
Benbonyathe 1064
Andamooka Opal Fields
Olympic Dam
Leigh Creek
Lake Torrens
Beltana
Parachilna
Lake Frome
Flinders Ranges
Malbooma
Tarcoola
L. Labyrinth
Kingoonya
L. Younghusband
L. Hanson
Woomera
Pimba
L. Harris
L. Hart
Lake Gairdner
Island Lagoon
Pernatty Lagoon
St. Mary Pk. 1168
Wilpena Cr.
L. Everard
Koonibba
L. Acraman
L. Macfarlane
Hawker
Cradock
White Cliffs
Barrier Range
472
Wilcannia
Stephens Creek
Cockburn
Broken Hill
Ceduna
Denial B.
Thevenard
Smoky Bay
Wirrulla
Nuyts Arch.
Pt. Brown
Streaky B.
C. Bauer
Pt. Westall
Poochera
Nukey Bluff 472
Port Augusta
Quorn
Carrieton
Olary
Mannahill
Yunta
Darling
Menindee L.
Cawndilla L.
Menindee
Tandou L.
Talyawalka
Ratcatchers
Streaky Bay
Minnipa
Wudinna
L. Gilles
Buckleboo
Iron Knob
Wilmington
Orroroo
963
Mt. Remarkable
C. Blanche
C. Radstock
Port Kenny
Kyancutta
Iron Baron
Whyalla
Kimba
Port Germein
Peterborough
Terowie
Jamestown
Popilta L.
Popio L.
Anxious Bay
C. Finniss
Elliston
Kopi
Lock
Port Pirie
Crystal Brook
Gladstone
Hallett
Mt. Bryan 934
Travellers L.
Pooncarie
Flinders I.
Investigator Group
Rudall
Cleve
Cowell
Port Broughton
Snowtown
Spalding
Burra
Mount Hope
Drummond Pt.
Eyre Peninsula
Arno Bay
Kadina
Wallaroo
Moonta
Clare
Port Wakefield
Balaklava
Robertstown
Morgan
Riverton
L. Victoria
Renmark
Wentworth
Mildura
Coffin Bay Pen.
Coffin B.
Coffin Bay
Ungarra
Cummins
Wanggary
Tumby Bay
Spencer Gulf
Maitland
Hamley Bridge
Kapunda
Waikerie
Murray
Berri
Barmera
Nuriootpa
Merbein
Gol Gol
Irymple
Red Cliffs
Pitarpunga L.
Yorke Pen.
Ardrossan
Angaston
Loxton
Meringur
Werrimull
Port Lincoln
C. Donington
Corny Pt.
C. Catastrophe
Sleaford B.
Thistle I.
ADELAIDE
Elizabeth
Gawler
Swan Reach
Mt. Mannum
Alawoona
Hattah
Euston
Robinvale
Balranald
Yorketown
Edithburgh
West Pt.
Gambier Is.
C. Spencer
Brighton
Mt. Barker
Murray Bridge
Peebinga
Ouyen
Kulwin
Willunga
Victor Harbor
Investigator Str.
Gulf St. Vincent
Strathalbyn
L. Milang
Alexandrina
Karoonda
Underbool
Cowangie
Pinnaroo
Patchewollock
Lameroo
L. Tyrrell
Swan Hill
Tyrrell
Kingscote
C. Borda
Kangaroo I.
Fleurieu Pen.
Goolwa
Tailem Bend
L. Albert
Meningie
Coonalpyn
Tintinara
Yaapeet
L. Albacutya
L. Hindmarsh
Hopetoun
Birchip
Kerang
Avoca
C. du Couedic
D'Estrees Bay
Encounter Bay
C. Gantheaume
Younghusband Peninsula
The Coorong
Keith
Bordertown
Kaniva
Nhill
Jeparit
Warracknabeal
Wycheproof
Charlton
Wedderburn
Dimboola
Donald
Horsham
Murtoa
St. Arnaud
Inglewood
Lacepede Bay
Kingston S.E.
C. Jaffa
Frances
Natimuk
Naracoorte
Lucindale
Robe
Edenhope
Glenelg
The Grampians
Dunolly
Maryborough
Stawell
Beachport
L. George
Mt. Burr
Rivoli B.
Millicent
L. Bonney
Penola
Casterton
Coleraine
Cavendish
Balmoral
Ararat
Maroona
Clunes
Kyneton
Daylesford
Ballarat
Mount Gambier
C. Northumberland
Port MacDonnell
Hamilton
Penshurst
MELBOURNE
Mortlake
Werribee
Discovery Bay
C. Bridgewater
C. Nelson
Portland
Portland Bay
Heywood
Port Fairy
Warrnambool
Camperdown
Terang
Geelong
Colac
Torquay
Lorne
Port Campbell
Apollo Bay
C. Otway
C. Wickham
King Island
Currie
Grassy
Stokes Pt.
Bass Strait
1
2
3
A
B
C
D
135
140
30
35
40
On same scale
C. Wickham
145
Curtis Group
Kent Group
Deal I.
Currie
King Island
Grassy
Stokes Pt.
Flinders Island
Palana
Prime Seal I.
Furneaux Group
Whitemark
C. Keraudren
Hunter I.
Three Hummock I.
Robbins I.
Cape Barren I.
Clarke I.
Banks Strait
Smithton
Stanley
Wynyard
Burnie
Penguin
Ulverstone
Devonport
Beaconsfield
George Town
Marrawah
Arthur
Bridport
C. Naturaliste
Eddystone Pt.
Sandy C.
Waratah
Savage River
Latrobe
Railton
Deloraine
Mole Creek
Launceston
Scottsdale
St. Helens
Rosebery
Mt. Ossa 1617
Westbury
1527
Ben Lomond
Longford
St. Marys
Zeehan
Strahan
Great L.
Campbell Town
Conara
Queenstown
Macquarie Harbour
Tarraleah
Ross
Bicheno
Hibbs Bay
Gordon
Bothwell
Swansea
Freycinet Pen.
Oatlands
TASMANIA
Kempton
Triabunna
Schouten I.
Maydena
New Norfolk
Bridgewater-Gagebrook
Maria I.
L. Pedder
Huonville
Sorell
Forestier Pen.
Port Davey
Bathurst Harb.
Cygnet
Hobart
Dover
Tasman Pen.
Port Arthur
South West C.
Storm Bay
Bruny I.
South East C.
ft
m
4500
1500
3000
1000
1200
400
600
200
0
0
200
600
2000
6000
4000
12 000
m
ft
Projection: Bonne
East from Greenwich

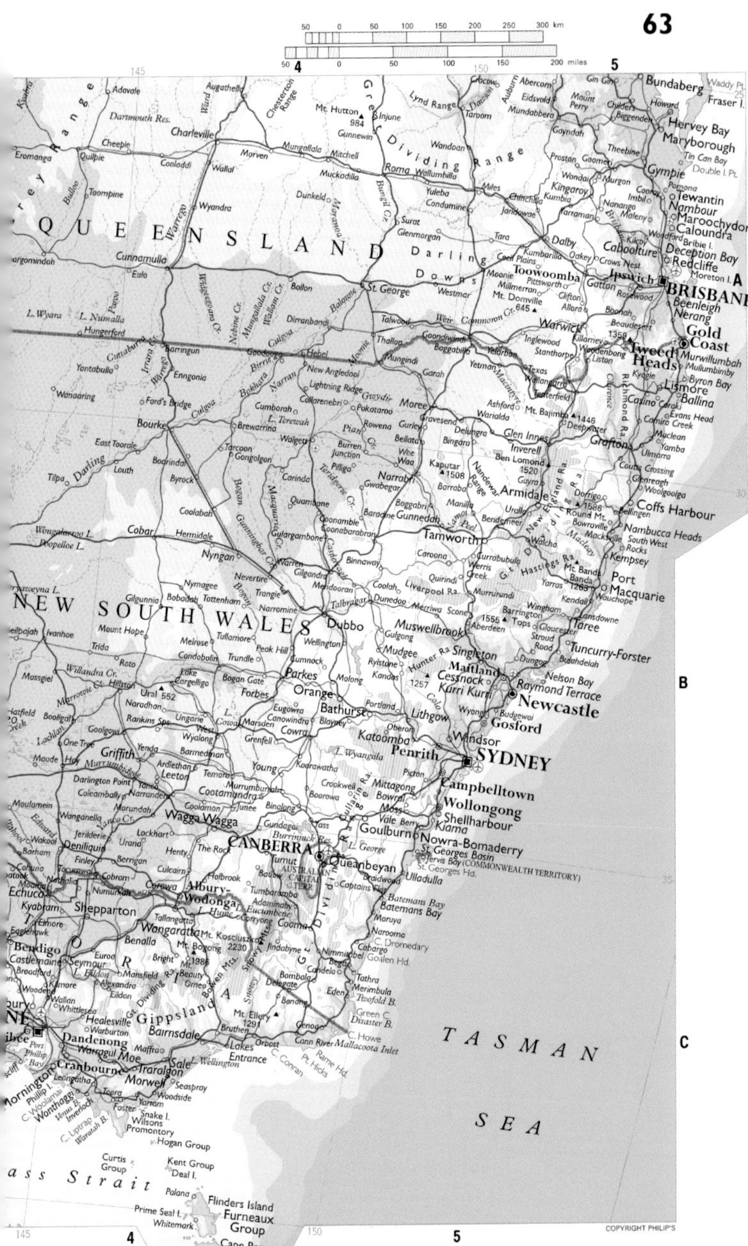
50 0 50 100 150 200 250 300 km
50 0 50 100 150 200 miles
4
5
145
150
A
B
C
QUEENSLAND
NEW SOUTH WALES
TASMAN SEA
Bass Strait
Great Dividing Range
Darling Downs
Bundaberg
Fraser I.
Hervey Bay
Maryborough
Gympie
Tewantin
Nambour
Maroochydore
Caloundra
Caboolture
Deception Bay
Redcliffe
Moreton I.
Ipswich
BRISBANE
Beenleigh
Nerang
Gold Coast
Tweed Heads
Murwillumbah
Mullumbimby
Byron Bay
Lismore
Ballina
Casino
Evans Head
Grafton
Yamba
Coffs Harbour
Nambucca Heads
South West Rocks
Kempsey
Port Macquarie
Wauchope
Taree
Tuncurry-Forster
Nelson Bay
Raymond Terrace
Newcastle
Maitland
Cessnock
Kurri Kurri
Singleton
Muswellbrook
Gosford
Windsor
Penrith
Katoomba
Lithgow
SYDNEY
Campbelltown
Wollongong
Shellharbour
Kiama
Nowra-Bomaderry
Goulburn
CANBERRA
Queanbeyan
AUSTRALIAN CAPITAL TERR.
Ulladulla
Batemans Bay
Moruya
Narooma
Bega
Eden
Cooma
Jindabyne
Mt. Kosciuszko 2230
Toowoomba
Dalby
Warwick
Stanthorpe
Tenterfield
Glen Innes
Inverell
Armidale
Tamworth
Gunnedah
Narrabri
Moree
Walgett
Dubbo
Orange
Bathurst
Parkes
Forbes
Cowra
Young
Wagga Wagga
Griffith
Leeton
Narrandera
Deniliquin
Albury-Wodonga
Wangaratta
Shepparton
Echuca
Bendigo
Seymour
Benalla
Dandenong
Cranbourne
Mornington
Moe
Traralgon
Morwell
Sale
Bairnsdale
Lakes Entrance
Gippsland
Wilsons Promontory
Bourke
Cobar
Nyngan
Charleville
Cunnamulla
St. George
Roma
Goondiwindi
Flinders Island
Furneaux Group
Cape Barren I.
Clarke I.
Banks Strait
COPYRIGHT PHILIP'S

NEW ZEALAND, CENTRAL AND SOUTH-WEST PACIFIC

PACIFIC OCEAN

North Island

Bay of Plenty

AUCKLAND

Hamilton

Whangarei

Rotorua

Gisborne

Napier

Hastings

New Plymouth

Wanganui

Palmerston North

Hawke Bay

Hauraki Gulf

North Taranaki Bight

South Taranaki Bight

Great Barrier I.

Northland

SOUTH-WEST PACIFIC

0 250 500 750 1000 km

0 250 500 750 miles

Projection : Mollweide's Homolographic

Micronesia

Melanesia

MARSHALL IS.

FEDERATED STATES OF MICRONESIA

NORTHERN MARIANAS (U.S.A.)

Caroline Is.

KIRIBATI

NAURU

TUVALU

SOLOMON IS.

VANUATU

FIJI

NEW CALEDONIA (Fr.)

Is. Wallis & Futuna (Fr.)

PAPUA NEW GUINEA

Coral Sea

AUSTRALIA

NEW ZEALAND

Tropic of Capricorn

International Dateline

Great Dividing Ra.

Brisbane

Auckland

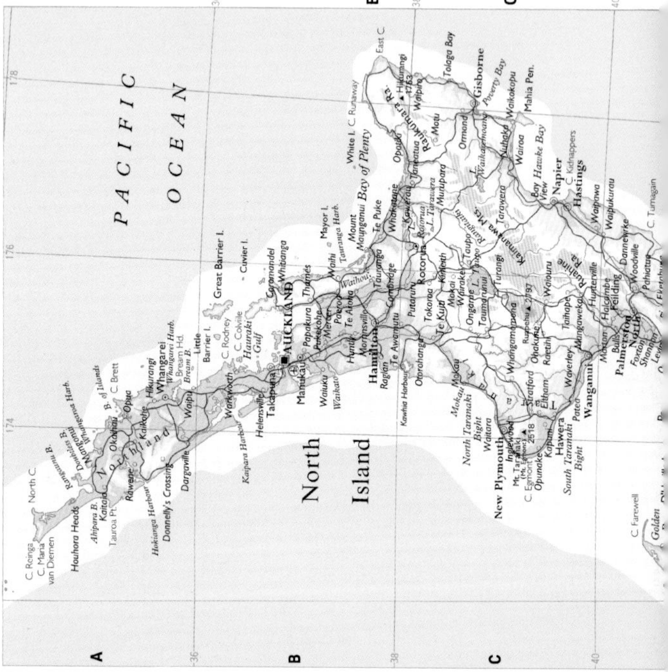

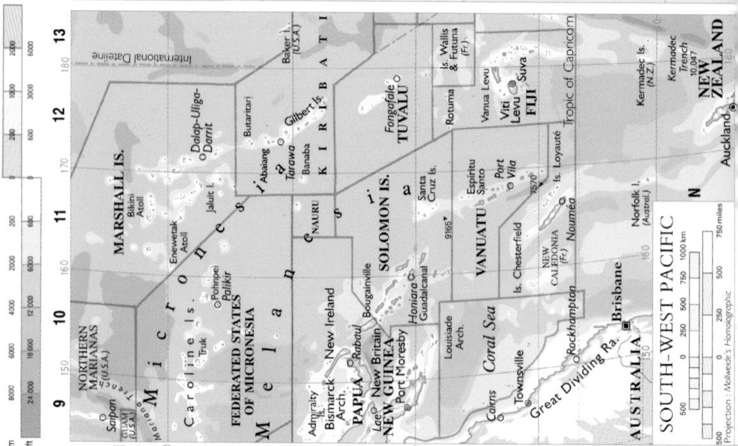

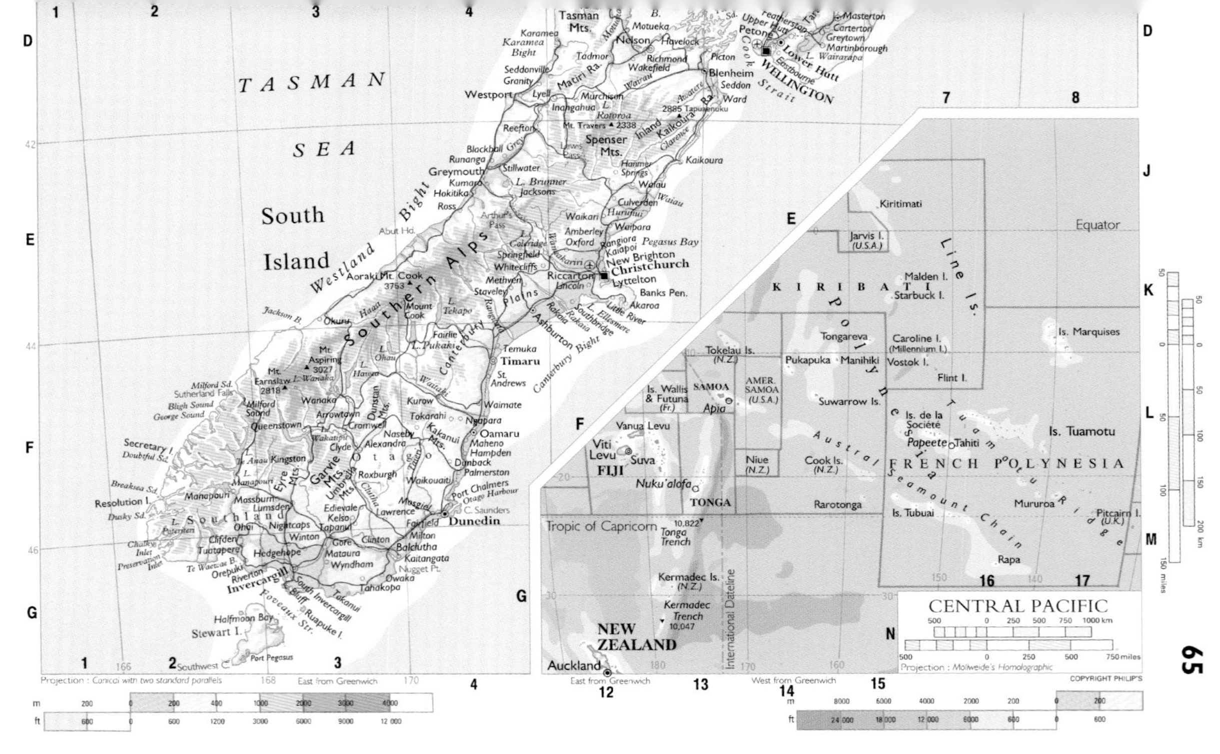
TASMAN SEA
South Island
Southern Alps
Westland Bight
Canterbury Plains
Canterbury Bight
Otago
Southland
Christchurch
WELLINGTON
Cook Strait
Dunedin
Invercargill
Timaru
Nelson
Blenheim
Greymouth
Westport
Hokitika
Oamaru
Queenstown
Lower Hutt
Aoraki Mt. Cook 3753
Mt. Aspiring 3027
Mt. Earnslaw 2818
Spenser Mts.
Tasman Mts.
Stewart I.
Foveaux Str.
Ruapuke I.
Resolution I.
Secretary I.
Milford Sound
Banks Pen.
Pegasus Bay
Kaikoura
Projection : Conical with two standard parallels
East from Greenwich
CENTRAL PACIFIC
Projection : Mollweide's Homolographic
West from Greenwich
Equator
Tropic of Capricorn
International Dateline
KIRIBATI
Line Is.
Kiritimati
Jarvis I. (U.S.A.)
Malden I.
Starbuck I.
Caroline I. (Millennium I.)
Vostok I.
Flint I.
Is. Marquises
Polynesia
Tongareva
Pukapuka
Manihiki
Suwarrow Is.
Tokelau Is. (N.Z.)
SAMOA
Apia
AMER. SAMOA (U.S.A.)
Is. Wallis & Futuna (Fr.)
Vanua Levu
Viti Levu
Suva
FIJI
Niue (N.Z.)
Cook Is. (N.Z.)
Rarotonga
Nuku'alofa
TONGA
Tonga Trench 10,822
Kermadec Is. (N.Z.)
Kermadec Trench 10,047
NEW ZEALAND
Auckland
Is. de la Société
Papeete
Tahiti
FRENCH POLYNESIA
Is. Tuamotu
Tuamotu Ridge
Austral Seamount Chain
Is. Tubuai
Mururoa
Rapa
Pitcairn I. (U.K.)
COPYRIGHT PHILIP'S

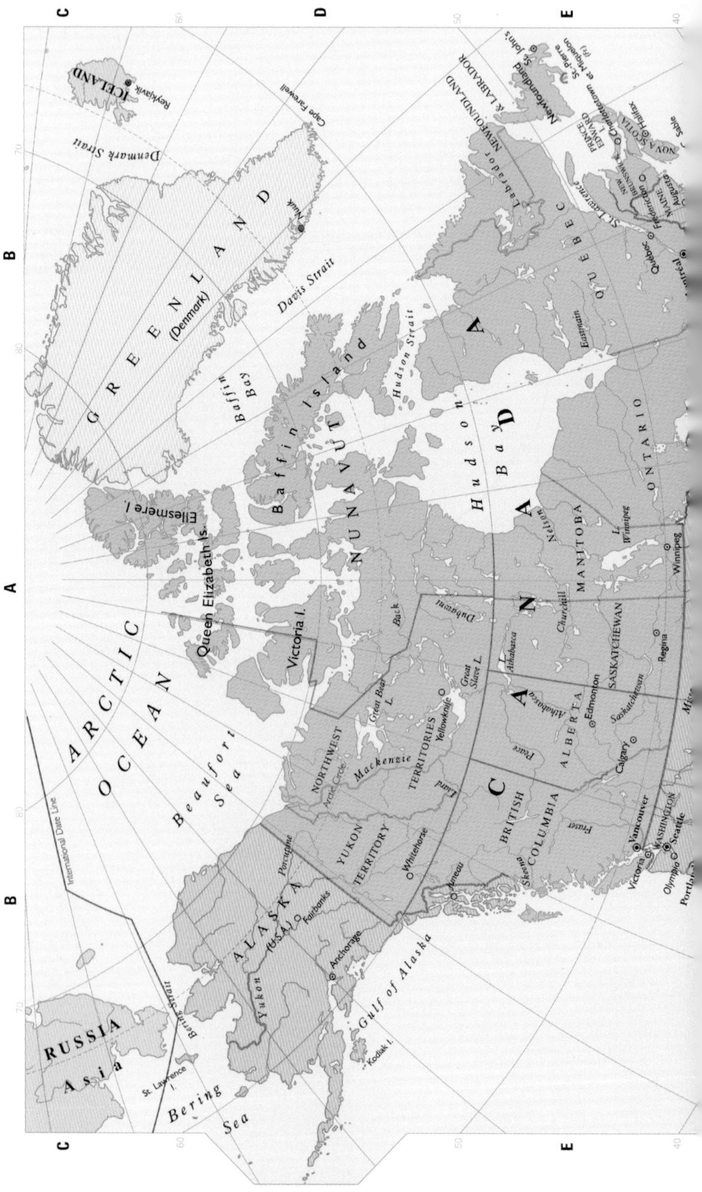
ARCTIC OCEAN
GREENLAND
(Denmark)
ICELAND
Reykjavik
Denmark Strait
Cape Farewell
Nuuk
Davis Strait
Baffin Bay
Baffin Island
Ellesmere I.
Queen Elizabeth Is.
Victoria I.
NUNAVUT
Hudson Strait
Hudson Bay
CANADA
NEWFOUNDLAND & LABRADOR
Labrador
Newfoundland
St. John's
St.-Pierre et Miquelon (Fr.)
PRINCE EDWARD I.
Charlottetown
NOVA SCOTIA
Halifax
NEW BRUNSWICK
Fredericton
MAINE
Augusta
QUEBEC
Quebec
Montreal
St. Lawrence
Eastmain
ONTARIO
MANITOBA
L. Winnipeg
Winnipeg
Nelson
Churchill
SASKATCHEWAN
Saskatchewan
Regina
ALBERTA
Edmonton
Calgary
Athabasca
L. Athabasca
Peace
Dubawnt
Back
NORTHWEST TERRITORIES
Great Bear L.
Great Slave L.
Yellowknife
Mackenzie
Arctic Circle
Liard
YUKON TERRITORY
Whitehorse
BRITISH COLUMBIA
Fraser
Skeena
Vancouver
Victoria
WASHINGTON
Seattle
Olympia
Juneau
ALASKA (USA)
Fairbanks
Anchorage
Porcupine
Yukon
Gulf of Alaska
Kodiak I.
Beaufort Sea
International Date Line
Bering Strait
Bering Sea
St. Lawrence I.
RUSSIA
Asia
A
B
C
D
E

NORTH ATLANTIC OCEAN
PACIFIC OCEAN
Gulf of Mexico
Caribbean Sea
UNITED STATES
MEXICO
MÉXICO
CUBA
BAHAMAS
HAITI
DOMINICAN REP.
JAMAICA
PUERTO RICO (U.S.A.)
GUATEMALA
BELIZE
HONDURAS
EL SALVADOR
NICARAGUA
COSTA RICA
PANAMA
COLOMBIA
VENEZUELA
South America
Washington D.C.
NEW YORK CITY
PHILADELPHIA
CHICAGO
LOS ANGELES
SAN FRANCISCO
Sacramento
San Jose
San Diego
Las Vegas
Salt Lake City
Phoenix
Tucson
El Paso
Albuquerque
Santa Fe
Denver
Cheyenne
Helena
Boise
Carson City
Bismarck
Minneapolis
Lincoln
Topeka
Kansas City
Oklahoma City
Dallas
Austin
Houston
Little Rock
Jackson
Baton Rouge
New Orleans
Memphis
Nashville
St. Louis
Springfield
Indianapolis
Cincinnati
Columbus
Detroit
Toledo
Lansing
Milwaukee
Madison
Cleveland
Pittsburgh
Buffalo
Toronto
Hartford
Providence
Baltimore
Richmond
Raleigh
Charlotte
Columbia
Charleston
Atlanta
Montgomery
Birmingham
Tallahassee
Jacksonville
Tampa
Miami
Nassau
Havana
Kingston
Port-au-Prince
Santo Domingo
San Juan
Monterrey
Hermosillo
Culiacan
Guadalajara
Puebla
Acapulco
Mérida
Belmopan
Guatemala
San Salvador
Tegucigalpa
Managua
San José
Panamá
Medellín
Barranquilla
Maracaibo
Bermuda (U.K.)
Turks & Caicos Is. (U.K.)
Cayman Is. (U.K.)
Revilla Gigedo Is. (Mex.)
Guadalupe (Mex.)
Tropic of Cancer
Florida Str.
Rio Grande
Mississippi
Colorado
Snake
Columbia
L. Michigan
L. Huron
L. Erie
L. Ontario
L. Nicaragua
OREGON
CALIFORNIA
NEVADA
IDAHO
UTAH
ARIZONA
NEW MEXICO
COLORADO
WYOMING
SOUTH DAKOTA
NEBRASKA
KANSAS
OKLAHOMA
TEXAS
IOWA
MISSOURI
ARKANSAS
LOUISIANA
MISSISSIPPI
ALABAMA
GEORGIA
FLORIDA
TENNESSEE
KENTUCKY
ILLINOIS
INDIANA
OHIO
MICHIGAN
WISCONSIN
VIRGINIA
W.V.
NORTH CAROLINA
SOUTH CAROLINA
PA.
NEW YORK
MASS.
N.J.
MD.
DE.
100 0 200 400 600 800 1000 1200 1400 km
0 200 400 600 800 1000 miles
F G H J
7 8 9 10 11 12
Projection: Bonne
West from Greenwich
■ MÉXICO Capital Cities
COPYRIGHT PHILIP'S

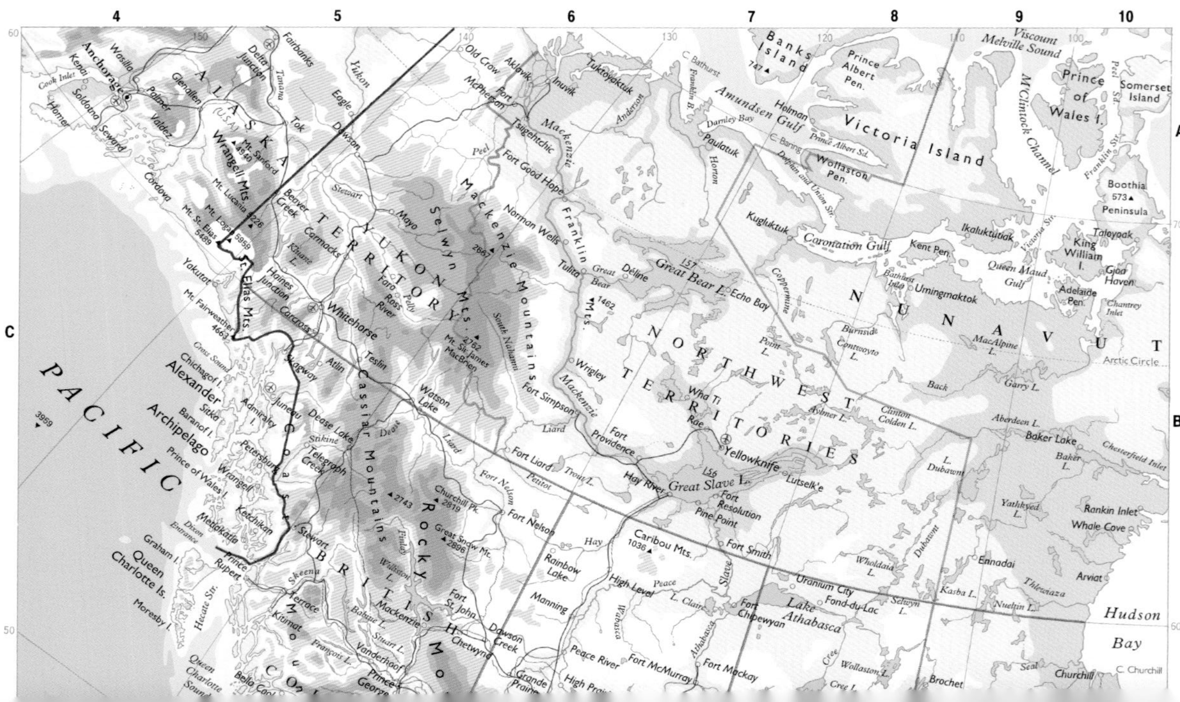

4
5
6
7
8
9
10
A
B
C
Anchorage
Wasilla
Kenai
Soldotna
Homer
Seward
Cook Inlet
Palmer
Glennallen
Valdez
Cordova
Delta Junction
Fairbanks
Tanana
Alaska
(U.S.A.)
Mt. Sanford 4940
Wrangell Mts.
Mt. Lucania 4226
Mt. Logan 5959
Mt. St. Elias 5489
St. Elias Mts.
Yakutat
Mt. Fairweather 4663
Tok
Eagle
Dawson
Yukon
Old Crow
Aklavik
Fort McPherson
Inuvik
Tuktoyaktuk
Tsiigehtchic
Peel
Mackenzie
Fort Good Hope
Anderson
Beaver Creek
Carmacks
Kluane L.
Haines Junction
Stewart
Mayo
Yukon Territory
Faro
Ross River
Pelly
Whitehorse
Carcross
Skagway
Atlin
Teslin
Selwyn Mts.
Mackenzie Mountains
2667
2762
Mt. Sir James MacBrien
South Nahanni
Norman Wells
Franklin
Tulita
Great Bear
1462
Mts.
Wrigley
Fort Simpson
Mackenzie
Watson Lake
Cassiar Mountains
Dease
Dease Lake
Stikine
Telegraph Creek
Liard
Fort Liard
Trout L.
Petitot
Fort Nelson
Fort Providence
Hay River
Juneau
Admiralty I.
Cross Sound
Chichagof I.
Sitka
Baranof I.
Alexander Archipelago
Petersburg
Wrangell
Prince of Wales I.
Ketchikan
Metlakatla
Dixon Entrance
Coast
Pacific
3959
Graham I.
Queen Charlotte Is.
Moresby I.
Hecate Str.
Prince Rupert
Stewart
Skeena
Terrace
Kitimat
Queen Charlotte Sound
Bella Coola
British Columbia
2743
Churchill Pk. 2819
Great Snow Mt. 2896
Rocky Mo
Finlay
Williston L.
Mackenzie
Babine L.
Stuart L.
François L.
Vanderhoof
Prince George
Fort St. John
Chetwynd
Dawson Creek
Grande Prairie
Banks Island
747
C. Bathurst
Franklin B.
Darnley Bay
Paulatuk
Horton
Amundsen Gulf
Holman
Prince Albert Pen.
Prince Albert Sd.
Victoria Island
C. Baring
Dolphin and Union Str.
Wollaston Pen.
Déline
157
Great Bear L.
Echo Bay
Kugluktuk
Coppermine
Coronation Gulf
Kent Pen.
Bathurst Inlet
Umingmaktok
Ikaluktutiak
Victoria Str.
Queen Maud Gulf
Viscount Melville Sound
M'Clintock Channel
Prince of Wales I.
Peel Sd.
Somerset Island
Franklin Str.
Boothia Peninsula
573
Taloyoak
King William I.
Gjoa Haven
Adelaide Pen.
Chantrey Inlet
Nunavut
Arctic Circle
Northwest Territories
Point L.
Burnside
Contwoyto L.
MacAlpine L.
Back
Garry L.
Wha Ti
Rae
Aylmer L.
Clinton Colden L.
Aberdeen L.
Baker Lake
Baker L.
Chesterfield Inlet
Yellowknife
156
Great Slave L.
Lutselk'e
Fort Resolution
Pine Point
Fort Smith
Dubawnt L.
Dubawnt
Yathkyed L.
Rankin Inlet
Whale Cove
Hay
Caribou Mts.
1036
Rainbow Lake
High Level
Peace
L. Claire
Slave
Manning
Wabasca
Athabasca
Wholdaia L.
Ennadai
Arviat
Thlewiaza
Kasba L.
Nueltin L.
Selwyn L.
Uranium City
Fond-du-Lac
Lake Athabasca
Fort Chipewyan
Hudson Bay
Peace River
Fort McMurray
Fort Mackay
High Prairie
Cree
Wollaston L.
Cree L.
Brochet
Seal
Churchill
C. Churchill
60
50
70
100
110
120
130
140
150

100 0 100 200 300 400 500 600 km

100 0 100 200 300 400 miles

ALASKA

100 0 100 200 300 400 500 600 km

100 0 100 200 300 400 miles

Projection : Bonne

West from Greenwich

m 0 200 600 1000 1500 2000 3000

ft 0 600 1200 3000 4500 6000 9000

m 0 200 2000 4000

ft 0 600 6000 12000

GREENLAND
(KALAALLIT NUNAAT)
(Denmark)
Kong Frederik VI's Kyst
Baffin Bay
Davis Strait
Labrador Sea
Baffin Island
NUNAVUT
Foxe Basin
Foxe Channel
Hudson Strait
Hudson Bay
Ungava Bay
Péninsule d'Ungava
Devon I.
Lancaster Sound
Somerset Island
Prince of Wales I.
Boothia Peninsula
Gulf of Boothia
Brodeur Peninsula
Bylot I.
Pond Inlet
Arctic Bay
Nanisivik
Borden Pen.
Clyde River
Qikiqtarjuaq
Cumberland Peninsula
Cumberland Sd.
Pangnirtung
Iqaluit
Hall Peninsula
Frobisher Bay
Resolution I.
Meta Incognita Peninsula
Kimmirut
Cape Dorset
Foxe Pen.
Nettilling L.
Amadjuak L.
Prince Charles I.
Air Force I.
Melville Peninsula
Igloolik
Sanirajak
Fury and Hecla Str.
Simpson Pen.
Pelly Bay
Committee B.
Rae Isthmus
Repulse Bay
Southampton I.
Coral Harbour
Bell Pen.
Coats I.
Mansel I.
Nottingham I.
Salisbury I.
Ottawa Is.
Roes Welcome Sd.
Wager B.
Arctic Circle
Igluligaarjuk
Rankin Inlet
Whale Cove
Arviat
Baker Lake
Chesterfield Inlet
C. Churchill
Churchill
Taloyoak
King William I.
Gjoa Haven
Adelaide Pen.
Chantrey Inlet
Peel Sd.
Franklin Str.
Ivujivik
Salluit
Kangiqsujuaq
Quaqtaq
Akpatok I.
Kangirsuk
Puvirnituq
L. Payne
Inukjuak
Kuujjuaq
Kangiqsualujjuaq
Hebron
Nain
Hopedale
Rigolet
Cartwright
C. Chidley
C. Harrison
George
Baleine
Caniapiscau
Arnaud
Nuuk
Qeqertarsuaq
Uummannaq
Upernavik
Ilulissat
Qasigiannguit
Kangerlussuaq
Maniitsoq
Sisimiut
Paamiut
Qaqortoq
Nanortalik
Tasiilaq
2850
2136
1890
2591
573
257
3309
1652

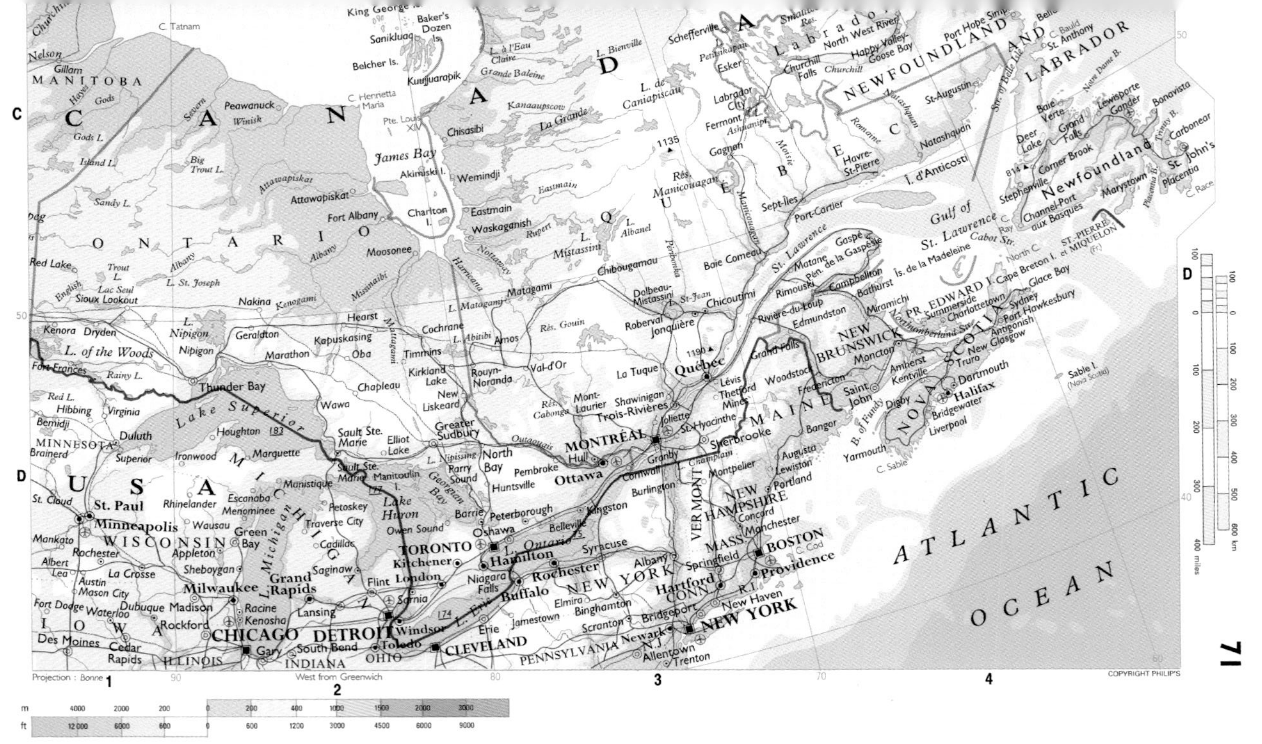
C A N A D A
U S A
O N T A R I O
Q U E B E C
MANITOBA
NEWFOUNDLAND AND LABRADOR
Labrador
Newfoundland
NEW BRUNSWICK
NOVA SCOTIA
PR. EDWARD I.
MAINE
NEW HAMPSHIRE
VERMONT
MASS.
CONN.
R.I.
NEW YORK
PENNSYLVANIA
N.J.
OHIO
INDIANA
ILLINOIS
IOWA
MINNESOTA
WISCONSIN
MICHIGAN
A T L A N T I C
O C E A N
James Bay
Gulf of St. Lawrence
Lake Superior
Lake Michigan
Lake Huron
L. Ontario
L. Erie
Georgian Bay
L. of the Woods
L. Nipigon
L. Mistassini
Rés. Manicouagan
B. of Fundy
Cabot Str.
Str. of Belle Isle
MONTRÉAL
Ottawa
Québec
TORONTO
DETROIT
CHICAGO
CLEVELAND
BOSTON
NEW YORK
Halifax
St. John's
Minneapolis
St. Paul
Milwaukee
Thunder Bay
Hamilton
Buffalo
Rochester
Providence
Hartford
Sherbrooke
Trois-Rivières
Kingston
Greater Sudbury
Sault Ste. Marie
Duluth
Fredericton
Moncton
Charlottetown
Corner Brook
Sept-Îles
Chicoutimi
Timmins
North Bay
Windsor
London
Kitchener
Grand Rapids
Lansing
Toledo
ST. PIERRE ET MIQUELON (Fr.)
Sable I. (Nova Scotia)
Projection : Bonne
West from Greenwich
COPYRIGHT PHILIP'S
m
4000
2000
200
0
200
400
1000
1500
2000
3000
ft
12 000
6000
600
0
600
1200
3000
4500
6000
9000
100 0 100 200 300 400 500 600 km
100 0 100 200 300 400 miles

NORTH-WEST USA

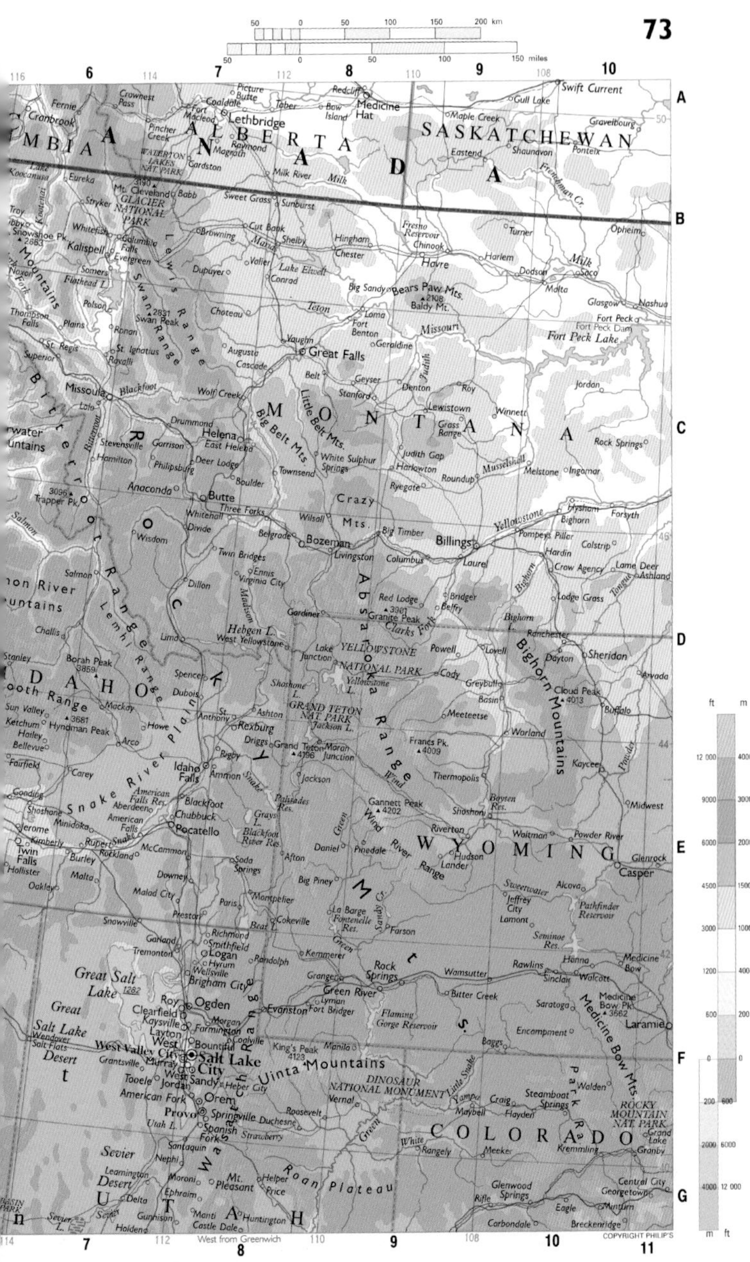
ALBERTA
SASKATCHEWAN
CANADA
MONTANA
IDAHO
WYOMING
UTAH
COLORADO
Lethbridge
Medicine Hat
Swift Current
Great Falls
Missoula
Helena
Butte
Bozeman
Billings
Casper
Sheridan
Pocatello
Idaho Falls
Ogden
Salt Lake City
Provo
Rock Springs
Laramie
Great Salt Lake
Fort Peck Lake
YELLOWSTONE NATIONAL PARK
GLACIER NATIONAL PARK
GRAND TETON NAT. PARK
DINOSAUR NATIONAL MONUMENT
ROCKY MOUNTAIN NAT. PARK
Bitterroot Range
Lemhi Range
Absaroka Range
Bighorn Mountains
Wind River Range
Uinta Mountains
Wasatch Range
Medicine Bow Mts.
Roan Plateau
Snake River Plain
Yellowstone
Missouri
West from Greenwich
COPYRIGHT PHILIP'S

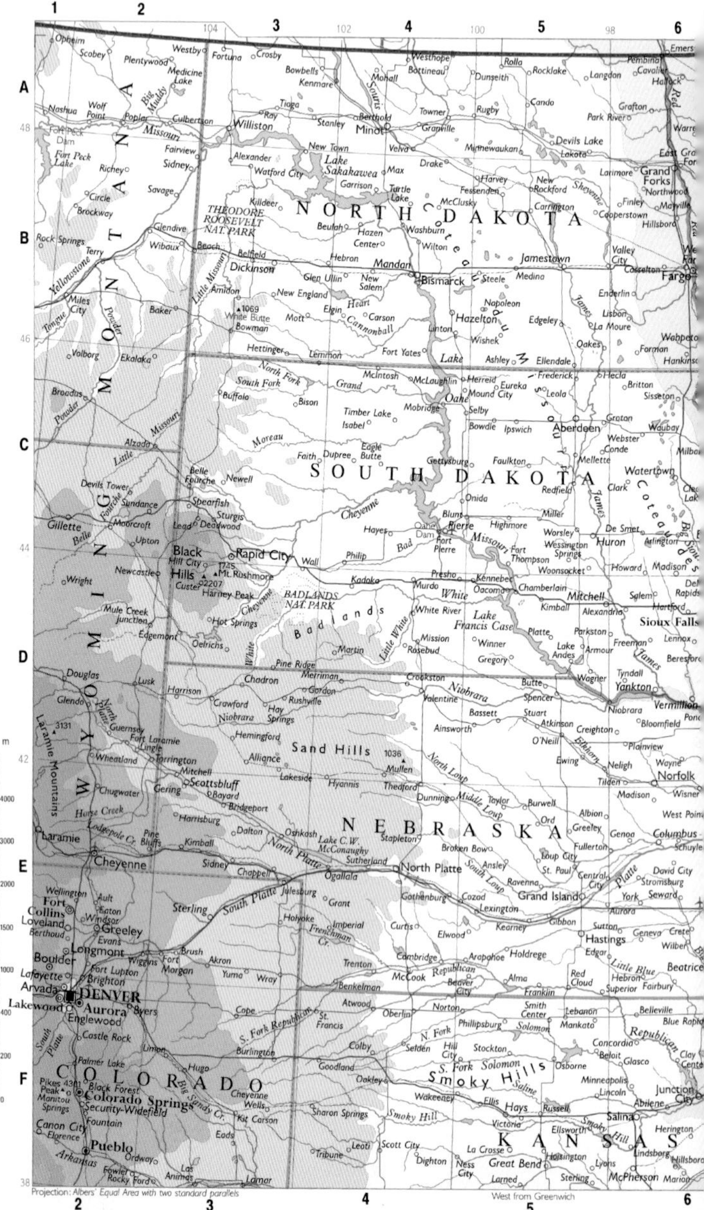
NORTH DAKOTA
SOUTH DAKOTA
NEBRASKA
KANSAS
COLORADO
WYOMING
MONTANA
Williston
Minot
Bismarck
Mandan
Dickinson
Jamestown
Fargo
Grand Forks
Devils Lake
Lake Sakakawea
THEODORE ROOSEVELT NAT. PARK
Aberdeen
Pierre
Rapid City
Black Hills
Mt. Rushmore
Harney Peak
BADLANDS NAT. PARK
Badlands
Huron
Mitchell
Sioux Falls
Yankton
Sand Hills
North Platte
Grand Island
Norfolk
Columbus
Hastings
Kearney
Scottsbluff
Cheyenne
Laramie
Casper
Gillette
Fort Collins
Greeley
Boulder
Longmont
DENVER
Aurora
Lakewood
Colorado Springs
Pueblo
Pikes Peak
Salina
Hays
Great Bend
Smoky Hills
Missouri
Yellowstone
Platte
South Platte
North Platte
Niobrara
Cheyenne
Republican
Smoky Hill
Lake Oahe
Lake Francis Case
Projection: Albers' Equal Area with two standard parallels
West from Greenwich
ft
m
12 000
9000
6000
4500
3000
1200
600
0
200
4000
3000
2000
1500
1000
400
200
0
600
A
B
C
D
E
F
1
2
3
4
5
6
104
102
100
98
48
46
44
42
38

50 0 50 100 150 200 km
50 0 50 100 150 miles
7 8 9 10 11
96 94 92 90 88
A B C D E F
C A N A D A
Lake of the Woods
Rainy Lake
Rainy River
Fort Frances
International Falls
VOYAGEURS NAT. PARK
Atikokan
Kabetogama
Thunder Bay
Northern Light L.
Cloud Bay
Grand Portage
Saganaga L.
Isle Royale
ISLE ROYALE NAT. PARK
Blake Pt.
183
LAKE SUPERIOR
Copper Harbor
Keweenaw Pt.
Keweenaw Pen.
Eagle River
Keweenaw B.
Pt. Abbaye
Hancock
Laurium
Houghton
Baraga
L'Anse
Ishpeming
Marquette
Negaunee
Gwinn
Ontonagon
Rockland
L. Gogebic
Wakefield
Bessemer
Watersmeet
Iron River
Crystal Falls
Iron Mountain
Norway
Kingsford
Powers
Menominee
Green Bay
MICHIGAN
Roseau
Warroad
Greenbush
Baudette
Karlstad
Thief River Falls
Upper Red L.
Lower Red L.
Red Lake Falls
Crookston
Big Falls
Little Fork
Big Fork
Northome
Vermilion L.
Ely
Tower
Cook
Grand Marais
Erskine
Fertile
Bagley
L. Winnibigoshish
Mountain Iron
Biwabik
Chisholm
Virginia
Hibbing
Eveleth
Bemidji
Cass Lake
Deer River
Grand Rapids
Ada
Mahnomen
Twin Valley
Leech L.
Walker
Hill City
Floodwood
Two Harbors
Apostle Is.
Chequamegon Bay
Hawley
Moorhead
Detroit Lakes
Park Rapids
Duluth
Superior
Cloquet
Bayfield
Washburn
Ashland
Ironwood
Hurley
Mellen
MINNESOTA
Barnesville
Perham
Wadena
Pine River
Aitkin
Moose Lake
Solon Springs
Breckenridge
Staples
Brainerd
Mille Lacs
Fergus Falls
Battle Lake
Baxter
Hayward
Park Falls
Eagle River
Hinckley
Long Prairie
Little Falls
Mora
Spooner
Phillips
Rhinelander
Alexandria
Wheaton
Sauk Centre
Melrose
Milaca
Pine City
Siren
Rice Lake
Prentice
Crandon
Laona
Glenwood
Sauk Rapids
Cambridge
St. Croix Falls
Ladysmith
Tomahawk
Big Stone L.
Morris
St. Cloud
Paynesville
Elk River
Barron
Merrill
Antigo
Ortonville
Big Stone City
Benson
Monticello
Blaine
New Richmond
Bloomer
Medford
Wausau
Oconto Falls
Marinette
Peshtigo
Oconto
Willmar
Litchfield
Coon Rapids
Brooklyn Park
Hudson
Chippewa Falls
Shawano
Sturgeon Bay
Montevideo
Minneapolis
St Paul
Menomonie
WISCONSIN
Green Bay
Algoma
Granite Falls
Hutchinson
Bloomington
Hastings
Eau Claire
Marshfield
Stevens Point
Clintonville
De Pere
Kewaunee
Glencoe
Burnsville
Lakeville
Red Wing
Durand
Neillsville
New London
Kaukauna
Canby
Ivanhoe
Redwood Falls
Whitehall
Wisconsin Rapids
Waupaca
Appleton
Two Rivers
Brookings
Marshall
Le Sueur
Northfield
Lake City
Alma
Black River Falls
Neenah
Manitowoc
New Ulm
Sleepy Eye
St. Peter
Faribault
Wautoma
Oshkosh
Chilton
Tyler
Tracy
Mankato
Owatonna
Winona
Necedah
Tomah
Adams
Berlin
Ripon
L. Winnebago
Sheboygan
Flandreau
Waseca
Kasson
Rochester
Holmen
Sparta
Onalaska
Montello
Fond du Lac
Pipestone
St. James
Stewartville
La Crescent
La Crosse
Mauston
Waupun
Plymouth
LAKE MICHIGAN
Luverne
Windom
Worthington
Albert Lea
Austin
Preston
Reedsburg
Portage
Beaver Dam
West Bend
Port Washington
Jackson
Fairmont
Blue Earth
Viroqua
Baraboo
Hartford
Rock Rapids
Richland Center
Watertown
Wauwatosa
Milwaukee
Canton
Estherville
Lake Mills
Northwood
Decorah
Waukon
Wisconsin
Rock Valley
Sibley
Forest City
Osage
Charles City
Prairie du Chien
Madison
Oconomowoc
Waukesha
Sheldon
Spencer
Mason City
West Allis
S. Milwaukee
Sioux Center
Emmetsburg
Clear Lake
New Hampton
McGregor
Dodgeville
Verona
Whitewater
Racine
Hawarden
Algona
Garner
Lancaster
Janesville
Delavan
Burlington
Sumner
Waverly
Guttenberg
Platteville
Geneva
Kenosha
Le Mars
Cherokee
Humboldt
Clarion
Hampton
Oelwein
Monroe
Beloit
Waukegan
North Chicago
Highland Park
Pocahontas
Eagle Grove
Cedar Falls
Manchester
Dubuque
Sioux City
South Sioux City
Storm Lake
Fort Dodge
Iowa Falls
Waterloo
Independence
Freeport
Woodstock
Arlington Hts
Wilmette
Evanston
Sac City
Webster City
Eldora
Grundy Center
Monticello
Rockford
Belvidere
Elgin
Dakota City
Ida Grove
Rockwell City
IOWA
Vinton
Anamosa
Maquoketa
Savanna
Oregon
St. Charles
CHICAGO
Carroll
Jefferson
Boone
Nevada
Marshalltown
Marion
Rochelle
De Kalb
Elmhurst
Onawa
Denison
Ames
Tama
Belle Plaine
Cedar Rapids
Clinton
Sterling
Dixon
Aurora
Cicero
Tekamah
Perry
Grinnell
Marengo
Tipton
Rock Falls
Joliet
Logan
Harlan
Audubon
Ankeny
Newton
Iowa City
Davenport
Bettendorf
Moline
Mendota
La Salle
Morris
Blair
Missouri Valley
West Des Moines
Des Moines
L. Red Rock
Montezuma
Muscatine
Rock Island
Geneseo
Princeton
Ottawa
Fremont
Omaha
Council Bluffs
Atlantic
Norwalk
Indianola
Pella
Washington
Kewanee
Kankakee
Wahoo
Bellevue
Winterset
Greenfield
Knoxville
Oskaloosa
Aledo
Galva
Henry
Streator
Dwight
Plattsmouth
Lincoln
Glenwood
Red Oak
Creston
Osceola
Albia
Ottumwa
Fairfield
Galesburg
Chillicothe
Pontiac
Nebraska City
Corning
Chariton
Mount Pleasant
Burlington
Monmouth
Peoria
Lexington
Shenandoah
Clarinda
Lenox
Corydon
Bloomfield
Fort Madison
Pekin
Normal
Paxton
Syracuse
Bedford
Centerville
Keokuk
Macomb
Canton
Bloomington
Rantoul
Auburn
Rock Port
Grant City
Princeton
Unionville
Kahoka
Carthage
Havana
ILLINOIS
Champaign
Maryville
Bethany
Milan
Kirksville
Rushville
Lincoln
Clinton
Urbana
Pawnee City
Wymore
Falls City
Mound City
Trenton
Edina
Canton
Mount Sterling
Beardstown
Decatur
Savannah
Chillicothe
Palmyra
Quincy
Springfield
Tuscola
Hiawatha
Marysville
Horton
Troy
Cameron
Macon
Hannibal
Monroe City
Pittsfield
Jacksonville
Taylorville
Sullivan
Mattoon
Frankfort
Atchison
St. Joseph
Pana
Shelbyville
Onaga
Holton
Excelsior Springs
Brunswick
Moberly
Louisiana
Vandalia
White Hall
Carrollton
Carlinville
Effingham
Tuttle Creek L.
Manhattan
Leavenworth
Liberty
Richmond
Carrollton
Fayette
Centralia
Litchfield
Newton
Wamego
Kansas City
Lexington
Marshall
Mexico
Montgomery City
Jerseyville
Staunton
Vandalia
Little Wabash
Kansas
Topeka
Overland Park
Independence
Columbia
Troy
Alton
Granite City
Alma
Lawrence
Kansas City
Warrensburg
Boonville
Fulton
St. Charles
ST. LOUIS
E. St. Louis
Salem
Flora
Centralia
Council Grove
Osage City
Olathe
California
Hermann
Washington
Belleville
Fairfield
Ottawa
Paola
Harrisonville
Sedalia
Jefferson City
Union
Mehlville
Waterloo
Mount Vernon
McLeansboro
Emporia
Osawatomie
Windsor
Clinton
Eldon
MISSOURI
Festus
Pinckneyville
Benton
West Frankfort
Burlington
Garnett
Butler
Harry S. Truman Res.
Lake of the Ozarks
Osage
Vienna
Sullivan
De Soto
Ste. Genevieve
Du Quoin
Mississippi
Missouri
Illinois
Wabash
Minnesota
Des Moines
Iowa
Cedar
Wapsipinicon
Skunk
Chippewa
Flambeau
Menominee
St. Croix
St. Louis
Grand
Chariton
Thompson
Little Sioux
Big Sioux
Kaskaskia
Black
Blue

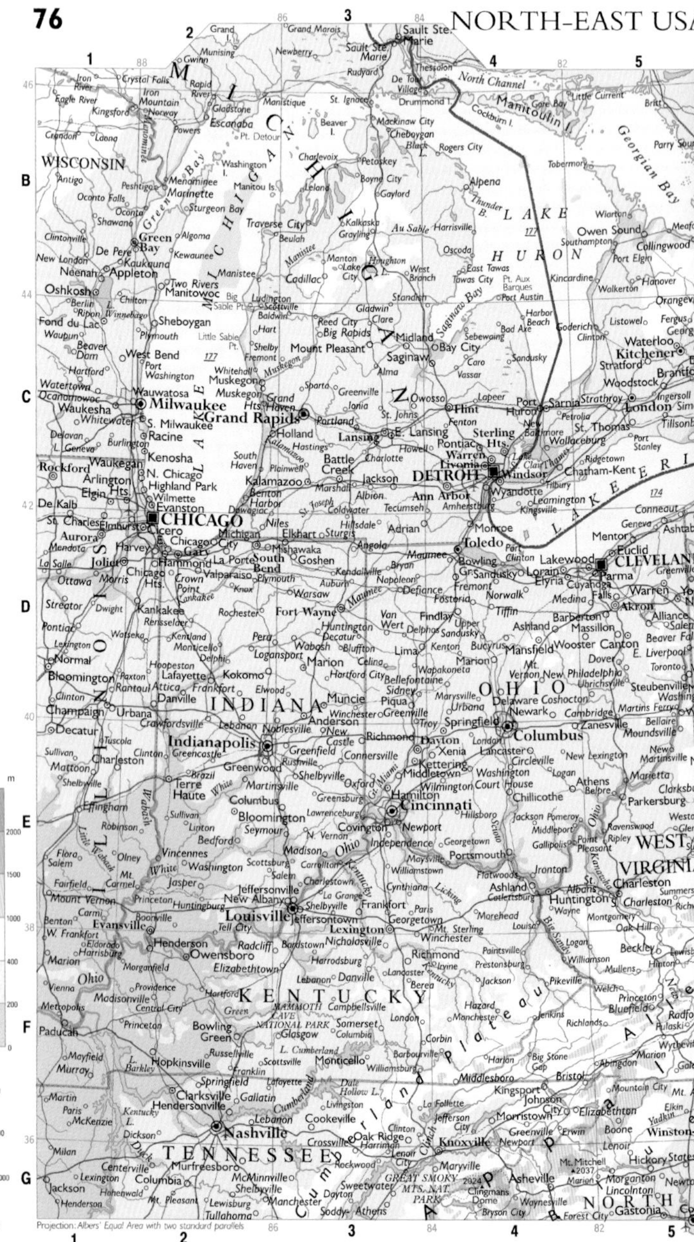

Projection: Albers' Equal Area with two standard parallels

50 0 50 100 150 200 km
50 0 50 100 150 miles
6
7
8
9
10
B
C
D
E
F
G
A
12
11
CANADA
MONTREAL
Sherbrooke
Granby
Magog
Coaticook
Cowansville
St-Jean-sur-Richelieu
Lachine
St-Hyacinthe
Lachute
Thurso
Hawkesbury
Rockland
Salaberry-de-Valleyfield
Buckingham
Hull
Ottawa
Arnprior
Carleton Place
Smiths Falls
Perth
Cornwall
Prescott
Brockville
Petawawa
Pembroke
Fort-Coulonge
Eganville
Renfrew
Barry's Bay
Bancroft
Huntsville
Bracebridge
Gravenhurst
Penetanguishene
Midland
Orillia
Lindsay
Peterborough
Bobcaygeon
Marmora
Madoc
Belleville
Trenton
Napanee
Picton
Kingston
Gananoque
New Tecumseth
Newcastle
Oshawa
Cobourg
Port Hope
TORONTO
LAKE ONTARIO
Hamilton
St. Catharines
Niagara Falls
Welland
Port Colborne
Lockport
Buffalo
N. Tonawanda
W. Seneca
Hamburg
Dunkirk
Fredonia
Gowanda
Salamanca
Olean
Jamestown
Erie
Rochester
Fairport
Batavia
Brockport
Medina
Newark
Canandaigua
Geneseo
Geneva
Seneca Falls
Auburn
Penn Yan
Dansville
Watkins Glen
Bath
Corning
Hornell
Wellsville
Elmira
Waverly
Sayre
Ithaca
Cortland
Syracuse
Oneida
Oswego
Fulton
Pulaski
Rome
Utica
Little Falls
Herkimer
Johnstown
Schenectady
Amsterdam
Saratoga Sps.
Glens Falls
Troy
Albany
Cobleskill
Hamilton
Cooperstown
Norwich
Oneonta
Sidney
Binghamton
Endicott
Catskill Mts.
Catskill
Saugerties
Kingston
Poughkeepsie
Newburgh
Beacon
Middletown
Peekskill
Liberty
Ellenville
Watertown
Carthage
Lowville
Adams
Boonville
Clayton
Alexandria Bay
Gouverneur
Ogdensburg
Canton
Potsdam
Massena
Malone
Plattsburgh
Dannemora
Saranac Lake
Tupper Lake
Long Lake
Adirondack Mts.
Ticonderoga
Port Henry
Lake George
Whitehall
Granville
Hudson Falls
NEW YORK
Burlington
Winooski
St. Albans
Montpelier
Barre
Middlebury
Randolph
Rutland
Fair Haven
Windsor
Springfield
Bellows Falls
Brattleboro
Bennington
Newport
Lyndonville
St. Johnsbury
Woodsville
VERMONT
Island Pond
Groveton
Lancaster
Berlin
Mt. Washington
Conway
Hanover
Lebanon
Claremont
Newport
Concord
Laconia
Franklin
Rochester
Dover
Manchester
Keene
Hillsborough
Nashua
Haverhill
Lawrence
Lowell
Lynn
Salem
Cambridge
Quincy
Brockton
BOSTON
Newton
Worcester
Fitchburg
Leominster
N. Adams
Greenfield
Pittsfield
Northampton
Holyoke
Springfield
Chicopee
MASS.
Attleboro
Taunton
Fall River
New Bedford
Hyannis
Cape Cod
Martha's Vineyard
Nantucket I.
Providence
Pawtucket
Woonsocket
Warwick
Newport
R.I.
Hartford
New Britain
Bristol
Waterbury
Meriden
New Haven
Norwich
New London
Danbury
Bridgeport
Norwalk
Stamford
Port Chester
Yonkers
CONN.
Long Island
Long Island Sound
Block I.
Montauk Pt.
Southampton
Riverhead
Patchogue
Levittown
Freeport
Jefferson
NEW YORK
Newark
E. Orange
Paterson
Jersey City
Elizabeth
Perth Amboy
New Brunswick
Long Branch
Asbury Park
Plainfield
Princeton
Trenton
Willingboro
Camden
NEW JERSEY
Hammonton
Vineland
Millville
Bridgeton
Pleasantville
Atlantic City
Ocean City
North Wildwood
Cape May
PHILADELPHIA
Norristown
Chester
Wilmington
Newark
Salem
West Chester
Coatesville
Lancaster
Reading
Pottstown
Allentown
Bethlehem
Easton
Pottsville
Hazleton
E. Stroudsburg
Wilkes-Barre
Scranton
Dunmore
Carbondale
Kingston
Nanticoke
Berwick
Bloomsburg
Shenandoah
Shamokin
Sunbury
Milton
Lock Haven
Jersey Shore
Williamsport
Harrisburg
Camp Hill
Carlisle
Lebanon
York
Columbia
Hanover
Gettysburg
Chambersburg
Shippensburg
Waynesboro
Altoona
Hollidaysburg
Huntingdon
Lewistown
State College
Bellefonte
Clearfield
Du Bois
Punxsutawney
Brookville
Clarion
Ridgway
St. Marys
Emporium
Coudersport
Wellsboro
Towanda
Port Allegany
Bradford
Kane
Warren
Corry
Meadville
Titusville
Oil City
Franklin
Butler
Kittanning
PENNSYLVANIA
Allegheny Plateau
PITTSBURGH
Penn Hills
Greensburg
Johnstown
Indiana
Somerset
Monessen
Connellsville
Uniontown
Allegheny Mountains
Cumberland
Frostburg
Hagerstown
Westminster
Frederick
Aberdeen
Towson
Dundalk
BALTIMORE
MARYLAND
Wheaton
Rockville
Annapolis
Arlington
WASHINGTON D.C.
Alexandria
Easton
Cambridge
Salisbury
Ocean City
Dover
Smyrna
Milford
Lewes
Seaford
DELAWARE
Delaware Bay
C. Henlopen
C. May
Chesapeake Bay
Berlin
Snow Hill
Pocomoke City
Chincoteague
Accomac
Onancock
Martinsburg
Brunswick
Charles Town
Winchester
Moorefield
Keyser
Romney
Fairmont
Grafton
Philippi
Buckhannon
Elkins
Petersburg
Front Royal
Luray
Franklin
Harrisonburg
Shenandoah
Culpeper
Fredericksburg
Orange
Dale City
St. Charles
Lexington Park
Leonardtown
Colonial Beach
SHENANDOAH NAT. PARK
Staunton
Waynesboro
Charlottesville
Ashland
Richmond
Hopewell
Petersburg
Williamsburg
West Point
Gloucester Point
Cape Charles
C. Charles
Hampton
Newport News
Norfolk
Portsmouth
Virginia Beach
Suffolk
Chesapeake
VIRGINIA
Lexington
Covington
Buena Vista
Lynchburg
Madison Heights
Bedford
Farmville
Salem
Roanoke
Blacksburg
Altavista
Blackstone
South Boston
Danville
Martinsville
Emporia
Franklin
John H. Kerr Res.
Murfreesboro
Ahoskie
Roanoke Rapids
Roxboro
Eden
Reidsville
Oxford
Henderson
Enfield
Elizabeth City
Edenton
Albemarle Sd.
Rocky Mount
Tarboro
Plymouth
Williamston
Manteo
Roanoke I.
Wake Forest
Greensboro
Burlington
Durham
Chapel Hill
Raleigh
High Point
Lexington
Siler City
Cary
Wilson
Belhaven
Greenville
Washington
Pamlico Sound
Asheboro
Sanford
Smithfield
Selma
Goldsboro
Kinston
New Bern
C. Hatteras
Salisbury
Kannapolis
Albemarle
Charlotte
CAROLINA
West from Greenwich
78
76
74
72
70
68
42
40
44
46
1281
1482
1605
1917
Edmundston
St-Leonard
Grand Falls
Fort Kent
Van Buren
Eagle Lake
Caribou
Ft Fairfield
Presque Isle
Ashland
Mars Hill
Perth-Andover
Hartland
Woodstock
Houlton
Eagle L.
Chamberlain L.
Chesuncook L.
Patten
Mt. Katahdin
Chiputneticook Lakes
Millinocket
Rockwood
Moosehead L.
Jackman
Greenville
Flagstaff L.
Milo
Dover Foxcroft
Lincoln
W. Grand L.
Calais
Woodland
MAINE
Bingham
Dexter
Orono
Old Town
Bangor
Brewer
Skowhegan
Pittsfield
Waterville
Machias
Ellsworth
Bar Harbor
Mt. Desert I.
ACADIA NAT. PARK
Belfast
Camden
Rockland
Penobscot B.
Augusta
Gardiner
Livermore Falls
Norway
Lewiston
Auburn
Lisbon Falls
Brunswick
Bath
Portland
S. Portland
Westbrook
Casco B.
Saco
Biddeford
Sanford
Rochester
Dover
Kittery
Portsmouth
Newburyport
Laconia
Conway
Mt. Washington
Berlin
Rumford
Groveton
Colebrook
Rangeley
Mooselookmeguntic L.
Farmington
Kennebec
Penobscot
St. John
Allagash
NEW HAMPSHIRE
ATLANTIC OCEAN
Continuation Eastwards On same scale
COPYRIGHT PHILIP'S

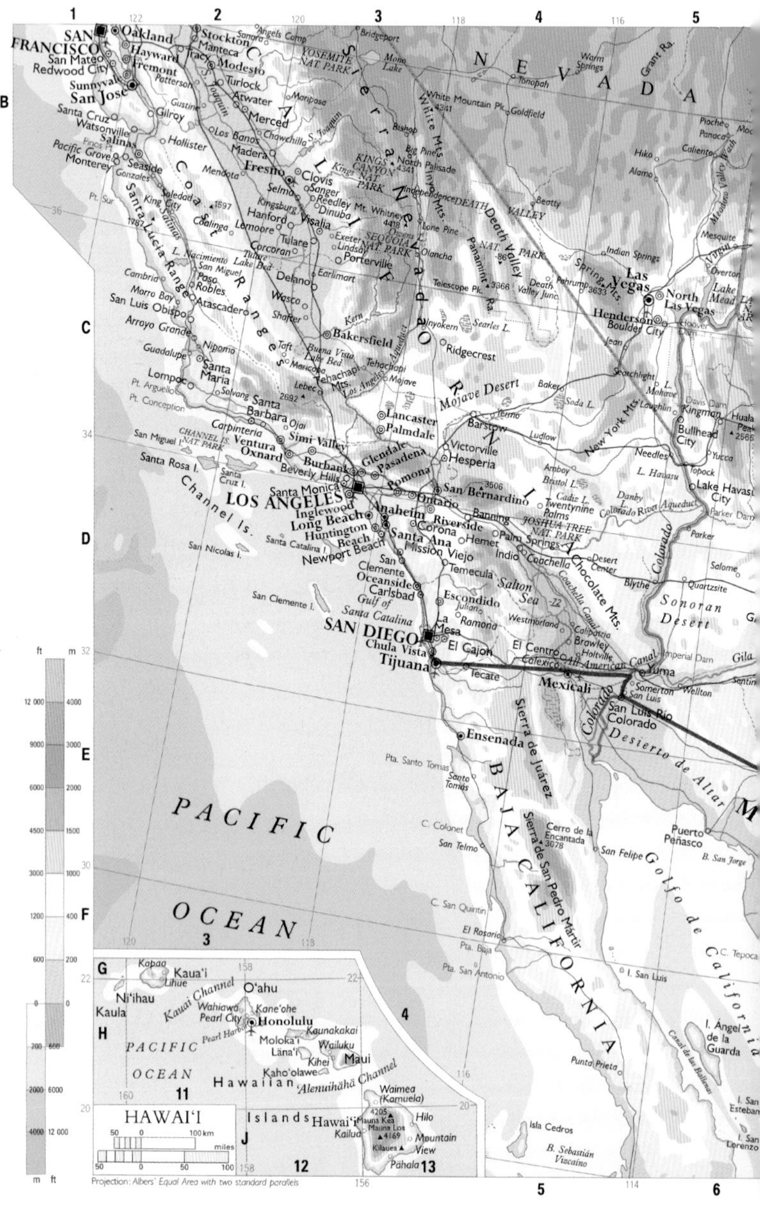
SAN FRANCISCO
Oakland
Stockton
San Jose
NEVADA
Sierra Nevada
Death Valley
Las Vegas
Bakersfield
Mojave Desert
LOS ANGELES
Santa Monica
Long Beach
Anaheim
San Bernardino
Riverside
Salton Sea
SAN DIEGO
Tijuana
Mexicali
Yuma
Ensenada
PACIFIC OCEAN
BAJA CALIFORNIA
Golfo de California
Desierto de Altar
Sonoran Desert
HAWAI'I
Kaua'i
O'ahu
Honolulu
Moloka'i
Maui
Hawai'i
Hawaiian Islands
Projection: Albers' Equal Area with two standard parallels

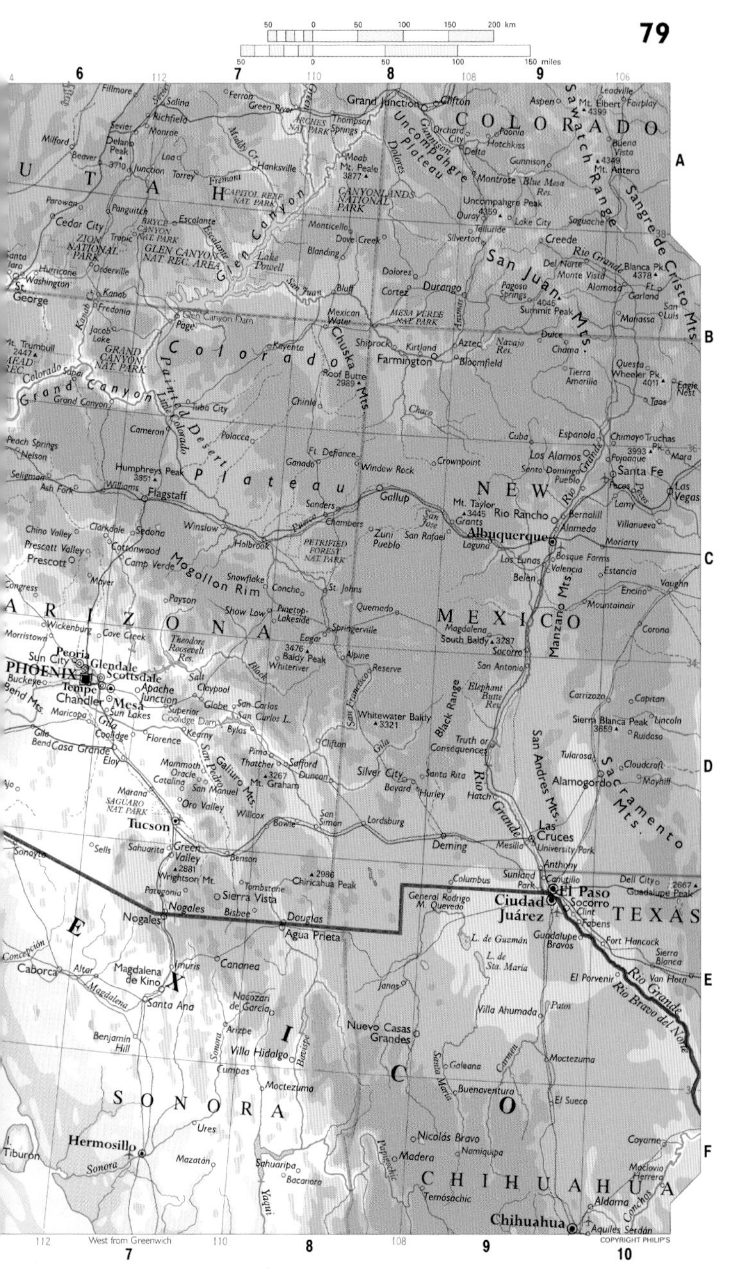
50 0 50 100 150 200 km
50 0 50 100 150 miles
6
112
7
110
8
108
9
106
A
B
C
D
E
F
COLORADO
UTAH
ARIZONA
NEW MEXICO
TEXAS
MEXICO
SONORA
CHIHUAHUA
Colorado Plateau
Painted Desert
Grand Canyon
Glen Canyon
Mogollon Rim
Uncompahgre Plateau
Sawatch Range
Sangre de Cristo Mts.
San Juan Mts.
Chuska Mts.
Manzano Mts.
San Andres Mts.
Sacramento Mts.
Black Range
Galiuro Mts.
Bend Mts.
Fillmore
Salina
Richfield
Sevier
Monroe
Milford
Delano Peak
3710
Beaver
Junction
Loa
Torrey
Fremont
Hanksville
Ferron
Green River
Grand Junction
Clifton
Thompson Springs
ARCHES NAT. PARK
Moab
Mt. Peale
3877
CAPITOL REEF NAT. PARK
CANYONLANDS NATIONAL PARK
Parowan
Panguitch
Cedar City
BRYCE CANYON NAT. PARK
Escalante
Tropic
ZION NATIONAL PARK
GLEN CANYON NAT. REC. AREA
Orderville
Hurricane
Washington
St. George
Kanab
Fredonia
Lake Powell
Monticello
Dove Creek
Blanding
Bluff
San Juan
Glen Canyon Dam
Page
Jacob Lake
Mt. Trumbull
2447
GRAND CANYON NAT. PARK
Grand Canyon
Kayenta
Mexican Water
Shiprock
Roof Butte
2989
Chinle
Tuba City
Cameron
Little Colorado
Polacca
Ft. Defiance
Ganado
Window Rock
Humphreys Peak
3851
Williams
Flagstaff
Ash Fork
Seligman
Peach Springs
Nelson
Sanders
Chambers
Puerco
Gallup
Winslow
Holbrook
PETRIFIED FOREST NAT. PARK
Zuni Pueblo
Chino Valley
Clarkdale
Sedona
Cottonwood
Prescott Valley
Prescott
Camp Verde
Mayer
Congress
Snowflake
Concho
St. Johns
Payson
Show Low
Pinetop-Lakeside
Wickenburg
Morristown
Cave Creek
Theodore Roosevelt Res.
Eagar
Springerville
Quemado
3476
Baldy Peak
Whiteriver
Alpine
Reserve
Peoria
Sun City
Glendale
PHOENIX
Scottsdale
Buckeye
Tempe
Chandler
Mesa
Apache Junction
Sun Lakes
Maricopa
Salt
Claypool
Globe
San Carlos
San Carlos L.
Superior
Coolidge Dam
Black
Gila
Gila Bend
Coolidge
Florence
Kearny
Casa Grande
Eloy
Bylas
San Francisco
Whitewater Baldy
3321
Clifton
Pima
Thatcher
Safford
3267
Mt. Graham
Mammoth
Oracle
Catalina
San Pedro
San Manuel
Duncan
Silver City
Santa Rita
Bayard
Hurley
Marana
SAGUARO NAT. PARK
Oro Valley
Willcox
Tucson
Bowie
San Simon
Lordsburg
Deming
Sells
Sahuarita
Green Valley
Benson
Sonoyta
Ajo
2881
Wrightson Mt.
2986
Chiricahua Peak
Patagonia
Tombstone
Sierra Vista
Nogales
Bisbee
Douglas
Agua Prieta
Columbus
General Rodrigo M. Quevedo
Concepción
Caborca
Altar
Magdalena de Kino
Imuris
Cananea
Magdalena
Santa Ana
Nacozari de García
Arizpe
Benjamin Hill
Sonora
Villa Hidalgo
Bavispe
Cumpas
Moctezuma
Ures
Hermosillo
I. Tiburon
Mazatán
Sahuaripa
Bacanora
Yaqui
Janos
Nuevo Casas Grandes
Galeana
Santa María
Buenaventura
Carmen
Nicolás Bravo
Namiquipa
Madera
Papigochic
Temósachic
Chihuahua
Aquiles Serdán
Aldama
Conchos
Coyame
Maclovio Herrera
L. de Guzmán
L. de Sta. María
Villa Ahumada
Patos
Moctezuma
El Sueco
Ciudad Juárez
El Paso
Socorro
Clint
Fabens
Guadalupe Bravos
Fort Hancock
Sierra Blanca
El Porvenir
Van Horn
Rio Grande
Rio Bravo del Norte
Dell City
Guadalupe Peak
2667
Sunland Park
Canutillo
Anthony
Mesilla
University Park
Las Cruces
Hatch
Truth or Consequences
Elephant Butte Res.
Rio Grande
Alamogordo
Tularosa
Cloudcroft
Mayhill
Sierra Blanca Peak
3659
Lincoln
Ruidoso
Carrizozo
Capitan
Corona
San Antonio
Socorro
Magdalena
South Baldy
3287
Mountainair
Encino
Vaughn
Estancia
Belen
Valencia
Los Lunas
Bosque Farms
Moriarty
Albuquerque
Laguna
San Rafael
Grants
San Jose
Mt. Taylor
3445
Rio Rancho
Alameda
Bernalillo
Villanueva
Lamy
Pecos
Santa Fe
Las Vegas
Santo Domingo Pueblo
Los Alamos
Pojoaque
3993
Truchas Pk.
Mora
Chimayo
Espanola
Cuba
Crownpoint
Chaco
Farmington
Kirtland
Aztec
Bloomfield
Navajo Res.
Animas
MESA VERDE NAT. PARK
Cortez
Dolores
Durango
Pagosa Springs
4045
Summit Peak
Dulce
Chama
Tierra Amarilla
Questa
Wheeler Pk.
4011
Eagle Nest
Taos
Manassa
San Luis
Ft. Garland
Alamosa
Blanca Pk.
4378
Monte Vista
Del Norte
Rio Grande
Creede
Silverton
Telluride
Ouray
4359
Uncompahgre Peak
Lake City
Saguache
Montrose
Blue Mesa Res.
Gunnison
Delta
Orchard City
Paonia
Hotchkiss
Buena Vista
4349
Mt. Antero
Mt. Elbert
4399
Leadville
Fairplay
Aspen
Muddy Cr.
Escalante
Kanab Cr.
West from Greenwich
COPYRIGHT PHILIP'S

1
2
3
4
5
A
B
C
D
E
F
104
102
100
98
36
34
32
28
COLORADO
KANSAS
NEW MEXICO
OKLAHOMA
TEXAS
CHIHUAHUA
COAHUILA
MEXICO
Sangre de Cristo Mts.
La Junta
Granada
Syracuse
Garden City
Jetmore
Hutchinson
Newton
Walsenburg
Lakin
Arkansas
Kinsley
St. John
Stafford
Cimarron
Dodge City
Pratt
Kingman
Wichita
4378
Blanca Pk.
Thatcher
San Luis
Springfield
Walsh
Johnson City
Ulysses
Bucklin
Greensburg
Derby
Trinidad
Kim
Hugoton
Meade
Coldwater
Medicine Lodge
Wellington
Winfield
Ashland
Anthony
Arkansas City
Raton
Elkhart
Liberal
Kiowa
Caldwell
1516
Black Mesa
Des Moines
Hooker
Beaver
Buffalo
Alva
Cherokee
Blackwell
Tonkawa
Wheeler Pk.
4011
Boise City
Guymon
Great Salt Plains L.
Ponca City
Taos
Springer
Carrizo Creek
Clayton
Texline
Perryton
Booker
Waynoka
Stratford
Gruver
Spearman
Lipscomb
Woodward
Fairview
Canton L.
Enid
Wagon Mound
Ute Creek
Dalhart
Higgins
Arnett
Seiling
Hennessey
Stillwater
Perry
3993
Mora
Truchas Pk.
Ray
Mosquero
Watrous
Trujillo
Nara Visa
Dumas
Channing
Canadian
Watonga
Guthrie
Las Vegas
L. Meredith
Fritch
Borger
Miami
Pampa
Thomas
Kingfisher
Chandler
Edmond
El Reno
Midwest City
Villanueva
Conchas Dam
Cheyenne
Wheeler
Elk City
Weatherford
Clinton
Oklahoma City
Shawnee
Tucumcari
Adrian
Vega
Panhandle
McLean
Sayre
Cordell
Pecos
Amarillo
Claude
Groom
Shamrock
Norman
Tecumseh
Santa Rosa
San Jon
Salt Fork Red
Anadarko
Grady
Hereford
Canyon
Clarendon
Wellington
Hobart
Chickasha
Purcell
Mangum
Apache
Lindsay
Vaughn
Friona
Happy
North Fork
Memphis
Hollis
Snyder
Marlow
Pauls Valley
Prairie Dog Town Fork Red
Fort Sumner
Altus
Lawton
Duncan
Yeso
Melrose
Clovis
Farwell
Dimmitt
Tulia
Silverton
Frederick
Walters
Childress
Earth
Muleshoe
Olton
Plainview
Portales
Quanah
Pease
Red
Waurika
Healdton
Sudan
Lockney
Vernon
Ardmore
Paducah
Burkburnett
Llano
Littlefield
Anton
Floydada
Iowa Park
Wichita Falls
Crowell
L. Kemp
Abernathy
Levelland
Morton
Ralls
Dickens
Guthrie
Henrietta
Nocona
Roswell
Lubbock
Crosbyton
Estacado
Slaton
Spur
Seymour
Bowie
Gainesville
Dexter
Munday
Brazos
Olney
W. Fork Trinity
Tatum
Plains
Tahoka
Jayton
Jacksboro
Hagerman
Artesia
Lovington
Denver City
Brownfield
Post
Aspermont
Haskell
Graham
Bridgeport
Denton
Decatur
O'Donnell
Possum Kingdom L.
Seagraves
Hamlin
Stamford
Gail
Snyder
Rotan
Hobbs
Seminole
Anson
Breckenridge
Mineral Wells
Arlington
Irving
Albany
Weatherford
Fort Worth
Lamesa
Colorado
Seminole Draw
Carlsbad Caverns Nat. Park
Carlsbad
Eunice
Sweetwater
Merkel
Abilene
Loving
Andrews
Coahoma
Colorado City
Cisco
Ranger
Eastland
Granbury
Alvarado
Big Spring
Stanton
Tuscola
Cleburne
Jal
Goldsmith
Stephenville
2667
Guadalupe Peak
Red Bluff Res.
Beals Cr.
De Leon
Dublin
Hillsboro
Guadalupe Mts. Nat. Park
Kermit
Wink
Odessa
Midland
Sterling City
Robert Lee
Coleman
Comanche
Garden City
Ballinger
Brownwood
Clifton
Pyote
Monahans
Hamilton
Waco
Pecos
San Angelo
Concho
Colorado
Gatesville
Hewitt
Crane
Goldthwaite
Grandfalls
Rankin
Copperas Cove
Killeen
Belton Lake
Temple
Kent
Van Horn
Big Lake
Mertzon
Eden
McCamey
Barnhart
Brady
San Saba
Lampasas
Belton
Balmorhea
Edwards
Menard
Mt. Livermore
2555
Davis Mts.
Fort Davis
Fort Stockton
Eldorado
L. Buchanan
Cameron
Ozona
Mason
Llano
Burnet
Rockdale
Valentine
Stockton Plateau
Sonora
Georgetown
Marfa
Alpine
Junction
Marble Falls
Round Rock
Taylor
L. Travis
Marathon
Plateau
Elgin
Austin
Fredericksburg
Sanderson
Pecos
Johnson City
2356
Chinati Peak
Rocksprings
Kerrville
Blanco
Bastrop
Balcones Escarpment
San Marcos
Lockhart
Langtry
Boerne
New Braunfels
Presidio
Camp Wood
Luling
Presa de la Amistad
Medina L.
Ojinaga
Rio Grande
Chisos Mts.
2388
Big Bend National Park
Del Rio
San Antonio
Seguin
Gonzales
Guadalupe
Brackettville
Ciudad Acuña
Sabinal
Hondo
Medina
Nixon
Yoakum
Uvalde
Spofford
Devine
Floresville
Poteet
Pleasanton
Quemado
Batesville
Pearsall
Jourdanton
Karnes City
Kenedy
Victoria
Bolsón de Mapimí
Eagle Pass
Piedras Negras
Crystal City
Dilley
Choke Canyon Res.
Frio
Three Rivers
Goliad
San Antonio
Zaragoza
Carrizo Springs
Asherton
Cotulla
Beeville
Refugio
Allende
Nava
Rio Bravo del Norte
Nueces
George West
L. Corpus Christi
Mathis
Rockport
Aransas Pass
Sinton
Nueva Rosita
Orange Grove
Portland
Sabinas
Alice
Salado
San Diego
Robstown
Corpus Christi
Benavides
Bishop
Nuevo Laredo
Laredo
Sabinas
Kingsville
Sierra Mojada
Hebbronville
Padre I.
ft
m
12 000
9000
6000
4500
3000
1200
600
0
200
4000
3000
2000
1500
1000
400
200
0
600
m
ft
Projection: Albers' Equal Area with two standard parallels
West from Greenwich

MISSOURI
ARKANSAS
TENNESSEE
MISSISSIPPI
LOUISIANA
TEXAS
MEXICO
GULF OF MEXICO
Memphis
Little Rock
Jackson
New Orleans
Baton Rouge
Shreveport
HOUSTON
DALLAS
Springfield
Tulsa
Boston Mts.
Ouachita Mts.
Continuation Southwards on same scale
COPYRIGHT PHILIP'S

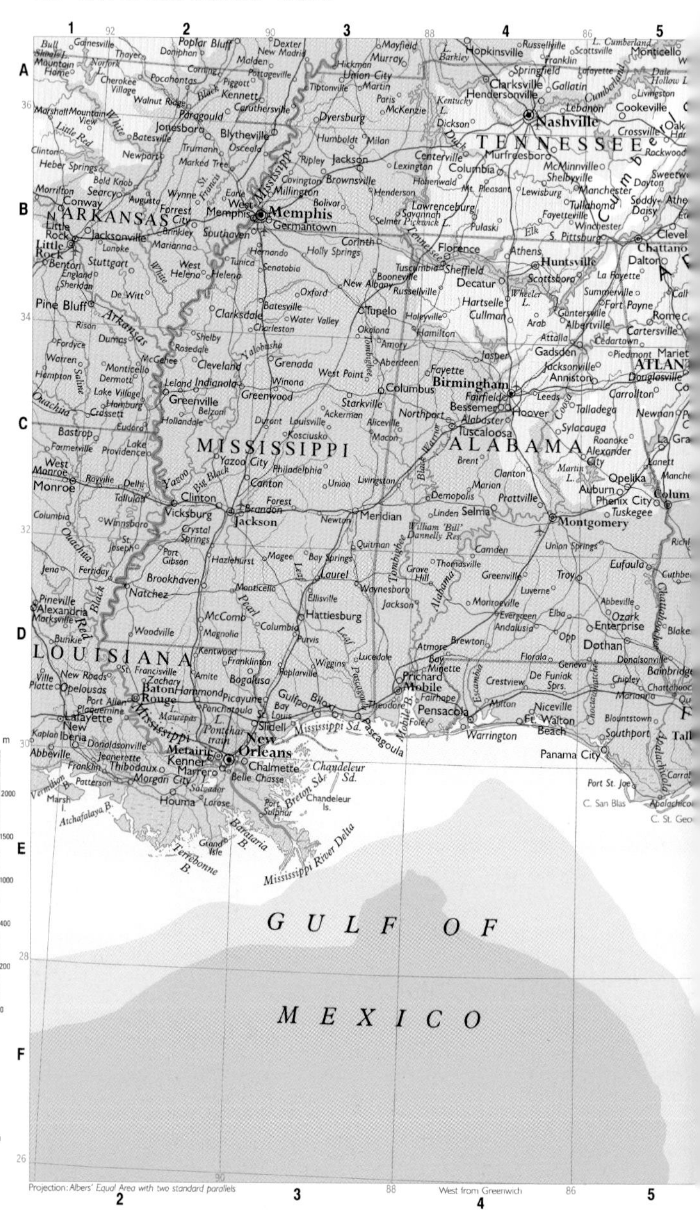

Projection: Albers' Equal Area with two standard parallels

West from Greenwich

50 0 50 100 150 200 km
50 0 50 100 150 miles
6
7
8
9
10
A
B
C
D
E
F
G
NORTH CAROLINA
SOUTH CAROLINA
GEORGIA
FLORIDA
ATLANTIC
OCEAN
BAHAMAS
Appalachian Mts.
Blue Ridge
Knoxville
Kingsport
Bristol
Johnson City
Asheville
Danville
Martinsville
Greensboro
Burlington
Durham
Chapel Hill
Raleigh
Winston-Salem
High Point
Charlotte
Gastonia
Concord
Fayetteville
Rocky Mount
Wilson
Greenville
Goldsboro
Kinston
New Bern
Jacksonville
Wilmington
Elizabeth City
Albemarle Sd.
Pamlico Sound
C. Hatteras
C. Lookout
Onslow Bay
C. Fear
Spartanburg
Greenville
Anderson
Columbia
Florence
Sumter
Myrtle Beach
Long Bay
Georgetown
Charleston
North Charleston
Mount Pleasant
Hilton Head Island
Athens
Augusta
Macon
Savannah
Brunswick
Valdosta
Okefenokee Swamp
Jacksonville
St. Augustine
Gainesville
Daytona Beach
Orlando
C. Canaveral
Melbourne
TAMPA
St. Petersburg
Clearwater
Sarasota
Lake Okeechobee
Fort Pierce
Port St. Lucie
West Palm Beach
Boca Raton
Fort Lauderdale
Hollywood
Miami Beach
MIAMI
Hialeah
Coral Gables
Naples
Cape Coral
The Everglades
EVERGLADES NAT. PARK
Grand Bahama
Freeport
Great Abaco I.
Little Abaco I.
84
82
80
78
76
36
34
32
30
28
26
COPYRIGHT PHILIP'S

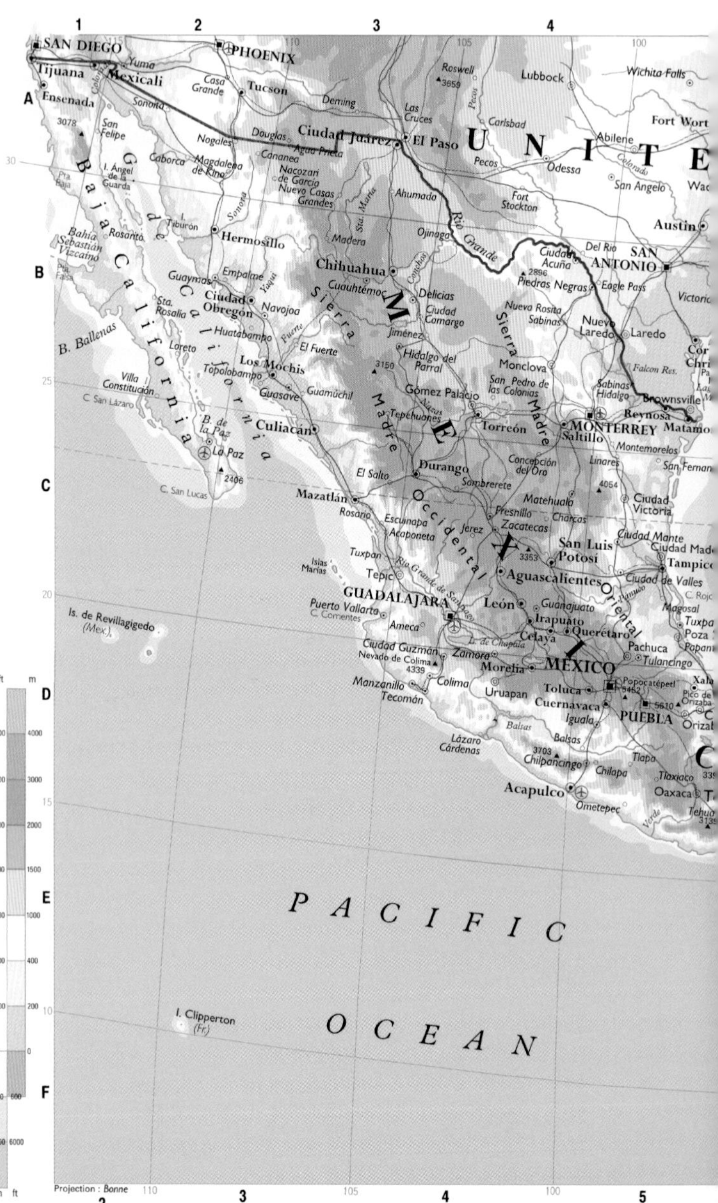
SAN DIEGO
PHOENIX
Tijuana
Mexicali
Yuma
Ensenada
Casa Grande
Tucson
Sonoita
San Felipe
Nogales
Douglas
Ciudad Juárez
El Paso
Agua Prieta
Cananea
Caborca
Magdalena de Kino
Nacozari de García
Nuevo Casas Grandes
Roswell
Lubbock
Wichita Falls
Deming
Las Cruces
Carlsbad
Fort Worth
Abilene
Pecos
Odessa
San Angelo
Fort Stockton
Ahumada
Ojinaga
Austin
Del Rio
SAN ANTONIO
Ciudad Acuña
Piedras Negras
Eagle Pass
Rio Grande
Baja California
Golfo de California
I. Ángel de la Guarda
I. Tiburón
Hermosillo
Bahía Sebastián Vizcaíno
Rosarito
Madera
Chihuahua
Cuauhtémoc
Delicias
Ciudad Camargo
Guaymas
Empalme
Ciudad Obregón
Navojoa
Sta. Rosalía
B. Ballenas
Huatabampo
Loreto
El Fuerte
Los Mochis
Topolobampo
Villa Constitución
C. San Lázaro
Guasave
Guamúchil
Culiacán
B. de la Paz
La Paz
C. San Lucas
Jiménez
Hidalgo del Parral
Sierra Madre Occidental
Sierra Madre Oriental
Nueva Rosita
Sabinas
Nuevo Laredo
Laredo
Monclova
San Pedro de las Colonias
Gómez Palacio
Torreón
Tepehuanes
Durango
El Salto
Mazatlán
Rosario
Escuinapa
Acaponeta
Sombrerete
Fresnillo
Zacatecas
Jerez
MONTERREY
Saltillo
Reynosa
Brownsville
Matamoros
Sabinas Hidalgo
Falcon Res.
Montemorelos
Linares
San Fernando
Concepción del Oro
Matehuala
Charcas
Ciudad Victoria
Ciudad Mante
Ciudad Madero
Tampico
San Luis Potosí
Aguascalientes
Ciudad de Valles
Islas Marías
Tuxpan
Tepic
Río Grande de Santiago
GUADALAJARA
Puerto Vallarta
C. Corrientes
Ameca
León
Guanajuato
Irapuato
Celaya
Querétaro
Pachuca
Tulancingo
L. de Chapala
Zamora
Morelia
Ciudad Guzmán
Nevado de Colima
Colima
Manzanillo
Tecomán
Uruapan
Toluca
MÉXICO
Popocatépetl
Pico de Orizaba
Cuernavaca
PUEBLA
Orizaba
Iguala
Balsas
Lázaro Cárdenas
Chilpancingo
Chilapa
Tlapa
Tlaxiaco
Oaxaca
Acapulco
Ometepec
Verde
Is. de Revillagigedo (Mex.)
I. Clipperton (Fr.)
PACIFIC OCEAN
MEXICO
UNITED
Projection : Bonne

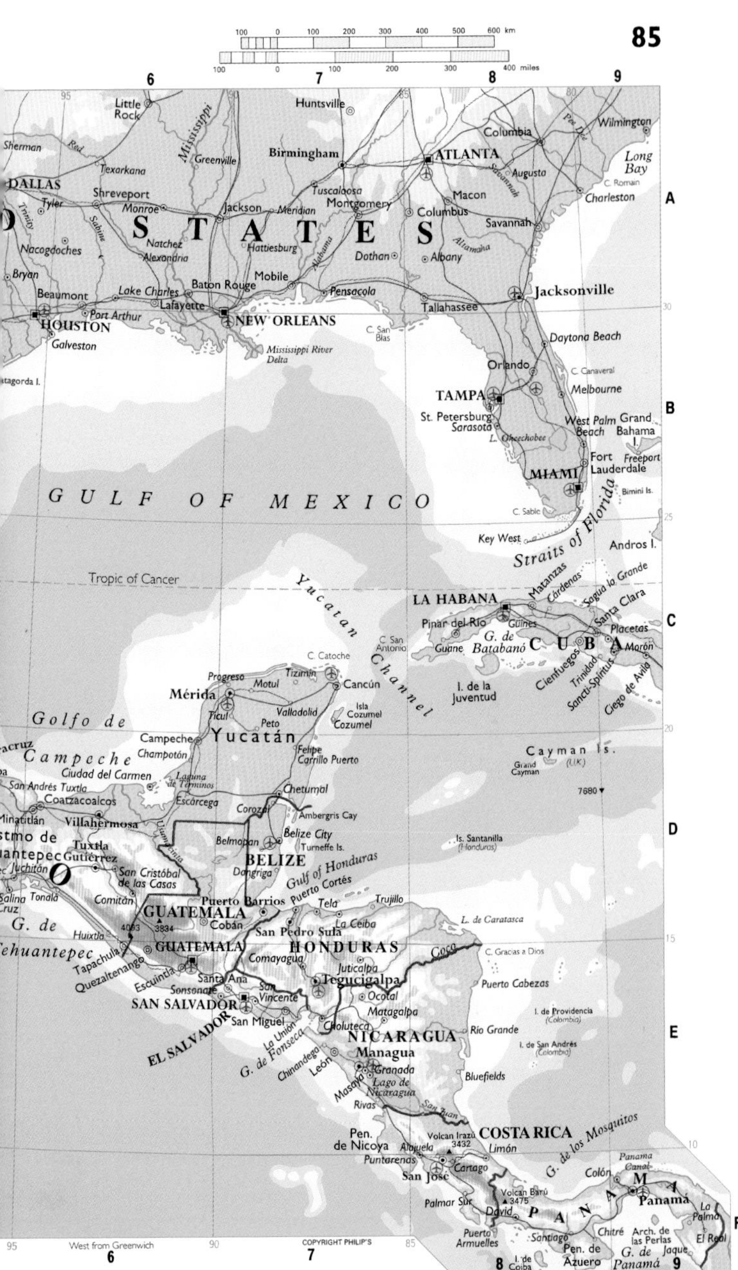

GULF OF MEXICO
STATES
Little Rock
Huntsville
Birmingham
ATLANTA
Columbia
Wilmington
Long Bay
Charleston
Augusta
Macon
Savannah
Columbus
Montgomery
Tuscaloosa
Meridian
Jackson
Greenville
Mississippi
Texarkana
Shreveport
Monroe
DALLAS
Tyler
Nacogdoches
Bryan
Natchez
Alexandria
Hattiesburg
Mobile
Baton Rouge
Lake Charles
Lafayette
Beaumont
Port Arthur
HOUSTON
Galveston
NEW ORLEANS
Mississippi River Delta
Pensacola
Dothan
Albany
Tallahassee
Jacksonville
Daytona Beach
Orlando
C. Canaveral
Melbourne
TAMPA
St. Petersburg
Sarasota
L. Okeechobee
West Palm Beach
Grand Bahama I.
Freeport
Fort Lauderdale
MIAMI
Bimini Is.
C. Sable
Key West
Straits of Florida
Andros I.
Tropic of Cancer
Yucatan Channel
LA HABANA
Matanzas
Cárdenas
Sagua la Grande
Santa Clara
Placetas
Pinar del Río
Güines
G. de Batabanó
CUBA
Morón
Guane
C. San Antonio
C. Catoche
Cienfuegos
Trinidad
Sancti-Spíritus
Ciego de Avila
I. de la Juventud
Progreso
Tizimín
Cancún
Mérida
Motul
Valladolid
Ticul
Peto
Isla Cozumel
Cozumel
Golfo de Campeche
Campeche
Champotón
Yucatán
Felipe Carrillo Puerto
Cayman Is. (UK)
Grand Cayman
Ciudad del Carmen
Laguna de Términos
San Andrés Tuxtla
Chetumal
7680
Coatzacoalcos
Escárcega
Corozal
Ambergris Cay
Minatitlán
Villahermosa
Istmo de Tehuantepec
Tuxtla Gutiérrez
Belmopan
Belize City
Turneffe Is.
Is. Santanilla (Honduras)
BELIZE
Dangriga
San Cristóbal de las Casas
Juchitán
Gulf of Honduras
Puerto Cortés
Salina Cruz
Tonalá
Comitán
Puerto Barrios
Tela
Trujillo
GUATEMALA
Cobán
La Ceiba
L. de Caratasca
G. de Tehuantepec
Huixtla
4093
3834
San Pedro Sula
HONDURAS
Coco
C. Gracias a Dios
Tapachula
Quezaltenango
Comayagua
Juticalpa
Tegucigalpa
Puerto Cabezas
Escuintla
Santa Ana
Sonsonate
San Vicente
Ocotal
SAN SALVADOR
San Miguel
Matagalpa
I. de Providencia (Colombia)
EL SALVADOR
La Unión
G. de Fonseca
Choluteca
NICARAGUA
Río Grande
I. de San Andrés (Colombia)
Chinandega
León
Managua
Granada
Masaya
Lago de Nicaragua
Bluefields
Rivas
San Juan
Pen. de Nicoya
Volcan Irazú 3432
COSTA RICA
G. de los Mosquitos
Alajuela
Limón
Puntarenas
Cartago
San José
Panama Canal
Colón
PANAMA
Panamá
Volcan Barú 3475
Palmar Sur
David
La Palma
Puerto Armuelles
Santiago
Chitré
Arch. de las Perlas
El Real
Pen. de Azuero
G. de Panamá
Jaque
I. de Coiba
West from Greenwich
COPYRIGHT PHILIP'S

GULF OF MEXICO
U.S.A.
Mississippi River Delta
Daytona Beach
Orlando
C. Canaveral
TAMPA
Melbourne
St. Petersburg
Sarasota
L. Okeechobee
West Palm Beach
Grand Bahama I.
Freeport
Great Abaco I.
Fort Lauderdale
MIAMI
Bimini Is.
New Providence I.
Nassau
Eleuthera I.
C. Sable
Key West
Straits of Florida
Andros I.
BAHAMAS
Cat I.
San Salvador
Great Exuma
Long I.
Tropic of Cancer
Yucatan Channel
LA HABANA
Matanzas
Cárdenas
Sagua la Grande
Santa Clara
Pinar del Río
Güines
Placetas
Morón
C. San Antonio
Guane
G. de Batabanó
CUBA
Camagüey
Cienfuegos
Trinidad
Sancti-Spíritus
Ciego de Avila
Nuevitas
Holguín
Great Inagua I.
C. Catoche
Progreso
Tizimin
Motul
Cancún
Mérida
Valladolid
Ticul
Peto
I. de Cozumel
I. de la Juventud
Victoria de Las Tunas
Bayamo
Banes
Manzanillo
2005
Santiago de Cuba
Guantánamo
Yucatán
Campeche
Felipe Carrillo Puerto
MEXICO
Greater
Cayman Is. (U.K.)
Grand Cayman
Windward
Jérémie
Escárcega
Chetumal
Corozal
Ambergris Cay
7680
Montego Bay
Mandeville
Spanish Town
Kingston
JAMAICA
Les Cayes
Belmopan
Belize City
Turneffe Is.
Is. Santanilla (Honduras)
BELIZE
Dangriga
Gulf of Honduras
Puerto Cortés
Puerto Barrios
Tela
Trujillo
Cobán
San Pedro Sula
La Ceiba
L. de Caratasca
GUATEMALA
HONDURAS
Juticalpa
Coco
C. Gracias a Dios
CARIBBEAN
Comayagua
Santa Ana
Tegucigalpa
Sonsonate
SAN SALVADOR
San Vincente
Ocotal
Puerto Cabezas
EL SALVADOR
San Miguel
Matagalpa
I. de Providencia (Colombia)
La Unión
Choluteca
Río Grande
G. de Fonseca
NICARAGUA
I. de San Andrés (Colombia)
Chinandega
León
Managua
Masaya
Granada
Lago de Nicaragua
Bluefields
Santa Marta
Rivas
San Juan
BARRANQUILLA
Soledad
Pen. de Nicoya
Volcan Irazú 3432
COSTA RICA
Cartagena
G. de los Mosquitos
Alajuela
Limón
Puntarenas
Panama Canal
G. del Darién
Sincelejo
San José
Cartago
Colón
Montería
Mompós
Volcan Barú 3475
Palmar Sur
PANAMA
Panamá
David
La Palma
El Real
Puerto Armuelles
Santiago
Chitré
Arch. de las Perlas
Pen. de Azuero
Jaque
Riosucio
I. de Coiba
G. de Panamá
2960
Barrancabermeja
Yarumal
Antioquia
PACIFIC
G. de Cupica
Bello
MEDELLÍN
Quibdó
C. Corrientes
Manizales
Pereira
Tolima 5215
Ibagué
Armenia
Girardot
OCEAN
Buenaventura
Palmira
CALI
Huila 5750
Neiva
Magdalena
Popayán
Volcan Puracé 4646
Projection : Bonne
West from Greenwich

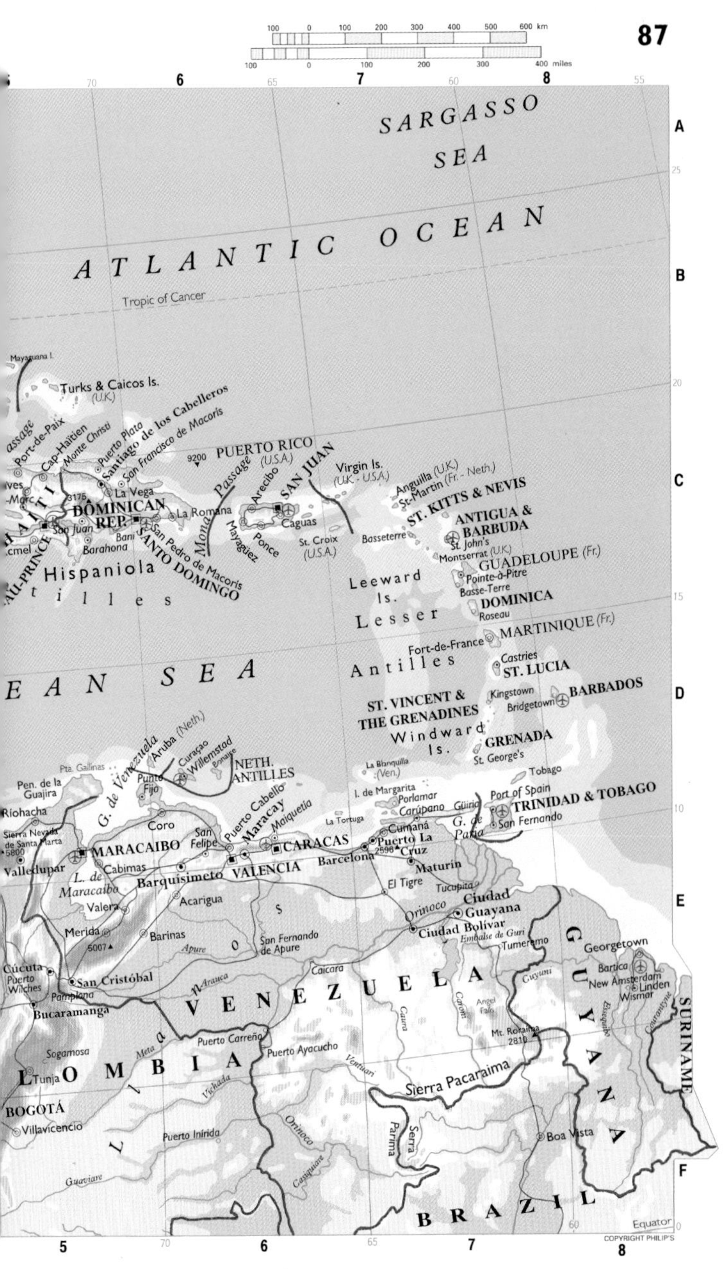
SARGASSO SEA
ATLANTIC OCEAN
Tropic of Cancer
Turks & Caicos Is. (U.K.)
Port-de-Paix
Cap-Haïtien
Monte Christi
Puerto Plata
Santiago de los Caballeros
San Francisco de Macorís
La Vega
DOMINICAN REP.
HAITI
Barahona
Bani
SANTO DOMINGO
San Pedro de Macorís
La Romana
Hispaniola
Mona Passage
PUERTO RICO (U.S.A.)
SAN JUAN
Arecibo
Mayagüez
Ponce
Caguas
Virgin Is. (U.K. - U.S.A.)
St. Croix (U.S.A.)
Anguilla (U.K.)
St-Martin (Fr. - Neth.)
ST. KITTS & NEVIS
Basseterre
ANTIGUA & BARBUDA
St. John's
Montserrat (U.K.)
GUADELOUPE (Fr.)
Pointe-à-Pitre
Basse-Terre
DOMINICA
Roseau
Leeward Is.
Lesser Antilles
MARTINIQUE (Fr.)
Fort-de-France
Castries
ST. LUCIA
Kingstown
ST. VINCENT & THE GRENADINES
Bridgetown
BARBADOS
Windward Is.
GRENADA
St. George's
Tobago
Port of Spain
TRINIDAD & TOBAGO
San Fernando
La Blanquilla (Ven.)
I. de Margarita
Porlamar
Carúpano
Güiria
G. de Paria
La Tortuga
Cumaná
Puerto La Cruz
Barcelona
Maturín
El Tigre
Tucupita
Ciudad Guayana
Ciudad Bolívar
Orinoco
Embalse de Guri
Tumeremo
Aruba (Neth.)
Curaçao
Willemstad
Bonaire
NETH. ANTILLES
Pta. Gallinas
Pen. de la Guajira
Ríohacha
Sierra Nevada de Santa Marta 5800
Valledupar
Punto Fijo
G. de Venezuela
Coro
San Felipe
Puerto Cabello
Maracay
Maiquetía
CARACAS
MARACAIBO
Cabimas
L. de Maracaibo
Barquisimeto
VALENCIA
Acarigua
Valera
Merida
5007
Barinas
Apure
San Fernando de Apure
Cúcuta
Puerto Wilches
San Cristóbal
Pamplona
Bucaramanga
Arauca
Caicara
VENEZUELA
Caura
Caroni
Angel Falls
Cuyuni
Georgetown
Bartica
New Amsterdam
Linden
Wismar
Essequibo
Courantyne
GUYANA
SURINAME
Mt. Roraima 2810
Sierra Pacaraima
Serra Parima
Boa Vista
Puerto Carreño
Puerto Ayacucho
Ventuari
Meta
Sogamosa
Tunja
COLOMBIA
BOGOTÁ
Villavicencio
Vichada
Puerto Inírida
Orinoco
Casiquiare
Guaviare
BRAZIL
Equator
CARIBBEAN SEA
9200
3175
2596
COPYRIGHT PHILIP'S

1
2
3
4
5
6
7
A
B
C
D
Tropic of Cancer
Equator
NORTH ATLANTIC OCEAN
Caribbean Sea
Gulf of Panama
G. of Guayaquil
G. of Darién
MEXICO
BELIZE
GUATEMALA
Guatemala
HONDURAS
Tegucigalpa
EL SALVADOR
San Salvador
NICARAGUA
Managua
COSTA RICA
San José
PANAMA
Panamá
CUBA
Havana
BAHAMAS
JAMAICA
Kingston
HAITI
Port-au-Prince
DOMINICAN REP.
Turks & Caicos Is. (U.K.)
PUERTO RICO (U.S.A.)
San Juan
Virgin Is. (U.K.)
ST. KITTS & NEVIS
Basse-Terre
ANTIGUA & BARBUDA
GUADELOUPE (Fr.)
DOMINICA
MARTINIQUE (Fr.)
Fort-de-France
ST. LUCIA
Castries
ST. VINCENT
Kingstown
BARBADOS
Bridgetown
GRENADA
St. George's
TRINIDAD & TOBAGO
Port of Spain
Aruba
Curaçao
VENEZUELA
Caracas
Valencia
Maracaibo
Barquisimeto
Ciudad Guayana
Orinoco
GUYANA
Georgetown
Essequibo
SURINAME
Paramaribo
FRENCH GUIANA
Cayenne
C. Orange
COLOMBIA
Bogotá
Medellín
Cali
Barranquilla
Cartagena
C. de la Aguja
Cúcuta
San Cristóbal
Bucaramanga
Magdalena
ECUADOR
Quito
Guayaquil
Galapagos Is. (Ecuador)
PERU
LIMA
Callao
Chiclayo
Trujillo
Chimbote
Cuzco
Iquitos
Napo
Marañón
Ucayali
Putumayo
BRAZIL
AMAZONAS
Manaus
Amazon
Japurá
Juruá
Purus
Madeira
Pôrto Velho
RONDÔNIA
ACRE
Madre de Dios
RORAIMA
Branco
PARÁ
Santarém
Belém
Marajó I.
Tapajós
Xingu
AMAPÁ
MATO GROSSO
TOCANTINS
Tocantins
Araguaia
MARANHÃO
São Luís
PIAUÍ
Teresina
Parnaíba
CEARÁ
Fortaleza
C. de São Roque
RIO G. DO NORTE
Natal
PARAÍBA
Campina Grande
PERNAMBUCO
Recife
ALAGOAS
Maceió
SERGIPE
Aracaju
BAHIA

PACIFIC OCEAN
SOUTH ATLANTIC OCEAN
CHILE
ARGENTINA
PARAGUAY
URUGUAY
MINAS GERAIS
ESPIRITO SANTO
MATO GROSSO DO SUL
SÃO PAULO
PARANÁ
SANTA CATARINA
RIO GRANDE DO SUL
R. DE J.
Brasília
Goiânia
Belo Horizonte
Vitória
Campos
Niterói
RIO DE JANEIRO
Juiz de Fora
Campinas
Ribeirão Prêto
SÃO PAULO
Curitiba
Pôrto Alegre
Pelotas
Montevideo
Río de la Plata
Arequipa
La Paz
Cochabamba
Santa Cruz
Sucre
Iquique
Antofagasta
Salta
San Miguel de Tucumán
Resistencia
Corrientes
Asunción
Pilcomayo
Paraguay
Paraná
Uruguay
Salado
Santa Fe
Paraná
Rosario
Córdoba
San Juan
Mendoza
BUENOS AIRES
La Plata
Mar del Plata
Bahía Blanca
Colorado
Negro
Viedma
Chubut
Comodoro Rivadavia
Gulf of San Jorge
Viña del Mar
Valparaíso
SANTIAGO
Talca
Concepción
Valdivia
Puerto Montt
Gulf of Penas
Punta Arenas
Magellan's Str.
Tierra del Fuego
C. Horn
West Falkland
FALKLAND IS. (U.K.)
Stanley
East Falkland
South Georgia (U.K.)
San Félix (Chile)
San Ambrosio (Chile)
Arch. de Juan Fernández (Chile)
Tropic of Capricorn
West from Greenwich
E F G H
1 2 3 4 5 6 7
20 30 40 50 60 70 80 90
100 0 200 400 600 800 1000 1200 1400 km
100 0 200 400 600 800 1000 miles
LIMA Capital Cities
Projection: Lambert's Azimuthal Equal Area

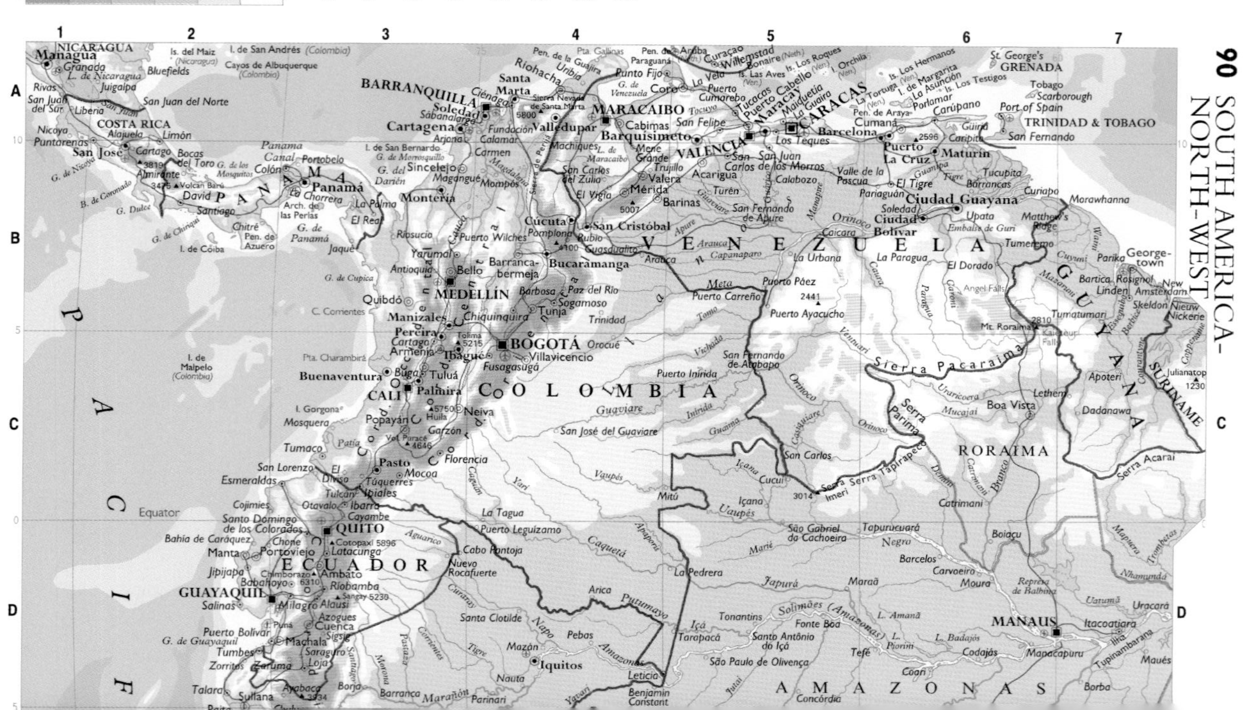

m 8000 6000 4000 2000 200 0 200 400 1000 1500 2000 3000 4000 6000
ft 24 000 18 000 12 000 6000 600 0 600 1200 3000 4500 6000 9000 12 000 18 000
NICARAGUA
Managua
Granada
L. de Nicaragua
Juigalpa
Bluefields
San Juan del Norte
COSTA RICA
San José
Puntarenas
Limón
Liberia
I. de San Andrés (Colombia)
Cayos de Albuquerque (Colombia)
PANAMA
Panamá
Panama Canal
Colón
Portobelo
David
Santiago
La Chorrera
Arch. de las Perlas
G. de Panamá
I. de Coiba
BARRANQUILLA
Cartagena
Santa Marta
Riohacha
Valledupar
Montería
Sincelejo
MARACAIBO
Barquisimeto
VALENCIA
Maracay
CARACAS
Barcelona
Cumaná
Maturín
Ciudad Guayana
Ciudad Bolívar
Puerto Ayacucho
San Fernando de Apure
San Fernando de Atabapo
San Cristóbal
Mérida
Cúcuta
Bucaramanga
MEDELLÍN
BOGOTÁ
Villavicencio
Manizales
Pereira
Ibagué
CALI
Buenaventura
Popayán
Pasto
Neiva
Florencia
Mocoa
Quibdó
Tunja
Leticia
Iquitos
MANAUS
QUITO
GUAYAQUIL
Cuenca
Machala
Riobamba
Ambato
Esmeraldas
Manta
Tumbes
Talara
Sullana
St. George's
GRENADA
Tobago
Scarborough
Port of Spain
TRINIDAD & TOBAGO
San Fernando
Georgetown
New Amsterdam
Nieuw Nickerie
Boa Vista
Lethem
V E N E Z U E L A
C O L O M B I A
E C U A D O R
G U Y A N A
SURINAME
R O R A I M A
A M A Z O N A S
P A C I F I C
Equator
Sierra Pacaraima
Serra Parima
Mt. Roraima 2810
Angel Falls
Orinoco
Solimões (Amazonas)
Negro
Caquetá
Putumayo
Napo
Japurá
Branco
Meta
Guaviare
Vaupés
Marañón
I. de Malpelo (Colombia)
I. Gorgona
G. de Guayaquil
Chimborazo 6310
Cotopaxi 5896
Sangay 5230

B R A Z I L
P E R U
B O L I V I A
C H I L E
ARGENTINA
P A R A G U A Y
A C R E
RONDÔNIA
P A C I F I C
O C E A N
Peru-Chile Trench
LIMA
Callao
LA PAZ
Cuzco
Arequipa
Trujillo
Chiclayo
Chimbote
Huancayo
Ica
Nazca
Puno
Juliaca
Tacna
Arica
Iquique
Calama
Oruro
Cochabamba
Santa Cruz
Sucre
Potosí
Tarija
Trinidad
Porto Velho
Rio Branco
Cobija
Pucallpa
Huánuco
Cerro de Pasco
Chincha Alta
Pisco
Machupicchu
Puerto Maldonado
L. Titicaca
L. de Poopó
Salar de Uyuni
Serra dos Parecis
Serra do Norte
Serra do Tombador
Chaco Boreal
Cáceres
Corumbá
Ilo
Moquegua
Mollendo
Camaná
Huaraz
Huascarán 6768
Tarapoto
Yurimaguas
Cajamarca
Chachapoyas
Moyobamba
Manicoré
Humaitá
Lábrea
Villa Montes
Tupiza
Villazón
Tocopilla
Pta. Angamos
West from Greenwich
Projection: Sanson-Flamsteed's Sinusoidal
COPYRIGHT PHILIP'S
100 0 100 200 300 400 500 km
100 0 100 200 300 400 miles

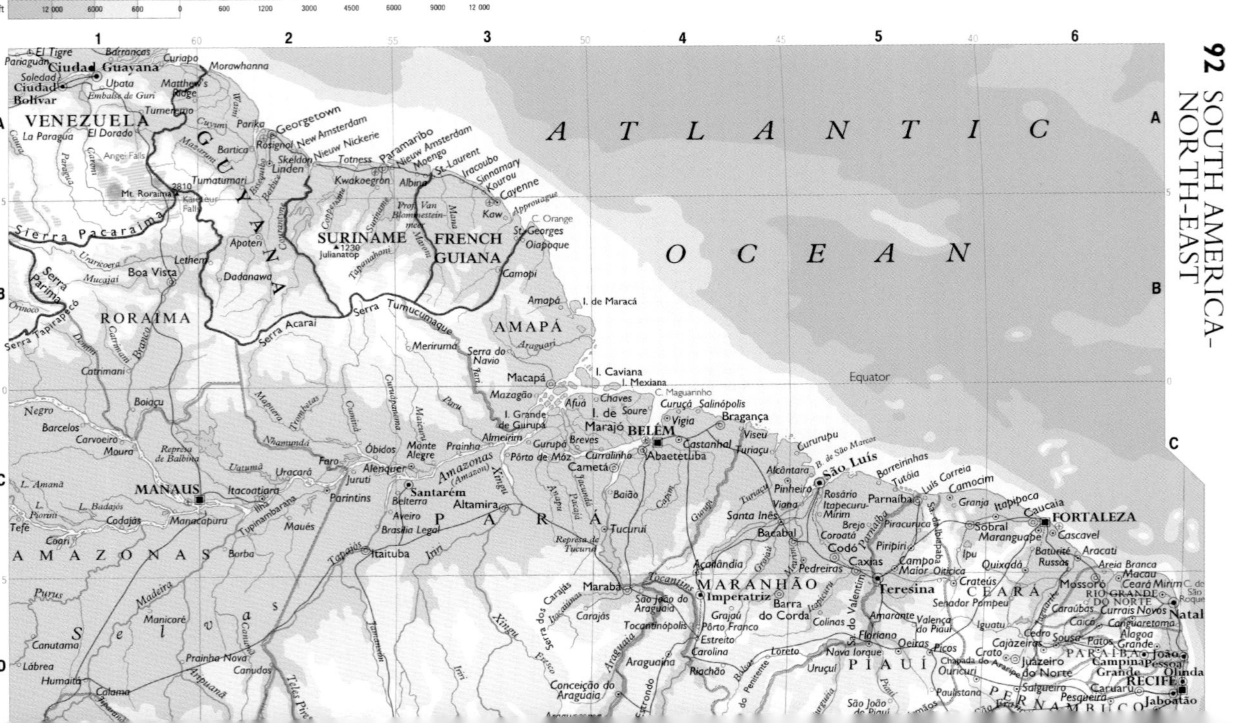

A T L A N T I C
O C E A N
Equator
VENEZUELA
GUYANA
SURINAME
FRENCH GUIANA
AMAPÁ
RORAIMA
AMAZONAS
PARÁ
MARANHÃO
PIAUÍ
CEARÁ
RIO GRANDE DO NORTE
PARAÍBA
PERNAMBUCO
Selva
Ciudad Guayana
Ciudad Bolívar
El Tigre
Georgetown
New Amsterdam
Paramaribo
Nieuw Nickerie
Cayenne
Kourou
St-Laurent
Oiapoque
Macapá
BELÉM
São Luís
FORTALEZA
Natal
RECIFE
Olinda
Jaboatão
João Pessoa
Campina Grande
MANAUS
Santarém
Teresina
Imperatriz
Marabá
Boa Vista
Lethem
Linden
Bragança
Parnaíba
Sobral
Mossoró
Caruaru
Juazeiro do Norte
Crato
Caxias
Codó
Altamira
Itaituba
Parintins
Óbidos
Humaitá
Lábrea
Tefé
Barcelos
I. de Marajó
I. Caviana
I. Mexiana
I. de Maracá
Sierra Pacaraima
Serra Parima
Serra Acaraí
Serra Tumucumaque
Mt. Roraima 2810
Julianatop 1230
Xingu
Tocantins
Araguaia
Negro
Purus
Madeira
Tapajós
Trombetas
Amazonas (Amazon)

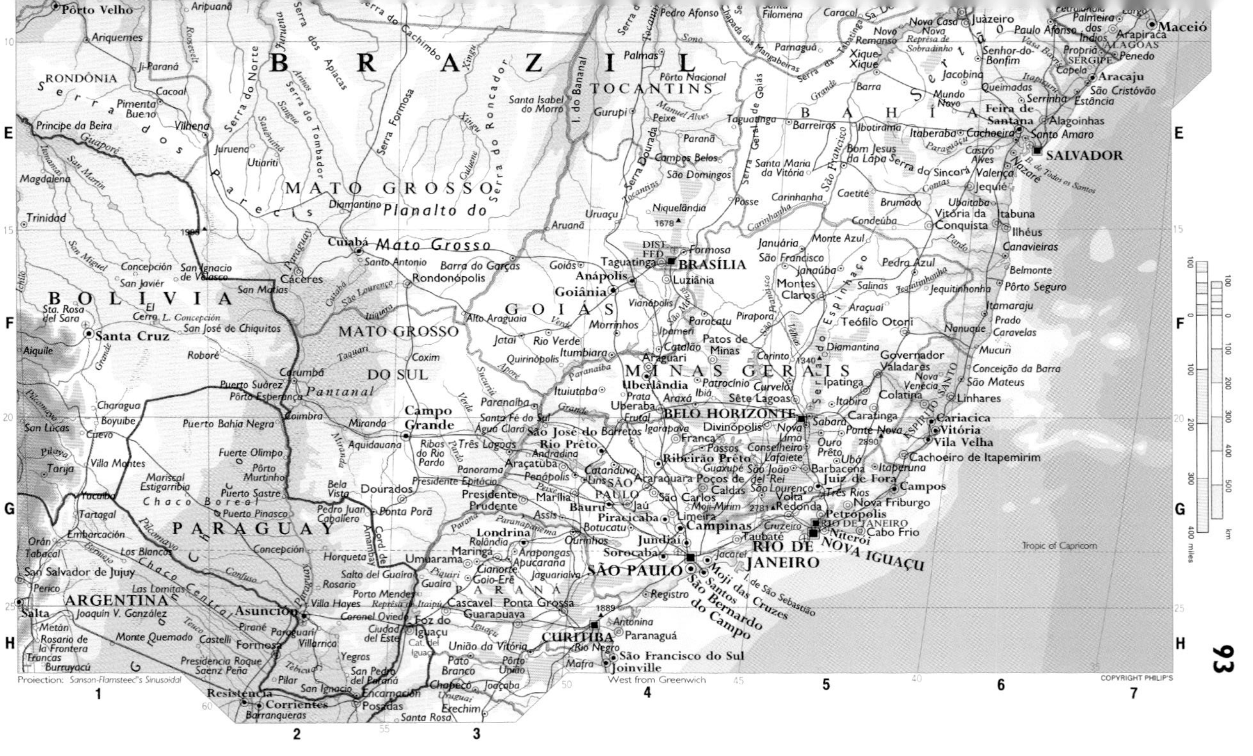

BRAZIL
BOLIVIA
PARAGUAY
ARGENTINA
RONDÔNIA
MATO GROSSO
MATO GROSSO DO SUL
TOCANTINS
GOIÁS
BAHIA
MINAS GERAIS
SÃO PAULO
PARANÁ
ESPÍRITO SANTO
RIO DE JANEIRO
SERGIPE
ALAGOAS
DIST. FED.
Planalto do Mato Grosso
Serra dos Parecis
Serra do Roncador
Serra Formosa
Serra do Tombador
Serra dos Apiacas
Serra do Norte
Serra do Cachimbo
Serra Geral de Goiás
Serra do Espinhaço
Serra do Sincorá
Serra da Tabatinga
Chapada das Mangabeiras
Serra Dourada
Chaco Boreal
Chaco Central
Pantanal
I. do Bananal
Tropic of Capricorn
BRASÍLIA
SÃO PAULO
RIO DE JANEIRO
BELO HORIZONTE
SALVADOR
CURITIBA
NOVA IGUAÇU
Asunción
Santa Cruz
Pôrto Velho
Cuiabá
Campo Grande
Goiânia
Anápolis
Uberlândia
Uberaba
Campinas
Santos
São Bernardo do Campo
Moji das Cruzes
Sorocaba
Jundiaí
Londrina
Maringá
Ribeirão Prêto
Juiz de Fora
Niterói
Petrópolis
Vitória
Vila Velha
Cariacica
Campos
Feira de Santana
Aracaju
Maceió
Vitória da Conquista
Ilhéus
Montes Claros
Governador Valadares
Joinville
Corrientes
Resistencia
Encarnación
Salta
San Salvador de Jujuy
Projection: Sanson-Flamsteed's Sinusoidal
West from Greenwich
COPYRIGHT PHILIP'S
km
miles

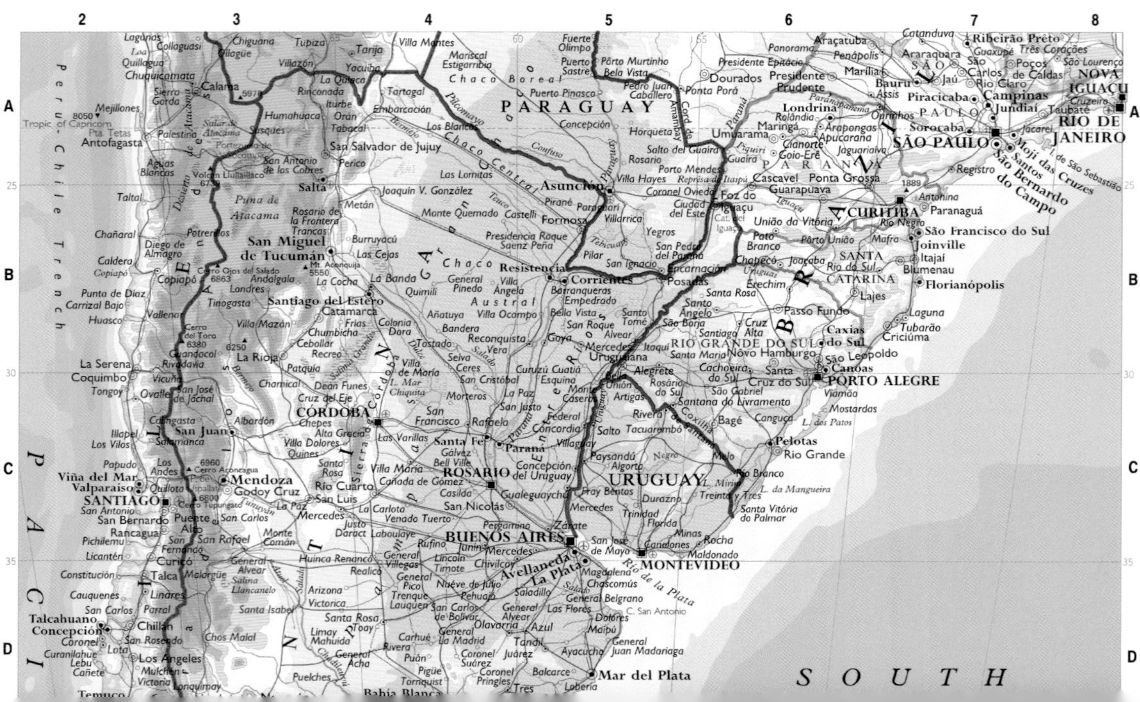

PARAGUAY
URUGUAY
BRAZIL
ARGENTINA
SÃO PAULO
PARANÁ
SANTA CATARINA
RIO GRANDE DO SUL
RIO DE JANEIRO
NOVA IGUAÇU
SÃO PAULO
Campinas
Santos
São Bernardo do Campo
CURITIBA
Florianópolis
PÔRTO ALEGRE
Pelotas
Rio Grande
Asunción
Resistencia
Corrientes
Formosa
Posadas
Encarnación
MONTEVIDEO
BUENOS AIRES
La Plata
Avellaneda
ROSARIO
Santa Fe
Paraná
CÓRDOBA
San Miguel de Tucumán
Santiago del Estero
Salta
San Salvador de Jujuy
La Rioja
San Juan
Mendoza
SANTIAGO
Valparaíso
Viña del Mar
Concepción
Talcahuano
Antofagasta
Calama
La Serena
Coquimbo
Mar del Plata
Río de la Plata
Chaco Boreal
Chaco Central
Chaco Austral
Peru-Chile Trench
Tropic of Capricorn
P A C I
S O U T H

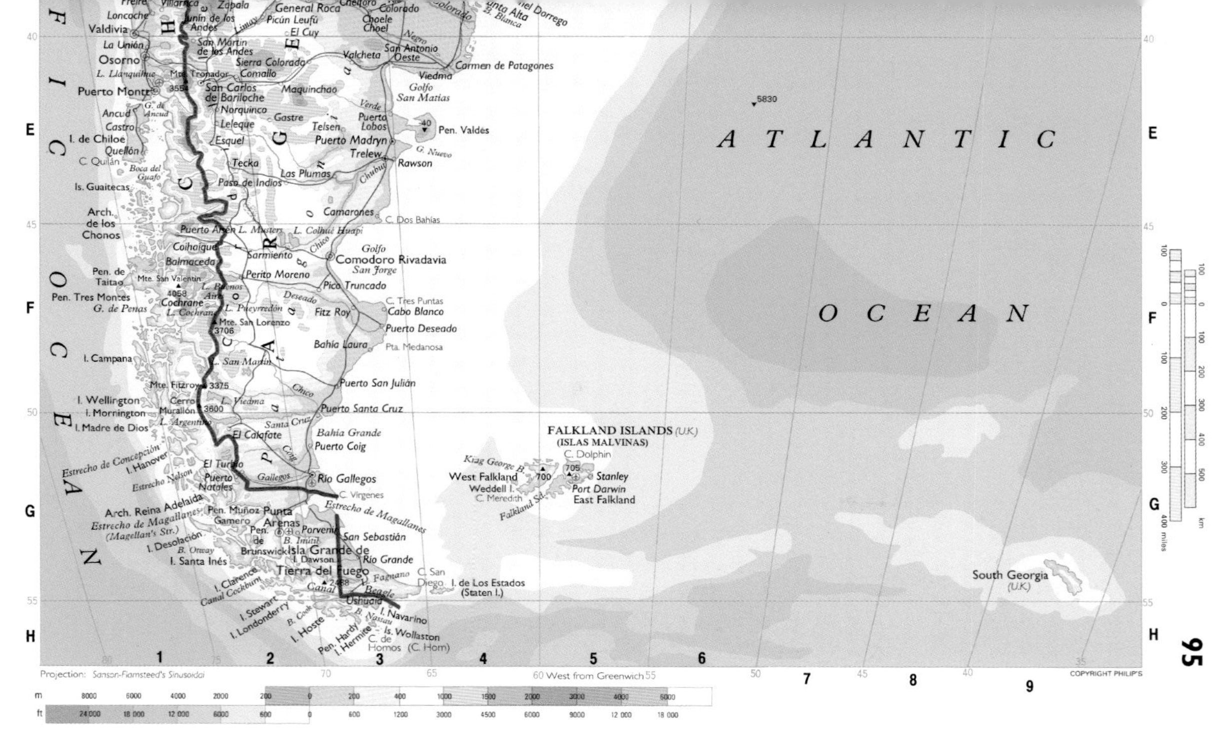
ATLANTIC OCEAN
PACIFIC OCEAN
PATAGONIA
CHILE
FALKLAND ISLANDS (U.K.)
(ISLAS MALVINAS)
C. Dolphin
West Falkland
East Falkland
Stanley
Port Darwin
Weddell I.
C. Meredith
Falkland Sd.
King George B.
South Georgia (U.K.)
Valdivia
Loncoche
Freire
Villarrica
Zapala
Junín de los Andes
General Roca
Picún Leufú
El Cuy
Choele Choel
Colorado
Carmen de Patagones
Viedma
San Antonio Oeste
Valcheta
La Unión
Osorno
L. Llanquihue
Mte. Tronador
Puerto Montt
San Martín de los Andes
Sierra Colorada
Comallo
San Carlos de Bariloche
Maquinchao
Golfo San Matías
Ancud
Castro
I. de Chiloe
Quellón
C. Quilán
Boca del Guafo
Norquinco
Leleque
Esquel
Gastre
Telsen
Puerto Lobos
Pen. Valdes
Puerto Madryn
Trelew
Rawson
G. Nuevo
Tecka
Las Plumas
Chubut
Paso de Indios
Is. Guaitecas
Arch. de los Chonos
Camarones
C. Dos Bahías
Puerto Aisén
L. Musters
L. Colhué Huapi
Coihaique
Sarmiento
Golfo San Jorge
Comodoro Rivadavia
Balmaceda
Perito Moreno
Pico Truncado
Pen. de Taitao
Mte. San Valentin
4058
L. Buenos Aires
Cochrane
L. Cochrane
Pen. Tres Montes
G. de Penas
Deseado
L. Pueyrredón
Fitz Roy
C. Tres Puntas
Cabo Blanco
Mte. San Lorenzo
3706
Puerto Deseado
Bahía Laura
Pta. Medanosa
I. Campana
L. San Martín
Mte. Fitzroy
3375
Chico
Puerto San Julián
I. Wellington
Cerro Murallón
3600
L. Viedma
Puerto Santa Cruz
I. Mornington
I. Madre de Dios
L. Argentino
Santa Cruz
El Calafate
Bahía Grande
Puerto Coig
Coig
Estrecho de Concepción
I. Hanover
El Turbio
Estrecho Nelson
Puerto Natales
Gallegos
Río Gallegos
C. Vírgenes
Arch. Reina Adelaida
Estrecho de Magallanes
(Magellan's Str.)
Pen. Muñoz Gamero
Punta Arenas
Porvenir
San Sebastián
I. Desolación
B. Otway
Pen. de Brunswick
B. Inútil
Isla Grande de Tierra del Fuego
Río Grande
I. Santa Inés
I. Dawson
L. Fagnano
C. San Diego
I. de Los Estados
(Staten I.)
I. Clarence
Canal Cockburn
2468
Canal Beagle
Ushuaia
I. Navarino
I. Stewart
I. Londonderry
B. Cook
I. Hoste
B. Nassau
Pen. Hardy
I. Hermite
Is. Wollaston
C. de Hornos (C. Horn)
5830
40
Projection: Sanson-Flamsteed's Sinusoidal
West from Greenwich
COPYRIGHT PHILIP'S
m 8000 6000 4000 2000 200 0 200 400 1000 1500 2000 3000 4000 6000
ft 24 000 18 000 12 000 6000 600 0 600 1200 3000 4500 6000 9000 12 000 18 000
100 0 100 200 300 400 500 km
100 0 100 200 300 400 miles

96 ANTARCTICA

100 0 200 400 600 800 1000 1200 1400 km

100 0 200 400 600 800 1000 miles

Projection : Zenithal Equidistant

Bases on King George Island:
Jubany (Argentina)
Com. Ferraz (Brazil)
Ten. Rodolfo Marsh (Chile)
Great Wall (China)
King Sejong (Korea)
Arctowski (Poland)
Artigas (Uruguay)

Ice cap

Permanent ice shelf

Maximum extent of sea ice

March (Summer) extent of sea ice

3488 / 3700 Surface elevation and depth of ice (in metres)

Stanley (U.K.) Permanent bases

Index to Map Pages

The index contains the names of all principal places and features shown on the maps. Physical features composed of a proper name (Erie) and a description (Lake) are positioned alphabetically by the proper name. The description is positioned after the proper name and is usually abbreviated:

Erie, L. **76 C5**

Where a description forms part of a settlement or administrative name, however, it is always written in full and put in its true alphabetical position:

Lake Charles . . . **81 D7**

Names beginning St. are alphabetized under Saint, but Sankt, Sant, Santa and San are all spelt in full and are alphabetized accordingly.

The number in bold type which follows each name in the index refers to the number of the map page where that feature or place will be found. This is usually the largest scale at which the place or feature appears.

The letter and figure which are in bold type immediately after the page number give the grid square on the map page, within which the feature is situated.

Rivers are indexed to their mouths or confluences, and carry the symbol → after their names. The following symbols are also used in the index: ■ country, ☒ overseas territory or dependency, □ first order administrative area, △ national park, ⌓ nature park or reserve.

A

B

C

D

E

F

G

H

I

J

K

L

M

N

O

Q

S

T

U

V

W

X

Y

Projection: *Hammer Equal Area*